WALKING MEDICINE

WALKING

The Lifetime Guide to Preventive and Therapeutic Exercisewalking Programs

---

Deena and David Balboa,
  M.S.W., M.B.A.
Steven Blair, PED
Nikola Boskovksi, M.D.
Elizabeth Boyce, R.N.
Myron Boxer, D.P.M.
Richard T. Braver, D.P.M.
Daniel A. Brzusek, D.O., M.S.
Edmund R. Burke, Ph.D.
Sheldon B. Cohen, M.D.
Kathryn Cox, M.D.
Charles Eichenberg, Ph.D.
Mark Forrestal, M.D.

Peter R. Francis, Ph.D.
Barry Franklin, Ph.D.
Stephen Gambert, M.D.
Steven B. Heymsfeld, M.D.
Harry E. Hlavac, D.P.M., M.Ed.
Jay Itzkowitz, M.S.
Joseph F. Kansao, D.C.
Susan Johnson, D.Ed.
Pamela Kovar-Joledano
Norman M. Kaplan, M.D.
Valery F. Lanyi, M.D.
Mark La Porta, M.D.
Arthur Leon, M.D.

MEDICINE

by
Gary Yanker and Kathy Burton

and 50 Medical Experts

Ruth Lerner, Ph.D.
Mort Malkin, D.D.S.
Francis McBrien, B.S.
William McLaughlin, Ph.D.
Claude Miller, M.D.
Howard L. Millman, Ph.D.
Robert Neeves, Ph.D.
David Roadruck, Ph.D.
Albert P. Rosen, M.D.
Jonathan Rosen, M.D.
Keith Sedlacek, M.D.
Othneil J. Seiden, M.D.

Neil Sheffler, D.P.M.
John C. Simpson, III, Ph.D.
Myra Skluth, M.D., Ph.D.
Terry Spilken, D.P.M.
Jack Stern, M.D.
Robert Thayer, Ph.D.
James Thomas, M.D.
David Toth, M.D.
J.E. Walker, M.D.
James D. Watson, M.D.
Kathryn Welds, Ph.D.
Mark Young, M.D.

McGraw-Hill, Inc.

New York   St. Louis   San Francisco   Auckland   Bogotá
Caracas   Lisbon   London   Madrid   Mexico   Milan
Montreal   New Delhi   Paris   San Juan   São Paulo
Singapore   Sydney   Tokyo   Toronto

Walking Medicine™ book series, Exercisewalking™ program, Walking Workouts™, Sportwalking™, Travelwalking™, and The Walking Atlas of America™ are trade and service marks claimed by Walking World.

First McGraw-Hill paperback edition published, 1993

    4 5 6 7 8 9 DOC DOC 9 5 4 3

ISBN 0-07-072234-X {HC}
ISBN 0-07-072265-X {PBK}

Library of Congress Cataloging-in-Publication Data

Yanker, Gary.
    Walking medicine: the lifetime guide to preventive and
    therapeutic exercisewalking programs/by Gary Yanker and Kathy
    Burton, and 50 medical experts.
        p.   cm.
    ISBN 0-07-072234-X :   —ISBN 0-07-072265-X (pbk.) :
    1. Walking—Therapeutic use.   I. Burton, Kathy.
II. Title.
RM727.W34Y36   1990
613.7′176—dc20
                                                    90-5443
                                                    CIP

Book design by Eve Kirch.
Project supervised by M 'N O Production Services, Inc.

WALKING WORLD STAFF

Editors: Gary Yanker and Kathy Burton

Managing Editors: Susan Henricks and Lisa Siegel

Researchers: Ariadne Antal, Deborah Cohen, Eric Kun, William O'Reilly, Margaret Salpukas, Miranda Spencer, Marie Szaniszlo, William A. Thomas, Bradford Verter, Laura Viola, Lisa Wu

Illustrator: Dawn Roland

ABOUT THE AUTHORS

Gary Yanker, America's foremost authority on walking, has authored seven books and two tapes on walking for exercise, sport, and travel. He holds a Juris Doctor and a Masters in Business Administration from Columbia University. He lives in New York City and exercisewalks 24 to 35 miles a week.

Kathy Burton is a free-lance writer and 15-mile-a-week exercisewalker with a Master's in Journalism and Business Administration from New York University. She lives in Sunnyside, New York.

This book is dedicated to

my father, Peter N. Yanker,
who wore his immigrant accent
like a badge of honor.
And to

L.M.M.

CONTENTS

BOOK 5: WALKTHERAPY
Become Stress Hardy and Gain Control of Your Life

BOOK 6: THE WALKING SHOE AND FOOT BOOK
Creating a Firm and Comfortable Foundation

ACKNOWLEDGMENTS

We'd like to thank the following people for reviewing our manuscript:

BOOK 1: Walking and Aging:
Dr. Myra Skluth (Chaps. 1 & 2), Dr. O. J. Seiden (Chaps. 1 & 2), Dr. Albert P. Rosen (Chaps. 3 & 4), Dr. Mort Malkin (Chap. 5), Dr. Steven Gambert (Chap. 6), Dr. J. E. Walker (Chap. 7)

BOOK 2: Walking for Arthritis, Back and Joints:
Dr. Mark Young (Chaps. 1, 2, & 6), Dr. Valerie Lanyi (Chap. 2), Dr. Daniel Brzusek (Chaps. 3 & 4), Ms. Pamela Kovar-Joledano (Chap. 3), Dr. Joseph E. Kansao (Chap. 4), Jay Itzkowitz (Chap. 5)

BOOK 3: Cardiowalking:
Dr. Steven Blair (Chaps. 1 & 2), Dr. James Thomas (Chap. 2), Dr. William McLaughlin (Chap. 3), Dr. Susan Johnson (Chap. 4), Dr. Norman Kaplan (Chap. 5), Dr. Robert Neeves (Chap. 5), Dr. Barry Franklin (Chap. 6), Dr. Jack Stern (Chap. 6), Dr. Mark Forrestal (Chap. 7), Dr. Jonathan Rosen (Chap. 8), Dr. Arthur Leon (Chap. 9), Dr. James D. Watson (Chap. 9)

BOOK 4: Walkshaping and Weight Control:
Dr. Peter Francis (Chaps. 1 & 3), Dr. Nikola Boskovski (Chaps. 1 & 2), Dr. David Toth (Chaps. 1 & 3), Dr. Steven Heymsfeld (Chap. 2), Dr. Edmund Burke (Chaps. 3 & 4), Ms. Frances McBrien (Chap. 4), Dr. Charles L. Eichenberg (Chap. 5), Dr. Kathryn Cox (Chap. 6)

BOOK 5: Walktherapy:
Dr. Keith Sedlacek (Chaps. 1 & 2), Dr. Claude Miller (Chap. 3), Dr. Howard Millman (Chap. 3), Dr. John Simpson, III (Chap. 4), Dr. Kathryn Welds (Chap. 5), Dr. Ruth Lerner (Chap. 5), Dr. Sheldon Cohen (Chap. 6)

BOOK 6: The Walking Shoe and Foot Book:
Dr. Myron Boxer (Chaps. 1 & 2), Dr. Harry Hlavac (Chap. 2), Dr. Mark LaPorta (Chap. 4), Dr. Neil Sheffler (Chap. 4), Dr. Terry Spilken (Chaps. 4 & 5), Mr. Richard Polk (Chap. 5)

Also, thanks to Richard Polk, president of Pedestrian Corp., and to Drs. Harry Hlavac and Richard Braver for their consultation on our Walking Shoe Questionnaire.

Walking: The Lifetime Approach

Walking is probably the best health remedy for adding more and better years to your life. Following a moderate exercise program like walking is as important as quitting smoking or reducing cholesterol if you want to avoid heart disease and cancer. Walking can help reduce your need for medication by fighting problems associated with arthritis, diabetes, and high blood pressure naturally. Moreover, walking can help you quit smoking, reduce stress and pain, lose weight, improve strength and self-confidence, and even look younger. In fact, walking addresses many of the problems, conditions, and diseases you'll face throughout your life, which is why *Walking Medicine* is a book for everyone: the old and the young, the infirm and the healthy.

The idea for *Walking Medicine* grew out of the numerous medical questions that walkers asked Gary Yanker at his exercisewalking clinics given throughout the United States over the last eight years. Many of the walkers' questions were related to previous sports injuries, illnesses, the effects of aging, or obesity. At first, Gary sent these walkers to doctors, feeling that he could not give them the specific advice they needed. He later realized that most of these doctors were not familiar with walking techniques and were often not prescribing a detailed walking regimen, telling their patients only to "walk more" or "walk regularly."

Few activities are broad enough or important enough to spark the development of their own medical field of research and treatment. Dance Medicine and Sports Medicine have evolved because of the need to treat injuries resulting from these activities. However, Gary felt that Walking as "medicine" could become the leading preventive and rehabilitative exercise—healing injuries from other sports, combating diseases and disabilities, and slowing the aging process. So he began searching for doctors who walked themselves and prescribed walking to their patients. These were the health professionals who would be at the forefront of the Walking Medicine movement.

The directory at the back of this book lists over 400 health professionals, researchers, and physicians who have responded to our search for walking doctors. Among them are the people who have helped us develop this book. Like a typical sports medicine clinic, we assembled leading walking doctors and health professionals from various disciplines (cardiology, nutrition, internal medicine, exercise physiology, and pharmacology, among others) into teams of advisors for each of the six sections of this book. These teams provide a comprehensive approach to the health problems covered here. The enthusiasm with which all the health professionals told us of their own experiences with walking are an indication that among the medical profession, walking is taking its place as a leading preventive and rehabilitative prescription.

But why read this book if you are healthy? The answer is simple and compelling—you are at risk. As you age (and the negative effects of aging start at 25), you will develop multiple health problems if you do not take preventative measures and stay active. Inactivity is increasingly indicted as the cause of disease and degeneration in older adults. Walking is the easiest and safest way to get active and remain active throughout your lifetime. But all styles of walking are not equal. The most effective way of walking is to use special techniques and programs known as *exercisewalking*. Exercisewalking combines dynamic arm and leg movements that turn walking into a total body exercise.

Exercisewalking techniques have already been introduced in three of Gary Yanker's previous books, *The Complete Book of Exercisewalking* for beginner walkers, *Walking Workouts* for intermediate walkers, and *Sportwalking* for advanced walkers. In *Walking Medicine*, these techniques have been modified, and others added, to form new walking routines and programs to address all aspects of your health, from helping with joint and back pain to calming your mind, improving the health of your heart, strengthening your muscles, keeping you trim, and slowing the aging process.

By following the exercisewalking routines in this book, along with the special diets and behavioral modification exercises (including how to quit smoking and how to stop overeating), you will be on your way to delaying the onset of or lessening the severity of such ailments as arthritis, heart disease, high blood pressure, high cholesterol, diabetes, and depression —all potentially fatal or debilitating conditions. And you can improve the quality of your whole life, too, by reducing aches and pains and avoiding injuries. Even the very sick or those with incurable conditions can benefit from our exercisewalking programs by strengthening their minds and bodies to better cope with the challenges they face.

Here are some of the major benefits from following a regular walking program:

1. Walking prevents or delays the onset of major diseases.

2. Walking lowers your biological age 10 to 20 years below your chronological age.

3. Walking improves your mood and self-confidence.

4. Walking helps you rehabilitate from injuries caused by more dangerous sports.

5. Walking lowers or eliminates your dependency on medications and addictive substances like nicotine, alcohol, and barbiturates.

6. Walking helps you lose weight and tones your body.

We have found most exercise and medical books deficient in the long view. They are usually aimed only at the young, ignoring the need for age-graded exercises or routines suited to different stages of life and to various disorders and conditions. *Walking Medicine* takes *the lifetime approach*, so that you can take precautions now against health problems that may occur in later years. You'll find walking programs for every age and fitness level, from the most unfit to the professional athlete.

One of *Walking Medicine*'s strengths is the self-administered tests found throughout the book that help you determine your present emotional and physical condition and your health risks (through constructing your own family health tree) and serve as a means of determining the areas in which exercisewalking can help you the most. Another is explanations of how the body works and how you can train it to perform most efficiently. We even use some medical terms, once arcane and relegated to the province of scientists, researchers, and doctors, so that until doctors learn to talk to patients, you can speak with your doctor in his or her language.

Another strength is the number of real walkers' stories used throughout the book, the result of our extensive grassroots research to seek out people who have been helped by following a regular exercisewalking program. (See the Walker's Questionnaire and the Doctor and Health Professional Questionnaire at the end of this book.) Some of these stories also come from the doctors we've recruited, who have "healed themselves" with walking and are among walking's biggest supporters.*

---

*Doctors and walkers who wish to be included in the next edition of this book should fill out a copy of the questionnaire and return it to us.

The stories are a great motivational force because they show that you don't have to slow down or weaken with age and that you can either overcome, or still lead a fulfilling life with, your health problems. These anecdotes make *Walking Medicine* not only a how-to manual, but an inspirational read-through book. You'll find stories of diabetics and heart and cancer patients who were told by their doctors that they had only a few months to live. With the help of walking, these same people have extended their lives 20 or 30 more years and are healthier and more optimistic than ever. There are amazing recoveries from heart attacks and strokes, automobile crashes, sports accidents, and high-impact exercise injuries. There are even stories of people who have used walking to help them cope with the loss of a daughter or husband or the uncertainty and pain of living with a terminal illness. Not all the stories are dramatic. Some are about people who just feel better and have more energy because they walk every day.

How to Use This Book

Walking Medicine is actually a seven-book series in one volume. Because of the depth of the material covered, we have divided it into six minibooks plus an extensive directory of health professionals so that you can easily go directly to the exact information you are seeking.

Each minibook covers a common medical problem and features one or more walking programs (complete with walking techniques), which are divided into five fitness levels, from poor (Level I) to excellent (Level V), and for the rehabilitative programs, three phases. Mileage, intensity, and walking speed increase with each level, and, depending on your goals, you can stay at one level or build to a higher one. You can follow the programs in *Walking Medicine* progressively, moving from one minibook to the next, but each program also stands on its own. That's why we call each section a minibook: It serves as a how-to book to help rehabilitate or prevent a health problem, whether it is heart disease, arthritis, or weight gain. Each minibook also functions as a maintenance manual for the body system most affected by that disease or disorder, so that the minibook that discusses heart disease is also a guide to keeping your heart, lungs, and vascular system healthy, and the minibook that deals with arthritis, back and joint pain also serves as a guide to your musculoskeletal system. Thus the minibooks of *Walking Medicine* come together to form a *complete lifetime guide* for your entire body. It is analogous to the maintenance and repair manual you get with a car. The factory manual tells you what your car can do, what can go wrong, and how to prevent and fix damages. *Walking Medicine* explains your body's capabilities, what can go wrong, and how to prevent and fix health breakdowns.

The exercisewalking programs contained in the six minibooks develop progressively. As you'll see from the following descriptions, the minibooks are ordered so that you first get an overview of your general health and then gradually learn walking techniques, starting with the basics in Book 2 and moving toward programs that require more strength and stamina (although there are programs for every fitness level within each book). After you have followed each program for 6 weeks, you can then go back to the program best suited to your needs. Here's how it works:

Your first step is to establish your walking needs and goals with the help of Book 1: Walking and Aging. This book introduces walking as an activity that can be modified for every age and fitness level and lists walking programs suitable for young children of 5 to old-old adults (over 75), so you know what your lifetime goals should be. This minibook also contains the diagnostic section of *Walking Medicine*: self-administered tests you can take to calculate both your fitness level and your physiological age (how young you really are). It also provides directions for making your own *family health tree* to help you determine which diseases or conditions you are at risk of inheriting from your parents and grandparents. Armed with all this information, you can set lifetime walking goals for yourself and your family members, concentrating on the programs in the following books if you have weaknesses or are at risk in one or more areas or following your age-graded program in this book if you are healthy.

Step two is to learn the basic walking techniques, outlined in Book 2: Walking for Arthritis, Back and Joints. These techniques are the backbone of exercisewalking and make walking an exercise that strengthens your muscles while it preserves your joints. This book will also help keep your musculoskeletal system running smoothly, both through walking and through stretching and strengthening exercises that promote joint and back health.

Book 2 provides special routines for walkers who have joint and bone weaknesses in their families or who want to stop the onset of osteoporosis, the leading cause of broken bones in the elderly. It is also a rehabilitative guide for those who come to walking already experiencing the aches and pains of arthritis, back, or joint problems due to injuries or accidents and who need to maintain their mobility.

In Book 3: Cardiowalking, you'll learn the third step, increasing your walking speed to strengthen your heart and lungs. The heart is the body's main pump, but it is also one of the organs most vulnerable to disease. Heart disease is the number one killer in the United States and one of the biggest killers worldwide. The cardiowalking program can lead you to a healthier heart, lungs, and vascular system, whether you are trying to prevent heart disease or already suffer from it. This program can also help you to lower your blood pressure and cholesterol levels. Included in this chapter are self-administered tests to help you choose the walking program to match your heart and lung fitness level, as well as schedules for both healthy heart walkers and those recovering from heart attacks, strokes, or lung diseases.

Once you've learned the basic techniques and have built up your walking speed, you are ready to shape your body. In Book 4: Walkshaping and Weight Control, you'll learn to build muscles as you reduce fat with calisthenic walking programs. This minibook is *Walking Medicine*'s answer to the myriads of diet books that appear annually. It shows how walking, combined with a diet developed especially for this book, will help you lose weight and build muscle. It is *not* the "look like a model in a week" approach to dieting, but rather a slow, steady lifetime maintenance approach to weight loss that will leave you feeling and looking healthy. Walkshaping also shows you how to use powerstepping and stroking techniques to burn fat and build muscle even more quickly.

Now that your basic skills are in place, Book 5: Walktherapy will teach you how to vary the distance, speed, and duration of your walks to reduce stress, energize yourself, and even improve your personality. Here you'll find self-administered tests to help you determine both the amount of stress you are under and how well you handle it. You'll learn how to stop smoking cigarettes, drinking alcohol, or using drugs with the help of walking and how walking gives you "stress hardiness" to fight cancer or other fatal illnesses or to cope with the death of a spouse or family member. You'll also read stories about executives of major companies who manage the ups and downs of their careers with therapeutic walking programs.

Book 6: The Walking Shoe and Foot Book provides leg exercises and information about footwear design and selection to help you better protect the Achilles heel of the walker—the foot. Through a survey of over 50 shoe manufacturers, numerous retail chains, and hundreds of walkers, we have developed the most in-depth analysis to date of walking shoes on the market. This information will help you choose a walking shoe that is right for your walking style and your specific foot construction.

Book 7: Walking Doctor and Health Professional Directory is a directory of over 400 health professionals, physicians, and researchers. This is your source for finding a walking doctor in your area (or in an area you might be visiting) who is sympathetic to your needs because he or she is, like you, a walker. It lists not only their addresses and telephone numbers, but how much each doctor walks and other facts about his or her personal connection to walking.

The Walking Philosophy

Above all, *Walking Medicine* will show you that walking is much more than an exercise. Gentle on the body and calming to the mind, walking symbolizes a moderate, balanced, active lifestyle. The walking philosophy does not embrace the hypercompetitive values that are prominent both in and out of most sports, nor does it support dangerous, risky behavior. It is the activity for those who follow the golden middle way.

As a part of this philosophy, we do not endeavor to represent walking as a magic solution to whatever ails you, but as a reasonable way of helping you to control, ameliorate, or perhaps prevent health problems, and make you feel younger and more energetic, and provide you with the strength, both physical and mental, for what life throws your way. We promise to tell you not only when walking can help, but also when it cannot or when there are other solutions.

Walking Medicine's special philosophy separates it from those health and fitness programs that promise the moon and the stars but rarely deliver the hoped-for results. Our society is filled with fitness frauds: exercise classes that promise the perfect body after 6 weeks, diets "guaranteed" to rid you of fat forever, drug remedies pledged to cure every condition and disease under the sun. Unlike these, our exercisewalking programs are for real people. We cannot promise that walking will make you look like Jane Fonda or Sylvester Stallone. It will not make you look 21 if you are 75. If you are short and 100 pounds overweight, it will not make you statuesque and painfully skinny. Walking can't change your genes or your basic body type, nor can it provide wonders overnight, but it can, if followed regularly throughout your life, help you to improve what you have, change what is transformable, and cope with what is not. What we can promise you is that walking is ultimately the easiest and safest solution for staying healthy or becoming healthy again.

WALKING AND AGING

*Add More and Better Years
to Your Life*

CONTRIBUTORS

Stephen Gambert M.D.

Dr. Gambert, a professor of medicine at New York Medical College in Valhalla, New York, is director of their Center for Aging and of the Westchester Medical Center's Geriatrics Division. He graduated from Columbia University College of Physicians and Surgeons in 1975 and has since been extremely active in conducting research in the fields of geriatrics, endocrinology, internal medicine, and metabolism. Dr. Gambert walks 40 miles a week and lives in Armonk, New York.

Mort Malkin, D.D.S.

Dr. Malkin is a staff dental surgeon at the Brooklyn Hospital in New York, where he performs oral-maxillofacial surgery. He designs and instructs aerobic walking programs nationally for heart, hypertension, and diabetic patients. Author of *Walking, the Pleasure Exercise*, Dr. Malkin has done many medical studies and medical literature reviews on walking. He racewalks 15 miles a week and lives in Brooklyn, New York.

Albert P. Rosen, M.D.

Dr. Rosen is a staff member in pediatrics at Columbia Presbyterian Medical Center in New York and at Valley Hospital in Ridgewood, New Jersey, where he was director of pediatrics from 1958 until 1976. He is retired from his position as assistant clinical professor at Columbia College of Physicians and Surgeons. He graduated from Downstate Medical College in Brooklyn, New York, in 1943. A long-time racewalker and hiker, Dr. Rosen has climbed many of the world's highest peaks. He lives in Fair Lawn, New Jersey.

Othneil J. Seiden, M.D.

Dr. Seiden is a general practitioner who left his private practice in the mid-1970s to become an author, writing primarily on health-related subjects. He also volunteers his time to Doctors to the World, a national organization of physicians who provide medical aid to both underdeveloped and recently stricken areas of the world. A graduate of the University of Maryland School of Medicine, Dr. Seiden is an endurance walker who competes in marathons—his best effort was a 78-mile triple marathon completed in 18 hours—and walks 4 to 6 miles a day, five to six times a week. He lives in Denver, Colorado.

Myra Skluth, M.D., Ph.D.

Dr. Skluth specializes in internal and preventive medicine and has a private practice in Norwalk, Connecticut. She graduated from the Albert Einstein College of Medicine

2

in New York. An avid walker, Dr. Skluth logs 12 to 15 miles a week and recommends walking to many of her patients. Dr. Skluth lives in Norwalk, Connecticut.

J.E. Walker, M.D.

Dr. Walker is clinical professor of neurology at the University of Texas Health Sciences Center in Dallas. His practice and research involve neurochemistry, neuropharmacology, and the treatment of epilepsy, multiple sclerosis, and chronic pain syndromes. Dr. Walker is a graduate of Baylor University College of Medicine in Houston, Texas. Walking is his primary form of exercise; he walks 10 miles a week and lives in Richardson, Texas.

1. Walking Through the Ages

Book 1: Walking and Aging is not about exercising when you are old, but rather about how to adapt an exercisewalking program to every period of your life. It shows you how walking can help to slow down the aging process and increase your vitality, and perhaps even your longevity. The sooner you start walking, the greater the benefits, but it is never too late, or too soon, to begin. Whether your age is 5 or 85, you can increase your strength and stamina, the capacity of your heart and lungs, and build self-esteem and a sense of well-being through walking.

In a monumental study done by the Institute for Aerobics Research and the Cooper Clinic in Dallas, researchers found that a complete lack of exercise is as dangerous to your health as smoking or having high cholesterol. The good news for walkers is that you don't have to be an athlete or marathon runner to increase your life expectancy. Even moderate amounts of exercise, according to Dr. Steven Blair, leader of the study, can substantially reduce your chances of dying of heart disease, cancer, and other causes. And the greatest health gains are for those people who move from being completely sedentary to being moderately active —walking for at least half an hour every day at a brisk pace.

The human body is in many ways similar to a complex machine like an automobile, and just as the parts of a car eventually wear out, so do parts of our bodies. To extend the life of a car, we know it is important to carry out routine maintenance: changing the oil, realigning the tires, replacing brake pads. If we don't, the car will keep breaking down.

To continue with the car analogy, we need to carry out maintenance

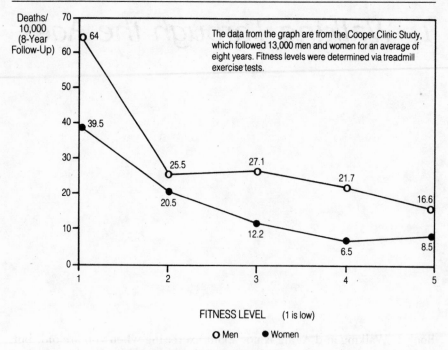

Deaths/10,000 (8-Year Follow-Up)

The data from the graph are from the Cooper Clinic Study, which followed 13,000 men and women for an average of eight years. Fitness levels were determined via treadmill exercise tests.

FITNESS LEVEL   (1 is low)

O Men   ● Women

Fitness Level versus Longevity

on our bodies to help them run better and last longer. Walking is probably the best and easiest form of body maintenance (prevention) and repair (rehabilitation). By following a regular walking program throughout your life, you will be on your way to ensuring that you don't suffer from health breakdowns, and in the process, improving the quality of your life.

Think of *Walking Medicine* as a repair and maintenance manual for your body. Just as a car is made up of systems, like an exhaust system and an electrical system, you can look at your body as a group of five systems: the musculoskeletal and skin systems (covered in depth in Books 2 and 6); the cardiovascular and respiratory systems, which include the lungs, heart, and blood vessels (Book 3); the metabolic, digestive, and excretory systems, which control how we gain and lose weight, use nutrients, and dispose of waste (Book 4); the central nervous system—the brain and nerves—which governs motor skills and processes information (Books 2 and 5); and what we call the "pyschoimmune" system, which is the interrelation between our emotions and the efficacy of the immune system in protecting us against disease (Book 5).

Book 1: Walking and Aging is your introduction to walking as a preventive, rehabilitative, and therapeutic medicine, and here and in each subsequent minibook you'll find an exercisewalking program that will help you maintain and repair each of the body's five systems. By following the walking programs in each chapter, you'll be able to say, "All systems are go!"

Although the word "aging" is often associated with old age, the truth is that we begin aging from the moment we leave the womb. The initial stages of aging are exhilarating: A baby learns to sit up, to walk and talk, and develops a distinct personality throughout childhood, adolescence, and early adulthood. Few of us in our teens or twenties can fathom that our bodies and minds are slowing down, no matter how many people we see grow old around us. It is only in our thirties and forties that we begin to experience changes in our bodies which signify that time is passing. Strength decreases, hairlines recede, and waistlines increase. But not all these changes have to be inevitable or, if they do occur, so dramatic.

All of us in essence reinvent the wheel as we age, often failing to learn from our elders that not taking our health seriously can lead to illness or premature death. The lesson we all must learn is that to some extent we are responsible for how healthy we are. What we hope for this section, as well as for the whole of *Walking Medicine*, is that you will learn from other walkers who have discovered the benefits of walking—feeling and looking younger, becoming mobile after surgery, allaying depression following an emotional crisis, relieving stress, or recovering from a near-fatal stroke or heart attack—and, in short, have improved the quality of their lives.

How to Use This Book

In this first chapter, Walking Through the Ages, you'll discover how and why the body deteriorates with age and in what ways walking can prevent, slow down, or reverse this decline. Many of the diseases or disorders you may encounter in your life are to some extent determined by genetics. In Chapter 2, Your Family Health Tree, you'll learn which medical problems are inherited and how to make your own family health tree to determine your health risks for everything from cancer to varicose veins. Armed with this information, you'll have an edge in preventing or fighting these medical disorders with a healthy lifestyle and an exercisewalking program.

Every age group has different concerns and emphasizes different health requirements that walking can address. Small children's activities center on developing motor skills, the average 40-year-old is most likely concentrating on keeping his or her weight down, and the 60-year-old wants to strengthen his or her body to prevent sickness or disease. Chapters 3 through 6, Kid Walkers, Teen Walkers, Walking Through Middle Age, and Walking for the Young, Middle, and Old-Old, take you through the specific changes that affect the five body systems during life's various phases and tell you how walking can enhance each of these stages. A detailed, age-graded walking program is included at the end of each chapter. Use these chapters as a reference guide for yourself, your children, your relatives, and your friends. The ailments, illnesses, and conditions you'll read about in these chapters are discussed in the decade in which they most commonly occur.

Chapter 7, What's Your Real Age?, is a series of self-administered tests to help you determine your biological age based on your muscle strength, your flexibility, and your heart and lung health. Through these tests you'll find out whether you are older or younger than your chronological age. After you've started an exercisewalking program, you can come back to these tests to see how much "younger" you've become.

How and Why We Age

There are several different theories on how and why we age. One, the "worn template" concept, posits that with every division of cells (the body replaces tissue through cell division), there is a greater chance that the copying mechanism will introduce errors, thus causing an eventual breakdown in the system. Another, the "accumulated toxins" theory, is that the body is gradually poisoned by toxins that it creates as by-products of normal bodily functions but which get trapped within the body. A third theory is that the immune system becomes less effective over the years, allowing viruses and other foreign organisms to attack the body undeterred. What

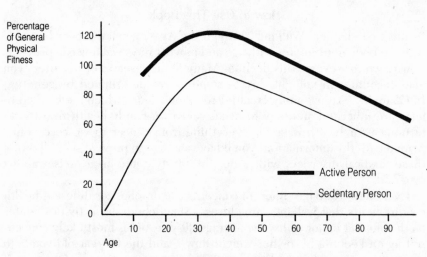

The Euro-American Curve

Source: *Exercise and Aging—The Scientific Basis* by Everet Smith and Robert Sertass.
(Hillside, NJ: Enslow Publications, 1981)

all these theories suggest is that aging is the wearing down of the body, either from prolonged use or from the ravages of disease.

Although the exact reasons for aging are not clear, we do know that the body is in a growth phase in the younger years, hitting an apex between ages 25 and 30. After that, the body starts on a long decline until death. (See the Euro-American curve on page 8.) The normal sedentary person experiences roughly a 1 percent decline in each of the body systems between the ages of 30 and 70. This means that by age 70, the body can perform at only 40 percent of its functional capability. (If you live longer than age 70, your functional capability will continue to deteriorate.) This reduction in overall functioning translates into a loss of muscle strength, endurance, and flexibility; an increase in body fat; and a decrease in coordination, agility, and balance. It also means that the heart pumps less blood with each stroke and cannot beat as fast during exertion. The lungs can transport less oxygen to the body's cells. The arteries become less flexible, and thus blood pressure increases. The bones become more fragile. Anxiety and depression increase, and mental agility and memory decrease. Many of the diseases and disabilities associated with growing older are caused by this overall deterioration, including heart attacks, arthritis, broken bones, strokes, and senility.

However, researchers believe that perhaps as much as half the decline normally associated with aging is actually due to disuse or underuse of the body. It is true that some results of aging are inevitable. Our hair turns gray and thin, our skin becomes thinner and dryer, and we develop wrinkles. Our voices begin to shake or become lower, and our speech slows down. Our hearing and eyesight grow less keen. Our joints wear down. In height, we tend to shrink, and in weight, we get heavier. But all the deterioration that the sedentary person experiences can be slowed down or reduced by staying moderately active with walking. As you can see from the figure on page 8, the active person still experiences a decline, but at a much less severe rate, perhaps losing only 20 percent of his or her functional capability between the ages of 30 and 70. Even if you have already begun to experience some of these effects of aging, you may be able to reverse them because walking's effectiveness as an antiaging tool increases with age, and as you approach your midsixties, lifestyle plays an increasingly important role in your speed of aging. For example, a 65-year-old who walks every day for 4 miles can have the same heart rate and lung capacity as a sedentary 25-year-old.

Examples of lifetime walkers abound, especially among artists and philosophers who found that walking helped them think clearly and creatively. Henry David Thoreau walked 250,000 miles in his lifetime, and Charles Dickens walked 180,000 miles. The average walker probably covers between 100,000 to 150,000 miles in his or her lifetime (this includes the normal walking done around your house, neighborhood, and office *and* an exercisewalking regimen).

Below you'll find a schedule of average miles walked at different levels of activity (Level I being the lowest and Level V the highest). Aim for a Level III lifetime mileage. Of course, when you are younger, you should walk more, and when you are older, you will probably walk less, but this chart assumes average daily mileage over your lifetime. Your walking speed may also decrease as you age, but even if you walk very slowly, you are still getting benefits in the form of increased circulation, increased muscle and bone strength, and ultimately protection against fatal diseases.

It is through a continuous, lifetime walking program that you can attain the best results. Many walkers interviewed for this book told us of being active as young adults but then suspending their walking program for several years during middle age. During the period they did not walk, many developed bad health habits, like eating an unbalanced, fatty diet or drinking too much, which, in turn, along with their lack of exercise, led to medical problems like heart disease or diabetes. These people were later able to control their problems with walking, but only when they made the decision to become active again. On the other hand, don't feel you have to catch up to the lifetime mileage goals if you are only starting a walking routine later in life. It is never too late to begin.

Obviously, we can do nothing about the march of the years. Human beings have a limited life span, thought to be about 110 years, and normal life expectancy for the United States is approximately 69 years for men and 77 years for women (life expectancy is highest in Scandinavia—72 years for men and 79 years for women). What we may be able to control is the quality of those years—*not* by depending on medicine to find the cure for diseases (after all, surgery can be dangerous and medication often has negative side effects), but by taking the active approach and adopting a healthy lifestyle.

Average Miles Walked at Different Activity Levels

LEVEL	AVERAGE DAILY MILEAGE*	LIFETIME MILEAGE
I	1–2	25,000–50,000
II	2–4	50,000–100,000
III	4–6	100,000–150,000
IV	6–8	150,000–200,000
V	8–10	200,000–300,000

*These numbers are calculated on walking every day for 70 years.

How Walking Helps the Body Systems

1. Central nervous system:
   Improves mental alertness and memory
   Primary rehabilitation for nervous system disorders
   Improves sexual vigor

2. Musculoskeletal and skin systems:
   Keeps skin firmer and smoother
   Improves posture
   Reduces stiffness in joints
   Improves flexibility
   Strengthens bones
   Builds muscles
   Improves balance
   Primary rehabilitation from autoimmune diseases (e.g., rheumatoid
      arthritis and muscular dystrophy)
   Important rehabilitation for accidents and injuries

3. Metabolic, digestive, and excretory systems:
   Helps control diabetes
   Reduces body fat
   Prevents constipation and related disorders

4. Cardiovascular and respiratory systems:
   Improves efficiency of heart and lungs
   Increases circulation
   Reduces cholesterol
   Reduces high blood pressure
   Increases lung capacity
   Primary rehabilitation from heart attack and stroke

5. "Psychoimmune" system:
   Strengthens immune system
   Reduces depression
   Helps psychological battle of disease
   Elevates mood
   Increases energy
   Helps control addictions to cigarettes, alcohol, and caffeine
   Improves self-esteem

2. *Your Family Health Tree*

ARE YOU AT RISK?

"You can't choose your parents," quipped Mady Bostain about the power of genetics. Her father suffered a heart attack at age 35. Although she did all the right things—"I've always been a walker, I've always been active," Mady says—Mady had a heart attack of her own at age 69.

Despite her heart attack and eventual quadruple bypass, Mady's precautions have actually paid off. Her heart problems struck her almost 35 years later than her father's did, and more important, Mady has left those problems far behind. Over the past year and a half, Mady has walked over 2000 miles, logging 10 to 16 miles daily, and she's shooting for a million. "I'll be in my nineties, but I'll still be chugging," she says.

Because Mady knew that heart disease lurked in her family, she took preventive measures to keep herself healthy. This chapter will teach you how to make your own family health tree, so that you, too, can determine your health risks. Armed with this knowledge, you can avoid or at least lessen the possible damage.

Many of the diseases and disorders discussed in *Walking Medicine* are thought to have what geneticists call a "familial component," meaning that the tendency to have the disease runs in a family. Risk for many diseases is also partially determined by race, gender, and cultural background, as well as by environmental circumstances. For example, you may have acquired certain habits from your parents, like eating fatty foods or smoking cigarettes, that put you at a greater risk for heart disease or lung cancer. Some diseases, like heart disease, are more common in men, and some, like rheumatoid arthritis, are more likely to appear in women. Blacks are more likely to have high blood pressure than whites.

Your lifestyle—your diet, how much you exercise, and whether you smoke cigarettes or drink alcohol excessively—is important in assessing your disease risks. In some instances, healthy habits are thought to be equally or even *more* important than genetic inheritance. You can also take extra precautions, like monitoring your health (with your doctor) to watch for early signs of the onset of a disease or illness. You can also use the information here to help you choose an exercisewalking program for the body system or systems that may be at risk. But even if you believe that your chances of developing a certain disease or disorder are small, it may be advisable to take the defensive and live a healthy lifestyle. Remember, even if you don't uncover any major diseases in your family tree, this may be due to healthy living on the part of your relatives, rather than superior genes.

As the extended family becomes a tradition of the past, many people, especially young adults, are not aware of the illnesses that have stricken their family members. This information is vital, as doctors often use it when prescribing a treatment or drug. (For example, women whose mothers have had breast cancer or a stroke will usually not be prescribed birth control pills.) You owe it to yourself and your offspring to determine the health risks that exist in your family.

Your parents' and siblings' (referred to by geneticists as "first-degree relatives") health histories are the most important, as these have the greatest repercussions on your own health risks. The health histories of "second-degree relatives" (your grandparents on both sides as well as aunts and uncles related by blood) are less important. If your grandparents died a long time ago, keep in mind that their reported cause of death may be inaccurate. (Remember, science wasn't as sophisticated 25 to 50 years ago as it is today.)

Many diseases are quite common, and thus the fact that they appear in your family may mean nothing. For example, a large number of people die of either cancer or heart disease (in that order) in industrialized countries, so there is bound to be at least one person in almost every family who has had one or both of these diseases. The two key factors to watch out for are (1) *multiple incidences of a disease in your family* (people not related to you by blood—stepparents, adoptive parents, aunts and uncles by marriage, brothers- and sisters-in-law—don't count) and (2) *early onset of a disease* (in the forties or fifties versus the sixties or seventies). These two elements generally indicate a genetic predisposition in the family. For example, if your mother died of a heart attack at age 80 and that is the only incidence of heart disease in your family, your chances of developing heart disease are probably not greater than average. However, if both

your parents had heart attacks in their forties or fifties, you are at greater
risk.

Interviewing Your Relatives

Below you will find instructions on creating your own family health tree
chart, as well as a personal health chart that will serve as a final summation
of the disorders and diseases to which you may be prone. Try to be as
complete as possible with your information: This means that you should
interview your relatives, not count on your own recollections. Often there
is one person in the family who is the keeper of family history, and he or
she may be able to give you information about many relatives. Use the
questionnaire below as your guide for querying your relatives. If they live
far away, send it to them. Fill out a questionnaire for each blood relative
in your family.

Don't take all information you get at face value. You'll also have to draw
some of your own conclusions. For example, in Kathy Burton's family
health tree (page 24) you'll note that her grandmother died a few days
after surgery for a broken hip. Therefore, we can conclude that she probably had osteoporosis (leading cause of broken bones among postmenopausal women). Also remember that the formal cause of death on a death
certificate may not tell the entire story. People with lung cancer, for
example, often technically die of pneumonia. However, the cancer is the
important illness to note. If someone has had heart disease, find out if he
or she also had high cholesterol or high blood pressure (often related
conditions). Remember that their lifestyle habits might either have protected family members or left them more vulnerable. Find out if they
smoked or drank excessively (the latter could indicate alcoholism). What
did your relatives do for a living? A highly stressful job might contribute
to a heart attack. If someone had cancer, it may have been caused by
occupational or environmental hazards. For example, an uncle who worked
in construction and had lung cancer might have been exposed to asbestos.
A coal miner or someone who worked in a petroleum refinery might also
be a candidate for lung cancer. A father who worked in a paint, rubber,
or textile plant or was a welder may have developed bladder or prostate
cancer from his exposure to dyes. Research has shown that a lag time of
up to 50 years can pass between exposure to toxic chemicals and the
development of cancer, so be sure to ask about jobs any cancer patients
held in their younger days, too.

Where your relatives lived is also important. People who live in cities
may be prone to a more stressful lifestyle or may be exposed to more
carcinogens than those who live in the country. Finally, find out how
physically active your family members were either in their jobs or in their
leisure time.

Family Health Questionnaire

Name: _____

Relation to you (including side of family, e.g., maternal grandmother):

_____

Height: _____ Weight: _____

Cause of death: _____

Age at death: _____

Please circle the diseases or disorders from which the person suffered. In the blank next to the circled item, list the age at which he or she first experienced the ailment.

Bones, Muscles, and Joints

1. Rheumatoid arthritis _____ 2. Osteoarthritis _____

3. Multiple sclerosis _____

4. Chronic joint problems (list joint affected, i.e., weak knees, shoulders, bone spurs, and initial cause of problem, such as accident or sports injury)

_____

_____

5. Broken hip or other bone _____ (list bone broken and cause)

_____

Family Health Questionnaire (Cont.)

6. Chronic back problems _____ (list initial cause of back problems,

i.e., pregnancy, accident) _____

_____

Heart, Lungs, and Circulation

1. Heart attack _____ 2. Bypass surgery _____

3. High blood pressure _____ 4. High cholesterol _____

5. Emphysema _____ 6. Hardening of the arteries _____

7. Chest pains (angina pectoris) _____

8. Leg cramps (intermittent claudication) _____

9. Varicose veins _____

Weight, Metabolic, and Digestive

1. Was this person very overweight? _____ If so, was this person

always overweight? _____ If not, at what age did he or she start to

have a weight problem? _____ 2. Diabetes _____

3. Alcoholism _____ 4. Hiatus hernia _____

Immune System

1. Breast cancer _____ 2. Lung cancer _____

3. Prostate cancer _____ 4. Colon cancer _____

Family Health Questionnaire (Cont.)

5. Lupus _____

6. Other cancer (please name _____) _____

Central Nervous System

1. Alzheimer's disease _____   2. Migraine headaches _____

3. Parkinson's disease _____

Miscellaneous

List any other chronic ailments or diseases here: _____

_____

Lifestyle Questions

1. Cigarette or pipe smoking or chewing tobacco (Please note number of

years smoked _____ and number of cigarettes per day _____)

2. Excessive drinking (more than two drinks a day) (Please note number of

years _____)

3. Activity level (circle one) *Note:* Exercise includes any physical activity

done for more than 20 minutes at a time (this includes physical labor).

Exercised 5 or more days a week for most of adult life.

Exercised between 3 and 5 days a week for most of adult life.

Exercised between 1 and 3 days a week for most of adult life.

Family Health Questionnaire (Cont.)

Exercised once every 2 weeks.

Rarely exercised.

4. Profession _____

Did or does this person have a particularly dangerous job (fireman, police-man)? _____

Did or does this person work in one of the following occupations or industries (circle appropriate one(s))?

Construction

Coal miner

Petroleum refineries

Welder

Manufacturing of rubber, paints, textiles, or leather goods

5. Eating habits (please answer yes or no to the following questions):

Did or does this person eat a high-fat diet? _____

Did or does this person eat a diet high in sugar? _____

How many times a week did or does this person eat red meat? _____

Was or is this person a vegetarian? _____

6. Where they lived or live.

In a large city? _____   In the country? _____

In a small city? _____   In the suburbs? _____

7. Was or is this person overweight? _____

Before you begin your investigation, however, you'll need to know what diseases or disorders are passed on from generation to generation. The following list, organized by body systems, includes the most common disorders discussed in *Walking Medicine* (this is by no means an exhaustive list of genetically transmitted diseases, but it does include those which may be prevented by walking or for which walking is a good rehabilitation).

Musculoskeletal System Disorders

Back Problems
Back problems due to body structural weaknesses are thought to be inherited, as is scoliosis (curvature of the spine). Women should note whether pregnancy in their mothers, aunts, or grandmothers brought on back problems. Of course, back pain caused by injuries is not inherited, but if several members of your family have had back problems (whatever the causes), you may be at risk.

Osteoarthritis
This is the common form of arthritis that will affect most people if they live long enough and what most older Americans are suffering from when they complain of aching and stiff hands, knees, and hips. You will be more likely to develop it, and develop it earlier, if someone in your immediate family had it at an early age (fifties).

Osteoporosis
Osteoporosis, in which the bones become excessively porous and fragile and are easily broken, occurs more often in women, especially small-boned women of northern European descent and those of Oriental ancestry. A rather large incidence of osteoporosis does occur in alcoholic men as well.

Rheumatoid Arthritis
Rheumatoid arthritis has a familial connection (although the incidence is small). In the general population, women are more apt to develop autoimmune diseases by a ratio of four to one over men. Rheumatoid arthritis is an autoimmune disease, i.e., one in which the body attacks itself. Other autoimmune diseases with familial connections include multiple sclerosis—a deterioration of the nervous system—and lupus—a disease that attacks blood vessels.

Cardiovascular and Respiratory System Disorders

Arteriosclerosis
Arteriosclerosis is a blockage or hardening of the arteries that generally leads to a heart attack or stroke. Most doctors and researchers believe that although the tendency for this disease does run in families, a healthy

lifestyle can go a long way toward protecting you. If any of your relatives had bypass surgery or angina pectoris (chest pains), they suffered from arteriosclerosis. If you are male, your chances of developing this disease are greater than if you are female (estrogen is thought to protect pre-menopausal women).

Emphysema

Emphysema, a disorder of the lungs that causes shortness of breath and chronic bronchitis, is most often thought to be a smoker's disease, but it can also be an inherited condition caused by an enzyme deficiency. If someone in your immediate family has emphysema (especially if they didn't smoke), you should avoid smoking, which could accelerate its onset in you.

High Blood Pressure

High blood pressure can lead to a heart attack and other lethal ailments, but fortunately, it can often be controlled through diet and exercise. If you have high blood pressure, you've probably inherited a sensitivity to salt, and the more salt you eat, the higher your blood pressure goes. Look for instances of this condition in family members, especially among those family members who have suffered heart attacks or heart disease. One in four blacks have high blood pressure, a much higher percentage than in whites.

High Cholesterol

High cholesterol is determined to a large extent by diet, but a tendency toward it is often found in families. As with high blood pressure, look for this condition in those family members who have had heart disease.

Varicose Veins

Varicose veins are the raised, blue, spidery veins that often appear on the backs of the thighs and calves. Although not a life-threatening disorder, the condition can be painful and unattractive. It is known to be passed on from generation to generation, usually from mothers to their daughters.

Immune System Disorders

Cancer

Certain types of cancers are inherited. However, since 25 to 30 percent of all people will develop some type of cancer, genetics is obviously not the only factor. Early onset in relatives and unusual tumors are signs of a hereditary risk for cancer.

Breast cancer, colon cancer, and prostate cancer are the three most common malignancies with familial connections. One in eleven women will eventually develop breast cancer, and about 5 percent of families clearly have a genetic disposition to this almost exclusively female disease (the female-to-male ratio for breast cancer is 150 to 1). If your mother or sister had breast cancer, your risk is increased; if they both had it, you have a 30 percent risk of developing it, too. Your risk is also increased if you started menstruating before age 12 or began menopause after age 55, if you have a tendency to get benign cysts in the breasts, and if you are a descendant of European Jews or northern Europeans or are an affluent American black. Women who become sexually active late in life, have their first child after age 35 (or are childless), haven't breast-fed a baby, or have been on birth control pills for more than 10 years are also statistically more likely to develop breast cancer.

There are 145,000 cases of colon and rectum cancer detected each year, and 60,000 of these result in death. Researchers have found evidence of a gene that protects against colon cancer and which is absent in some colon cancer patients. If a first-degree relative has colon cancer, your risk of developing a malignancy is two to five times greater than average.

Your risk for prostate cancer, an exclusively male disease, increases threefold if your father or brother also has had it. The incidence of prostate cancer among blacks is higher than for other racial groups.

Metabolic, Digestive, and Excretory System Disorders

Alcoholism

Alcoholism can weaken the immune system, make you age more rapidly, or cause life-threatening diseases such as cirrhosis of the liver. Alcoholism does run in families, and studies have shown that genetics are responsible for 35 to 40 percent of all alcoholics. If one (or both) of your parents is an alcoholic, you are four times more likely to become an alcoholic than if you were a child of nonalcoholic parents. Studies have also found that males are more likely to inherit this trait from alcoholic fathers, and women from alcoholic mothers.

Diabetes

Diabetes, or high blood sugar, is the exception to the early-onset rule. Diabetes that develops in children or young adults (called *juvenile diabetes*) is much less likely to be inherited than *adult-onset diabetes* (90 percent of all diabetics suffer from the latter variety). If you are the child of an adult-onset diabetic, you have a 60 percent chance of developing the disease before age 60. If you are overweight, your risk increases (doubles, in fact, for every 20 pounds of extra weight).

Hiatus Hernia

Hiatus hernia is a weakening of the muscles and ligaments (the tissue that links muscles) surrounding the stomach and is thought to be an inherited tendency; it can also be caused by aging tissues and muscles. Obese women over age 40 are especially susceptible to hiatus hernias.

Obesity

Researchers have found that obesity, defined as being 20 percent or more above the proper weight for your height, sex, and age, does run in families.

Central Nervous System Disorders

Alzheimer's Disease

Alzheimer's disease is thought to be responsible for 50 percent of all dementia that occurs later in life. Government statistics show that if all four of your grandparents live past age 75, there is a greater than equal chance that at least one will develop the disease. Your risk is increased only if a member of your immediate family (first-degree relatives) has suffered from Alzheimer's (some sources put this risk figure at 10 to 15 percent). In a small percentage of families, researchers have found a dominant gene for Alzheimer's, which increases the likelihood of contracting it to roughly 50 percent. Your risk is higher if there have been multiple occurrences in your family or if the disease appeared at an early age (forties) in a first-degree relative.

Migraine Headaches

Migraine headaches afflict women more than men (estrogen is thought to play a role in migraines, as the headaches often cease after menopause). If one of your parents suffered from migraines, you only have a 4 percent chance of having them, but if both parents experienced migraine headaches, your chances jump to 70 percent.

How to Draw Your Family Health Tree

The more family members you have, the more branches your tree will have (remember this sort of family tree *does not* include your aunts and uncles by marriage, stepparents or stepchildren, half brothers or half sisters, or cousins—because half their genes are determined by another family). For each row, list the appropriate relatives' names. Underneath each name list any of the familial conditions or diseases from which they suffered and the age of onset. List the cause of death, if deceased, and the age at death. You should also note any environmental factors, such as occupational hazards, poor nutrition, or bad habits. (See Kathy's and Gary's family health trees.)

As you can see, Gary and Kathy both have disease themes running through their family health trees. Here's a quick look at their interpretations of their own health risks to help give you some insight on how to analyze your own family health tree.

Gary's Family Health Tree

MOTHER'S SIDE   FATHER'S SIDE

Grandparents:

Dr. Franz Krauter.....Maria Krauter		Casper Yanker........Elizabeth Yanker	
1885–1969 (84)	1890–1956 (66)	1896–1955 (60)	1899–1983 (84)
Died of prostate	Died of pneumonia	Died of stroke–	Died of cerebral
cancer	High blood pressure	cerebral hemorrhage	hemorrhage
Smoked until age 45	and atherosclerosis	After an accident at	Atherosclerosis (74)
Walked daily	Did not drink or	48, developed blood	Did not smoke or
	smoke	clots that traveled	drink
	Walked daily	up from the legs	Very active
		Did not smoke or	
		drink	
		Very active	

Parents:

Elizabeth Yanker ....Peter Yanker
1925–   1922–
Arthritis (60)   Very active
Very active

My generation:

	Gary	Kristen	Peter
	1947–	1951–	1954–
	Muscle spasms (40)	Back problems (36)	Squeezed disk (30)
	and calcium deposit	from lifting	Hikes, swims, bikes
	in right shoulder	Swims, skis, hikes	
	Walks daily, skis,		
	bikes		

Gary, age 43, feels that his biggest danger is the high incidence of back and joint pain in his family. His mother has arthritis, and both his brother and sister have back problems. He feels that his brother and sister have exacerbated their back problems by being overweight. Although almost 10 years of serious walking has helped Gary control his weight and has strengthened his back so that he has avoided back problems, he still has experienced some shoulder pain (which seems to worsen when he is tense). Walking with a rigorous arm pump does seem to reduce the pain when it occurs.

Kathy, age 28, feels that her health weaknesses lie in heart health. Both her paternal grandparents had heart or vascular diseases, and her father has had triple bypass surgery. Although she is female and thus is protected from heart disease for the time being, she started walking this year to help improve her cardiovascular system.

While both her grandmothers had osteoporosis, Kathy is not as worried about developing this condition, since it was most likely a lack of exercise that brought on the osteoporosis (in fact, her maternal grandmother was bedridden for many years, which explains why her osteoporosis was so severe).

Kathy's Health Tree

MOTHER'S SIDE		FATHER'S SIDE	

Grandparents:

Jim Weimar	Em Weimar	John Burton	Mary Burton
1885–1977 (81)	1897–1978 (81)	1885–1971 (86)	1885–1966 (81)
Died of cirrhosis of the liver	Parkinson's disease (64)	Emphysema (seventies)	Heart attack (68)
Was a lifelong smoker and heavy drinker	Osteoporosis (late sixties)	Arteriosclerosis (seventies)	High blood pressure
	(broke hip twice, wrist twice, back, and pelvis)	Lifelong heavy smoker	Osteoporosis (died 2 days after hip surgery)
	Mild smoker		

Parents:

Mary W. Burton	Jim N. Burton
1926–	1921–
Active	Triple bypass surgery (63)
	Low HDL:LDL ratio (should be high)
	Smoked until age 63
	Active

My generation:

Jack	Scott	Kathy
1954–	1957–	1962–
	Walks	Walks, practices gymnastics

To Draw Your Family Tree:

Designate the right side of the paper for your mother's family and the left side for your father's.

1. In the first row, write the names of your four grandparents.

2. In the second row, list your parents' names in the center of the page. List your mother's siblings to the right of your mother's name and your father's to the left (without spouses)

3. The third row is your generation. List yourself and any siblings.

4. If you have children and want to determine their health risks, you will have to do a family tree for your family and your spouse's family. Although you may want to begin this tree with your spouses grandparents, for genetic purposes, your children's risks will be more determined by their parents (you and your spouse) and grandparents rather than great-grandparents.

What Does It Mean for You?

Now that you have a chart of your family, analyze what it says about your health risks or weaknesses. You can transfer the information to your own personal chart (see page 26).

First, look at the longevity factor in your family. Discounting family members who died in accidents, did the majority of the women live into their eighties? Did the majority of the men live past age 75? If so, you have a good chance of living a long life as well, provided you take care of your health. Discounting accidents, write down the average age at death in your family on your personal chart. For example, in Kathy's chart, both the men and the women (smokers and nonsmokers) lived into their eighties. This means that Kathy's life expectancy is comparable.

Family-Related Illnesses

Now, using the worksheet on page 26, list all the family-related diseases or disorders in your family. Then, for each illness, write down the number of times it has occurred in your family tree; the names of the family members who suffered from the disease or disorder, and the age when each first became ill with it. Then, in the space provided, give yourself 2 points for every case of the illness that struck a family member under the age of 60. In the next column, give yourself 2 points for each case of the illness affecting a parent or a sibling. In the same column, give yourself 2 points if your father has or had the disorder and his father or mother had it as well; 2 points if your mother has or had the disorder and her father or mother had it as well; 2 points if your father has or had the disorder and one or more of his siblings had it as well; and 2 points if your mother has or had the disorder and one or more of her siblings had it as well.

Now add up the numbers in the second and third columns for each disease and total that row. If the number is 2 or more, circle the name of the disease or disorder on the worksheet.

The diseases and disorders you log in on your personal chart are those for which you are at a higher than average risk. Now you can turn to other sections of *Walking Medicine* to find out how walking can help you prevent or recover from these diseases and conditions.

Remember, being at risk does not mean that you will necessarily develop the disease or disorder. However, if you are aware of your tendency toward the problem, you may be able to prevent its onset by following the walking and dietary advice in this book. If the disorder or disease is not a preventable one (like multiple sclerosis or rheumatoid arthritis) and you do develop it, you can use the walking and diet programs in this book to help rehabilitate yourself or to reduce the effects of the disease.

Worksheet: Family-Related Illnesses

FAMILY-RELATED DISEASES OR DISORDERS	NUMBER OF KNOWN OCCURRENCES IN FAMILY TREE	FAMILY MEMBERS AFFECTED BY THE ILLNESS	AGE WHEN FIRST AFFECTED	2 POINTS FOR EACH ONSET UNDER AGE 60	2 POINTS FOR EACH PARENT, SIBLING, PARENT'S PARENT, PARENT'S SIBLING

Your Personal Chart

IMMUNE DISEASES

CENTRAL NERVOUS SYSTEM DISEASES

_____

_____

_____

_____

METABOLIC/DIGESTIVE DISEASES

CARDIOVASCULAR DISEASES

_____

_____

_____

MUSCULOSKELETAL DISEASES

_____

_____

3. Kid Walkers

IT'S NEVER TOO EARLY TO START

More children are overweight today than they were 20 years ago, and one third of all children (some as young as 3 or 4) have elevated cholesterol levels. Thirteen percent of school-age children exercise less than twice weekly, and the average child watches 25 hours of television a week. In fact, everyone's health has improved over the last two decades except for children and teenagers.

This trend toward inactivity and poor health needs to be combated. Exercise is extremely important for children and teens. The period from birth to age 25 is the prime growth stage, and exercise enhances the growth cycle by making all areas of the body stronger. It also prevents children from being fat later in life, since most of our fat-storing cells are created during these early years.

The latest tack taken by health professionals in the effort to improve fitness levels among our youngsters is to instill good health habits in the *very* young, beginning with kindergarten-aged children. This approach works. In a survey done by the Metropolitan Life Foundation and Louis Harris & Associates, children in grades 3 through 12 who had at least 3 years of health education were less likely to drink alcohol, smoke cigarettes, or take other health risks than those children with one year or less of such education. Those with more health education were also more likely to exercise regularly, eat breakfast every day, and take care of their teeth.

What better way to train our children than with walking? For one, walking is a natural exercise that doesn't seem like an exercise. It is cheap and accessible, and even if parents or their children are not athletic,

27

everyone enjoys going for a walk. For older children, walking is a means
of independence and exploration. And exposing your children early on to
the joys of walking will encourage them to make it a lifelong exercise.
They may leave walking in their twenties or thirties to participate in team
sports, but many will come back to walking and readopt it as an exercise
as they get older.

So, if you are a parent or grandparent, read this chapter to find out
how you can instill a lifelong walking habit in your child.

Teaching Baby Steps

Human beings are designed to walk, and even in the first few weeks of
life, infants begin to learn skills to prepare them for walking. If infants
are held up with their feet touching the ground, they will instinctively
take a step as if they were walking.* Along with this natural reflex, infants
develop mental and sensory systems that increase the desire to be mobile.
When 7-month-old infants see a shiny red object across the floor, they
want to go over and explore. Infants develop at a surprisingly rapid speed.
In roughly 11 to 14 months they go from being dependent and immobile
to walking on their own. In between, they learn the building-block skills
to walking, such as sitting up, creeping, crawling, and pulling themselves
up to a standing position.

Although learning to walk is a skill that doesn't need to be taught,
parents, sitters, or other people who spend time with the infant can influence the development of some of these basic motor skills and thereby
help determine how active a child becomes. Parents can initially help
stimulate motor skills in a very young infant by holding the baby's feet or
hands and pumping his arms and legs. Even a child as young as two and
a half months will be amused by this activity and push and pull his limbs
with his parents' help.

When your child is three to four months old, you can begin to teach
him to sit up with assistance. With your baby lying on his back, take hold
of his hands and pull him up into a sitting position. At first, his head will
fall back because the muscles in the neck are not fully developed. Within
two months or so, however, your child will learn to move his upper body
as a single unit and will even pull his head forward as he sees your hands
moving to take his. You can also help him learn to sit after the fourth
month by holding him in a sitting position. Again, after two or three
months, your child will have learned to sit by himself.

In the seventh to ninth month, infants learn to move across the floor
on their stomachs, using their arms and legs for propulsion (crawling), and

---

*This reflex disappears after 3 months and reappears when the child learns to walk.

scooting backward across the floor in a sitting position. Later, they learn how to creep on their hands and knees. In the beginning, a child may just pull with his arms, letting his legs drag behind, but eventually, he will use both his arms and his legs and finally learn to move his left arm with his right leg, and vice versa. You can encourage motion by providing your child with adequate room to creep and crawl and by placing objects around the area that he can travel to and investigate.

As your infant gets older, you can encourage motor development by providing objects such as low tables or chairs or even a rope ladder hung in a doorway with which he can pull himself into a standing position. (Make sure there is nothing with sharp edges that he could hurt himself with if he fell.) It is not, however, advisable to force a child to learn to stand and walk before his muscles are ready.

Although children seemingly learn to walk in a few months, they do not walk "correctly,"—that is, with the proper techniques—until about the age of 6. These techniques include swinging the arms, keeping the feet pointed straight ahead, and extending the leg fully when taking a step. These walking gait developments happen separately and gradually.

In the initial stages of walking, at approximately one year, children usually hold their arms above their heads, in what is called the "guarded position." The stance is usually wider than an adult's for increased balance, and the toes are often turned out in a duck-footed, somewhat flat-footed walk, which also seems to add stability. These gait habits will be left behind in most cases as your child becomes steadier on his feet.

A Child's Locomotor Development

SKILL	AVERAGE AGE OF DEVELOPMENT
Crawling	4–5 months
Sitting	6–7 months
Creeping	7–9 months
Standing	10–11 months
Walking with help	11–12 months
Walking alone	12–14 months
Walking sideways, walking backwards	16–17 months
Walking upstairs with help	20–21 months
Walking upstairs and downstairs alone (leads with the same foot)	2 years

As a child masters walking, he will begin to swing his arms, moving them in opposition with the feet. He'll also learn to extend his knee and hip when he walks, and step so that his heel rather than the ball of his foot, hits the ground first.

By age two, children can walk very fast, averaging about 170 steps per minute. Their stance becomes narrower to accommodate this speed. They can climb up and down stairs unaided as well, although they tend to lead with the same foot, instead of alternating feet as adults do.

You can play walking games with your child once he has reached 2 or 2½ years of age. Good choices are "Simon Says" or "Follow the Leader," which can include hopping on one foot (a good exercise for developing balance and coordination) and, for children above four years of age, skipping.

Until children can walk well on their own (after the age of 5 or so), include children in your walking routine by placing them in a stroller or, with infants, in a backpack or frontpack. One walker told us that she has formed a group of mothers who walk with their young children. It allows the mothers to keep fit (more than regular walking would, since they are carrying or pushing extra weight), and the children to enjoy fresh air and the world around them.

Child Walkers

Walking is a beneficial exercise for youngsters because it strengthens the heart, lungs, and bones but is gentle on the joints and is a noncompetitive social activity. Walking energizes children, increases their attention spans, and calms any hyperactivity.

A recent federal study found that children with active parents are active themselves and tend to be more physically fit. Yet the parents' activity may not suit the child. Many runners, for example, find that their children don't like jogging because it is not playful. Up to the age of eight, children tend to expend energy in bursts, which match their attention spans. Walking suits younger children better, not only because it lets them stop and explore along the way, but also because it keeps them active and improves their motor skills. Plus, walking can be done with other kids, and doesn't seem like an exercise. If parents push physical fitness on their children, making it another chore, like picking up toys or making their beds, their children will never develop a positive attitude toward exercise.

Robert Sweetgall, who has spent the last few years walking all fifty states promoting walking to school children, has created a "wellness walking" curriculum, found in his two books *Walking for Little Children* and *Walking Wellness,** that educators and parents can follow to teach children

*Copies of these books and a newsletter for elementary educators, "The New Teacher," are available from Creative Walking Inc., P.O. Box 50296, Clayton, MO 63105.

anything from good health habits to mathematics and geography. Below are several walking programs and some walking activities (including some from Sweetgall's books) for elementary-aged school children.

A walking program for kids is in many ways similar to one for adults. Children should do warm-ups, stretches, and cool-downs. They should be taught to walk at different speeds and to follow a day of fast walking with a day of strolling. Children, like adults, should be encouraged to walk every day.

The motivation is also the same. Neither group will want to walk if it is not enjoyable. So don't overdo the amount you and your children walk, and most important, make it fun.

One of the primary concerns in designing your child's walking program is to understand a child's limit. You cannot, for example, plan a 12-mile hike with your 5-year-old. On the other hand, ½ to 1½ miles is a suitable distance for a kindergartner. Young children will benefit from a walk even if it's only 10 minutes long.

Teach your child to use different walking speeds. A slow speed, 2.5 miles an hour, might be used to walk to school. A medium speed is 3 miles an hour, and a fast speed is 3.5 miles an hour. Different walking speeds can be combined with different terrains. Hill walks should be slower than walks on flat ground, for example. If you have done a fast walk one day, it should be followed by a slow, longer walk the next day to let any sore muscles recover. If you use this method, your child won't experience exercise burnout. You can also use the different walking speeds to give your child a beginning anatomy course. Point out that the faster he walks, the harder he breathes, the more he sweats, the more tired he gets, and the faster his heart pumps. You can show you child how to take his pulse and explain that the pulse is a way to count and feel how fast the heart is beating.

Follow the chart below to plan your child's walking schedule. Use a slower walk as a time to open your child's eyes to colors and shapes, nature, machines and buildings, and smells and sounds. Make your walk into a mini-field trip by visiting the local post office, fire station, or museum. The faster speeds (Level III and higher) can be used to relax your child and expend pent-up energy.

Making walking into a game will keep your child interested. By age 6, most children are proficient climbers, and stairwalking or ladder climbing can be added as part of an obstacle walking course in a playground or along a walking route. Climbing is a good way to build cardiovascular health, and it is also something most children like to do.

There are simple walking techniques that your child should be taught, and again, you can use walking games to make your point. The main walking techniques mentioned in the infant's section were the pelvic tilt, arm pump, landing on the heel of the foot, keeping the feet pointed straight ahead. You should also teach your child to keep proper posture, with the head up and back straight.

Have your child walk while balancing a book on his head. If he slouches or looks down as he walks, the book will fall to the ground. He can start off slow and increase his speed as his postural technique improves.

Although children have learned the arm swing by age 16, they often prefer to walk with their hands in their pockets or hanging immobile by their sides. Show your child the difference between swinging and arm pumping. Explain that swinging your arms is for a slow walk, like strolling in the park or on the way to school, and arm pumping is for a more vigorous walk because it helps you move faster. In arm pumping, the elbows are bent at a 90-degree angle and are moved back and forth, held close to the body (see page 99 of Book 2 for detailed instructions). Teach the arm pump to your child by playing "Follow the Leader" and having him imitate your arm-pumping technique. Many children also shuffle their feet when they walk. Having them follow you in a heel walk (walking only on your heels) will teach them to pick up their feet and place their heels on the ground first when they walk.

To teach and reinforce proper foot placement, have your child study his own footsteps. The best ways are to have him step in a puddle (he will be fond of this part) and then make visible footprints with his wet feet. Or take him for a walk on the wet hard sand at the beach. How wide is his stance? Does he walk duck-footed or pigeon-toed? (The usual stance should be hip width apart.) If your child is walking incorrectly, use the footprints as a visual aid to point out the problem, and then show him how to correct it.

You can also use walking as a way to improve balance and coordination. Try getting your son or daughter to walk on a painted line, practicing the heel placement technique simultaneously with balancing skills.

For children 10 and older, walking will become a way to assert independence. They can walk with friends in woods or around the neighborhood, or they can join organizations like the Boy or Girl Scouts that give merit badges for walking. If the streets have sidewalks and it is safe for children to walk alone, have your child walk as a means of transportation; it's the perfect opportunity to promote an active lifestyle.

Walking Programs for Ages 5–12

Start the following walking programs at Level I and build to Level III. Some children may want to walk more and can increase to Level IV or V.

Walking Program for Kindergartners (Ages 5–6)

LEVELS	I	II	III	IV	V
Distance per day or session (miles)	0.25–0.5	0.5–0.75	0.75–1.25	1.25–1.5	1.5–1.75
Top speed (mph)	2	2.5	3.0	3.25	3.5
Frequency per week					
At top speed	1–2	2–3	3	4	4
Total days*	2–3	3–4	4–5	5–6	6–7
Time per aerobic session (minutes)†	5–15	15–20	20–30	30–45	45–60
Weekly distance (miles)	0.5–1.5	1.5–3	3–6	6–9	9–12

*On non-top-speed days, you should walk at a slower pace than your top speed.

†This equals an average time per session. On aerobic days, you may walk for a shorter period of time, and on strolling days, longer. Be sure to meet your daily mileage goals by walking several times a day, if necessary.

Walking Program for First-Graders (Ages 6–7)

LEVELS	I	II	III	IV	V
Distance per day or session (miles)	0.5–0.75	0.75–1.25	1.25–1.5	1.5–1.75	1.75–2
Top speed (mph)	2	2.5	3.0	3.25	3.5
Frequency per week					
At top speed	1–2	2–3	3	4	4
Total days*	2–3	3–4	4–5	5–6	6–7
Time per aerobic session (minutes)†	5–15	15–20	20–30	30–45	45–60
Weekly distance (miles)	1–2	2–5	5–8	8–11	11–14

*On non-top-speed days, you should walk at a slower pace than your top speed.

†This equals an average time per session. On aerobic days, you may walk for a shorter period of time, and on strolling days, longer. Be sure to meet your daily mileage goals by walking several times a day, if necessary.

Walking Program for Second-Graders (Ages 7–8)

LEVELS	I	II	III	IV	V
Distance per day or session (miles)	0.75–1	1–1.5	1.5–1.75	1.75–2.25	2.25–2.5
Top speed (mph)	2	2.5	3.0	3.25	3.5
Frequency per week					
At top speed	1–2	2–3	3	4	4
Total days*	2–3	3–4	4–5	5–6	6–7
Time per aerobic session (minutes)†	5–15	15–20	20–30	30–45	45–60
Weekly distance (miles)	1.5–3	3–6	6–9	9–12	12–16

*On non-top-speed days, you should walk at a slower pace than your top speed.

†This equals an average time per session. On aerobic days, you may walk for a shorter period of time, and on strolling days, longer. Be sure to meet your daily mileage goals by walking several times a day, if necessary.

Walking Program for Third-Graders (Ages 8–9)

LEVELS	I	II	III	IV	V
Distance per day or session (miles)	1–1.5	1.5–2	2–2.5	2.5–3	3–3.5
Top speed (mph)	2	2.5	3.0	3.25	3.5
Frequency per week					
At top speed	1–2	2–3	3	4	4
Total days*	2–3	3–4	4–5	5–6	6–7
Time per aerobic session (minutes)†	5–15	15–20	20–30	30–45	45–60
Weekly distance (miles)	2–5	5–8	8–13	13–18	18–24

*On non-top-speed days, you should walk at a slower pace than your top speed.

†This equals an average time per session. On aerobic days, you may walk for a shorter period of time, and on strolling days, longer. Be sure to meet your daily mileage goals by walking several times a day, if necessary.

Walking Program for Fourth- to Sixth-Graders (Ages 10–12)

LEVELS	I	II	III	IV	V
Distance per day or session (miles)	1.5–2	2–2.5	2.5–3.5	3.5–4	4–4.5
Top speed (mph)	2.5	3	3.5	4	4.5
Frequency per week					
At top speed	1–2	2–3	3	4	4
Total days*	2–3	3–4	4–5	5–6	6–7
Time per aerobic session (minutes)†	15–20	20–30	30–45	45–60	60–75
Weekly distance (miles)	3–6	6–10	10–18	18–24	24–32

*On non-top-speed days, you should walk at a slower pace than your top speed.

†This equals an average time per session. On aerobic days, you may walk for a shorter period of time, and on strolling days, longer. Be sure to meet your daily mileage goals by walking several times a day, if necessary.

Goals for All Walkers

LEVELS	I & II	III	IV & V
Expected heart rate (expressed as percentage of maximum)	50–65%	65–75%	75–85%

LEVELS	I–III	IV & V
Physical response	Easy breathing Can talk easily Minimal sweating Minimal muscle fatigue	Hard breathing Sweating Greater muscle fatigue

4. Teen Walkers

HOW TO RECLAIM OUR LOST YOUTH

Teenagers are also setting themselves up for an unhealthy adult life by smoking, drinking alcohol, eating a fattier diet, and exercising less than in past decades. Thirty-four percent of high school students smoke, compared to 27 percent of all adults. Nearly half of all high school juniors and seniors admit to driving after drinking. Only 21 percent look for nutritious food to buy. The change has even been noticed by the U.S. Army: 10 percent of the recruits entering basic training can't pass the minimum strength and endurance tests.

Parents, however, should not throw up their hands, because such risk-taking and antisocial behavior is *not* a natural part of adolescence. Studies on adolescents have shown that despite the "rebel without a cause" attitude usually associated with adolescents, 80 percent of all teenagers do not undergo violent mood swings or engage in rebellious, unreasonable risk-taking behavior.

Thus adolescents can be persuaded to take a reasonable approach to their health. If they have not been exposed to walking for exercise and activity as young children, encourage them to walk now. And teach them the importance of a balanced diet as well, since many health problems that affect adults begin to develop in the teen years.

Even if teens and young adults are involved in other sports, a brisk walking regimen can still be a part of their overall aerobic program. And for nonathletic teens, walking is the perfect introduction to aerobic activity, and it's safe for growing young bodies. What is especially unfortunate about this neglect of fitness among adolescents is that it is during the late

36

teens and early twenties that the body is at its physical peak. The heart and muscles are at their strongest, and the lungs are at their most powerful. The more children and young adults exercise, the greater their functional capacity will be when they reach physical maturity and the less will be their chances of losing an inordinate amount of capacity as they hit middle and old age (especially if they continue exercising throughout their lives).

Introduce walking as something that young teens can do with the family. If they enjoy it then, they may take it up as something to do on their own. Parents can encourage this by urging them to walk as their transportation rather than always begging a ride from Mom or Dad.

If your child would like some competitive sport but does not show any real aptitude or interest in the usual fare, you might suggest racewalking. It is an excellent aerobic exercise that is more demanding physically than running but does not strain the joints. The competition is not as fierce as in other track and field events, so that children who are only moderate athletes can still excel.

If competition is not your child's bag, hiking or long-distance walks might be a good way for him or her to exercise while developing a sense of independence and exploration. These are also good activities for adolescents to pursue with the opposite sex. The relaxing environment of being out of doors and the soothing action of walking itself will tend to calm teenagers, especially teenage boys who are nervous around girls. Talk tends to flow more naturally while walking.

Let's look at the teenage and young adult body in terms of the five major body systems. This will give you an idea of what is happening during this "peak performance" stage. You'll also learn how walking can address the aging process during these younger years.

Cardiovascular System

As we said earlier, the lungs, heart, and blood vessels are at their strongest during the teens and twenties. A 20-year-old's maximum heart rate is 200 beats per minute, which translates into a lot of stamina, because blood and oxygen are delivered to the muscles at a rapid rate. Exercising will lower the resting heart rate so that the heart will pump more slowly but more efficiently. Although most experts feel that aerobic exercise is good for all ages (even young children), it is during the teens that it becomes an important health practice. This is so because many diseases of the arteries and heart have already developed by this time. Statistics show that two thirds of all teenagers with moderately high blood pressure will have high blood pressure as adults. Other risk factors for heart disease that may show up in teens include cigarette smoking, obesity, high cholesterol, and a sedentary lifestyle. If you encourage your teenager to start a walking habit now, these risk factors can be reduced.

Musculoskeletal System

After age 20, the blood supply to the back's disks begins to recede, and the disks become less pliant. As the disks harden, the muscles surrounding the spine need to be strengthened to ensure that the spine stays aligned and free of pain or injury. Walking can do the job. The teen years are also when scoliosis, curvature of the spine, often appears (in about 5 percent of all teens). Along with a doctor's care, walking with proper posture can help correct scoliosis.

The bones will not reach their maximum density until approximately age 35, but teenagers should be concerned about building bone strength now. Teenage girls, especially, need to consume about 1000 milligrams of calcium a day (from food, not from calcium pills, which are thought to be ineffective), as well as walk regularly, to build strong bones and avoid osteoporosis and broken bones later in life. Although women are much more prone to bone weakening than men, teenage boys should also walk regularly to promote bone strength. Both boys and girls should be careful of overtraining, especially in sports like jogging that can cause stress fractures (stress fractures among walkers are almost nonexistent). Young women who overtrain can also halt their menstrual cycle, a condition known as *amenorrhea*. Amenorrhea has been shown to lead to bone deterioration because of a decrease in estrogen (which has been linked to bone strength in women). X-rays taken of 20-year-old women who were competitive athletes and had stopped menstruating showed bone deterioration equal to that of a 70-year-old woman.

Girls between the ages of 11 and 13 and boys between the ages of 13 and 16 often experience dramatic growth spurts. These can cause muscle tightness, so a long warm-up before walking is good idea.

Metabolic System

An area of concern during the teenage years is weight control. Being overweight can damage self-esteem, which at this stage of life tends to be fragile. Fat or chubby kids are often teased, and gym classes for such youths can be hell. Parents can do their children a favor by getting them involved in a walking program. Walking is better than other exercises for the overweight (both adults and kids) because it is not as embarrassing as jogging (excess flesh jiggles around too much) or swimming (because you only wear a bathing suit). The weight will come off slowly and fairly easily, and your child will be introduced to a rewarding exercise that doesn't demand an enormous amount of coordination.

Ideally, females in this age group should have 25 percent body fat or less. Males should have 16 percent or less. Because the teen years are a time of such rapid growth, any weight gain is distributed evenly over the body. In later years it will tend to collect in certain areas, depending on gender and genes.

Central Nervous and "Psychoimmune" Systems

Teens are under a great deal of stress, since both their bodies and their roles are changing drastically during these years. Walking is a known stress reducer, and a teen can benefit as much from a brisk walk after a hard day at school as adults do after a hard day at the office. Walking as a family is also a great way to iron out problems. One doctor wrote us that he and his son were able to have a very serious talk about their relationship while on a walk, a conversation the doctor contends would never have taken place had they been sitting together in the kitchen or living room.

Walking Programs for Ages 13–24

Start at Level I and build to Level III. Those teenagers and young adults who want to can build to Levels IV and V.

Walking Programs for Ages 13–14

LEVELS	I	II	III	IV	V
Distance per day or session (miles)	3–3.5	3.5–4	4–4.5	4.5–4.75	4.75–5
Top speed (mph)	3	3.5	4	4.5	4.75
Frequency per week					
At top speed	1–2	2–3	3	4	4
Total days*	2–3	3–4	4–5	5–6	6–7
Time per aerobic session (minutes)†	20–30	30–45	45–60	60–90	90–120
Weekly distance (miles)	6–11	11–16	16–23	23–29	29–35

*On non-top-speed days, you should walk at a slower pace than your top speed.

†This is an average. On days when you are walking at your top speed, you may walk for less time, and on other days, for longer. Be sure to meet your daily mileage goals by walking several times a day, if necessary.

Walking Program for Ages 15–17

LEVELS	I	II	III	IV	V
Distance per day or session (miles)	3.5–3.75	3.75–4.25	4.25–4.75	4.75–5.25	5.25–5.5
Top speed (mph)	3.25	3.75	4.25	4.75	5
Frequency per week					
At top speed	1–2	2–3	3	4	4
Total days*	2–3	3–4	4–5	5–6	6–7
Time per aerobic session (minutes)†	20–30	30–45	45–60	60–90	90–120
Weekly distance (miles)	7–11	11–17	17–24	25–32	32–39

*On non-top-speed days, you should walk at a slower pace than your top speed.

†This is an average. On days when you are walking at your top speed, you may walk for less time, and on other days, for longer. Be sure to meet your daily mileage goals by walking several times a day, if necessary.

Walking Program for Ages 18–24

LEVELS	I	II	III	IV	V
Distance per day or session (miles)	3.75–4.5	4.5–4.75	4.75–5	5–5.5	5.5–6.5
Top speed (mph)	3.5	3.75	4.5	5	5.5
Frequency per week					
At top speed	1–2	2–3	3	4	4
Total days*	2–3	3–4	4–5	5–6	6–7
Time per aerobic session (minutes)†	20–30	30–45	45–60	60–90	90–120
Weekly distance (miles)	8–14	14–19	19–25	25–33	33–46

*On non-top-speed days, you should walk at a slower pace than your top speed.

†This is an average. On days when you are walking at your top speed, you may walk for less time, and on other days, for longer. Be sure to meet your daily mileage goals by walking several times a day, if necessary.

Goals for All Walkers

LEVELS	I & II	III	IV & V
Expected heart rate (expressed as percentage of maximum)	50–65%	65–75%	75–85%

LEVELS	I–III	IV & V
Physical response	Easy breathing Can talk easily Minimal sweating Minimal muscle fatigue	Hard breathing Sweating Greater muscle fatigue

It is probably only in their late teens or early twenties that young adults will begin to realize how much walking can help them. Before this time, even though they are reaping the health benefits of walking, they may only think of walking as an activity to do with parents or friends, a means of transportation, or a sport. But after they leave home, either to attend college or to begin a career, they may come to appreciate the health and psychological benefits of following a regular walking program—whether it's to unwind after a day's work or to reduce the infamous "freshman 10" (the 10 pounds often gained during the freshman year of college). From these early years, the appreciation for walking will only grow.

5. Walking Through Middle Age

HOW TO IMPROVE YOUR PRIME

Sarah Gardner, age 27, recently took up racewalking. Although she is svelte and athletic—the results of an active lifestyle and a healthy diet—she is already worried about some of the first manifestations of aging. She knows that after age 25, the metabolism slows down and fat tends to collect on a woman's hips and upper thighs. While she shows no signs of these yet, she is afraid of developing what she calls "office butt": flabby thighs and buttocks from sitting at a desk all day.

Sarah turned to racewalking because her other exercises were no longer right for her. Jogging had worn down the cartilage in her knees so much that she could no longer run any distance without pain. Swimming kept her in good shape, but it was inconvenient and expensive to join a pool and she missed exercising out of doors.

Sarah never expected to like racewalking as much as she does. "I never thought it could be as strenuous as jogging," she said, "but when I woke up that first morning after trying racewalking and felt how sore my butt muscles were, I knew this was for me." She also enjoys the upper body movement of walking.

In addition, walking is a plus for her social life. "When I used to swim every night, I would get home late and have less time to spend with Brad [her fiancé]. Now he comes walking with me, and it is a chance for us to talk and exercise together."

A pessimist might say that after age 25 it is all downhill, especially in view of the aging curve you saw in Chapter 1. To most people, "middle age" probably designates the forties and fifties, but we cover the twenties and thirties in this chapter because that is when the effects of aging that become apparent in the middle years actually begin. With proper diet and exercise, the ailments and diseases that often strike during these years may be put off into the seventies, eighties, or even nineties.

Many people consider their thirtieth birthday as the first landmark on the way to old age and the final dividing line between youth and adulthood. However, the effects of aging at this initial stage of decline may be very small: You may only notice that you cannot eat as much as you used to without gaining weight, for example, or that your energy level is not what it once was. At this age you'll probably want to walk as a weight-reduction and body-toning tool, as well as a way to reduce stress.

As you cross over into your forties, the effects of aging become more obvious. In addition to graying hair and a few wrinkles, you may see your stomach or hips expand, and you may begin to experience aches in your knees, trouble with your back, or stiff muscles from a weekend softball game or an extralong hike. During your fourth decade, you may want to concentrate on the walking techniques and routines that will help you maintain your flexibility and strength, delay the effects of osteoarthritis and back pain, and prevent osteoporosis.

The fifties are the time when major health worries first come on the scene. Heart disease is not uncommon for men, and women go through menopause (after which they also face an increased risk for heart disease). Both men and women may choose to concentrate on walking techniques and programs that will improve their heart and lung health, as well as those that will help control or prevent diabetes, another serious disease that often strikes in the fifties.

Let's look at six body systems to see the major changes that will happen to the average sedentary male and female as he or she ages and how walking can help combat aging during the middle years.

Central Nervous and "Psychoimmune" Systems

Dr. Hampton Roy, a 52-year-old opthamologist specializing in eye surgery, walks 7 miles from his house to his office three times a week. The walk takes him about 1½ hours. Walking, he knows, lowers his blood pressure and is, in general, a great exercise. Aside from keeping his heart and lungs healthy, he's found that walking is good for his disposition. He started walking in his early thirties, but after keeping up a regular routine for 8 years, he stopped. During the three years he was inactive, he noticed a negative change in his overall mood. Egged on by his wife, he took up walking again, and hasn't stopped since. Roy uses his walking for "pondering time." He wears no watch and dons no headsets. "I like listening to the birds and watching the sun come up," he says.

During your thirties, forties, and fifties, you will deal with some of the biggest stresses of your life. Family responsibilities abound; these are the primary parenting years, and you may also have to care for ailing parents or in-laws. Work-related stress is endemic, and it gets worse as your job responsibilities grow. At some point you will probably have to deal with career successes and failures, leaving jobs, and starting new ones—all stressful situations.

Because of the multiple challenges of work and family, these years are often characterized by a midlife crisis. The psychological adjustments of entering middle age are complicated by more pronounced body changes, like weight gain, loss or thinning of hair, and the development of wrinkles. For the first time, we must begin to face the fact that we are getting older.

As life's stresses are on the rise, the body's stamina and energy levels are simultaneously decreasing. Walking is a good way to relieve the stresses of a job and to take time away from your work and family to ponder your problems or to allow your creative muses to work uninhibited. Walking will reduce the headaches, muscle tension, and bad moods. It will also make you more "stress-hardy" by strengthening your muscles, lungs, and heart, even undoing the effects of aging on these organs. Your feeling better will boost your self-esteem and perhaps even lessen the effects of the self-questioning you may undergo during these years.

Of all the neurological and psychological changes that take place during middle age, the most unsettling is an increase in absentmindedness. While much of this forgetfulness is probably due to stress, the brain does go through some anatomic changes during these years that may cause forgetfulness. The brain becomes slightly smaller, and it pulls away from its cover, the cortical mantle. Billions of neurons, or nerve cells, are lost. These changes do not, however, affect intelligence or our decision-making processes. As we reach our fifties, however, we often experience a decrease in reaction time, probably because messages don't travel as fast as they once did across synapses.

An experiment done on 55- to 70-year-olds at the Veteran's Administration Medical Center in Salt Lake City found that those put on a 4-month period of walking briskly for an hour three times a week increased their response time, their visual organization, and their memory over other participants in the program who remained sedentary or did flexibility and strengthening exercises that were not aerobic. Other studies have found that older people who exercise have a quicker response time than unfit 25-year-olds. Increased circulation of oxygen and blood is thought to be behind these improvements, as well as changes in the brain's biochemistry.

Playing "mind games" also improves memory. You can train both your mind and your body at once by learning a language or listening to books on tape while walking. Studies have also shown that memory can be improved to "younger" levels by using mnemonic devices. For example, if you have problems remembering peoples' names, create a mental picture that will make a person's name and face stick in your mind. If George Green is a banker, imagine a bright green dollar bill with his face in the center instead of George Washington's.

Finally, keep in mind that enhanced performance and overall feelings of well-being are the product of a proper night's sleep. Unfortunately, men over 30 and women over 50 begin to experience disturbances in their sleep patterns due to a loss of brain cells in the area of the brain that controls sleep. Thus we lose some of sleep's rejuvenating properties as we age. It takes increasingly longer to fall asleep, and we spend less time in REM sleep (when you dream and thus stimulate the brain) and NREM sleep (very deep sleep without dreams) and, in general, spend less time in uninterrupted sleep of any kind. Taking a brisk walk at least 2 hours before bedtime will induce fatigue and help you to fall asleep more quickly. It may also encourage an increase in REM and NREM sleep. Gary says that from his own experience, long weekend walks (over 12 miles a day) have similar results.

Musculoskeletal and Skin Systems

The first signs of back and joint pain tend to show up in the thirties and forties owing to a decrease in muscle strength and flexibility. A regular walking program can increase agility, flexibility, and strength.

After age 25 or 30, the normal sedentary person starts to lose muscle as the muscle cells atrophy. Because walking exercises the large muscles of the body, it will increase both muscle strength and endurance. Walking also exercises muscles evenly—both the front and the back of the legs are toned and both the stomach and the back are strengthened. Flexibility, which is determined by collagen fibers in the tissue connecting muscles to muscles and bones, begins to decrease after age 35. As this happens, our joints become stiff and we may get muscle spasms (continued contraction of the muscles). Stretching exercises (see pages 102 to 103 in Book 2), however, can restore flexibility, and continued stretching of your arms, legs, and back may even make you more flexible than you were in your youth. The heel-to-toe action of walking naturally tightens the muscles at the backs of the calves, so stretching the lower legs is particularly important for people over age 35, as is stretching the muscles at the backs of the thighs (the hamstrings) and in the lower back.

The blood supply to the disks (the shock absorbers of the back) has totally ceased by age 30, and they must now get their nutrients from lymph, a transparent fluid found in the body's tissue. The decrease in nutrients means that if you injure your back, it will heal more slowly, so precautions should be taken to avoid any jarring actions. Walking is both a preventive and a rehabilitative exercise for the back. Since walking is a low-impact exercise that is smooth and rhythmic, it does not place stress

on the bones of the spine. Rather, walking strengthens the muscles surrounding the spine and thus reduces the likelihood of a muscle spasm,
which is a common cause of back pain. Strong muscles will also help you
maintain proper posture. You may begin to lose height, roughly ⅛ inch
between the ages of 30 and 40 on average and ¼ inch between the ages
of 40 and 50. If you don't hold your back straight, you will place added
pressure on the already compacted disks.

After age 35, both men and women begin to lose more bone than they
make, especially of the more porous variety known as *trabecular bone
tissue*. Although all bones are made up of both trabecular bone tissue and
a harder cortical layer, the hips, wrists, and spine are made primarily of
trabecular bone (this is why these often break in older adults). The density
of your bone at its maturity is dependent on how much you exercised and
the type of diet you followed during your childhood and early adulthood.
The more density you have built up prior to age 35, the less dangerous
will be your bone loss. If you have not built up an adequate amount of
bone, you may develop osteoporosis (an extreme loss of bone density),
which puts you at risk for bone breaks and back problems.

Bone density in both sexes is lost at the rate of 0.3 percent a year after
age 35, but after menopause, women lose bone density at an average rate
of 1 percent a year, with the most rapid loss occurring between the ages
of 50 and 65, and mostly in the trabecular bone. This dramatic bone loss
after menopause in women is thought to be due to the loss of estrogen,
which helps in transferring calcium from the blood to the bone. A sedentary
man's rate of bone loss continues at roughly 0.3 percent a year.

Walking, because it is a weight-bearing exercise, increases bone density. The gentle shocks (equal to one or one and one-half times your body
weight) the bones absorb with every step are thought to stimulate the
bone to grow, or "lay down," an extra layer of bone matter, which makes
them thicker. In addition to walking, women especially should also eat
1200 milligrams of calcium daily in the form of dairy products and vegetables.

The skin experiences the most apparent signs of aging. In women, these
signs may first appear in the thirties and forties, although the skin has
been changing from childhood. Men's skin usually ages 10 years later than
women's because it is thicker and oilier. Although it is far from life-
threatening, wrinkling often has a devastating effect on people simply
because it is a visible sign of growing older. The main cause of wrinkles
is a change in the bottom-most layer of skin, called the *dermis*, which
loses moisture and elasticity and thus shrinks with age. As the dermis,
which houses blood vessels, glands, and nerve endings, becomes smaller,
the epidermis (the outer skin that we see) loosens and wrinkles. The skin
thickness is also modified, becoming thicker and leathery in some places

and thinner in others (especially under the eyes). Walking can help in a number of ways. One is that it increases circulation and thus nourishes the collagen fibers which hold the dermis together. It may also make the fibers more elastic, thus helping the skin remain firm and smooth. Walking also builds the muscles underneath the skin, smoothing out the wrinkles slightly.

The first wrinkles to appear (for women in their forties and for men in their fifties) are crow's-feet around the eyes and laugh lines around the mouth. In the next decades, dark circles may develop under the eyes and the skin may hang more loosely on your cheeks and neck. When you walk outdoors, protect your skin with sunscreen (especially your face), and wear a hat. A large percentage of adults over age 50 suffer from skin cancer. What level of protection you use depends on your skin type. Very fair people should use a product rated 15 to 20 for sun protection; people with very dark, even black, skin should use a sunscreen with a rating of 8.

Digestive and Metabolic Systems

After age 25, your metabolism (how fast your body burns fuel) slows down (at a rate of roughly 1 percent a year), and fat becomes harder to lose. In the sedentary person, body fat generally increases as muscle decreases. Although a 1 percent increase in body fat per decade is acceptable, women in their fifties should not have more than 27 percent body fat, and men, not more than 18 percent. Women's higher percentage of fat is associated with their childbearing and reproductive roles. Weight gain in the thirties and forties for women is primarily in the hips and thighs; for men it is in the abdomen and chest. After age 50, however, both sexes gain weight in the abdomen.

Walking is an effective weight-loss exercise. Walking at a brisk but comfortable pace will help you lose weight slowly and steadily. Although walking (or anything else) will not allow you to spot reduce, it will tone muscle in the thighs, buttocks, and abdomen, so your body looks trimmer and less flabby. If you need to lose a great deal of weight, combine an exercisewalking program of at least 12 miles per week with a low-calorie diet (see Book 4 for diet suggestions).

Along with the increase in body fat and the decrease in muscle mass, a general dehydration of cells also occurs in middle age. So as we get older, it is more important to drink water before and during exercise, especially in very hot weather.

The digestive system loses speed with age, and thus it takes longer for food to move through it. This slowdown can lead to stomach cramps, gas, constipation, and perhaps even colon cancer in adults over age 45. Dietary fiber and a regular exercisewalking program can help to reestablish good function. Wait more than 1 hour after eating before walking to avoid cramps, or plan to walk slowly.

Type II diabetes, a potentially dangerous metabolic disease that often arises in the forties or fifties, is brought on by an insensitivity to insulin, a hormone manufactured by the pancreas that allows the cells to remove sugar from the blood for fuel. Thus a diabetic cannot store or use glucose efficiently, which can lead to fatigue as well as other symptoms. This form of diabetes, also known as non-insulin-dependent diabetes, often can be controlled with exercise, diet, and (if need be) oral medication. Diabetics frequently have circulatory disorders because the disease causes small blood vessels to degenerate. Cuts in the legs and feet often don't heal properly or quickly because of poor circulation. Diabetics also have a greater than average risk of developing heart disease, high blood pressure, and cataracts, a clouding of the lens of the eye that leads to vision impairment.

Walking makes the body more sensitive to the effects of insulin and thus allows more glucose to be absorbed by the cells. Walk at night if possible, since blood sugar levels tend to be highest then. Many diabetics taking oral medication are able to reduce their dosages or eliminate it altogether after starting a regular walking program.

Cardiovascular and Respiratory Systems

Maximal heart rate begins to decrease after age 25 in the sedentary person. You may not notice the decline while doing a nonstrenuous activity like carrying a bag of groceries, but as the activity becomes more strenuous, say hiking up a steep, long hill, you might feel the effects. By age 35, maximal oxygen uptake has already decreased by roughly 10 percent in a sedentary person, and by age 45, it has decreased 20 percent. This means that the body takes in and delivers to the muscles 20 percent less oxygen than it could at age 25. Walking can prevent some of this loss by increasing the efficiency with which the muscle cells take oxygen from the blood, as well as by deterring the shrinkage of lung tissues and increasing the development of chest muscles (this aids in inhalation and exhalation).

The arteries become less flexible with age and can become clogged with cholesterol (a fatty substance). Both factors cause a narrowing of the arteries, which slows down blood flow to the heart, but walking helps to open up the arteries and flush out the cholesterol or at least deter further buildup. Eating a healthy diet also becomes increasingly important as you reach your thirties and forties, especially if you are male and have a history of heart disease in your family. This does not mean that women are without risk. Although it is rare for women to have a heart attack before menopause (roughly age 55), they should begin watching their diets for high-choles-terol foods and start a walking program before menopause.

High blood pressure is another worry in the middle years. Blood pressure tends to rise naturally with age, but not all doctors are convinced that it is a safe or good thing. Walking helps reduce blood pressure because it both opens narrowed arteries and helps reduce weight (being overweight is one cause of high blood pressure, because the cardiovascular system cannot efficiently cope with the extra weight). High blood pressure often turns up in men in their forties, but once women reach their fifties, their chances of developing high blood pressure are actually greater than those of men. After age 55, 30 percent of all women have high blood pressure, compared to 28 percent of all men. After age 65, 36 percent of women and 32 percent of men have high blood pressure.

By lowering your blood pressure and reducing the viscosity of your blood, walking also will help you avoid strokes, which frequently strike in middle and old age; in fact, strokes are the third biggest killer of women in their fifties. Walking is also one of the major rehabilitative exercises for stroke patients.

The forties are also when varicose veins, a less serious circulation dis-order, can arise. (Pregnant women of any age may also develop them.) Although varicose veins are usually painless, adults who develop them (they are four times more likely in women) are apt to experience more serious problems, such as phlebitis (blood clots in the legs), than those who don't. Walking increases circulation in the legs and helps prevent or minimize varicose veins and related circulatory problems.

Reproductive/Sexual System

Middle age is the time for rearing children. These days more couples are waiting until at least their thirties to have a baby. Although a woman's body is most efficient at delivering oxygen and nutrients to a fetus during her twenties, women in their thirties remain at peak fertility (ovulating 80 percent of all cycles) until age 35 (after age 35, women are fertile less often). There is no medical link between walking and fertility, but walking will definitely keep the lungs, the heart, and the circulatory system, as well as the mother's musculature (especially the abdominal and back mus-cles so important to a mother's comfort during pregnancy), young and strong until she is ready to conceive. Walking can also help tone the muscles that help push the baby through the birth canal and may help older women avoid the necessity for a cesarean section. Walking can also reduce complications, like diabetes, hypertension, and heart disease, that appear in 20 percent of the women over age 40 who try to conceive.

Ten percent of all women over age 35 (and a much smaller number under age 35) experience severe premenstrual syndrome (PMS), which can cause distressing changes in the body, including depression, aggression, headaches, constipation, backache, fatigue, or weight gain a week or two before menstruation. Following a *regular* walking program four times a week can help alleviate these symptoms (research shows that isolated periods of aerobic activity don't do much to combat PMS) and will also reduce the effects of molimina (a less intense version of the symptoms of PMS that many women normally experience right before their periods). A regular walking program can also reduce some of the side effects of menopause, like depression, numbness, headaches, and appetite loss.

Men reach their sexual peak in their late teens. In their thirties and forties they may notice a decline in sexual vigor, for example, that it takes longer to get an erection, that the angle of erection is not as steep, and that it takes longer to reach orgasm. As men get older, they also produce less sperm. Moderate exercise like walking has been shown to increase levels of testosterone in men (although intense exercise lowers testosterone levels), which in turn enhances sexual performance. Walking also helps avoid physical fatigue and stress, which are both causes of impotence (common in men over age 50) and the inability to maintain an erection.

For both sexes, walking will help build endurance, strength, and overall vigor, which will make sex more enjoyable for both partners.

Walking Programs for Ages 25–59

Walking Program for Ages 25–29

LEVELS	I	II	III	IV	V
Distance per day or session (miles)	3.75–4.25	4.25–4.5	4.5–5	5–5.25	5.25–5.5
Top speed (mph)	2.5	3.5	3.75	4.5	5
Frequency per week At top speed	1–2	2–3	3	4	4
Total days*	2–3	3–4	4–5	5–6	6–7
Time per aerobic session (minutes)†	10–20	20–30	30–45	45–60	60–90
Weekly distance (miles)	8–13	13–18	18–25	25–32	32–39

*On non-top-speed days, you should walk at a slower pace than your top speed.

†This is an average. On days when you are walking at your top speed, you may walk for less time, and on other days, for longer. Be sure to meet your daily mileage goals by walking several times a day, if necessary.

Walking Program for Ages 30–39

LEVELS	I	II	III	IV	V
Distance per day or session (miles)	3.75–4.25	4.25–4.5	4.5–5	5–5.25	5.25–5.5
Top speed (mph)	2.5	3.5	3.75	4.5	5
Frequency per week					
At top speed	1–2	2–3	3	4	4
Total days*	2–3	3–4	4–5	5–6	6–7
Time per aerobic session (minutes)†	10–20	20–30	30–45	45–60	60–90
Weekly distance (miles)	8–13	13–18	14–25	25–32	32–39

*On non-top-speed days, you should walk at a slower pace than your top speed.

†This is an average. On days when you are walking at your top speed, you may walk for less time, and on other days, for longer. Be sure to meet your daily mileage goals by walking several times a day, if necessary.

Walking Program for Ages 40–49

LEVELS	I	II	III	IV	V
Distance per day or session (miles)	3.5–4	4–4.25	4.25–4.5	4.5–4.75	4.75–5
Top speed (mph)	2.0	3.0	3.25	4	4.53
Frequency per week					
At top speed	1–2	2–3	3	4	4
Total days*	2–3	3–4	4–5	5–6	6–7
Time per aerobic session (minutes)†	10–20	20–30	30–45	45–60	60–90
Weekly distance (miles)	7–12	12–17	17–23	23–29	29–35

*On non-top-speed days, you should walk at a slower pace than your top speed.

†This is an average. On days when you are walking at your top speed, you may walk for less time, and on other days, for longer. Be sure to meet your daily mileage goals by walking several times a day, if necessary.

Walking Program for Ages 50–59

LEVELS	I	II	III	IV	V
Distance per day or session (miles)	3.5–4	4–4.25	4.25–4.5	4.5–4.75	4.75–5
Top speed (mph)	2.0	3.0	3.25	4	4.5
Frequency per week					
At top speed	1–2	2–3	3	4	4
Total days*	2–3	3–4	4–5	5–6	6–7
Time per aerobic session (minutes)†	10–20	20–30	30–45	45–60	60–90
Weekly distance (miles)	7–12	12–17	17–23	23–29	29–35

*On non-top-speed days, you should walk at a slower pace than your top speed.

†This is an average. On days when you are walking at your top speed, you may walk for less time, and on other days, for longer. Be sure to meet your daily mileage goals by walking several times a day, if necessary.

Goals for All Walkers

LEVELS	I & II	III	IV & V
Expected heart rate (expressed as percentage of maximum)	50–65%	65–75%	75–85%

LEVELS	I–III	IV & V
Physical response	Easy breathing Can talk easily Minimal sweating Minimal muscle fatigue	Hard breathing Sweating Greater muscle fatigue

Preparing for the Outdoors

If you walk in bright sunlight, wear sunglasses, as eyes that have been overexposed to the ultraviolet rays of the sun are more likely to develop cataracts.

You can take precautions when walking outdoors to keep your hair healthy. Besides graying with age, hair also becomes dryer and less shiny.

Use hot oil treatments to counteract the effects of sun and heat, or wear a hat.

You will undoubtedly face many changes and challenges in your life during your middle years. Whether you want to quit smoking, lose weight, tone your body, increase your energy level, reduce your blood pressure, relieve stress, or just feel younger, walking can help.

6. Walking for the Young-, Middle-, and Old-Old

IT'S NEVER TOO LATE TO START

"I was all set to buy one of those Lay-Z-Boy chairs so I could keep my movement to a minimum, when I decided to start walking," says Marjorie Taylor, age 68, who suffered from the aches and pains of mild osteoarthritis in her legs. Now she and her husband Eldred, also age 68, have logged over 1000 miles in a year and a half, and both feel and look better for it.

About 10 years before he (officially) retired, Eldred started taking some mild medication—50 mg of hydrochlorothiazide—for his elevated blood pressure. After 9 months of walking, he was able to discontinue his medication. In 1988—the year he started walking—Eldred strode 830 miles.

Marjorie's hip pain was so bad that she couldn't lie on either side when she slept, and sometimes she would get a pain in one knee, for which she wore a brace. In church, when the congregation was told to get up and sing, she was rising "slower than a 91-year-old woman." During her first 11 months of walking, she logged 530 miles, and now the pain in her legs has diminished so much that she can sleep on either side and get up from a sitting position without any problem. She says that now she moves like a much younger woman, and people don't believe that she is 68.

The Taylors walk 6 days a week, Monday through Saturday. In bad weather, they walk in their local mall. They start out first thing in the morning and have breakfast when they return. Although they walk at the same time, they don't walk together because they have different paces. Marjorie walks 2 miles a day, taking about 40 minutes. Eldred walks closer to 3 miles, in about 48 minutes.

Since they've started walking, the Taylors sleep better at night and feel more relaxed. They watch their cholesterol and eat a cereal they prepare themselves out of oatmeal, oat bran, yogurt, raisins, pecans, and orange juice. They avoid salt, butter, beef, and fried foods. When he was 47 years old, Eldred weighed 168 pounds. Today, more than 20 years later, he has gained only 7 pounds. Marjorie is a little overweight, but since she started walking, she's lost 10 pounds and is holding her weight at a steady level. People tell the Taylors they look 54, "and we feel at least that young!" says Eldred.

Frank Forsythe, age 80, has been walking since the spring of 1983—3 miles a day, 4 days a week. In October of 1985, Frank underwent bypass surgery. At his hospital, surgery is a three-phase process. Phase 1 is the operation, phase 2 is a mild exercise program, and phase 3 is a more rigorous exercise program. Frank came through the operation so strongly that he was allowed to skip phase 3. According to his cardiologist, Frank's speedy recovery was a result of his regular walking program.

Frank has been suffering from osteoporosis for the past 20 years, and he suffers back pain because of compression fractures. When his back starts acting up, he says, he just walks around a little and the pain goes away. He notes that he breathes more easily than he did before he started walking.

Frank doesn't mind walking outside, but he much prefers the mall. "It's a good place to meet a lot of friendly people," he says. He himself is of a cheerful disposition. This, too, he believes, is due in part to his walking. "My friends who don't walk are depressed," he says. "Even those younger than me don't seem to care if the world goes on or not."

Gerontologists and sociologists refer to the years from age 60 to 75 as the "young-old," from age 75 to 84 as the "middle-old," and age 85 and over as "old-old," but as the Taylors and Frank Forsythe show, even if you fall into these categories, you don't have to feel old.

Surveys conducted by the President's Council on Fitness have found that many older people believe that their need to exercise diminishes with age. They also tend to exaggerate the dangers of exercise and their inability to exercise. The example of walkers in this book is proof not only that almost anyone at any age can walk, but also that they will feel better for it.

Walking's major benefit for the young-old is to make them stronger both physically and psychologically. Walkers at this age are experiencing an increased threat of developing fatal or serious ailments such as cancer, heart disease, Parkinson's disease, Alzheimer's disease, heart attacks, and strokes. The strength and mood enhancement such people can gain from a daily walking regimen may help them fight against illness.

The middle- and old-old also benefit from the psychological and physiological boost that walking affords, but perhaps most important, walking represents increased independence through mobility for this age group, which is often thought of (by others as well by themselves) as frail and helpless.

Central Nervous and "Psychoimmune" Systems

The sixties, seventies, and years beyond are recognized as a time of increased depression in adults, especially following retirement. Over 2 million Americans over age 60 are alcoholics; about a third of these did not abuse alcohol in the first five decades of their lives. Retirement, loss of spouse, illness of self or loved one, realization of growing old—all contribute to this rise in alcohol abuse. These particular stresses are among the most difficult to deal with, even more than the earlier-age responsibilities of family and work, which provide a structure that may actually keep a potential alcoholic from drinking.

Walking can become your structure. If you have a problem with alcohol abuse, try combining a walking program (either in a walking club or on your own) with formal counseling or support groups like Alcoholics Anonymous.

Research has shown that just starting a walking program in your eighties or nineties may provide positive benefits. Dorothea Warner, a nurse and former staff education coordinator at a nursing home in Mystic, Connecticut, found that the residents at the home became more social, independent, and aware and less alienated when they followed a regular walking program. After only 3 months, residents were visiting friends on their own and taking part in recreational activities thanks to their newfound mobility. Crippling arthritis pain and circulatory problems associated with diabetes were also reduced among this group.

As Ms. Warner's program shows, contact with the rest of the world is perhaps one of the most important by-products of walking in your later years. Even walking among strangers on a sidewalk or in a gym or mall will make you feel part of society and therefore more vital. Being mobile means you can cultivate friendships with people of all ages, as well as keep in touch with your family. Taking a walk with your adult children provides a good time for conversation, and walking is also a relaxing activity for grandparents and grandchildren.

Perhaps the most frightening neurological disease that the young-, middle-, and old-old experience are senile dementia and, more specifically, Alzheimer's disease, both of which often strike in the sixties and seventies. (Alzheimer's disease is responsible for 50 percent of all occurrences of senile dementia, the other 50 percent are caused by numerous factors, including medication side effects and depression). Lesions (called *neuritic plaques*) and tangles of the nerve fibers (called *neurofibrillary tangles*) develop in the brain and interfere with the transmission of nerve impulses from one brain cell to another. Although we all develop these irregularities as we age, they are particularly prominent in people with Alzheimer's disease. According to a study done by researchers at Harvard Medical School, 10.3 percent of all adults over age 65 are believed to have the disease, as are 47.2 percent of those over age 85.

Although walking cannot cure or prevent Alzheimer's disease, it can help people with this disease by keeping them mobile, helping them sleep better at night, and providing a constructive means of expending energy (people with Alzheimer's often have a lot of nervous energy).

Musculoskeletal System

Accidental falls account for a large majority of deaths after age 65. Strokes, Parkinson's disease, and osteoporosis can contribute to falls by weakening the leg muscles and disturbing balance (due to age or the side effects of medication). Following a walking routine and learning proper walking techniques will decrease the likelihood of falls in the young-old and the old-old, both by increasing muscle and bone strength and by improving balance, coordination, and motor skills. Walking regularly will also improve confidence. If a walker is afraid of falling, he or she may become sedentary, which will weaken the body and thus increase the risk of falling.

One of the main causes of falls is loss of bone density. By age 70, a sedentary woman may have lost up to 30 percent of her total bone mass; a sedentary man, roughly 10 percent. By age 65, one in four women has osteoporosis. The bones become brittle and can spontaneously break, causing falls (the falls don't always cause the break). However, it is never too late to improve bone density. Studies have shown that walking as little as 30 minutes three times a week, even in women 80 years old, can slow down and even reverse bone loss.

Stride length usually decreases naturally with age, but this adds to instability. Thus if you are over age 60, you should practice the walking techniques found in Book 2 of this book. The most important technique for the older adult is the stride stretch. A stride length of less than 16 inches puts you in danger of falling, and you should endeavor to increase your stride length to 24 inches. You should also walk with a hip-width stance and pick your feet up sufficiently so that you do not stumble on uneven ground. Wear low-heeled shoes that offer support and stability.

If you are unsure of your balance, try this test (with someone spotting you in case you begin to fall). Imagine you are walking on a 4-inch-wide line, placing one foot directly in front of the other. If you cannot walk without straying from this line, then you may have a balance problem. If this is the case, you can follow a modified walking program using a walker.

Walking is a primary rehabilitative exercise for many diseases and disorders. For example, walking has been widely used for Parkinson's disease, a central nervous system disorder that causes tremors and a slow paralysis and affects about half a million Americans over age 50. Walking very deliberately and concentrating on foot placement can help to retrain muscles, make them stronger, and improve motor performance, which (combined with medication) decreases the effects of the disease.

Following a walking program will also keep you strong in case you need surgery on your joints or bones. Susan Cable, a physical therapist who specializes in geriatrics, told us about a 90-year-old woman who had undergone surgery for a hip fracture. This patient was up walking sooner than any other patient, regardless of age, who Cable had ever seen. It turns out that this woman was a dedicated walker. "She said that every morning she opened her window, took a shower, and went out for a walk, and she always took the stairs to her second-floor apartment."

Our nervous systems become less sensitive to temperature as we age. In older adults, drops in temperature are often not perceived unless they are extreme. This, coupled with a decreased ability to regulate body heat (by shivering, for example), means that people over age 65 are at a greater risk of hypothermia (a body temperature of below 94.6°F caused by overexposure to cold). If you walk outside in winter, be sure to dress warmly. You may prefer indoor walking in a mall or at a track.

Metabolic and Digestive Systems

During middle age, adults worry about weight gain, but after age 65, you may begin to lose weight again, especially if you are female, because of a decrease in appetite. A daily walk can help boost your appetite, ensuring that you are getting enough nutrients (especially important because the body becomes less efficient at absorbing nutrients from food as we age).

The ability to remove sugar from the bloodstream also decreases with age, and can lead to adult onset diabetes. Walking can combat diabetes by increasing the body's efficiency in metabolizing sugar, and by helping you to slim down. (Being overweight is a risk factor for developing the disease.)

Cardiovascular and Respiratory Systems

After age 65, women's death rate from heart disease is almost as high as that of men. And if a woman suffers a heart attack, her chances of having another are two to three times greater than a man's. Walking can help you recover from a heart attack (and lessen your chances of a second one) even if you are in your seventies or eighties.

Reginald Arnold is an 82-year-old racewalker who can complete 1500 meters (just shy of a mile) in under 14 minutes (faster than most 50-year-olds). At age 78, while preparing for national racewalking competition, he suffered a heart attack. Reginald's active lifestyle actually saved his life, since he came from a family in which two siblings had died of heart attacks and one had undergone a quadruple bypass. Within 6 months of his heart attack, Arnold won a Senior Olympic gold medal in racewalking. So far, he has improved his health so much that he has averted the need for heart surgery. In addition, walking has allowed him to throw away the diabetic medication he had taken for the last 30 years.

"At this moment, my 1-hour aerobic racewalk each morning is as important to me as my breakfast," says Arnold. "It has been a lifesaver for me, and there is no question that it has improved the quality of my life. My doctor told me, 'You are in better health than 90 percent of the people your age.'"

Walking Programs for Ages 60–99

Walking Program for Ages 60–68

LEVELS	I	II	III	IV	V
Distance per day or session (miles)	1.5–2	2–2.5	2.5–3.25	3.25–3.5	3.5–3.75
Top speed (mph)	2.5	2.75	3.25	3.75	4
Frequency per week					
At top speed	1–2	2–3	3	4	4
Total days*	2–3	3–4	4–5	5–6	6–7
Time per aerobic session (minutes)†	5–15	15–20	20–30	30–45	45–60
Weekly distance (miles)	3–6	6–10	10–16	16–21	21–26

*On non-top-speed days, you should walk at a slower pace than your top speed.

†This is an average. On days when you are walking at your top speed, you may walk for less time, and on other days, for longer. Be sure to meet your daily mileage goals by walking several times a day, if necessary.

Walking Program for Ages 69–74

LEVELS	I	II	III	IV	V
Distance per day or session (miles)	1–1.5	1.5–2	2–3	3–3.25	3.25–3.5
Top speed (mph)	2.0	2.5	3	3.5	3.75
Frequency per week					
At top speed	1–2	2–3	3	4	4
Total days*	2–3	3–4	4–5	5–6	6–7
Time per aerobic session (minutes)†	5–15	15–20	20–30	30–45	45–60
Weekly distance (miles)	2–5	5–8	8–15	15–20	20–25

*On non-top-speed days, you should walk at a slower pace than your top speed.

†This is an average. On days when you are walking at your top speed, you may walk for less time, and on other days, for longer. Be sure to meet your daily mileage goals by walking several times a day, if necessary.

Walking Program for Ages 75–84

LEVELS	I	II	III	IV	V
Distance per day or session (miles)	0.75–1.25	1.25–1.75	1.75–2.25	2.25–2.75	2.75–3
Top speed (mph)	2.0	2.5	3	3.25	3.5
Frequency per week					
At top speed	1–2	2–3	3	4	4
Total days*	2–3	3–4	4–5	5–6	6–7
Time per aerobic session (minutes)†	5–15	15–20	20–30	30–45	45–60
Weekly distance (miles)	2–4	4–7	7–11	11–17	17–21

*On non-top-speed days, you should walk at a slower pace than your top speed.

†This is an average. On days when you are walking at your top speed, you may walk for less time, and on other days, for longer. Be sure to meet your daily mileage goals by walking several times a day, if necessary.

Walking Program for Ages 85–99

LEVELS	I	II	III	IV	V
Distance per day or session (miles)	0.5–.75	0.75–1.5	1.5–1.75	1.75–2	2–2.5
Top speed (mph)	1.5	2	2.5	3	3.25
Frequency per week					
At top speed	1–2	2–3	3	4	4
Total days*	2–3	3–4	4–5	5–6	6–7
Time per aerobic session (minutes)†	5–15	15–20	20–30	30–45	45–60
Weekly distance (miles)	1–2	2–6	6–9	9–12	12–18

*On non-top-speed days, you should walk at a slower pace than your top speed.

†This is an average. On days when you are walking at your top speed, you may walk for less time, and on other days, for longer. Be sure to meet your daily mileage goals by walking several times a day, if necessary.

Goals for All Walkers

LEVELS	I & II	III	IV & V
Expected heart rate (expressed as percentage of maximum)	50–65%	65–75%	75–85%

LEVELS	I–III	IV & V
Physical response	Easy breathing Can talk easily Minimal sweating Minimal muscle fatigue	Hard breathing Sweating Greater muscle fatigue

Walter Heppner, now age 68, has always enjoyed walking for exercise. But in July of 1988, after he retired from his job as a senior vice president at Ocean Spray, he began a regular racewalking program, which he practices 6 days a week for about 5 miles a session. By January of 1990, Walter plans to build his pace to 6 miles an hour.

Thanks to Walter's year of serious walking (he logs about 30 miles a week), he is in better shape than he was in high school. As a student he was fat (235 pounds on a 5'7" frame). He now weighs 153 pounds and has less than 17 percent body fat. His resting pulse (now a very low 44 to 47 beats per minute) and blood pressure have decreased since he started walking, and his cholesterol level, once high, is now at an acceptable level.

"Walking," says Walter, "has made me physically fit, increased my confidence, and helped me ignore my age."

7. What's Your Real Age?

For the past 5 years, May Smith, age 69, has been getting up every weekday morning to walk for an hour around an Atlanta mall. Before she started walking, May had felt the ache of arthritis in her fingers and wrist, for which her doctor had prescribed medication. She had gained weight over the years and had been told to watch her cholesterol. At one time she had had chronic bronchitis.

Walking has seemed to turn back the tide, however. May has discontinued her arthritis medication, depending instead on her walks and a few aspirin. She's been able to keep her weight down, maintain a healthy cholesterol level, and rid herself of her breathing problems. Even a car accident 2½ years ago, which injured her back, hasn't daunted her, and her doctor claims that the strong back muscles she developed from walking probably saved her from a much worse injury.

Then there is Dr. Robert Rosner, an 82-year-old ophthamologist who walks every day, 12 to 15 miles a week. A lifetime of walking and other activities like swimming and playing tennis, along with "following all the rules of good health," has allowed Dr. Rosner to live longer than the combined ages of both his parents, who both died from tuberculosis.

People like May Smith and Dr. Rosner walk because it makes them feel better and younger, but walking's effects are not only psychological. People who follow a regular walking program feel younger because, in fact, they have stemmed the aging process of their tissue, muscles, bones, and organs and thus biologically *are* younger. Even though May Smith is

69 years old, her body looks like and works like that of a 60-year-old. Dr. Rosner says that, biologically, he has the body of a 50-year-old.

We all have two ages: *chronological*, the number of years we have been alive, and *biological*, the age of our body in terms of how well it functions. It is generally fairly easy to determine someone's age just from looking at them. A brief glimpse at someone's skin, hair, eyes, how they move, and how slim or fat they are will tell you if they are in their twenties or are closer to 40. Your guess will probably be fairly accurate. Yet we've all had the experience of meeting a man or woman who was wrinkled and stooped like a 70-year-old but was only 60 or a slim, athletic person who looked 50 but was actually 70. That's the influence of biological age.

Biological age doesn't only apply to the body's exterior, however. As you learned from previous chapters, doctors and researchers have mapped out the biological changes that occur in the body of a sedentary person as he or she ages, from the demineralization of bones to the loss of stamina in the muscles (including the heart), the decreased capacity of the lungs, the increase in body fat, and the decrease in the brain's reaction time. To determine your biological age, use the tests below to measure your heart capacity and the strength and stamina of your muscles, as well as their flexibility. For each age, from 6 to 99, different averages are given. Take the test and then compare your score to the accompanying chart. You may be surprised to find out that you have several biological ages, all of which are different from your chronological age. For example, although you've just had your fortieth birthday, you might be 45 years old in terms of flexibility, 35 years old in terms of strength, and 30 years old in terms of heart endurance.

Be forewarned that some aspects of age will probably be easier than others to combat (for example, it might be quite difficult to return to the same weight you were in high school), but you can, depending on your age and fitness level, be living proof of the potential for looking and feeling younger by walking regularly. The nicest thing about biological age is that you can keep on reducing it through training.

Also use these tests to help plan your walking program. If you are strong in heart capacity but weak in flexibility and strength, you'll want to do more of the stretching exercises outlined in Book 2: Walking for Arthritis, Back and Joints. If the reverse is true, concentrate on a walking program like the one found in Book 3: Cardiowalking, which will increase the stamina and strength of your heart. You should also analyze the results of these tests in terms of your family health tree. If, for example, you know that back problems run in your family, you should be concerned if you are not strong or flexible. If osteoarthritis runs in your family, you will want your muscles to be stronger than normal to help take stress off the joints. If heart disease is a dominant concern, you'll want to increase your aerobic capacity. In short, knowing where your risks lie will be a further incentive to make yourself younger.

Finally, to calculate your overall biological age, just average all the numbers for the four tests.

The Four Fitness Tests

Heart Health

The most scientific way to measure your cardiovascular fitness (the strength and endurance of your heart) is to determine your maximum heart rate —the highest number of beats your heart can reach. This number usually decreases with age, and the accepted formula for maximum heart rate is to subtract your age from 220. Yet this is only a general rule. Let's take an example from real life. Dr. Mort Malkin, an oral surgeon who also teaches aerobic walking techniques, is in his early fifties. A former pole vaulter, Dr. Malkin was on the track team in high school and college, as was a close friend. Dr. Malkin began walking several years ago, while his friend stayed sedentary. Now Malkin has a maximum heart rate of 190 (the heart rate of a 30-year-old); his friend has a heart rate of 120 (the heart rate of a 100-year-old). Maximum heart rate is normally measured in a laboratory, but you can use a 1-mile walk test to determine your heart health. Measure out a mile on flat terrain (either on a premeasured track or on a section of flat road). Walk the mile at a brisk pace and then record your time. Your maximum heart rate controls how efficiently your body can pump blood (and oxygen carried in the blood) throughout your body. If, as happens with sedentary adults, the amount your heart can beat decreases significantly as you age, you will get tired sooner.

Look up your walking time on the following chart. Then look across at the age column. Your physiological heart age falls somewhere within that decade.

Number of Minutes Required to Walk 1 Brisk Mile

	TIME (IN MINUTES)	
AGE	MALES	FEMALES
6–9	14–17	14–18
10–15	12–15	13–15
16–19	11–13	12–13
20–29	12–13	13–14
30–39	12–13	13–14
40–49	14–16	16–17
50–59	16–17	17–18
60–69	17–19	18–20
70–79	19–21	20–22
80–89	21–23	22–24
90–99	23–26	24–28

Your chronological age: _____

Your biological age: _____

Flexibility

Flexibility is an important sign of fitness. As we age, our muscles lose flexibility, although this trend can be combatted effectively with stretching exercises. Flexibility is imperative to muscular health. The following test was developed by the Chrysler Fund Amateur Athletics Union.

Place a yardstick or a measuring tape on the floor, and sit at the zero end with the tape or stick running between your legs (your heels should be about a foot apart). Your heels should line up with the 15-inch mark on the tape or stick. Keep your legs straight and flat against the floor (have someone hold your legs down at the thigh to avoid bending your knees). Bend forward at the waist, with your arms outstretched and your hands overlapped, palms down, and see how far down you can reach on the tape or stick without bouncing. Once your hands are on a mark, stay in that position for a few seconds. Take a deep breath and let it out slowly while trying to reach forward even farther. You should be able to increase the · distance a bit. Now look at the appropriate part of the following chart to find you biological age for flexibility.

Children's Flexibility (in Inches)—Ages 6–18

	6 YEARS		7 YEARS		8 YEARS		9 YEARS		10 YEARS	
FLEXIBILITY	BOYS	GIRLS	BOYS	GIRLS	BOYS	GIRLS	BOYS	GIRLS	BOYS	GIRLS
Average	15	17	16	17	15	17	16	17	15	17
Excellent	17	19	18	20	18	20	18	21	18	21

	11 YEARS		12 YEARS		13 YEARS		14 YEARS		15 YEARS	
FLEXIBILITY	BOYS	GIRLS	BOYS	GIRLS	BOYS	GIRLS	BOYS	GIRLS	BOYS	GIRLS
Average	16	18	16	19	16	20	16	20	17	21
Excellent	18	21	18	21	18	23	19	23	20	23

	16 YEARS		17 YEARS	
FLEXIBILITY	BOYS	GIRLS	BOYS	GIRLS
Average	18	21	17	21
Excellent	20	23	20	24

Adult's Flexibility (in Inches)

AGE	18–29	30–39	40–49	50–59	60–69	70–79	80–89	90–99
Men	17–20	15–16	13–14	13–14	12–11	12–11	5–10	0–4
Women	21–24	19–20	17–18	17–18	13–16	13–16	9–12	0–8

Your chronological age: _____

Your biological age: _____

Strength

It is necessary to keep up your muscle mass as you grow older. If you don't, you will be more prone to injury and tire more easily. Muscles also help to keep your weight down (since muscles require more nourishment and therefore burn more calories than fat). Below are two strength tests —one for stomach muscles and another for the upper arms. A strong stomach helps hold proper posture and thus prevents back injuries. Upper body strength is important for the arm-pumping technique in exercise-walking (see Book 2: Walking for Arthritis, Back and Joints).

Sit-Up Test

This test measures how many sit-ups can be done in 1 minute (you can stop and rest whenever need be in that minute). Do the sits-ups as follows: Lie down with your feet flat on the floor, your knees bent at a 90-degree angle, and your heels about a foot from your buttocks. Brace your feet under an object or have someone hold them in place. Fold your arms across your chest so that your right hand is touching your left shoulder, and vice versa. Sit up, touching your arms to your knees (your arms should be held flat against your chest throughout the sit-up). Then lower yourself back down until your lower back and middle back are on the floor (you do not have to touch your shoulders to the floor). Always make sure that you are sitting up with your back straight, not arched. Use the appropriate section of the following chart to find your biological age for stomach strength.

Children's Sit-Up Chart

	6 YEARS		7 YEARS		8 YEARS		9 YEARS		10 YEARS	
	BOYS	GIRLS	BOYS	GIRLS	BOYS	GIRLS	BOYS	GIRLS	BOYS	GIRLS
Health goal	20	20	24	24	26	26	30	28	34	30

	11 YEARS		12 YEARS		13 YEARS		14 YEARS		15 YEARS	
	BOYS	GIRLS	BOYS	GIRLS	BOYS	GIRLS	BOYS	GIRLS	BOYS	GIRLS
Health goal	36	33	38	33	40	33	40	35	42	35

	16 YEARS		17 YEARS		18 YEARS	
	BOYS	GIRLS	BOYS	GIRLS	BOYS	GIRLS
Health goal	44	35	44	35	44	35

Adult's Sit-Up Chart

AGE	20–29	30–39	40–49	50–59	60–69	70–79	80–89	90–99
Men	37–42	29–36	24–28	19–23	14–18	10–13	9–13	7–10
Women	33–38	25–33	19–24	15–18	10–14	7–9	6–8	0–5

Your chronological age: _____

Your biological age: _____

Push-Up Test

Push-ups test your upper body strength and stamina. Since females and children have less upper body strength than adult males, women, girls, and boys under age 10 will do modified push-ups, and men will do traditional push-ups.

For this test, do as many push-ups as possible until you cannot go on or until 1 minute has elapsed, whichever comes first. Do not rest. For the modified push-up, get down on all fours with your hands placed underneath your shoulders and your stomach pulled in so that your back is straight. Lift your feet off the ground, so only your knees are in contact with the floor, and lower your upper body until your nose is touching the ground. Then push back up to the starting position, keeping your back straight throughout the exercise.

For the regular push-up, lie flat on the ground with your hands placed under your shoulders. Raise yourself up so that you are supporting yourself with your arms and your toes. As in the modified push-up, it is important to keep your back straight. In addition, as you raise and lower your body, touching your nose to the ground, take care not to bend at the waist.

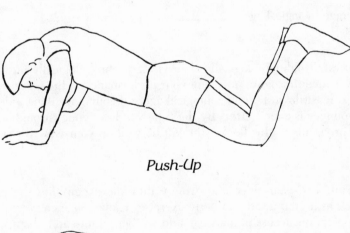

Push-Up

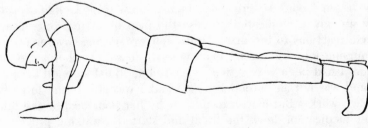

Modified Push-Up

Children's Push-Up Chart

| | 6–9 YEARS | | 10–13 YEARS | | 14–19 YEARS | |
	BOYS	GIRLS	BOYS	GIRLS	BOYS	GIRLS
Average	10–15	10–15	20–30	20–30	30–40	20–30
Outstanding	16–30	16–30	31–40	31–40	41–50	31–40

Adult's Push-Up Chart

AGE	20–29	30–39	40–49	50–59	60–69	70–79	80–89	90–99
Men	35–44	25–34	20–24	15–19	10–14	7–9	5–8	0–4
Women	17–33	12–16	8–11	6–8	3–5	1–2	1–2	1

Your chronological age: _____

Your biological age: _____

Your average biological age: _____

If you rated older biologically than you are chronologically on any of the tests, concentrate on improving your performance in those areas until you are at least down to your biological age. Of course, ranking a decade or two younger is even better. By the time you have gone through all the walking programs in this book, you will be well on your way to reaching your age goals.

Ruby Brun, a 65-year-old walker from California, exemplifies the power of walking as a total mind and body exercise. Eleven years ago, after the breakup of an unsuccessful marriage and a rebound into an unhappy one, Ruby began having severe pains in her chest (called *angina pectoris*). Ruby was given medication to ease the pain of angina, but because of adverse reactions to the drugs, Ruby felt worse. She was forced to quit her nursing job, and wasn't even able to do simple chores around the house. "I had been very active," says Ruby, "but I stopped because my husband was not an outdoors person and I was still trying to make the marriage work." But driven to despair by her poor health, she dumped all her medication down the toilet and started a walking program. She increased her walking distance every few days until she had walked a mile,

Pull-Up

and then joined a local hiking club and went on outings with them. "At times I had to stop and rest, or turn back and wait at the cars," remembers Ruby, but with persistence she was finally able to keep up with the group. Ruby says that walking has helped lower her cholesterol level and has made her legs firmer, although she weighs 10 pounds more than she'd like. She plans to add another mile to her 2-mile-a-day, 6-day-a-week walking program to try to lose the extra weight.

"Walking is the most important thing in my life—it is my life. It makes it possible for me to work at 65 and enjoy so many things. . . . I've heard it said that an angel rides on your shoulder and whispers in your ear when you walk," says Ruby. "I believe it."

WALKING FOR ARTHRITIS, BACK AND JOINTS

Strengthen Your Muscles and Bones

CONTRIBUTORS

Daniel A. Brzusek, D.O., M.S.

Dr. Brzusek is director of physical medicine and rehabilitation at Northwest Rehabilitation Associates, Inc., in the state of Washington and co-director of physical medicine and rehabilitation at Overlake Hospital Medical Center in Bellevue, Washington. He received the Doctor of Osteopathic Medicine degree in 1970 from Philadelphia College of Osteopathic Medicine, and in 1976 he received the Master of Science in Rehabilitative Medicine degree from the University of Washington. Dr. Brzusek walks 10 miles a week and lives in Bellevue, Washington.

Jay Itzkowitz, M.S.

Mr. Itzkowitz is the exercise physiologist at the ArthroFitness Center in New York City, where he treats patients predominantly for bone and joint diseases such as rheumatology and osteoporosis. Mr. Itzkowitz has a masters degree in exercise physiology from Adelphi University in Garden City, New York, and has received a stress testing certification from the American College for Sports Medicine as an exercise test technologist. He has also been certified by the National Athletic Trainers Association. He walks 5 miles a day with patients at the ArthroFitness Center and at least 10 miles a week in and around New York City, where he lives.

Joseph F. Kansao, D.C.

Dr. Kansao received the Doctor of Chiropractic degree from Texas Chiropractic College in Houston. He is director of chiropractic medicine for the American College of Sports Medicine (professional organization), as well as the director of Park Chiropractic Center in New York City. In addition to being medical editor of *Running News* newsletter and author of a monthly article for *Athletic Magazine*, Dr. Kansao lectures at sports medicine symposiums, at various health institutions, and on the radio. Dr. Kansao is an avid walker who logs 36 miles a week and lives in New York City.

Pamela Kovar-Joledano

Pamela Kovar-Joledano is a physical therapist who specializes in musculoskeletal diseases and arthritis treatment. She is currently working on her doctoral dissertation in Health Education at Columbia University in New York City, concentrating on arthritis education for patient, professional, and community populations. Ms. Kovar-Joledano walks 7½ miles a day, 3 days a week. She lives in New York City.

Valery F. Lanyi, M.D.

Dr. Lanyi is a physiatrist with a private practice in New York City. She also holds the posts of director of rehabilitation medicine at Bellevue Hospital, acting director of rehabilitation medicine at St. Clare's Hospital, and is an associate clinical professor of rehabilitation medicine at New York University Medical Center. Dr. Lanyi graduated from the University of Budapest Medical School. She walks 3 to 4 days a week and lives in New York City.

Mark Young, M.D.

Dr. Young now specializes in physical medicine and rehabilitation at Albert Einstein College of Medicine in New York. He has published a number of articles on physical medicine, including one on bone fracture and hypogonadism in the *New England Journal of Medicine*. Dr. Young is a graduate of the University of Health and Sciences/ The Chicago Medical School. He walks 25 or more miles a week and lives in the Bronx, New York.

1. Walking Out the Aches

The musculoskeletal system is the body's frame, responsible for protecting the inner organs and governing our mobility. Unfortunately, this system —the 200 bones, the hundreds of muscles, and the ligaments and tendons that link them together—is perhaps the body system most susceptible to injury and disease. Even the healthiest of us have suffered from sore muscles, a sprained ankle, a stiff neck, or even a broken bone. And time is against us. By age 40 or 50, we all show signs of joint deterioration (known as *osteoarthritis*) in our knees, hips, ankles, and shoulders. By middle age, the bones and muscles of sedentary adults have already begun to weaken. As we grow older, our ability to bounce back from sports injuries or accidents declines, while the probability of getting injured increases.

Along with the normal decline in the musculoskeletal system, diseases can also strike. Among the most common are rheumatoid arthritis, an autoimmune disease in which the body attacks itself, eating away at the joints; osteoporosis, a dramatic loss of bone density; and neurologic disorders that affect muscle movement, among them multiple sclerosis and Parkinson's disease. These diseases strike million of Americans.

A regular exercisewalking program (including stretching and strengthening exercises) can be effective in battling both the natural aging process and diseases. Walking is among the best preventive exercises because it is a gentle, nonjarring activity that promotes bone density and builds muscles and thus counteracts and slows the onset of degeneration of the musculoskeletal system. Moreover, although walking cannot prevent diseases such as Parkinson's disease, multiple sclerosis, or certain forms of arthritis, walking is a major rehabilitative exercise. Not only for the same reasons, walking is also recognized as a preventive exercise, but because it is functional—walking is how we move, our means of independence.

How to Use This Book

This minibook is *Walking Medicine*'s answer to a sports medicine manual. However, unlike sports medicine, which is a reactive approach to medicine, this minibook provides both reactive and preventive walking programs for your bones, muscles, and joints.

Chapter 1, Walking Out the Aches, explains why walking is one of the most often prescribed exercises for maintaining a healthy back and healthy joints and muscles.

Chapter 2, Your Joints and Your Back: What Can Go Wrong? gives you explanations of the major joint, back, and muscular ailments, including various forms of arthritis, multiple sclerosis, and Parkinson's disease. You'll also learn about common sports injuries, including a list of the most dangerous sports (in terms of injuries) and the safest.

In Chapter 3, Arthrowalking Techniques and Prevention Program, you'll learn the right way to walk. We coined the word "arthrowalking" (from the Greek word *arthro*, for "joint") to signify that this five-level preventive program is healthy and safe for your joints.

In Chapter 4, Walking for a Bad Back, and Chapter 5, Walking Joint by Joint, you will learn how to regain mobility of your injured back or joints through walking and stretching and strengthening exercises. If, after taking the tests in Book 1, you discovered that your arms or legs need strengthening or flexibility training, you'll find the exercises here to help you build up and limber up your muscles.

Chapter 6, The Arthrowalking Comeback Program: Over Land or Water, will take you from your first day out of bed after an injury or bout with joint or back pain and get you on the road to recovery. Two programs are offered: one on terra firma and another in the pool, where walking shares all the benefits of swimming (a nonimpact, aerobic exercise) without any of the disadvantages.

Why Walking?

The benefits of walking are clear. It improves the efficiency of the heart and lungs, burns fat and calories, and builds muscle and bone strength. Yet exercises like aerobic dancing and running can also boast these attributes, so what makes walking better?

The most important difference is that walking is easier on the joints and back. When you run or execute aerobic dance movements, your foot hits the ground with a force equal to three to four times your body weight. This force, transmitted throughout the entire body, must be absorbed by the bones and muscles. Walking only exerts a force of one to one and one-half times your weight on your back and joints.

The impact forces of running and walking are measured in biomechanics laboratories (*biomechanics* is the study of how the body moves and functions). The amount of impact force your body experiences is dependent on how high your center of gravity moves during an activity. When you run, your arms and legs swing upward, and thus your center of gravity is higher than when you walk. To test this theory for yourself, stand on a bathroom scale and swing your arms upward. The scale will register more weight when your arms are in the air than when you are standing with your arms held at your sides. Now try walking in place on the scale and pumping your arms at chest height. The scale will register an increase of roughly 50 percent above your actual weight (70 percent if you pump your arms overhead). If you tried running in place on your scale (something we don't suggest, since you may end up breaking it), it would register a weight three to four times heavier than what you actually weigh.

The sports medicine community contends that the bodies of people with normal, healthy joints can absorb the extra forces of running or other high-impact sports without damage. Furthermore, the sports medicine community claims that normal, healthy people, if they exercise on a regular basis, can actually prolong the onset of osteoarthritis. Yet a significant number of health professionals and walkers interviewed for *Walking Medicine* have switched from aerobic dancing or running precisely because they experienced chronic pain in their legs or back—pain they don't feel when they walk.

Why did these people develop joint damage and pain from high-impact exercise? Most likely because they have weak joints or joints that aren't built for the strain of running. You may, too, although you might not know it yet. Do your parents or siblings suffer from a "trick" knee or a bad back? If so, you may have inherited a structural weakness. (Refer to your family health tree in Book 1 to determine your risks.) Or you may be running or exercising incorrectly, perhaps because you are bowlegged or knock-kneed, which will place unnatural forces on your joints and thus weaken them. Or maybe you've already had a sports injury, a broken bone, for example, a common predecessor to chronic joint and back problems. If any of these scenarios are true and you continue to regularly engage in high-impact exercises, you will wear down your joints and start to experience pain.

Maintaining both strength and flexibility in the muscles is the best way to ensure joint and back health. Walking strengthens more muscles than running. For example, running just builds the muscles at the front of the thighs and the back of the calves, while walking builds muscles at both the front and back of the entire leg. Running provides no upper body strengthening, while walking (with the use of the arm-pumping technique you'll learn in Chapter 3) does. Aerobic dance may exercise all the major muscles, but the movements are not smooth, as in walking, and the jerky arm swings and leg kicks can wrench the joints. Learning and using all of the techniques outlined in Chapter 3 will ensure that you walk with smooth, controlled movements that promote strength as well as flexibility.

Because the overall impact forces are much less for walking than for running, so are the forces on individual joints. For example, running places twice the amount of force on the hip, six times on the knee, and two times on the ankle than walking (these forces are caused both by impact and by muscular pull on the joints). Other sports, in general, are much more prone to injury than walking, which is virtually injury-free. There are no injuries named after walking—no "walker's knee" or "walker's elbow."

Walking has been proven a safe exercise for joints that are already damaged (something that cannot be said for running). A multiyear study performed at the University of Missouri at Columbia found that participants of all ages with arthritis could increase their walking speed without further damaging their joints. Researchers found that the participants were less depressed and had more stamina for everyday activities than before they began walking. Twenty percent were also able to decrease their pain medication.

Walking has the lowest dropout rate of any exercise. This is so because walking is accessible—you can do it anywhere and you don't need special equipment except some comfortable clothing and shoes. Walking is also inexpensive, and it can be incorporated into your daily routine (walk to the store instead of driving). It offers variety (you can hike one day, take a stroll the next, and do a brisk walk the next), it's a social activity that can be done with friends, and it's appropriate for all age groups and fitness levels.

Walking is also an effective tool for weight loss, and there is a large correlation between obesity and joint and back problems. Walking also improves balance and coordination, decreasing the likelihood of falls, a common cause of injuries.

Now you know the advantages of walking, but you may still wonder why you should exercise at all? Because if you don't *use* your body, then you will *lose* your ability to use it. Our muscles and joints stiffen and atrophy when they are not exercised regularly. Think of exercise as the joint's means of lubrication. You must exercise to keep your body movable, much like you need to grease the axle and wheels of your car to keep it movable. Walking strengthens muscles, too, and good muscle tone is what saves you from joint pain. For even if you do exercise, researchers have found that you will undergo *some* joint deterioration as you age. If your muscles are strong, however, you will probably not feel any pain. That's because strong muscles ensure that your joints are held in proper alignment (which reduces the amount of forces they must withstand during normal movement or exercise).

The lesson behind Book 2: Walking for Arthritis, Back and Joints is to take the defensive. If you strengthen your frame—both your muscles and your bones—you'll be less apt to get injured and you'll help keep your joints moving painlessly and easily as you grow older. If you have already experienced back, joint, or muscle pain, whatever the cause, in this book you can learn how to use walking as a rehabilitative tool to regain mobility.

Walking's Benefits for the Musculoskeletal System

1. Walking is a total-body exercise.

2. Walking strengthens the bones.

3. Walking is gentle on the joints.

4. Walking with proper techniques protects the joints and muscles from injuries.

5. Walking is one of the best rehabilitative exercises for muscle, bone, and joint injuries.

2. Your Joints and Back

WHAT CAN GO WRONG?

In Book 1 you took a series of tests to determine your flexibility and your strength, and you may have discovered that you are at risk of developing joint or back problems. You also drew your family health tree, through which you may have uncovered joint or back weaknesses or diseases that afflict the joints or muscles in your family. Perhaps you uncovered no weaknesses, but you are nevertheless worried about damaging your back or joints in an accident or during an exercise session.

In short, anyone concerned about joint or back health should read this chapter. It provides an overview of the kinds of disorders and diseases that can crop up and explains how walking can be your means to prevention or rehabilitation. Armed with the knowledge of precisely what can go wrong, you can react promptly to any aches or pains you experience or take the first steps toward overcoming a disease or disability.

Osteoarthritis

All of us will experience osteoarthritis (also known as *degenerative joint disease*) as we age. It most commonly strikes the hips, knees, ankles, hands,* and spine, and if symptomatic, it manifests itself in stiff, swollen, aching joints. One study found that osteoarthritis can be detected (with

---

*Two common hand disorders caused by arthritis are Herberden's nodes (which causes disfiguring bony spur formation in the first joints of the fingers) and Bouchard's nodes (which strike the knuckles).

the use of x-rays) in 35 percent of 30-year-olds' knees, and by age 65, 86 percent of women and 78 percent of men will have signs of osteoarthritis. Although not everyone will feel pain, 16 million Americans do experience its debilitating effects.

To understand the deterioration that occurs as we age, you first need to understand the anatomy of a normal joint. The joint's function is to allow for movement while still providing enough support that you don't fall over. The muscles and tendons (which connect muscle to bones) are responsible for movement, and the ligaments (fibers that connect bones to one another) provide stability. If you could look under the skin at the knee or ankle, you would see that at the ends of the bones that meet to form the joint there is a smooth and rubbery substance. This is the cartilage, a shock absorber and cushion that keeps the two bones from rubbing against one another as the joint moves.

Osteoarthritis is a fraying of the bone and a depletion of cartilage that leaves the two bone ends rubbing together. It is known as the "wear and tear" disease because unusual wear seems to bring it on (normal usage does not, however). For example, ballet dancers often develop arthritis in their feet, baseball pitchers in their shoulders, and soccer players in their hips. (Exercisewalkers, as a rule, will not develop osteoarthritis because the joints are exercised evenly and nonballistically—with smooth rather than jerky motions.)

Scientists now believe that as joints are moved, an enzyme is released that digests old cartilage, while simultaneously, new cartilage cells are replacing those lost. Osteoarthritis is thought to occur when the cartilage is broken down faster than it is replaced, either because too much enzyme is released or because the repair process is slowed down, or some combination of the two.

As the cartilage is depleted, the space between the bones is reduced, and this puts increased stress on the ligaments and muscles. Bone surfaces

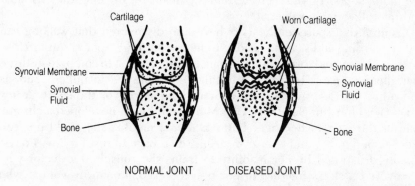

NORMAL JOINT   DISEASED JOINT

Comparison of a Normal and a Diseased Joint

become thicker from rubbing against each other without a cushion in between, and spurs (jagged lumps) form on the bones. The joints stiffen and swell, and movement becomes restricted and painful. Osteoarthritis can also cause tendonitis (the inflammation of a tendon). Osteoarthritis tends to run in families, perhaps because a slightly imperfect match in the way joints fit together is passed on from one generation to the next.

Underuse of a joint increases the severity of the condition. Joints don't have a blood supply of their own. That's why the joint of a chicken leg is white and not red. The only way a joint can get nutrients and rid itself of wastes is through movement. Walking exercises the entire body and, if done correctly, will keep all the joints aligned and moving together in harmony, which will aid in preventing the disease or at least in stopping further joint damage.

Sports and Exercise Injuries

Dorothy Schatz, age 71, discovered first hand not only the rehabilitative powers of walking, but also that being in good physical condition helps in recovery from exercise injuries. Dorothy and her husband live in upstate New York, where winters are cold and snowy. They walk daily at their local mall, where Dorothy has logged over 1400 miles since 1986, the year she first started a walking regimen.

In April of 1989, Dorothy broke her hip while cross-country skiing. It was a clean break with no bone splintering or displacement. The orthopedic surgeon placed four pins in her hip, assuring Dorothy that because she had developed such good circulation from her daily walks, her hip would repair itself quickly. In fact, Dorothy's physical condition was so fine that within 6 weeks she was back walking in the mall on crutches and in 8 weeks her hip was completely healed. After 9 weeks Dorothy was walking without a cane or crutches. "Starting to walk in the mall has helped my recovery," said Dorothy, "because of both the exercise and the moral support I've received from my husband, my long-time friends, and my fellow mall walkers."

Competitive sports enthusiasts have also discovered that walking can be a rewarding and safe alternative to more "harmful" sports. Susan Henricks, a 33-year-old former long-distance runner, used to compete in three marathons a year. Her intense training schedule led to pulled tendons and other injuries, but Susan accepted them as par for the sport. A few years ago, after the New York City Marathon, Susan developed a chronic pain at the base of her right buttock. For 2 months she could not run more than 5 miles, and after every run, she'd have to rest for 3 or 4 days. Finally, frustrated by her inability to train, she consulted a doctor who discovered a stress fracture in her pelvis (very common in women who run). The doctor also told her that she had probably run the marathon with this fracture.

Susan then realized that she was abusing her body and would have to find a gentler alternative to running. That alternative was racewalking. Racewalking demands more muscle strength than running (and is therefore more challenging) and places significantly less stress on the leg and back joints. In fact, although Susan still competes in marathons (walking), she has yet to be injured. And her new sport has provided even more competitive excitement than marathon running—manifested by Susan's silver medal at the 1989 New York State Empire Games.

Sports injuries and accidents are perhaps the leading cause of secondary osteoarthritis (that not associated with aging) or other chronic joint or back pain. Sports injuries fall into two categories: intrinsic and extrinsic. *Intrinsic injuries* are those that are inherent in a sport, like tennis elbow or runner's knees. They are caused by movements repeated over time that traumatize the joint, eventually wearing away cartilage or stretching ligaments and tendons beyond their natural length. An *extrinsic injury* is one caused by an outside event, like Dorothy Schatz's fall.

Aside from its role as a therapy or rehabilitation from a sports injury, walking is a relatively risk-free preventive exercise. Running has the most intrinsic injuries, twenty-seven, even more than a contact sport like football, and even swimming, thought by many to be one of the safest exercises, has three intrinsic injuries: shoulder injuries, back strains, and buttocks strains (from doing the dolphin kick). Walking has only two intrinsic injuries associated with it: muscle cramps, especially in the buttocks and arms, and shin splints, a pulling away of the muscle from the shin bone. Both these ailments disappear as the arm and leg muscles become stronger and are usually only the complaint of the beginning walker.

Doctors have also prescribed walking to serious athletes to supplement their training, especially if they have an injury that keeps them from their main sport. If you're an aerobic dancer or a jogger who doesn't want to give up your sport completely, at least alternate your high-impact exercise with low-impact walking, especially if members of your family have had arthritis or back problems.

Most sports tend to build muscles unevenly. For example, if you play tennis, your arm and back muscles will be more developed on your dominant side, and this muscle imbalance can pull your back out of alignment. If you bicycle, your legs will be developed, but your upper body, including your back, will be relatively weak and thus prone to injury. By alternating such exercises with walking, you'll develop a more balanced body and build more overall body stamina.

Whether intrinsic or extrinsic, sports and exercise injuries can be divided into seven types (in order of severity): cramps, muscle spasms,

Number of Different Injuries Associated with 16 Selected Activities

SPORT	NUMBER OF INJURIES
Running	27
Football	25
Tennis	16
Gymnastics	15
Ballet dancing	13
Basketball	11
Wrestling	10
Skiing	10
Baseball	8
Soccer	7
Weight training	7
Cycling	6
Aerobic dance	5
Swimming	3
Hiking	3
Walking	2

strains, sprains, joint inflammation, dislocation, and fractures. *Cramps* are caused by an involuntary temporary contraction of a muscle (lasting only a few minutes at most), usually brought on by muscle fatigue or dehydration. Avoid overtraining. Also, warm up sufficiently before you begin walking and drink plenty of liquids before and during exercise to help

Most Common Joints Injured in These Selected Activities

INJURY	NUMBER OF ACTIVITIES IN WHICH THEY COMMONLY OCCUR
Knee injury (dislocation, sprain, or torn cartilage)	12
Shoulder injury (dislocation, separation, rotator cuff tear)	7*
Ankle sprain	7
Shin splints	6
Calf strain (also known as "tennis leg" —when the muscle pulls away from the Achilles tendon)	5
Stress fractures in the back	3

*Some sports have more than one shoulder injury associated with them.

prevent cramps. However, if you are exercising a muscle group you don't ordinarily use, you will probably experience cramping nonetheless. Stretching or massaging the muscle when you first feel pain will help to relieve cramps.

If muscle cramps are not addressed, they can lead to muscle spasms, a prolonged tightening of the muscle that can last for days or even weeks. Muscle spasms are caused by muscle fatigue, which eventually drives a muscle into a state of permanent contraction. Range-of-motion exercises, which move a joint through its entire range of motion (or at least as much of its range as is possible), can prevent a spasm and reduce pain. Let's say you have a stiff neck that keeps you from looking over your right shoulder. Every time you start to move your neck to your right, your neck muscles contract to keep you from moving into the "pain zone." If you don't try to regain movement, however, the muscles will keep "putting on the brakes" until they go into a permanent spasm. Gently moving a joint as much as you can through its range of motion, although painful at first, should force the surrounding muscles to relax, countering the tendency to spasm. If the spasm does not resolve itself in 48 hours, seek medical attention, as muscle spasm will also place stress on neighboring muscles, eventually creating a domino effect of spasms. If you have a muscle that often goes into a spasm, concentrate on strengthening it. (See Chapter 4 and 5 for exercises.)

A *strain* is usually defined as a pulled muscle or tendon in the back, arms, or legs. Strains fall into three categories. A *first-degree strain* is a mild stretching of the muscle or tendon fibers. A *second-degree strain* means some muscle or tendon fibers are torn, although the majority are still intact. And a *third-degree strain* is the tearing of a majority of the fibers in the affected muscle or tendon. Strains can be avoided by warming up sufficiently before you exercise, as well as by avoiding overuse of a muscle or tendon.

A *sprain* occurs when the ligaments (the fibers that connect bone to bone) are pulled or torn because the joint is pushed beyond its normal range of motion. When you sprain your ankle, for example, you have twisted or otherwise forced the ankle into an abnormal position. Sprains, like strains, come in three degrees of severity, depending on how much tearing the ligaments undergo.

You may get strains and sprains when you walk, but only if you fail to stretch and warm up enough before your exercise (see more on stretching and warming up in the following chapters), you overexercise, or you happen to fall or turn your ankle on an uneven surface (the techniques in Chapter 3 will help you avoid falls).

Strains and sprains can be relieved with the RICE principle—*Rest* the joint, apply *Ice*, apply *Compression* with an Ace bandage (be sure it is not wrapped too tightly, which will cut off circulation), and *Elevate* the injury. All these steps will reduce swelling of the joint within 24 to 48 hours.

Joint inflammation covers a wide variety of conditions, whose names usually end with "-itis." Arthritis, bursitis, and tendonitis are just a few. "-itis" means inflammation, which translates into a joint that is red, swollen, painful, warm to the touch, and difficult to move. All these symptoms result because blood flow to the injured area increases.

The two most common types of "-itis" caused by sports injuries are tendonitis and bursitis. *Tendonitis* is an inflammation of the fibrous band that connects muscles to bones. Generally, tendonitis hurts most when you first begin exercising and will go away once you've warmed up. But after you stop activity, the pain will flair up again. *Bursitis* is an inflammation of the bursae, small fluid-filled sacks that, along with cartilage, cushion the joints. Prolonged pressure on a joint often brings on bursitis (clergymen often develop bursitis in their knees from kneeling for long periods of time), as does minor injuries. Generally, you will not develop bursitis or tendonitis walking (unless your shoes aren't suitable for walking). If you do have bursitis or tendonitis, you may want to move your walking routine to a pool until the pain subsides.

Dislocation occurs when one of the bones of a joint slips out of alignment. This is perhaps the most painful of sports injuries. A dislocated joint needs to be treated by a physician, who will realign it. Usually rehabilitation involves strengthening exercises, including walking (if the injury is in a weight-bearing joint), to ensure that the problem does not recur.

Fractures are any break in a bone. The least severe is a hairline, or stress, fracture, which is common in runners. Although these breaks are only small fissures, they are painful. They may or may not require splinting, and they will heal with rest. Walking can be done in a pool while the fractures are healing.

More severe fractures, either simple, which don't break the skin, or compound, which do, usually occur in contact sports, but they also can happen with any fall. Depending on the kind or location of the fracture, your doctor may tell you to walk as part of your rehabilitation.

Osteoporosis

Tricia Stevens, age 53, has been racewalking for 3 years. She started because of ankle and hip pain she developed in her late forties and the fear that she would develop osteoporosis like her mother, who had broken both her hips. Tricia now walks 3 days a week, averaging 4 miles a day, and this has alleviated her pain.

Although we all lose some bone density as we age, osteoporosis is a dramatic loss of bone density. Symptoms include loss of height and a rounding of the back (called a *dowager's hump*), which is accompanied by back pain. The main result of osteoporosis is broken bones, especially at the hip, wrist, and back. White women who are thin and small boned and who have a history of fractures are at most risk for this disease, which affects about 15 to 20 million Americans and causes approximately 1.3 million fractures every year. Male alcoholics also suffer this disease.

The disease is tied to a decrease in estrogen in females, which explains its presence in women who have entered menopause. Although men, in general, are less prone to osteoporosis, hormones may be behind their osteoporosis as well. A recent study reported in the *New England Journal of Medicine* reported that subnormal levels of testosterone in men increase their prevalence of bone breaks twofold. Risks of acquiring the disease can be reduced by eating dairy foods, not smoking (women who smoke reach menopause earlier than nonsmokers), not drinking more than 2.5 cups of coffee a day (caffeine is thought to inhibit the body's absorption of calcium), and not consuming more than two alcoholic drinks per day.

Bones are composed of two different tissues, dense cortical bone and porous trabecular bone. As with other tissue in the body, new layers of bone are always being laid down as old layers die, but as we age, more trabecular bone disappears than is replaced. The onset of osteoporosis greatly increases this difference. The bones of the hip, wrist, and the vertebrae of the back are almost entirely made up of trabecular bone, which is why osteoporosis affects these areas the most. By the time a sedentary woman reaches age 80, she has lost 47 percent of her trabecular bone, compared to 14 percent in men of the same age. The bone becomes so fragile that it can fracture spontaneously (especially common in the vertebrae). Such fractures often cause falls in older people.

One study found that one quarter of all white women had had fractures of their vertebrae by age 50 and one half had had fractures by age 70. Unlike fractures of the arm or leg, spinal fractures can go unnoticed except for a small loss of height and sometimes, though not always, back pain.

Osteoporosis is life-threatening in older adults. Fewer than half of all women who break their hips will regain normal function. Fifteen percent will die soon after the break, and 30 percent will die within 1 year. Overall, a hip fracture in later years reduces life expectancy by 12 percent.

Weight-bearing exercise like walking promotes bone growth. Astronauts who have gone up into space lost significant bone density as a result of weightlessness. Osteoporosis is best battled by starting to walk when you're young and continuing throughout your life. However, a study done at Washington University in St. Louis, Missouri, found that women with osteoporosis who walked 3 days a week, including up stairs and on a level surface, for 1 hour a day increased their bone density at the spine (and presumably at other parts of their body) by 6 percent over 9 months. This finding suggests that some bone loss can be regained through walking (although you will not regain height or undo a dowager's hump once it has already developed).

Rheumatoid and Other Forms of Arthritis

Rheumatoid Arthritis

When Gail Kirshner Riggs was 20 years old, her orthopedic surgeon told her she would be in a wheelchair by the time she was 50. But instead, her fiftieth year has been marked with a bronze medal in a national table tennis competition. Gail was also recently voted "Tucson Woman of the Year."

Gail has suffered from arthritis throughout most of her life, and it has damaged her body so severely that she now has four artificial joints. Gail had juvenile arthritis and experienced dramatic inflammation of her joints when she was in her late teens and twenties. The juvenile arthritis gave way to adult rheumatoid arthritis, and by the time she was 30, both hips had been implanted with plastic cups (bilateral cup arthroplasties).

At 40, she had two artificial knees, and her toes, gnarled from arthritis, were wired together to make them straighter and aid mobility.

Because rheumatoid arthritis has also severely damaged her ankles, Gail cannot walk for long distances. Yet every day she strolls for several blocks around the campus of the University of Arizona, where she is an associate director in the division of restorative medicine, and once a week she follows an abbreviated uphill walking regimen to help build up her cardiovascular system.

Gail is proof that walking can be an important part of an exercise program no matter how severe the affliction. Despite her limited mobility, Gail says walking has made her more independent and self-sufficient.

Arthritis is really a collection of more than 100 different diseases that cause inflammation and pain in the joints. Although osteoarthritis is the most common, other types, such as the juvenile and rheumatoid arthritis that Gail suffers from, are far more serious and seem to be caused by a very different medical phenomenon. They are *systemic* diseases, meaning that they usually travel throughout the body attacking several joints at once. The cause of these types of arthritis remains unknown. (One recent hypothesis is that they may be the result of a virus.)

Rheumatoid arthritis is the most prevalent of the systemic arthritis diseases, afflicting 2.1 million Americans. It is a disease that in most cases waxes and wanes. In periods of remission, joints may be only slightly painful or stiff; at other times, there will be terrible pain, so severe that a person cannot even stand the pressure of sheets and blankets on his or her joints. Rheumatoid arthritis strikes the synovium, the joint membrane that excretes synovial fluid, a substance resembling egg yolk that lubricates and nourishes the joint. During an attack of arthritis (called a *flare-up*), the joint swells as a result of an excess of synovial fluid and an increase in the production of synovium cells. This overflow of cells, known as *pannus*, is forced out over the side of the joint. Eventually the cartilage in the joint begins to break down until bone is rubbing against bone.

Research indicates that there is a familial predisposition to the disease, and scientists have located "genetic markers" that indicate susceptibility, although many people at risk never acquire the disease.

The disease afflicts 6 million Americans (1 to 2 percent of the population) and strikes women three times as often as men, usually beginning in their forties or fifties. In one in six cases, the disease causes severe crippling or deformity, although, as demonstrated by Gail's case, physical therapy and medication are thought to reduce these odds.

If you have rheumatoid arthritis, you should exercise your joints daily to maintain their mobility (see the exercises in Chapter 5) and follow a personalized daily walking program to strengthen your whole body and increase your stamina. However, *don't* actively exercise an arthritic joint during a flare-up (isometric exercises are permitted, and the afflicted joint should be moved passively by a physical therapist at least once a day). If you have severe rheumatoid arthritis of the weight-bearing joints, you may want to adapt our land-walking techniques to water (Chapter 6 will tell you how). You can also combine walking with bicycling, rowing, or swimming. Physiatrists (doctors specializing in rehabilitation), rheumatologists, and physical therapists emphasize that people with arthritis must combine walking with separate strengthening and stretching exercises, especially for the muscles surrounding the affected joints.

Other Forms of Systemic Arthritis

Juvenile Rheumatoid Arthritis
Like rheumatoid arthritis, this usually strikes more than one joint and afflicts children under age 18. Juvenile rheumatoid arthritis afflicts from 60,000 to 200,000 children and six times as many girls as boys.

Systemic Lupus
This autoimmune disease can lead to the destruction of the body's connective tissue, as well as the heart, lungs, skin, and joints. About 130,000 Americans have lupus, and women are eight times as likely as men to contract the disease.

Gout
Once thought to be caused by high living, gout is now known to result from the accumulation of uric acid, initially in the joint of the big toe, but later spreading to other joints. Gout afflicts 1 million Americans and four times as many men as women.

Multiple Sclerosis

Multiple sclerosis, often referred to as MS, is included in this chapter because it responds to many of the same exercise and walking solutions as does arthritis, although it is not an arthritic disease. MS destroys the central nervous system—eating away at nerve cells that transmit messages from the brain to the muscles. Like arthritis, it is thought to be an autoimmune condition. MS afflicts 250,000 Americans, striking women twice as often as men. Its major symptoms are weakness in the legs, spasticity (rigidity) of the muscles, blurred vision, and coordination and balance problems. MS patients with less severe forms of the disease (two thirds of all the people with MS are not disabled and are ambulatory with or without walking aids) are encouraged to follow a moderate exercise program like walking, which helps keep the muscles from becoming rigid, builds strength in the legs, and improves balance. MS sufferers, however, should be careful of exercising too strenuously during warm weather, since heat is thought to trigger symptoms of the disease.

Moira Griffin, who has multiple sclerosis, was formerly a runner, but she started walking because running tired her too quickly and caused her to fall frequently. Moira, who has just written a book about living with multiple sclerosis and other disabilities, called *Going the Distance*, tries to walk every day at a brisk pace for ½ to 1 mile. Moira emphasizes that following a regular program of exercise is of extreme importance to people with MS and that each person should do as much as he or she can in order to maintain mobility.

Parkinson's Disease

Parkinson's disease is a degenerative central nervous system disorder in which some nerve centers are destroyed and two brain chemicals, dopamine and norepinephrine (called *neurotransmitters*), that help relay impulses to the muscles are no longer produced. Because of this glitch in the body's communications network, Parkinson's disease causes tremors, rigid muscles, and a spastic, shuffling gait. Posture becomes stooped, movement is very stiff, and range of motion is reduced. Balance is also affected. In advanced stages of the disease, the patient's gait becomes very quick in order to keep from falling. Lack of norepinephrine and dopamine also causes depression.

The cause of Parkinson's disease remains unknown, although some researchers believe it may be the result of aging of nerve cells. Men contract the disease slightly more often than women (the ratio is three to two).

Although some drugs have been found to eradicate the symptoms of Parkinson's disease, none has yet proven to be effective over many years. Walking and other exercises involving gross motor skills (large muscle groups) are imperative for the treatment of Parkinson's disease and can reduce the rigidity of muscles and improve posture and range of motion, as well as balance. Stretches for affected areas also should be included. Some rehabilitation centers use visual and audio cues to help retrain persons with Parkinson's disease to walk properly. Step length is regulated by having the person walk on a square-tiled floor and asking him or her to touch every third block with his or her feet.

For patients with MS and Parkinson's disease, learning and using walking techniques, which demand a conscious effort, are good ways to train the muscles and regain lost motor skills.

Now that you have a better understanding of some major muscle, bone, and joint disorders and how walking can help you prevent them or rehabilitate from them, you are ready to learn how to exercisewalk.

3. Arthrowalking Techniques and Prevention Program

Everyone needs to learn to walk correctly. "I've been walking since I was 1 and haven't had any problems so far," you are probably thinking, but there is plenty you can be doing wrong—and putting your joints and back at risk in the process.

Walking faults abound. For example, a large percentage of Americans walk duck-footed or pigeon-toed, have poor posture, or shuffle their feet. Such habits can eventually damage your knees, hips, and back. Learning proper walking techniques will ensure that your body is correctly positioned and aligned and that your joints aren't experiencing unnatural and harmful forces. Even if you don't have any of these bad habits, you still need to be aware of the proper way to walk to avoid slipping into bad walking form when you are tired or injured.

Walking Techniques

While learning the techniques outlined below, stand in front of a mirror or, better yet, get someone to observe you from the side and front and perhaps even videotape you. Once you learn how to walk properly, you'll begin to notice, and be surprised by, how many people stand and walk incorrectly.

The most important elementary technique is to maintain proper posture while standing, sitting, and walking. When you think of standing straight, you may imagine soldiers at attention. But this thrusting out of the chest, coupled with a swayed back, is not healthy because it places too much strain on the lower back. To achieve proper posture: (1) keep your chin tucked in and your head straight (don't tilt it to one side or the other); (2) don't shrug your shoulders (keep them down, back, and relaxed); and (3) tighten your stomach, tuck your pelvis under your torso, and don't arch your lower back.

Improper head placement will throw your entire posture out of whack. To align your head, imagine a string running along your spine and out the top of your head pulling you upward. Feel your torso stretching and lifting off your hips and your head centered over your chest and back. Then, with your arms at your side, drop your shoulders down and slightly back, which will spread out, or "open up," your chest, adding to the "lifting" sensation. Tuck your chin gently into your neck (like a Marine), so that your ear is aligned with your shoulder. Focus on a spot at eye level about 15 feet in front of you, which will keep you from hanging your head. If your head is too far forward or back, your neck and shoulder muscles will be pulled unevenly, causing fatigue and muscle spasms. The muscles in the back of the neck are stronger than those in the front because they fight against gravity to hold your head up. By tucking your chin into your neck, you are stretching those muscles in the back of your neck and strengthening those in the front. If you can balance a book on your head when you walk, then you're using correct head placement.

The pelvic tilt—pulling in your stomach and flattening the small of your back by tucking your buttocks under your spine—is an important postural control. Without it, your lower back will arch, causing strain and pain. To master the pelvic tilt, stand sideways in front of a mirror, first as you normally would, and then doing the pelvic tilt. Notice how much your back flattens, and remember this image to help you stand and walk correctly. You may need to strengthen your stomach muscles to perform the pelvic tilt correctly. (See Chapter 4 for stomach strengthening exercises.)

Once you have learned these postural techniques, have someone look at you from the side. Does your body form a straight line, one section stacked upon the next? Your head should be centered on your shoulders, back, and chest; these should, in turn, be centered over your hips. Your feet and legs should be directly under your hips. From the side, your ear, shoulder, hip, and ankle bone should be in a straight line perpendicular to the floor.

Proper posture may be easy to maintain while standing still, but once you try it on the move, especially after you've walked several miles and are tired, you may find yourself getting sloppy. You will need to concentrate on your technique in the beginning until it becomes second nature. Below are some common postural mistakes to watch out for.

Pelvic Tilt

Leading with Your Chin

You may jut your chin out as you walk. This mistake, if not corrected, can lead to a muscle spasm in your neck. Tuck your chin into your chest. This may feel uncomfortable at first, but doing some simple neck stretches (see Chapter 4) will help.

Hanging Your Head

If you find yourself looking at the ground as you walk, you are hanging your head. This will strain both your neck and upper back and restrict breathing. Lift up your head and focus on a spot 15 feet in front of you.

Arching Your Back

This may happen after you've walked several miles and begin to tire or if you try to walk too fast before you have mastered proper technique. An aching lower back is a sure signal that you are not practicing the pelvic tilt.

Spend time every day strengthening your stomach muscles if you tend to arch your back. Also try standing with your back to a wall so that your shoulders, lower back, buttocks, and heels are all flat against it. (Your heels should be 4 to 6 inches away from the wall.)

Leaning Forward or to the Side as You Walk

Another cause of lower back pain is bending forward at the waist as you walk. Many beginners do this when they are trying to walk fast. Concentrate on the pelvic tilt and leaning from the ankles (about 5 degrees), not the waist.

Hunched Shoulders

Hunched shoulders are a symptom of tight chest muscles and weak upper back muscles. As with other bad postural habits, giving in to them will cause pain and exacerbate any existing problem. Gently bring your shoulder blades down and together if you feel them hunching. This helps to "open up" your chest and will also make your breathing deeper and more relaxed.

As you begin to practice walking with proper posture, take note of your body position every few minutes. Are your shoulders down and back? Is your chin tucked in? Going over a mental checklist of postural pitfalls will get you on the track to walking correctly.

Once your posture and stance are set, you are ready to learn the proper stepping action: (1) the hip- to shoulder-width stance, (2) the heel strike, (3) the outer edge heel-toe roll, (4) the toe-off, and (5) the stride stretch. If you've read other walking books, gone to other people's walking clinics, or just taken note of how you move when you are strolling down the street, you may realize that these five techniques represent a slightly exaggerated version of how we "normally" walk. The techniques of exercisewalking are purposely exaggerated to enhance the exercise value of walking. They demand more muscle control and move your joints through a wider range of motion. The muscles are stretched farther, promoting flexibility.

Understanding the mechanics of walking will help you to understand how the following walking techniques were developed. If you were to watch a slow-motion film of someone walking correctly, here's what you'd see: The heel strikes the ground first. As the body moves forward, the weight falls to the outside of the foot. At this moment the foot is rigid, acting much like the bottom of a rocking chair. At the end of the rock forward, the weight shifts toward the inside of the foot and up onto to the toes (called the *toe-off position*). At the same time that the front foot is rolling from heel to toe, the other leg is stepping forward. As the stepping leg reaches the front of the body, the knee straightens and the ankle bends upward in preparation for the heel strike that begins the next step.

As your head guides the position of your upper body, proper stance and foot placement ensure the correct positioning of your lower body. Your feet should be parallel and pointing forward. Relax your knees, keeping them slightly flexed. Many people believe that you should walk with a very narrow stance, placing one foot directly in front of the other. This is fine for racewalkers (it helps increase speed), but beginners or people with some joint weakness in the leg should walk with their feet hip- to shoulder-width apart (meaning that your stance is as wide as the distance between your hips or shoulders). This stance lowers the body's center of gravity and thus decreases your likelihood of falling. (A hip- to shoulder-width stance is taught in many forms of karate because of its stability.)

The heel strike locks your ankle into a stable place, thus keeping your weight from shifting as it moves over your foot and protecting your knee and ankle from injury. A proper heel strike also forces you to lift your feet, so you'll be less likely to trip on uneven surfaces.

Begin by placing your foot at a 45-degree angle to the ground and fully extending your front leg. The foot will be at a 90-degree angle with the leg and in a neutral position, neither turning out nor in. You'll feel a tension in your shin, a sign that you're pulling your foot high enough to properly execute the heel strike. Practice this technique by standing with your legs together and then taking a step forward and placing your foot in the heel-strike position. Return to your starting position and repeat with your other leg. This exercise also will improve your balance. Another heel-strike exercise is to walk on your heels for several yards. (Don't do this if you have an ankle injury.)

To execute the heel-toe roll, turn your foot slightly outward (enough to place two fingers underneath your arch) as you roll from the heel strike to the toes. The heel-toe roll works the ankle through its range of lateral motion and exercises the calf muscle, helping to pump blood back up to the heart. To get accustomed to the heel-toe roll, try to rock up on your toes and then come back down so that you land on your heels with your toes off the ground. Repeat this six to twelve times. If you have problems keeping your balance, hold onto the back of a chair or a wall for support.

As the heel of your front foot strikes the ground, your back foot is in the toe-off position, ready to push you forward into the next step. Take a step and freeze. Look at your back foot to make sure it's parallel with your front foot and that you are pushing straight forward from your toes (you get the most speed from pushing off the toes, not the ball of the foot). Many beginners push to the side, which wastes energy and throws off the next step. If you have difficulty keeping your feet parallel, widen your stance.

The stride stretch, or hip extension, helps you increase your step length 3 to 8 inches. The secret is in the hip. Normally when you walk, your hips are square to the line of travel. By letting your hip rotate downward and forward as your leg reaches forward, you can cover more ground. The stride stretch exercises the muscles surrounding the hips more effectively than "normal" walking and helps increase flexibility. Don't be afraid to let your hips extend forward as you walk. Not only does this look more natural than moving your body side to side as in a John Wayne walk, but it will help avoid back strain. However, if you have a bad back you should limit the hip rotation and stride stretch.

Many people consider walking to be a workout for the legs only, but if you pump your arms back and forth, you will transform walking into a total-body exercise. Arm pumping almost doubles walking's aerobic benefits and builds and tones muscles in the arms, upper and lower back, and shoulders. Just five minutes of pumping your arms will convince you that walking can be a strenuous exercise.

There is a difference between pumping and swinging the arms. Your arms naturally swing forward and back (the right arm moves with the left leg, and vice versa) from the shoulder joint as you walk, but this swing demands almost no muscle strength. Arm pumping, moving your arms briskly back and forth as you walk, demands much more strength and control in your arms, chest, and back and actually helps to propel the body forward. Pumping also takes stress off the shoulder joint by forcing all the muscles in the upper back to share the strain of movement.

The basic arm-pump position is with the elbow bent at a 90-degree angle. Make a loosely clenched fist with your hand. Move your right arm straight forward and back, brushing the sides of your body. Holding your arms too far away from your body is tiring and puts added stress on the shoulders. Your elbow should travel in a rather wide arc throughout the pump, coming to chest height in the front of the body and almost shoulder height in the back. Although it may seem more natural to let your arms cross toward the center of your body in the front pump, pumping straight forward and back demands more muscular control, is a gentler movement for the shoulder joints, and prevents low back pain.

For a slower, less athletic walk, use the straight arm pump, which uses the same shoulder and back muscles but is done with the arms extended. This arm-pump looks more "normal" and is perfect for the walker who doesn't want to call attention to himself or herself. If you use the straight arm pump, you can also extend the fingers rather than holding them in a loosely clenched fist.

As you build arm and back strength, you can adapt a slight cross pump (but don't let your fist go beyond the midpoint of your chest), which will help you propel your body forward even faster. As with the other techniques, practice the arm pump standing in front of a mirror until you understand the basic movement.

Now you are ready to put all your techniques together. Go through the

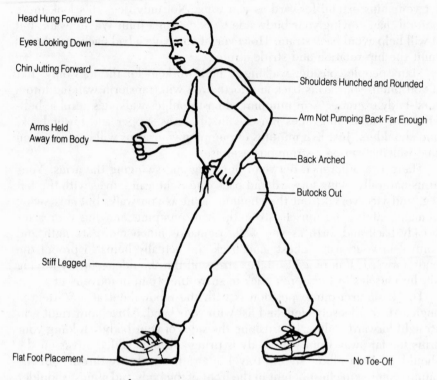

Head Hung Forward

Eyes Looking Down

Chin Jutting Forward

Shoulders Hunched and Rounded

Arm Not Pumping Back Far Enough

Arms Held
Away from Body

Back Arched

Butocks Out

Stiff Legged

Flat Foot Placement

No Toe-Off

Incorrect Walking Technique

motion of walking at an extremely slow pace, concentrating on your posture and parallel foot placement, as well as the heel strike, the heel-toe roll, the toe-off, the stride stretch, and the arm pump. The exaggerated slowness of the movement not only will give you time to concentrate on all the movements, but also will strengthen your muscles (it is hard work to move more slowly than is natural).

Warming Up to Walking

Before you tear off down the track or around the block, you need to warm up. If you don't, you will certainly increase the likelihood of injuring yourself.

"Warm-up" is not synonymous with "stretching." In fact, for any physical activity—including exercisewalking—the warm-up always precedes the stretching exercises, which both precede the main event, the workout.

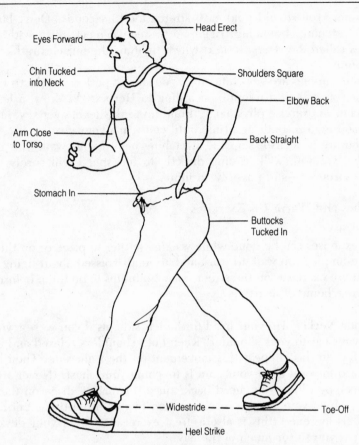

Eyes Forward

Head Erect

Chin Tucked into Neck

Shoulders Square

Elbow Back

Arm Close to Torso

Back Straight

Stomach In

Buttocks Tucked In

Widestride

Toe-Off

Heel Strike

Correct Walking Technique

A warm-up exercise increases circulation to the extremities and makes stretching easier.

The easiest warm-up is to walk. Start slowly and gradually increase speed. Do this for as long as it takes to build up a mild sweat, usually about 5 to 10 minutes. During the warm-up walk, you can also perform some range-of-motion exercises for your upper body—for example, circling your straightened arms clockwise and counterclockwise over your head (see description of this and other warm-up exercises on pages 102–103).

Stretching exercises lengthen the muscles, increase flexibility, and allow us to retain the range of motion in our joints. Stretching and strengthening work together. Every muscle you strengthen should be stretched (and vice versa). Exercise physiologists usually suggest that each stretch last for at least 15 seconds. After the first 5 seconds, the muscles begin to relax, and the stretch occurs in the latter 10 seconds, so even if you are a beginner, you should hold each stretch for 15 seconds. Don't bounce while stretching. Bouncing triggers a protective mechanism within the muscles called the *stretch reflex*, which tightens the muscles rather than lengthening them.

If your muscles are very inflexible, you should perform each stretching exercise for at least a minute, according to Herbert de Vries, a leading researcher in exercise physiology. Build up to this level over several sessions, adding 5 seconds at a time until you reach your goal.

If you are in a rush, skip the stretching before your walk, but never skip the warm-up walk. Going directly to top speed will surely cause muscle soreness—and possibly an injury.

Stretches and Warm-Up Exercises

Warm-Up
These exercises can be done while walking (either in place or on the go). If, for example, you walk to work and are embarrassed about being seen doing these exercises on the street, take 2 minutes to do them before you leave your home or apartment.

For Your Neck: Tip your head to the left side, as if you were trying to touch your ear to your shoulder. Keep both shoulders relaxed and down when you do this. Repeat this movement on the right side. Then bring your head forward until your chin is touching your chest. (Never stretch your neck by tilting your head back, since this places stress on the vertebrae.) Move your head in each position two or three times until your neck feels loosened (this is also a great exercise to do at your desk, especially if you sit for much of the day).

For Your Shoulders and Arms: Arm circles (also called *windmills*) help increase circulation to your shoulders, arms, and hands. Start with straightened arms at your side. Swing your straightened right arm counterclockwise over your head (with your palm facing the ceiling on the upswing) while swinging your left arm clockwise. After 30 seconds, switch directions. This shoulder exercise will ready your shoulder for the smooth, rhythmic arm pump.

Stretches
As mentioned earlier, you can skip stretches before your walking workout if you are in a hurry, but it is better, especially if you are a beginning walker, to do the following four stretches before you go out. Repeat each stretch twice. You can complete all the stretches in roughly 3 minutes.

For Your Shins: Standing with your feet hip width apart, roll up onto your toes and back down again. Repeat ten to twenty times.

For the Backs of the Calves: Here you can use the classic runner's calf stretch. Face a tree or wall and lean against it with your arms straight and placed at shoulder height. Step forward with your right leg and try to keep your left heel on the ground (keeping your left knee slightly bent) as you lean into the wall or tree, bending your arms. Hold for 15 seconds and repeat on the other side.

For the Fronts of Your Thighs: This stretch, the lunge, will stretch the front of your upper leg as well as your hip. Take a giant step forward so that your right knee is bent and your right thigh is parallel to the ground. Your right knee should be over your ankle, and both your right and left feet should be facing forward. Try to sink down as far as possible, feeling the stretch in your left thigh. You can put your arms out to the side for balance or place your hands on your hips. Hold for at least 15 seconds. Switch legs.

For the Backs of Your Thighs: Place the heel of one leg on the back of a chair or park bench (preferably so that it is raised to hip height). Keeping the knee and back straight and turning your foot inward, lean forward and reach forward on your leg as far as you can. Hold for 15 seconds and release. Now repeat with your foot held straight and then again with it turned out. Then repeat with the other leg.

It's important to keep your joints covered up while warming up and walking. If you are walking in athletic clothes, start out wearing a loose, long-sleeved top and pants unless it is very hot. If you feel you will be too hot after you've walked for a while, wear shorts and a short-sleeved shirt under your top layer, which you can shed once you start to sweat. Covering your arms and legs until you warm up thoroughly will help prevent injuries. Even if you are wearing business attire, you might want to start out with a sweater or jacket, which you can take off as you get hot. Remember that any kind of clothes is good for walking as long as the clothes are loose and don't restrict your movements.

Finally, end every walking session with a cool-down walk. Slow your speed over the last 5 minutes, as stopping abruptly is not good for the heart or muscles. If you have time, it is a good practice to end each walk with a brief stretch (using the same exercises you did before you walked). This is particularly helpful for beginning walkers who may be experiencing pain in their calves or shins from muscle fatigue.

The Preventive Walking Program

This program is designed for people who need to strengthen their muscles, increase flexibility, and learn the basic walking techniques. Advancement from one level to the next is based on distance walked, not speed. You

How Far and How Often to Walk

YOUR LEVEL	MILEAGE PER DAY	DAYS PER WEEK
Level I	⅛ to 1 mile	At least 3
Level II	1 to 2 miles	At least 3
Level III	2 to 5 miles	At least 4
Level IV	5 to 8 miles	At least 4
Level V	Over 8 miles	At least 4

cannot increase walking speed efficiently until your muscles are strong and you know how to walk correctly. Follow this preventive program for 6 weeks. If you have reached Level III *and* feel comfortable with the walking techniques at that time, then you can move on to Book 3: Cardiowalking, where you'll learn how to safely increase your walking speed. If you are not at the desired level after this period, continue for another few weeks until you have satisfied both criteria. Use the chart above as a guideline of how far and how often you should walk. Unless you have been

Tracking Your Mileage Progress over 6 Weeks

STARTING MILEAGE (PER DAY)	AFTER 3 WEEKS YOU WILL WALK (PER DAY)	AFTER 6 WEEKS YOU WILL WALK (PER DAY)
⅛ mile	⅝ mile	1⅜ miles
¼ mile	¾ mile	1½ miles
½ mile	1 mile	1¾ miles
1 mile	1½ miles	2¼ miles
1½ miles	2 miles	2¾ miles
2 miles	2½ miles	3¼ miles
2½ miles	3 miles	3¾ miles
3 miles	3½ miles	4¼ miles
3½ miles	4 miles	4¾ miles
4 miles	4½ miles	5¼ miles
4½ miles	5 miles	5¾ miles
5 miles	5½ miles	6¼ miles
5½ miles	6 miles	6¾ miles
6 miles	6½ miles	7¼ miles
6½ miles	7 miles	7¾ miles
7 miles	7½ miles	8¼ miles
7½ miles	8 miles	8¾ miles
8 miles	8½ miles	9¼ miles
8½ miles	9 miles	9¾ miles

completely sedentary for some time, begin walking at Level II. If you don't feel you can walk at least a mile, start with Level I.

While you are walking, practice one walking technique for 5 minutes and then move onto the next. For example, concentrate on the heel-toe roll for 5 minutes, then forget about that and think only about arm pumping for 5 minutes, and then concentrate on holding proper posture for 5 minutes. Once you've gone through all the techniques, practicing them consciously, you can think about whatever you like. Slowly, over the 6 weeks, you will begin to use the techniques without even thinking.

Every week, increase your mileage by ¼ mile. If you walked 1½ miles per session during the first week, walk 1¾ miles per session during the second week, and so on. Although you shouldn't concentrate on increasing your speed, you'll probably notice that you are naturally walking faster as you become stronger.

Use the chart on page 104 to track your overall mileage progress over 6 weeks. Find your starting mileage in the first column and increase your mileage accordingly.

4. Walking for a Bad Back

Robert Ross, age 64, is a truck driver who began walking several years ago for a back injury that hadn't responded to other treatment—but it was alleviated by walking. He is now a cheerleader for walking for every reason under the sun.

According to Robert, 80 percent of truck drivers have bad backs as a result of lifting heavy cargo and prolonged sitting behind the wheel. Drivers' backs are further aggravated by the bumpy rides of big trucks. One day in 1984, Robert severely strained a muscle when he attempted to reach over and pull a pin on a truck wheel by hand rather than with a crow bar. He wound up hospitalized for many months.

Robert was put in traction and on various types of pain-relief drugs. All different types of therapy followed, none of which alleviated the excruciating muscular pain. Bed rest had atrophied his muscles, and an orthopedic surgeon told him to walk in order to regain some of the strength in his back.

In tandem with physical therapy (aerobic exercises in a pool, which he still does), Robert began walking with the Westdale Mallwalkers, a 700-member group in southwest Cedar Rapids. At this point he was still on crutches, but he was encouraged to use his legs as much as possible. At first, walking was very difficult, but with the support of friends and family, Robert kept on walking every day and soon experienced dramatic improvement. "Walking was the best thing in the world for me," says Robert.

Robert has logged more than 1000 miles at Westdale Mall. He also keeps a treadmill at home, on which he logs 3 to 4 miles at a time—

starting slowly, pacing steadily for about a mile, and then doing a cool-down. Robert still takes an occasional ibuprofen for his back. He also watches his diet—he is a bit overweight—but walking, he says, helps that, too. "If I exercise . . . if I get stiff or upset, I walk and it alleviates everything," he avers. He also gets psychological benefits: "a tremendous uplift."

About 80 million Americans suffer from back pain, and virtually all people will experience some sort of back problem or discomfort in their lifetime. A tendency toward back difficulties is inherited, but problems often arise because of bad posture, which weakens the back muscles. If you then lift something incorrectly or fall or have some other accident that traumatizes your back, you'll end up with back pain. Most problems can be avoided by exercising the back and abdominal muscles regularly with walking and doing some preventive stomach-strengthening exercises.

To understand what can go wrong with your back, you'll need to un-derstand a little about its structure. The spine is made up of twenty-four vertebrae* that are connected by facet joints. Each vertebra is covered with a thin layer of cartilage. The vertebrae are separated by a disk, a cushion that not only helps bind the vertebrae together, but also acts as a shock absorber. Muscles on either side of the spine keep it aligned. The vertebrae not only serve as a support for the upper body, but also protect the spinal cord, the network center for nerves running up, down, and across the body.

Back problems are usually difficult to diagnose, since the pain can be caused by any combination of tendon, ligament, muscle, and joint prob-lems. Lower back injury and pain are the most common, happening about three or four times more often than upper back ailments. The most fre-quent back afflictions are muscle stiffness, especially in the neck (least severe), muscle strain (slightly more severe), back sprain—the tearing or stretching of a tendon or ligament (moderately severe), and disk problems (the most severe).

Muscle stiffness can be alleviated through stretching and strengthening exercises (see pages 111–114). Back strains and sprains should be treated by applying ice for the first 48 hours (for 10 to 15 minutes at least twice a day). Switch to moist heat (such as an old-fashioned hot water bottle or a hydrocollator—a cloth bag filled with silicone that is boiled, wrapped in a towel, and placed on a joint) on the following days, to be applied before you do stretching exercises.

Temporary structural malposition of the vertebrae can be caused by a muscle spasm on one side of the back. The temporary curvature can be corrected by walking (which strengthens the back muscles) and doing the

---

*There are really thirty-three vertebrae in the back, but nine in the lower back are fused together to form the sacrum and coccyx.

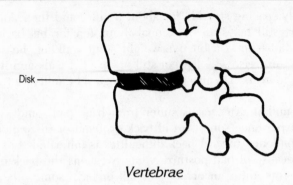

Disk

Vertebrae

back exercises on pages 111 to 114, which will help to ensure that muscles on both sides of the spine are pulling evenly.

Not only will walking relieve muscle spasms and cramps in the back, but it will also strengthen muscles and keep them from going into spasms in the future. In fact, chiropractors report that patients who walk need less manipulation for proper back adjustment and each manipulation lasts longer because muscles are stronger. In addition, walking places less stress on the back than sitting or standing. Doctors now tell their patients with severe back pain to confine bed rest to less than 2 days if possible, because the muscle atrophy that occurs after 48 hours of bed rest usually complicates the problem and causes further pain.

Disk injuries are more complicated to treat. The three most common injuries are a flattened disk, a herniated disk, and a ruptured disk. Disks are often described as being like stale jelly donuts, somewhat hard on the outside and gooey on the inside. A *flattened disk* means that the disk is squashed and the space between the vertebrae is reduced. The muscles and ligaments surrounding the injured disk then pull unevenly on the spine. A *herniated disk* protrudes beyond its normal space, placing pressure on spinal nerves and causing surrounding muscles to spasm. A *ruptured disk* is so called because the center ruptures into the harder outer portion of the disk, leaving less shock absorption between the vertebrae. Disk problems are often associated with sciatica, a pain that runs from the buttocks and down the leg and is caused by a pinched sciatic nerve (which runs from the base of the spine down the leg). You will need to consult a doctor if you have disk problems, but walking may relieve some of the pain and will not cause further damage.

If your back pain makes walking on land too painful, follow Robert Ross's example and take your exercisewalking techniques to your local pool (see Chapter 6 for more details on water walking), although you should try to walk a little around your home or workplace, at least ¼ mile, to maintain mobility.

Exercisewalking Techniques

While you walk, pay attention to the postural techniques described in Chapter 3:

1. Tuck your chin into your neck (see page 95).

2. Do the pelvic tilt (see page 95).

3. Don't lean forward at the waist. This puts additional strain on your back. To avoid leaning forward, imagine that someone is gently pushing their finger into the middle of your back.

4. Pump your arms vigorously. This will help relieve stress that may collect in the upper back from sitting at a desk all day and thus help you to avoid muscle spasms. Pumping has also been shown to relieve pain in patients who have developed signs of osteoporosis in the upper back (see page 99).

Walking styles should also differ depending on the site of your back pain. If you have a weak lower back, you should adopt a narrower than normal stance (the feet just inches apart or even placed one in front of the other rather than the hip- to shoulder-width stance recommended on page 98) and use a shorter stride length (3 to 8 inches) for part of the workout. This narrower stance will force you to rotate your hips more as you walk. This rotation will in turn gently rotate the lower spine and quickly build strength in the muscles of the lower back. You only need to walk with the narrow stance for ¼ mile and then switch back to a regular brisk walk with a longer stride. If you have arthritis of the hip or have disk problems in the lower back, the narrow stance is not advised.

Exercises for the Back

If you have back problems (or fear that you are susceptible to such problems), you should perform these exercises every day in addition to your regular walking program. How many of each exercise you do depends on your back pain. Use the following pain scale to decide how many repetitions are right for you. A rating of 1 represents the worst pain you have ever felt, and 10 is the least. If pain is severe, *don't* push yourself. One or two repetitions of each may be all you can comfortably do and thus all you should do. It is better to do fewer of each exercise more often during the day than a lot of them all at once. Listen to your body, and remember that the following chart is only a guideline.

The idea behind the pain scale is that you should be able to eventually get to Phase 3. However, if you have arthritis in your back, your pain may never completely disappear. In that case, exercise as much as you can without increasing your pain.

Pain Scale

Worst pain

$\left.\begin{array}{c} 1 \\ 2 \\ 3 \end{array}\right\}$ Follow Phase 1 prescription on the following chart

$\left.\begin{array}{c} 4 \\ 5 \\ 6 \\ 7 \end{array}\right\}$ Follow Phase 2 prescription on the following chart

$\left.\begin{array}{c} 8 \\ 9 \\ 10 \end{array}\right\}$ Follow Phase 3 prescription on the following chart

Least pain

According to the chart below, if you are in Phase 1, you would repeat each strengthening exercise one to six times and hold each stretch for 15 seconds. As you get to Phases 2 and 3, repeat each group of repetitions (known as a "set" in athletic jargon) more than one time per exercise session.

As you can see from the chart, the more pain you are in, the more often you should try to do these exercises. At some pain-management centers where patients learn to live with chronic pain (back pain is the most common type of pain treated at these centers), patients perform exercise routines ten times a day in the initial stages.

Some of these exercises can be done sitting down, others lying down, and others standing. If you do the prone exercises on the floor, place a 3- to 4-inch pad underneath your head and back. (An exercise pad folded in three works well.)

Exercise Prescriptions per Phase

YOUR PHASE	NUMBER OF REPETITIONS*	SECONDS TO HOLD†	FREQUENCY PER SESSION	TIMES PER DAY
Phase 1	1–6	15	1	4
Phase 2	7–10	15	2	2–3
Phase 3	11–15	15	2	1

*For strengthening exercises.

†For stretching exercises.

Neck

A Stretch

Bend your head forward until your chin is touching your chest. Keep your shoulders down and relaxed while you do this exercise. Next, try to bring your right ear as close as possible to your right shoulder, again relaxing your shoulders. Repeat on the left side. Finally, turn your head as far as possible to the right. Then to the left. Doing this exercise in front of a mirror helps you to be sure you are stretching the same amount in all directions.

Strengthening Exercises

The following are resistance exercises.

1. Place your left hand on the side of your head. Try to move your head toward your left shoulder, and resist that movement by pushing against your head with your left hand. Repeat on other side. Hold each for 10 seconds.

2. Place your hands behind your head. Try to move your head backwards while pushing against your head with your hands. Then place your hands on your forehead to create resistance as you try to move your head forward toward your chest. Hold each position for 10 seconds.

Trunk Turns (to Stretch the Lower Back)

1. This exercise can be done either sitting in a chair or standing. Cross your arms in front of you as if you were an Indian chief. Keeping your arms at chest height, twist to the right, following your right elbow with your eyes and turning as far as possible to the right. Repeat the twist on the left side, following your left elbow with your eyes.

2. This exercise improves your back's range of motion. Sit on the front of a chair. Make a circle with your upper body, first leaning forward slightly from the waist, then bending to the left side, then leaning back, and finally bending to the right. Repeat, circling to the right. (This can be done standing as well.) Keep your back straight during this exercise.

3. Stand with your hands above your head. Bend to the right laterally about 30 degrees, come back to the middle, and then bend to the left. Repeat the exercise with your arms at your side and then your hands on your hips.

Shoulder and Back Stretch

Hold your arms straight out to the side as if you were a scarecrow. Swing your arms to the front of your body, touching your hands together. Then hug yourself. This exercise stretches your shoulders and upper back muscles.

Leg Stretches (Very Important for Lower Back Problems)

1. Lie on your back. Bend your left leg, keeping its foot flat on the floor. Then bend your right leg and pull it into your chest. Release after 15 seconds and switch legs.

2. Lie on your back. Bend your leg, keeping your foot flat on the floor. Bend your right leg and bring it to your chest. Then extend your right leg (without locking your knee) to the ceiling. Your foot should be flexed (opposite of pointed). Hold for 15 seconds and switch legs. This exercise stretches the hamstring (muscles in the back of the leg) and replaces the traditional "bending over and touching your toes."

3. Lie on your stomach, propped up on your arms. Raise one leg as far as you can, keeping the knee straight. Repeat with the other leg.

Stomach Exercises (Very Important for Lower Back Problems)

1. Lie on your back with your hands across your chest (left hand touching right shoulder, and vice versa). Lift only your shoulders off the floor, no higher than 30 degrees. Don't "puff out" your abdominal muscles, as this places stress on the neck and back.

2. Lie on your back and place a hand on your abdominal muscles. Contract your abdominal muscles so that your lower back is pushed into the floor. Hold for 6 seconds and release.

3. Pelvic tilt: Lying on your back with knees bent and feet flat on the ground, lift your buttocks off the ground. Keep your arms at your side for support.

4. Lie on your back with your knees bent (so your thighs and calves form a 90-degree angle and your thighs form a 90-degree angle with the floor). Slowly lower your feet to the floor and bring them back to the starting position. Don't tense your neck and shoulders during this exercise, and make sure your push your lower back into the floor.

5. Lie on your stomach, each arm held straight out to the side (at a 90-degree angle to your body). Squeeze your buttocks and tense your stomach muscles, and then lift your shoulders off the ground. Hold that position for 5 seconds.

6. Sit in a chair and inhale using your diaphragm, so that your upper abdomen fills with air. As you exhale, push your stomach into the back of the chair. (This is a good stomach exercise for a bus, subway, car, or train ride). Hold for 6 seconds.

Leg Stretches

Stomach Strengthener

Leg Twist

Leg Twist

Lie on your back, knees bent, but with your feet flat on the floor. Move both legs to the left until your left thigh is touching the floor. Repeat on other side. People with sciatic nerve pain should cross their legs (so that they are moving their right thigh to the left, and vice versa), since this releases tension in the lower back. Don't try this modification, however, if you have knee inflammation.

After you've done these exercises, look at Chapter 6 for a rehabilitative walking program you can follow while your back is healing.

5. Walking Joint by Joint

Bernice Burkeholder, now in her seventies, turned to walking as a last resort after more than 20 years of pain caused by twice tearing a ligament in her right knee. About 6 years ago, the University of Missouri offered an exercise class (which included walking) for people with arthritis. Bernice joined, and after the 12-week class was over, she had improved so much—decreasing pain in her knee and increasing movement—that she signed up for the class a second time and that summer also began an aquatic exercise program that included walking in water. People began telling her how well she looked. After the summer she began to walk at her local mall 5 days a week, covering a little over a mile in 20 minutes. Although Bernice may still have to have knee replacement surgery eventually, walking has kept her in the mainstream, meeting new people, improving her health and sense of well-being, and most important, reducing her pain.

Exercise is imperative if a person with arthritis or a joint injury is to maintain function in his or her sixty-eight joints. As Bernice's story shows, even if mobility is limited, joint problems and pain can be reduced with walking.

As with back problems, stretching and strengthening the muscles and increasing the range of motion around an injured or damaged joint are keys to the rehabilitative process. Since the cartilage, tendons, and ligaments will never regenerate, the muscles must take over, and in order to do so, they need to be strong and flexible.

This chapter is divided up into sections that cover the major joints—

115

the ankles, knees, hips, and upper body (shoulder, elbow, wrist, and hand)—and you'll find exercises to improve joint strength, flexibility, and range of motion. If you've injured a joint or have arthritis, you need to do these exercises in addition to walking to enhance the performance of your muscles and joints. The exercises become even more important if you've been bedridden or in a cast, since you will need to rebuild muscle strength. Even if you had a joint injury that is now healed, you should use these exercises as part of your warm-up before your regular walking program to ensure that the joint stays healthy.

There are two main ways to strengthen a muscle, either *isometrically* (without moving the joint) or *isotonically* (moving a muscle against resistance, like a weight or even gravity).* Isometric exercises are the only exercises prescribed to athletes with a swollen joint, or to patients during a flare-up or after some types of surgery. If you have rheumatoid arthritis and the joint is red, swollen, and warm to the touch, active movement of the joint *can cause permanent damage.* Isometric exercises strengthen the muscles surrounding a joint without damaging the joint and help to prevent muscle atrophy. Those exercises below which are isometric are so marked.

Keeping the joints moving through their range of motion helps to avoid muscle spasms and keeps the joint from "freezing," which can happen quite rapidly if a damaged or injured joint is held in one position for too long. One woman with arthritis reported that if she doesn't move her legs during her bus trip across town, she can't stand up at the end of her ride. You can do many of the strengthening and stretching and range-of-motion exercises inconspicuously while waiting in line or seated on a bus or subway.

If you have an injury or disease that affects one or more of the weight-bearing joints, you'll probably begin to adopt an unnatural and compensatory walking gait. For example, people with arthritis of the ankle may waddle when they walk or swing one of their legs out to the side. These compensations, because they are unnatural, place further strain on the injured joints. Under each of the following joint categories, you'll find common gait "abnormalities" and how you can combat these mistakes with proper walking technique.

If your joint is severely swollen, ice the joint until the swelling is reduced, elevate the limb, and *don't exercise it.* Once the swelling recedes (probably after a day or two), do gentle warm-up exercises to recover range of motion in the joint. As the joint heals, begin stretching and strengthening exercises. Use an ice bag or a package of frozen vegetables (frozen peas seem to work best), placing a towel between your skin and the cold pack. No more than 10 to 15 minutes is needed.

---

*There is a third way, called *isokinetic exercise*, which is often used in hospital and rehabilitation programs. This type of exercise will not be discussed in the chapter.

Taking a warm bath or shower and placing hot compresses on stiff joints are particularly effective early in the morning and prior to exercise. Mild wet heat (like a hydrocollator, a cloth bag that is boiled and then wrapped around a joint) rather than dry heat (like a heating pad) works best, but it shouldn't be kept on the joint for more than 20 minutes.

Massage also relieves pain and helps warm up the muscle for exercise. You can apply self-massage if you have a muscle cramp, which will usually go away after several seconds of rubbing the sore area. For people with arthritis or serious injuries, a longer massage session may be helpful. Don't use the "pressure point" type of massage that digs deeply (and painfully) into a muscle but rather use smooth, long strokes that gradually work deeper into the muscle tissue between the bones, coaxing the tension from the muscle. Use baby powder, baby oil, or menthol gel to help your fingers glide over your skin. If the joint feels very tight or resistant, you can use arnica oil or Tiger Balm in conjunction with warm compresses to loosen up the area.

If you have arthritis in your hands or feet, try a contrast bath. Begin by soaking in warm water (about 110° F) for 3 minutes, and then switch to cold (65° F) for 1 minute. Repeat three times, ending with a warm bath. This method can also be used for a sprained ankle or sports injuries to the foot or wrist.

How the Program Works

Look under the headings below to find the recommendations and exercises for the joint you have injured. The rehabilitation process is divided into three phases. As you progress from one phase to another, increase the number of repetitions you do of both the range-of-motion and strengthening exercises and the number of seconds you hold a stretch or isometric exercise. (Not all types of exercises are listed for each joint.) These exercises should be done in conjunction with one of the walking programs you will find in the next chapter.

If you have arthritis, your pain may never go away completely. In this case, do as many exercises as you can without increasing your pain (if your joints hurt two hours after exercising, you've done too much).

Follow *Phase 1* guidelines if you've just had a flare-up, you've just come out of joint surgery, you've been bedridden for more than 2 days, or you have just had a cast taken off. *Phase 2* is an intermediate level. Follow these guidelines if you've had a muscle sprain or have mastered Phase 1 (this should take 1 to 3 weeks depending on the severity of your injury). Follow *Phase 3* if you've had a muscle strain or have mastered Phase 2 (this should take 1 or 2 weeks depending on the severity of your injury).

According to the following chart, if you are in Phase 1, you would repeat each range-of-motion or strengthening exercise one to six times and hold

Exercise Prescriptions per Phase

YOUR PHASE	NUMBER OF REPETITIONS*	SECONDS TO HOLD†	SECONDS TO HOLD‡	FREQUENCY PER SESSION	TIMES PER DAY
Phase 1	1–6	15	2	1	4
Phase 2	7–10	15	4	2	2–3
Phase 3	11–15	15	6	2	1

*For range-of-motion and strengthening exercises.
†For stretching exercises.
‡For isometric exercises.

each stretch for 15 seconds, as well as each isometric exercise for 2 seconds. As you get to Phases 2 and 3, you should repeat each group of repetitions (known as a "set" in athletic jargon) more than one time per exercise session. Do the exercises several times a day at the beginning of your rehabilitation period, and level off as you can do more during each session.

Remember that the preceding schedule is only a guideline. The most important thing to remember when exercising an injured or damaged joint is to *listen to your body. If you are in pain, stop exercising.* Although exercise is invaluable, overexercising is damaging.

You can also use the following pain scale to decide what phase to follow: Rate yourself from 1 to 10 (1 being the worst pain you've experienced, and 10 the least). If your pain falls between 1 and 2, you should rest or do only isometric exercises. Between 3 and 5, follow Phase 1 guidelines; between 6 and 8, follow Phase 2; and between 9 and 10, follow Phase 3.

Pain Scale

Worst pain

$\left.\begin{array}{l} 1 \\ 2 \end{array}\right\}$ Rest the joint and do only isometric exercises

$\left.\begin{array}{l} 3 \\ 4 \\ 5 \end{array}\right\}$ Follow Phase 1 rehabilitation guidelines

$\left.\begin{array}{l} 6 \\ 7 \\ 8 \end{array}\right\}$ Follow Phase 2

$\left.\begin{array}{l} 9 \\ 10 \end{array}\right\}$ Follow Phase 3

Least pain

Don't be discouraged if some days you feel better than others and can thus do more. This variableness is a natural part of the rehabilitation process.

If you have rheumatoid arthritis or osteoarthritis in several joints, you may want to begin by taking account of your pain. Relax, close your eyes, and concentrate on each part of your body from your toes to your head. Note which areas are tight, which seem painful, which seem neutral. Imagine you're in a warm climate, and feel the sun warming your muscles. After a minute or so of this "imaging," you can begin moving. This routine should be repeated at the end of your exercise session as well, so you can take stock of any joint or back pain.

The following exercises are done standing, sitting in a hard chair (with or without arms) or on a stool, or lying on the ground. If you do the exercises on the floor, place a 3- to 4-inch pad underneath your head and back (an exercise pad folded in three does the trick).

Hips

The hips are most often damaged by osteoporosis, stress fractures (especially among runners), and rheumatoid arthritis, which strikes the hip joint in 50 percent of all cases.

Sylvia Isler, age 56, from Juneau, Alaska, has arthritis in her hip. She began walking 15 years ago for weight control, and at her most active, she was walking 5½ miles a day. Her arthritis has gotten worse, and although she can no longer endure her old workout, her doctor is emphatic that she try to walk every day, as much as she can. She finds she can reduce her hip pain by walking as little as ½ to 1 mile a day.

If you're recuperating from hip replacement surgery, you may adopt a "Marilyn Monroe" gait, swinging your hips excessively from side to side as you walk. One reason you may walk with such a swagger is because of weak buttocks muscles (called *gluteals*). Follow the hip-strengthening exercises below.

Severe arthritis in the hip will also cause this Marilyn Monroe walk. If the swaying is very severe, you will usually be fitted with crutches or a cane by your doctor, since this movement will further traumatize the hip joint. If you must use walking aids, follow the water walking program in the next chapter to maintain leg strength safely.

Walking Techniques

If your hip is injured, you will tend to take smaller strides when you first start walking for rehabilitation. As the muscles that surround the hip, as well as those in the buttocks and upper leg, become stronger, you can gradually increase your stride to a normal length. Once you can walk easily with a regular stride, you should concentrate on the stride-stretching technique to help increase the hip's range of motion and reduce pain (see pages 98–99). One doctor, 81-year-old Robert Rosner, said that the stride stretch was the only therapy he had found to effectively reduce his hip pain, the result of a daily tennis game. Make sure to walk with a hip- to shoulder-width stance, as a narrower one can strain the hip.

Exercises

See the chart on page 118 for your repetition and set prescription.

Range-of-Motion Exercises

1. Hold on to the side of a chair or the wall for balance. Step with one leg to the front, then to the side, and finally to the back. Repeat on other side.

2. Holding on to the side of a chair for balance, kick your legs in front of you like a cancan dancer, always kicking across your body.

Strengthening Exercises

1. Stand with your feet together. Raise your right hip as high as possible so that your right foot is not touching the floor. Repeat on the left side.

2. While sitting down, raise your right hip off the chair seat. Hold for 2 to 6 seconds depending on your phase. Repeat on the left side.

3. Sit back in a chair. By lifting your right and left hips off the chair, "walk" to the end of the chair and back.

Stretching Exercises

This exercise is often called the "butterfly." Sit on the floor and bend your knees so that the soles of your feet are touching. With your hands, push down gently on your thighs as you try to touch your knees to the floor. Hold for 15 seconds. (Only the most flexible walker will be able to touch his or her knees to the floor, but the stretch is effective no matter how far away your knees are from the floor.)

Knees

Chuck Hunter is a 52-year-old who does 100-mile walking marathons with a complete right knee replacement. Chuck first injured his knee, tearing a ligament and the cartilage, while playing semiprofessional football in his early twenties. He started running marathons a few years later, but he soon discovered that his knee could not take it. Chuck then switched to long-distance walking (100-mile races). Although walking is less damaging to the joints than running, the large number of miles Chuck was logging took their toll—arthritis set in and his knee degenerated. Some days Chuck couldn't walk at all, and he started to walk bow-legged to compensate for his injury. It was time for a total knee replacement, in which every piece of cartilage was replaced with plastic cushions.

Chuck's rehabilitation took an entire year. He started out lifting light weights, sitting on a bench and raising and lowering his foot (he wore a weighted boot). He then progressed to a stationary bicycle. Both these exercises helped build his upper thigh muscles (quadriceps), which take much of the force off the knee.

"Throughout the first year I could walk," said Chuck, "but nothing strenuous." He used a cane in the beginning and racewalked in a pool for exercise. Toward the end of his rehabilitation, he started stair climbing.

Four years after surgery, Chuck competed in a 100-mile race, finishing in 22 hours. Even though Chuck walks over 100 miles a week, he no longer has any discomfort in his knee.

Virginia Howell, who's in her early seventies, began walking a year ago to rehabilitate from arthritis in her left knee, which was swollen to 1 inch larger than her right. After only 5 days of walking 2¼ miles at her local mall, her knee was back to the normal level and has stayed that way.

As these two examples show, walking is an integral part of knee re-habilitation, whether you've had joint replacement surgery or suffer from the aches and swelling of arthritis.

The knee is the most often injured joint. It bears more forces than any other joint when we walk. A severe injury is often rehabilitated with isometric exercises initially, followed by weight training, until the quad-riceps muscles (those in the fronts of the thighs) are strong enough to take pressure off the knee when you walk. Walking in a pool, as Chuck Hunter did, is often part of therapy after knee replacement surgery, a torn liga-ment, torn cartilage, or a resutured muscle (a badly torn muscle that is sewn together).

If you've had a knee injury, you may find that you snap the knee of your forward leg back into a straightened position as your body moves over the leg. This snapping action is usually a compensation for weak thigh muscles (the quadriceps), and can be rectified by climbing stairs or hills to build the muscles back up. Even if you've never injured your knee, incline or stair walking is recommended. Such preventive exercises are much more dependable than relying on a prophylactic knee brace. Studies have shown that athletes who wear such braces suffer more knee and leg injuries than those who do not (this is not true of rehabilitative or functional braces that are worn after an injury and do help restore function to the knee).

However, if you already have had a knee injury or have arthritis of the knee, as did a former football player Gary met in one of his clinics, you may have to avoid climbing hills because of pain. Although climbing helps build leg muscles, it can place too much force on the permanently weakened joint. You might also have to refrain from hyperextending your back leg when you walk (a technique common among racewalkers).

Walking Techniques

Once you are strong enough to walk on land, you may still find that you hunch over slightly when you walk and that you bend your injured knee when executing the heel strike. To overcome this irregular gait (if continued, it will further damage the knee), concentrate on the following techniques:

1. Extend the leg completely for the heel strike (see page 98). Stepping with an extended knee and landing on the heel ensures that the whole leg takes the impact force. (In running, in which you land on a bent knee, the knee must bear much more of your weight.)

2. Use proper posture (see page 95).

3. Make sure your weight is on the outside of your foot in the initial stages of the heel-toe roll (page 98). Women especially have a tendency to overly pronate (when one's weight moves excessively toward the inside of the foot over the course of the heel toe roll) because their weight naturally falls more than men's toward the inside of the foot (this is so because women's hips are wider than men's and thus their legs tend to form a V from their hips to their feet). Overpronation can lead to knee problems because the knees bear most of these lateral forces.

Exercises

See the chart on page 118 for your repetition and set prescription.

Stretching Exercise (for the Upper Thigh)

Lie on your stomach and bend your right knee. Try to touch your heel to your buttocks. Repeat with the left leg. The following are isometric exercises.

1. Sit in a chair. Place your legs together and squeeze. This exercise can also be done by placing a pillow or semi-inflated beach ball between your knees.

2. Place your leg next to the leg of a chair and push against it. Hold this for a count of six. Repeat with the other leg.

Strengthening Exercise

Sit at the end of a table or on a high stool. Place a light ankle weight (up to 1 pound) or wear a hiking boot on the foot of your injured leg. Raise your foot until your knee is straight. Then lower to the starting position.

Ankle and Lower Leg

Joe T. jumped up to throw a football one day and felt a rip in the back of his leg. He had torn his Achilles tendon, the cord that connects the heel with the calf muscle, a painful and common sports injury. His tendon was reattached surgically, and he spent 6 weeks in a cast, his foot held in a pointed position. Once the cast came off, Joe began rehabilitation to stretch the muscles in the back of his calf and strengthen the muscles surrounding his ankle. Because he couldn't bend his foot up enough for the heel strike, he walked flat-footed. The tightness in his ankle also caused Joe to walk with a straight knee (if you bend your knee as your weight moves over your foot, your ankle must also bend forward to support the weight), which caused further strain.

Joe's predicament is not unusual. Many ankle problems, whether a sprain, a break, or osteoarthritis, can lead to an improper heel strike and an abnormal gait: waddling from side to side or swinging the injured leg to the side—anything to avoid bending the ankle. Joe stretched his calf muscles and Achilles tendon over several weeks, working up to a proper heel strike by degrees and learning to rock all the way up to his toes rather than pushing off from a flat foot.

Walking Techniques

Concentrate on the heel strike (see page 98), which ensures that your foot hits the ground in a stable position, and the heel-toe roll (see page 98), which exercises the ankle through its full lateral range. Also try walking for several yards on your heels, toes, and the outside of your feet to strengthen and stretch the muscles surrounding your ankle.

Exercises

See the chart on page 118 for your repetition and set prescription.

Stretching and Strengthening Exercises

1. While seated or standing, extend your right leg out in front of you. Flex and then point your foot. Repeat with your left leg.

2. Extend your right leg out in front of you and rotate your ankle clockwise and counterclockwise. Repeat with the left ankle.

3. Stand next to a chair or wall you can hold on to for balance. Rise up on your toes and then roll back down until you are balancing on your heels.

4. Tie a bicycle innertube or surgical tubing around your feet and try to pull your toes apart while keeping your heels together. Then try to pull your heels apart while holding your toes together. (These are isometric exercises.)

Shoulders, Hands, and Wrists

The most common upper body injuries are a shoulder dislocation (usually a result of contact sports) and arthritis of the hands and wrist. These injuries will not prevent you from walking the distances prescribed in the preventive walking program outlined in Chapter 3, but you may have to modify the arm-pumping techniques.

If you have a shoulder injury and can't rotate your arm around the shoulder socket to execute the arm pump, you can still get some upper body exercise with the *bend-and-extend arm pump*. This technique resembles a bicep curl in weight lifting. Keeping your shoulder static, bend your left arm upward as your right leg steps forward. Your right arm should be extended. As your left leg steps forward, the right arm bends and the left straightens. This arm pump is not very effective for propelling you forward, but it does exercise your arms and helps to raise your heart rate, thus increasing the aerobic benefits of your walking workout.

If arthritis or injury stiffens your elbow, you may want to alternate the usual bent arm pump with a straight arm pump. The straight arm pump uses the same muscular action at the shoulder to glide the arm back and forth smoothly, but the arms are straight, instead of bent at a 90-degree angle. Switch back and forth every 5 minutes to keep your joints from freezing in one position. If you're experiencing a flare-up (or have an injury) in the elbow and don't want to bend it at all, use only the straight arm pump. Don't hyperextend the elbow, and make sure the arms pass close to your body on the forward and back swings.

If you've got hand injury, you may want to replace the loosely clenched fist position with an open hand and extended fingers. If you have arthritis in your fingers, alternating between the two every 5 to 10 minutes will keep your fingers from freezing into a bent position.

Exercises

See the chart on page 118 for your repetition and set prescription.

Warm-Up/Range-of-Motion Exercises

1. With your arms held at your sides, circle your shoulders clockwise. Make as large a circle as you can, bringing your shoulders up to your ears and pushing them down as far as they will go. Repeat circling the shoulders counterclockwise.

2. Move your arms as if you were swimming the crawl stroke. Make sure your arms cross in front of your body.

3. Beginning with your arms stretched out in front of you, bring them behind you laterally until you are "pinching" your scapulae (shoulder blades) together.

4. Starting with your arms at your sides, raise them (laterally) until they are over your head, turning your palms up on the way up and down on the way down.

5. Swing your arms forward and back, making as wide an arc as possible. In the forward swing, turn your palms up. In the backward swing, turn them down.

6. Rotate your forearms as if you were turning a doorknob.

7. Circle wrists in both directions.

8. With your hand held straight, spread your fingers apart as far as they will go. Then move your fingers together. For an extra challenge, try separating your index finger from your other fingers, then move your middle finger next to your index finger, then your ring finger, and finally your pinky. Repeat starting with your pinky.

9. Make an O with your thumb and index finger. Repeat this motion with your thumb and your other fingers.

Stretching Exercises

1. Sit in a chair. Turn to look behind you and pretend to reach for something on the ground (you don't need to actually touch the ground), then something at shoulder height, and then something above your head. Repeat this process to the side and to the front.

2. Bring one arm straight across your body at shoulder height. Use your other hand to push your arm (at the elbow) closer to your chest. Repeat with other arm.

3. Reach behind you (over your head) with your right hand and try to touch your left shoulder blade. Pull your elbow with your left hand. Repeat on the other side.

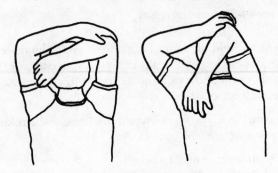

Shoulder Stretch

Strengthening Exercises

1. Modified push-up: Lie on your stomach, palms on the ground underneath your shoulders. Keeping your legs and pelvis on the ground, push your upper body off the floor.

2. Extend your right arm in front of you. With a series of five to ten "jerks," move your hand to your shoulder. (This strengthens your bicep—the muscle of your upper arm.)

Two Isometric Exercises

1. With your arms held straight at your sides, push them against your body.

2. Push your forearms against the arms of a chair or against some other solid object.

Once you've gone through the exercises for your injured joint or joints, you can move on to the appropriate walking program in the next chapter (or, if you have an upper body injury, to the preventive walking program). Return to these exercises throughout the day to ensure that your joints remain supple and your muscles strong.

6. The Arthrowalking Comeback Program

OVER LAND OR WATER

We can teach you how to walk, but it is harder to motivate you to walk. The most compelling motivators are fear and knowledge—fear of what will happen if you don't exercise and knowledge that exercise can make you stronger, healthier, and more in charge of your life. If you've experienced joint pain, either from arthritis or some injury or disease, you may feel fragile. You don't want your pain, or your condition, to worsen, so you might not be motivated to walk. Yet walking is critical to rehabilitation and pain reduction.

Kathleen Lewis, a registered nurse who suffers from lupus, has experienced both the physical and psychological benefits of walking. Kathleen used to enjoy outdoor activities like tennis and swimming, but now, she says, "It's difficult to find an exercise I can do without making my condition worse." Kathleen has found enjoyment in walking (although she cannot walk for long periods outside because sunlight can activate the symptoms of lupus). She admits that it is hard to be motivated when you're in pain, but she exercises regularly because she knows it makes her "stress-hardy"—able to cope with day-to-day aggravations.

Each of us must design our own personalized walking program based on our needs and limitations. General guidelines are provided below to help you do this. If you are under the care of a doctor, show him or her the program for approval before you begin.

For the rehabilitation period, a walking program can be done on land or in a pool. Whichever you do (and some people will do both) depends

127

on the severity of your joint damage and your pain. Even if you do the bulk of your walking program in a pool, continue to walk on land as much as possible, perhaps ¼ mile throughout the day around your neighborhood, office, or home just to maintain your mobility. Once you've strengthened your leg and back muscles in the pool, you may be able to increase your walking time on land.

If you've had joint surgery or have broken a bone (and are building back strength after the cast comes off), you will probably begin by walking with a cane or crutches. To build up to the point where you no longer need a walking aid, walk at least three or four times a day, every day, for 10 minutes (even if it is just around your apartment or home), until you can walk for 30 minutes at one time. People with joint replacements are told by their doctors to walk every day for the rest of their lives in order to keep the joint and muscles working properly.

Anyone with injuries or arthritis of the weight-bearing joints should walk on a flat and cushioned surface, like a track, or a treadmill (using no resistance). Walking down hills or down stairs places extra stress on the legs and back, which should be avoided during the early rehabilitative phases. As you regain your strength, expand your walking routine to include walking up moderate inclines or stairs. Take some of the stress off your back and feet when stairclimbing by walking down backwards. However, if you have permanent joint damage in your ankles, knees, or hips, incline and stair walking may not be a suitable workout.

To protect joints from excess shock, wear shoes with well-cushioned soles. Add an arch support to absorb shock and help force your weight to the outer edge of your foot as you walk. If you have severely fallen arches, a podiatrist or physiatrist can prescribe orthotics (see Book 6: The Walking Shoe and Foot Book). Other features to look for in a shoe are a firm heel cup, a hard plastic form on the inside of the heel of the shoe (which prevents over pronation), and a high toe area, called the *toe box* (especially important if you have arthritis in your feet or suffer from bunions, calluses, corns, or hammertoes).

Your warm-up should include the exercise in Chapter 4 (if you have a back problem) and Chapter 5 (if you have a joint problem). Then follow up with the four exercises and slow walk described in Chapter 3. Although the comeback program is designed so you walk several times a day, you do not need to do all these exercises every time you walk. It will suffice to do them at the beginning of your first session of the day and at the end of your last session.

Cover both your arms and legs when walking, unless it is very warm. If there's a slight breeze (even a warm one), keep your joints covered, as the air moving over your body will evaporate the sweat and expose the muscles to rapid cooling, causing spasms, cramps, and stiffness. On the other hand, wearing too many clothes will make you sweat excessively, leaving damp cloth next to your skin, which will also cool the muscles.

Wearing several layers of clothing will allow you to adjust to changes in temperature (both your body temperature and the air temperature) by adding or taking off clothes as needed. This technique is borrowed from ballet dancers and gymnasts (athletes most prone to joint injuries), who often wear tights under sweatpants and T-shirts under sweatshirts when they begin a workout. Keep the layer of clothing closest to your skin as dry as possible, and change it if it gets too wet.

If it's cold, keep your extremities covered. The cold slows down your circulation, so your hands and feet will feel the cold the fastest, and the warmest part of the body will be the upper torso because it is closest to the heart. Even in 50-degree weather, you may want to wear a light pair of gloves. Wearing a hat will prevent you from losing 80 to 90 percent of your body heat, since heat escapes through your head. A scarf also keeps in much body heat, and covering your neck, upper back, and shoulders sufficiently will keep you from hunching them against the cold. Even in mild weather, a cotton or light wool scarf will help warm up stiff shoulders, back, or neck.

If you walk in hot, humid weather, slow down the pace. Humidity causes fatigue. Don't walk faster than 2 miles an hour if the humidity is above 80 percent and the temperature is over 80°F.

Some people with rheumatoid arthritis are sensitive to weather and can experience increased symptoms when the barometer is falling. It is not the low pressure that brings on the symptoms, but rather the *change* in weather conditions. If you are sensitive to weather changes or the climate is very hot or cold, you may want to walk indoors. Many malls have walking clubs and special hours for walkers, and you can find a track or treadmill at many health clubs, YMCAs, YWCAs, or university gyms (which are sometimes open to the community). If your arthritis or joint condition is very severe and you don't want to stray far from your home, plan a route through your house or apartment building. If you are afraid of falling, walk by the walls or by furniture you can grab on to should you begin to lose your balance or else walk when someone is there to supervise.

Progress, as with the preventive program, is measured in terms of distance walked. If you are recovering from surgery, a broken bone, or a flare-up, you will be measuring your walking program not in miles, but in yards. This is Phase 1 of the program, when your goal is to move around your room. In Phase 2, you can begin to build distance in multiples of 100 yards, and finally, in Phase 3, in terms of miles. Once you can walk at least 1 mile, you can move on to the preventive program for another 6 weeks. According to the American College of Sports Medicine, short exercise periods of increasing frequency put less strain on arthritic joints.

Thus through this phasic program you will slowly build up distance by walking short distances separated by rest periods. As you regain strength, your walking sessions increase and rest periods decrease.

Throughout the rehabilitative stage, you will not be walking at a speed sufficient to rapidly improve your cardiovascular health. However, any speed above zero miles per hour will exercise the heart and lungs and will improve circulation. As one woman with rheumatoid arthritis said, "We won't die from arthritis, but we can die from heart disease." So don't be discouraged if you can't walk far or fast. Every step helps.

The following 10-point pain scale (with 1 being the worst condition and 10 being the best) can be useful in quantifying your physical condition and will help you to decide what level of intensity and at what distance you should walk each session. If you rate your pain as a 1, do not exercise. If your pain falls between 2 and 3, follow the Phase 1 program on pages 131–132 (you may want to walk in a pool if one is available). If you rate your pain between 4 and 7, follow the Phase 2 program, and if you fall between 8 and 10, follow Phase 3. Each day rank yourself on your pain level and follow the appropriate program. If you have a joint injury, your pain should decrease over several weeks until your muscles regain strength and you become pain-free. If you have arthritis, however (especially rheumatoid arthritis), then you may always feel some pain. Walk as far as you can without increasing your present level of pain. Keep adding 10 percent to your walking distance each week (as long as you aren't experiencing more pain) until you hit your distance goal. After a flare-up, you won't be able to walk as far, but don't be discouraged. All the walking you did before will help you to build up your distance again quickly.

Pain Scale

Worst pain

1	Rest
2 3	Follow the Phase 1 program
4 5 6 7	Follow the Phase 2 program
8 9 10	Follow the Phase 3 program

Least pain

When you should walk is a strategic decision. If you are taking anti-inflammatory medication (whether over-the-counter or prescription), it is best to walk when that medication is working at its peak. For medication you take two times a day, the peak is normally 6 to 8 hours after ingestion. For medication taken four times a day, the peak is every 2 hours, and for aspirin, the peak is 30 minutes to 1 hour after ingestion (the peak for coated aspirins is slightly longer).

In addition to the technique modifications you learned in the last chapter, if you have an injury or arthritis in your ankle, knee, or hip, you will also tend to take shorter steps and spend less time on the weakened leg. It is better to take shorter steps in the beginning with both the weak and strong legs rather than to limp—taking a longer step with the good leg and a shorter one with the injured one—which strains the good leg. As you build strength, try to take normal-length strides, and finally, attempt the stride stretch. In your home, try walking to a metronome. First, set it on a quick speed (so that you will be taking small, quick steps of even length), and then gradually slow it down as you can take longer strides. This method will help you increase your stride without limping.

Researchers specializing in biomechanics have determined that walking slowly (about 1 mile per hour) creates 30 percent less impact on your joints than walking at a moderate speed (3 miles an hour), which creates a force of 1.3 times your body weight. Therefore, a joint-injured person should walk slowly, although the specific speed should be self-selected. Walk as slow or as fast as is comfortable. Walking slower than feels natural to you actually places increased stress on the joints because the muscles are working harder to decelerate the body. As for top speed, researchers have found that if you have an injured or damaged leg or back, you shouldn't walk faster than 3.7 miles an hour at the most.

Land Walking Program

Phase 1: Following a Flare-Up, Injury, or Surgery

Along with the range-of-motion, stretching, and strengthening exercises (isometric or otherwise) listed in Chapters 4 and 5, you can begin walking in your room either with or without a walking aid (if you've had joint replacement surgery, you may be walking with a cane for up to one year after surgery). At this phase, progress is measured in steps. Don't be discouraged if it's slow going; this is the stage where you need the most courage.

If your problem is back pain, you may move relatively quickly from Phase 1 to Phase 2. Your progress will be slower if you've had surgery where muscle has been cut or if you've been in a cast. At this point, practice the walking program at least twice a day.

Land Walking Program: Phase 1

NUMBER OF DAYS OUT OF BED (OR WITHOUT EXERCISE)	DISTANCE WALKED	STEP LENGTH*	NUMBER OF TIMES PER DAY YOU SHOULD WALK
1	2 feet	½ to 1 foot	2
2–5	5–100 feet	1 to 1½ feet	3
6–10	100–300 feet	1 to 1½ feet	3
11–14	300–600 feet	1 to 1½ feet	4

*Step length is measured from the heel of your back foot to the toe of your front foot. The easiest way to measure your step length is to place a yardstick on the floor and place your heel at the 1-inch mark. Then take a normal step and see at what mark your foot lands.

Your doctor may start you off with a non-weight-bearing exercise, like walking in water, which builds leg strength quite quickly. After a few sessions of aquatic walking, you'll be weaned from the water by splitting up sessions or alternating sessions between land and water walking. If a pool isn't available, the walking can be alternated with stationary bicycling or rowing. (If you're in a gym, you can begin on the bicycle and every 5 minutes switch to a treadmill for 1 minute. Repeat this process until you've exercised for about 20 minutes. Over several sessions you can decrease time on the bicycle and increase time on the treadmill.)

Phase 2: Regaining Your Strength

Once you have mastered walking 600 feet (about ⅛ mile) on your own, you can move to Phase 2.

Land Walking Program: Phase 2

	DISTANCE WALKED	STEP LENGTH*	NUMBER OF TIMES PER DAY
Week 1	⅛ mile†	1½ to 2 feet	4
Week 2	⅛ mile	1½ to 2 feet	4
Week 3	3⁄20 mile	1½ to 2 feet	3
Week 4	3⁄20 mile	1½ to 2 feet	3
Week 5	⅕ mile	1½ to 2 feet	3
Week 6	⅕ mile	1½ to 2 feet	3

*Step length is measured from the heel of your back foot to the toe of your front foot.

†⅛ mile = approximately 2.5 blocks; 3⁄20 mile = approximately 3 blocks; ⅕ mile = approximately 4 blocks.

Phase 3: Getting Up to Speed

In Phase 2, you will be walking a little more than a half a mile throughout the day, but in Phase 3 you will be increasing your mileage until you can walk a mile all at once with a step length of about 2½ to 3 feet. If your arthritis or injury is severe, this may be a challenge, but many people with arthritis or sports injuries start off this way and after several months can walk an average of ¼ to 1½ miles or more. Don't be embarrassed to stop and rest. In fact, you should plan your walking route around convenient rest stops. It's better to take two or three small walks than one long one that will cause you pain or further injury. Once you've mastered Phase 3, you can move on to Level I of the preventive walking program in Chapter 3.

Don't stop dead. Take another 5 minutes to slow down your walking pace, gradually decreasing speed. Finish your last walking session of the day by stretching out your muscles with the same stretches you performed in the beginning of the workout (like those for the fronts of the thighs and the fronts and backs of the calves, as well as the muscles surrounding weakened or damaged joints). This will reduce soreness after exercise and keep the muscles from going into spasm as they cool off.

Physical therapists report that if your joints hurt more than 2 hours after you've finished exercising, you've done too much. Unfortunately, there is no way to tell if you're doing too much *during* your exercise, so *listen to your body.* Although some pain when you exercise is normal if you have arthritis, a joint injury, or a bad back, you need to differentiate between expected and extreme pain. *Don't tough it out. If it hurts too much, stop.*

To keep track of how much you exercise and your level of discomfort afterwards, keep an aches and pain diary. This is a journal of what you did during your workout, including types and number of repetitions in range-of-motion and stretching exercises, and the distance walked. If you

Land Walking Program: Phase 3

	DISTANCE WALKED	STEP LENGTH*	NUMBER OF TIMES PER DAY
Week 1	¼ mile	2 to 2½ feet	4
Week 2	¼ mile	2 to 2½ feet	4
Week 3	⅓ mile	2 to 2½ feet	3
Week 4	⅓ mile	2 to 2½ feet	3
Week 5	⅔ mile	2 to 2½ feet	2
Week 6	1 mile	2 to 2½ feet	1

*Step length is measured from the heel of your back foot to the toe of your front foot.

PAIN DIARY

DATE: _____

LIST WARM-UP, STRETCH, AND STRENGTH EXERCISES (BEFORE WALK):

TOTAL AMOUNT YOU WALKED: _____

LIST EXERCISES DONE AFTER WALK:

hurt after exercising, reduce the intensity for several sessions. You may find that certain exercises bring on pain. If this is the case, drop those exercises from your repertoire.

Water Walking Techniques

Although the name is somewhat mystical, water walking is not complicated. In fact, it is the same as walking on land, except that the water supports 90 percent of your body weight, making it a completely safe and comfortable exercise if you have severe pain in one or more of your weight-bearing joints.

The advantage of water walking is that because the joints take such little stress, you can usually walk and do other exercises for 20 to 30 minutes without fatigue. For motivational purposes, water walking is a godsend, since people who cannot walk without a walker or cane on land can walk in water. The warmth of the water also seems to reduce pain and stiffness in the joints.

One health professional, Jean Dattner, told us about Arthur, a 73-year-old who had suffered three strokes and lost function in his right arm and leg. He needed a walker to get around on land and thought he would never be able to walk unassisted. Dattner put Arthur in the pool to get him to build up his weakened right side. The first few sessions, Arthur stood in the shallow end, holding on to the sides, but gradually he built up confidence until he could walk for 4 feet in the water unassisted. Recently, with a helper walking with him for support, Arthur walked the whole width of the pool (25 yards), and now he has done this as many as four times in one session. He has also been able to improve his walking technique and has learned the heel strike (he had a tendency to walk on his toes) and proper posture (he walked hunched over). Arthur was also able to build upper body strength by making circles on the surface of water with his hands (similar to the motion used to tread water) as he walked. Arthur will be able to move on to a more traditional arm swing when his coordination improves. As yet, Arthur does not have the skill to pump his arms and move his legs simultaneously.

Any size pool will work for water walking. The water, which should be at least 83° F, can be anywhere from thigh to chest high, and the deeper the water, the more the resistance and the more your muscles must work. If the shallow end is too small to walk in, put on a life vest or belt and "walk" in deeper water. Even though you can't touch the floor, you can propel yourself forward with walking movements. Physical therapists have their patients "walk" in very deep water when they don't want the joints to bear any weight at all.

Start out in the shallow end if possible, walking the width of the pool, and move to greater depths as you gain strength. The shallow end of most pools is roughly 3 feet deep, so depending on your height, you will be walking in water that is thigh to waist deep.

Follow the schedule on page 136 to increase your walking time and distance in the pool. If you have easy access to a pool (or other body of water), walk every day. If not, try to walk at least three times a week. Do stretches before and after your workouts (these can be done in the water or on land).

Once you've built up to 30 or 40 minutes of walking, try walking in deeper water. Spend 5 minutes walking at a new level, and increase by 10 minutes every subsequent session so that by the end of four sessions you'll be spending your whole exercise time at the new deeper level.

Water Walking Schedule

	WARM-UP WALK	WALKING WORKOUT	COOL-DOWN WALK
Week 1	5 minutes	10 minutes	5 minutes
Week 2	5 minutes	20 minutes	5 minutes
Week 3	5 minutes	30 minutes	5 minutes
Week 4	5 minutes	40 minutes	5 minutes

Rough Conversion of Laps into Miles*

NUMBER OF LAPS	MILES
5	1/14 mile
10	1/7 mile
15	1/5 mile
20	1/4 mile
25	1/3 mile
35	1/2 mile
45	9/10 mile
55	9/10 mile
60	9/10 mile
70	1 mile

*This is based on the assumption that most pools are 25 yards wide. A water walking lap is one width of the pool.

Your warm-up and cool-down walks will be slower than your main walking sessions. All three will be slower than your walking speed on land.

Aside from practicing proper walking techniques, you can also try various steps to work different muscles. For example, take advantage of the buoyancy to raise your knees high off the ground, thus working your thighs and hips much more than you would on land. Practice an exaggerated stride stretch, too (you don't have to be worried about falling over if you get carried away).

Water Exercises

These are additional exercises you can do in the pool to strengthen specific joints.

Hip

1. Walk in place in waist- to chest-deep water, lifting your legs high. Stand on your "good leg" and lift the hip of the injured leg so that your

foot is off the ground. Swing the injured leg back and forth. Lifting the hip strengthens the buttocks, which can be weak after surgery or atrophied from being in a cast.

2. Face the shallow end of the pool and walk sideways, first leading with the left leg and following with the right. On the way back down the pool, lead with the right leg. Then try crossing the right leg over the left as you walk.

Knees and Calves

1. To strengthen the knees, jump off the bottom of the pool and bend your knees deeply as you land back on the bottom of the pool. This will strengthen the thigh muscles and the buttocks muscles.

2. Walk backward for several laps. This exercises both the calf and thigh muscles.

You can continue to walk in water even after you're healed, and you can even convert some of the walking calisthenics in Book 4: Walkshaping and Weight Control, to water walking exercises, as water walking burns more calories than land walking. But if you do want to return to land walking, you can do so as soon as your pain has decreased. You'll be surprised how toned your muscles have become.

The lesson of Book 2: Walking for Arthritis, Back and Joints is that you *can* be helped by following a regular walking program. Walking can help you rehabilitate from injuries or from the pain of arthritis. And even if your joints are healthy, walking will strengthen your muscles and bones and help to keep you free of injury and pain.

BOOK

3

CARDIOWALKING

Increase Your Stamina and Speed

CONTRIBUTORS

Steven Blair, PED

Dr. Blair, director of epidemiology at the Institute for Aerobics Research in Dallas, Texas, is the editor of the American College of Sports Medicine's *Guidelines for Exercise Testing and Prescriptions*, third edition. Dr. Blair's teaching appointments include adjunct professor of epidemiology and biostatistics at the School of Public Health, University of South Carolina, and adjunct professor at the School of Public Health, University of Texas Health Sciences Center, Houston. Dr. Blair received the Physical Education Doctor (PED) degree from Indiana University. Dr. Blair walks or runs every day and logs 35 miles a week. He lives in Dallas.

Mark Forrestal, M.D.

Dr. Forrestal is a phlebologist at the Vein Clinics of America in Chicago, Illinois, where he performs operation-free removals of varicose veins. A 1979 graduate of the Autonomous University of Guadalajara, Mexico, Dr. Forrestal received board certification in internal medicine in 1984. Dr. Forrestal walks 10 miles a week and lives in Chicago.

Barry Franklin, Ph.D.

Dr. Franklin is director of cardiac rehabilitation at the Barnum Health Center in Birmingham, Michigan. Dr. Franklin received a Ph.D. in physiology from Pennsylvania State University in 1976, and he walks 8 to 12 miles a week. He lives in West Bloomfield, Michigan.

Susan Johnson, D.Ed.

Dr. Johnson is director of continuing education at the Aerobics Research Institute in Dallas, Texas, and is director and editor of *Reebok Instructor News*, a fitness publication, and clinician/consultant for the President's Council on Physical Fitness and Sports in Washington, D.C. Dr. Johnson is a past member of the International Dance and Exercise Association (IDEA) Continuing Education Committee. In 1986–1987, Dr. Johnson received an "Outstanding Training Organization" award from IDEA for a fitness program that she developed, coordinated, and instructed. The author of numerous articles on aerobic fitness training, Dr. Johnson has addressed the issue of walking and fitness in a book entitled, *The Walking Handbook*. Dr. Johnson received the Doctor of Education degree from the University of North Carolina at Greensboro. She walks 21 miles a week and lives in Dallas.

Norman M. Kaplan, M.D.

Dr. Kaplan is professor of internal medicine and head of the Hypertension Division at the University of Texas Southwest Medical Center in Dallas, where he received the Doctor of Medicine degree in 1954. Dr. Kaplan walks 30 minutes a day and 15 to 20 miles a week. He lives in Dallas.

Arthur Leon, M.D.

Dr. Leon is professor and director at the Applied Physiology-Nutrition Section of the University of Minnesota School of Public Health in Minneapolis and has published over 100 articles in the fields of cardiology, biochemistry, exercise physiology, and clinical pharmacology. Dr. Leon, who received the Doctor of Medicine degree from the University of Wisconsin, Madison, walks every day, 20 miles a week. He lives in Minneapolis.

William McLaughlin, Ph.D.

Dr. McLaughlin is an now exercise physiologist and director of the Cardio Fitness Center in New York City, which specializes in creating corporate fitness programs. He helps many of the country's leading executives stay fit and stress free. Dr. McLaughlin has a Ph.D. in health education and exercise physiology from the University of Maryland and walks a varied amount each week, 6 days a week. He lives in New York City.

Robert Neeves, Ph.D.

Robert Neeves is an associate professor of exercise physiology and co-director of the Human Performance Laboratory at the University of Delaware in Newark, Delaware. He teaches courses in nutrition and human performance, cardiac rehabilitation, and exercise prescription. Dr. Neeves also serves on the Governor's Task Force on Wellness Education and Delaware's Advisory Committee on Teaching and Learning. He received his doctorate from the University of Utah in Salt Lake City, where he specialized in cardiopulmonary physiology. He walks 15 miles a week and lives in Newark, Delaware.

Jonathan Rosen, M.D.

Dr. Rosen is a pulmonary specialist and assistant professor of medicine at Albany Medical College in Albany, New York. A 1979 graduate of the Downstate Medical Center in Brooklyn, New York, Dr. Rosen walks 4 miles a day five times a week and hikes 5 to 10 miles on weekends. He lives in Albany.

Jack Stern, M.D.

Dr. Stern is medical director of Canyon Ranch Health Resort in Tucson, Arizona. A graduate of the University of Maryland Medical School, Dr. Stern is also coauthor of *The Home Medical Handbook*. Dr. Stern speed walks 8 miles a day 5 to 6 days a week and lives in Tucson.

James Thomas, M.D.

Dr. Thomas is a staff cardiologist at Massachusetts General Hospital and graduated first in his class from Harvard Medical School. He is working in the field of rehabilitative medicine and does research in echocardiography. Dr. Thomas is also an assistant professor of medicine at Harvard Medical School. He walks daily and also takes mountain walking vacations in Colorado and Switzerland. Dr. Thomas lives in Boston.

James D. Watson, M.D.

James Watson is director of cardiac rehabilitation at the Montana Deaconess Medical Center in Great Falls, Montana. He also practices clinical and invasive cardiology at the Great Falls Clinic. A graduate of the Medical College of Pennsylvania, Dr. Thomas walks 5 to 7 days a week, averaging 10 hours a week.

1. Walking for a Healthy Heart

Without a steady flow of blood to the heart, brain, and rest of the body, our organs will die and their life-giving functions will cease. Our lives literally depend on a healthy heart and vascular (blood vessel) system. Yet this system is constantly under siege, both from environmental factors and from bad health habits that eventually lead to *coronary heart disease*, an umbrella term for a number of heart disorders, including heart attacks, chest pains (angina pectoris), and atherosclerosis, a buildup of fat deposits in the arteries that impedes blood flow to the heart and is the leading cause of heart attacks.

Coronary heart disease is the number one killer in America. According to the National Center of Health Statistics, it accounted for 24 percent of all deaths, in 1987. More than 1.25 million heart attacks occur each year. There is no cure for coronary heart disease, but doctors and researchers have found that by changing your lifestyle you can substantially lower your chances of having a heart attack. Lack of exercise, cigarette smoking, a diet high in fat and cholesterol, and a Type A personality have all been linked to coronary heart disease. The most sensible approach is thus to reduce these factors (called "risk factors" by the medical profession). Walking is the main tool to help you change your unhealthy ways and reduce the risk.

Unfortunately, some people are more susceptible to heart attacks than others. There are people who do all kinds of unhealthy things and yet never have a problem with their hearts. For others, the kind of life they lead has a direct impact on their health. Since it is difficult and expensive to test for the presence of heart disease, doctors tend to rely heavily on risk factors in determining overall heart health. In short, because the symptoms of heart disease lie dormant until the disease has progressed to an advanced level, you'll never *really* be able to know if your bad habits are putting you at higher risk for a heart attack. But isn't it better to be safe than sorry and take the preventive approach?

If you have already developed some form of heart disease or have been diagnosed as having high blood pressure or high cholesterol levels (another risk factor), it's still not too late to act. In fact, at this point, the risk factors *must* be managed if you are to avoid serious problems.

The cardiowalking program will show you how walking can improve your heart health no matter how good or bad it is—whether you've had a heart attack or heart surgery, have high blood pressure or other risk factors, or are healthy and want to stay that way.

How to Use This Book

The cardiowalking book is an in-depth health guide to your heart, lung, and circulatory system and features a two-tiered exercise walking program to help you prevent heart disease or, if you are already a heart patient, to lead you back to health.

The first chapter, Walking for a Healthy Heart, tells you how the heart works and explains some of the ailments that can attack the heart as it ages. While diet is certainly half the battle, you'll learn how cardiowalking can help you better manage your health and improve your lifestyle.

In Chapter 2, Reducing the Risks, you'll find out how walking can help you overcome the seven major contributing factors to heart disease and how you can assess your own likelihood of having a heart attack.

Chapter 3, Testing Your Heart with Your Feet, is your key to customizing a cardiowalking program for your fitness level. With one or two easy tests, you can determine a starting point that's safe for you.

The Cardiowalking Prevention Program, Chapter 4, outlines a basic preventive walking program, organized around five levels of fitness, to improve the efficiency of your heart, build stamina, and reduce your chances of developing heart disease. You'll also learn walking techniques that help build muscle strength and speed.

Chapters 5 through 8 explain heart and lung disorders in detail, prescribing applications to the preventive program for a number of common heart problems: Chapter 5, Walking to a Lower Blood Pressure, Chapter 6, Walking Through Angina Pain, Chapter 7, Walking for Stronger Veins, and Chapter 8, Walking for Better Breathing.

Chapter 9, The Cardiowalking Comeback Program, is a rehabilitation program for patients who have had a heart attack, heart or lung surgery, or a stroke that takes you from your hospital bed to a home walking regimen.

How Your Heart Works: The Walking Connection

The heart is the body's main pump. Located at the center of your chest, this eggplant-shaped muscle, about the size of your fist, beats 100,000 times per day—about 70 times per minute at rest and 90 to 200 times per minute while walking—pumping blood throughout your body. The blood carries nutrients and oxygen—via red blood cells—to all the organs, muscles, and bones and exchanges these for wastes and carbon dioxide, which are expelled by the kidneys and lungs. The heart itself is hollow, weighing only 7 to 12 ounces; the walls of the heart—called the *myocardium* (*myo* means "muscles" and *cardium* means "of the heart")—do all the work. As the myocardium contracts, the blood spurts out of the heart, and as the muscle relaxes, the heart fills with blood.

There are four chambers of the heart, a right and left ventricle and a right and left atrium. The atria are the receiving chambers, and the ventricles are the pumping chambers. The fresh, oxygen-rich blood leaves the lungs, flows into the left atrium, and then through the left ventricle, the heart's biggest pumping chamber. From there it is pumped into arteries, which carry the blood away from the heart. The veins carry oxygen-depleted blood back to the heart, entering at the right atrium, flowing through the right ventricle and into the lungs, where carbon dioxide is released and oxygen is picked up. Both sides of the heart are always filled with blood, the two atria contracting at the same time as the blood moves to the ventricles and the two ventricles sending blood out of the heart, either to the lungs or the arteries, simultaneously. The atria and ventricles are separated by valves, one-way swinging doors that keep the blood from backing up.

Walking increases aerobic power, the rate at which the muscles use oxygen. If you're in good shape, your muscles can take up to 20 percent more oxygen from the blood during exercise than those of a sedentary person can.

As you walk or perform any physical activity, the heart increases its *stroke volume*—the amount of blood that is squeezed out during each contraction of the left ventricle—because the muscles are demanding more oxygen than if you remained in a state of rest. With training your stroke volume will remain at a higher level, so that if you walk regularly your resting heart rate will be lower, and you'll tire less easily.

The role of the arteries and veins (the circulatory system) cannot be separated from that of the heart, which is why the two are referred to together as the cardiovascular system (*vascular* means "vessel"). This is a 70,000-mile network of elastic-like tubes with smooth walls that allow blood

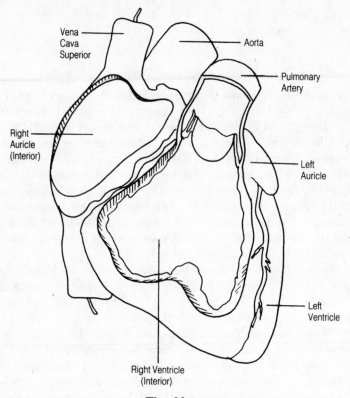

Vena Cava Superior

Aorta

Pulmonary Artery

Right Auricle (Interior)

Left Auricle

Left Ventricle

Right Ventricle (Interior)

The Heart

to flow easily through them. The aorta, the large artery (about the diameter of your thumb), leaves the heart and passes through your chest and abdomen and branches into the smaller arterioles and finally into the capillaries—the smallest vessels leading to the cells, where the exchange of oxygen and nutrients for waste and carbon dioxide takes place. The blood then flows back to the heart from the capillaries to venules and into the larger veins and finally back to the heart by means of the vena cava (the body's largest vein).

Walking also improves circulation, because the arterioles open during exercise to allow more blood to reach the muscles and to release the heat generated by the increased blood flow.

The heart itself needs nourishment, and thus there are two coronary arteries that branch off from the aorta and wrap around the heart, leading into its interior with smaller and smaller branches. The left branch of the coronary artery forks into two branches, so that doctors usually talk about the coronary arteries as three vessels. It is in these arteries that atherosclerosis strikes. This is a form of arteriosclerosis in which the arteries harden and become blocked with plaque, a waxy substance made up of cholesterol and other fats. A blockage develops over many years, much like rust accumulates inside an old pipe. As more plaque collects, it becomes harder and harder for the blood to pass through and nourish the waiting heart. If left untreated, the blood flow will become a mere trickle and a heart attack will ensue.

Together the cardiovascular system and the lungs (the pulmonary system) deliver fuel and oxygen to the cells. The healthier your systems, the stronger is the heart muscle, the greater is the capacity of the lungs, the freer the vessels are of fats and other debris, and the more efficiently your body will work.

Walking's Benefits

Walking is also the exercise of choice for 95 percent of all cardiac patients and the most prescribed exercise by doctors. This is so because walking is a natural movement that is inexpensive to do and can easily be incorporated into your daily routine. And most people will stick with walking because it is less boring than other exercises.

In the preceding minibook you learned that walking can help keep you moving, and in Book 3: Cardiowalking you'll learn how walking, by improving the efficiency of the heart and lungs, increases your stamina and endurance. Not only so you can exercise more, but also so you can enjoy life to the fullest. The more you walk, the more active you can be, whether the activity is traveling, working, or playing with your children or grandchildren.

Walking is the number one exercise for heart health because it:

1. Improves circulation, which means your muscles and organs get the oxygen and nutrients they need

2. Increases ability to take oxygen from the blood

3. Reduces the amount of workload on the heart

4. Increases your total blood volume

5. Lowers your blood pressure

6. Makes breathing easier and deeper

7. May widen your blood vessels and keeps them flexible

8. Increases HDL ("the good" cholesterol that impedes plaque buildup)

9. Deters plaque formation and the occurrence of blood clots

10. Increases your chances of surviving a heart attack and decreases your chances of having a second heart attack

11. Reduces the effects of lung disorders like emphysema and bronchitis

12. Increases your overall stamina and reduces fatigue from daily activity

2. Reducing the Risks

Risk factors are those elements in your background that increase your likelihood of developing diseases. In the case of heart disease, health professionals have identified eleven such characteristics. Assuming you live a moderate lifestyle with no risk factors, your chances of having a heart attack are relatively low. But the probability climbs with the number of risk factors you have. That's why it is so important to be aware of these factors and get them under control. Walking is an important means of reducing your risk of having heart problems and of improving your heart health.

Risk factors fall into two categories, ones that can be changed and ones that cannot. It is important to remember that even if you have unchangeable risk factors, your lifestyle can save you from heart disease. Physicians consider heart disease a man-made phenomenon, more influenced by lifestyle than by genes.

Here are some of the most important unmodifiable risk factors.

1. A family history of heart disease or related risk factors, like high blood pressure.

2. You are over 40 years of age.

3. You are male.

4. You belong to an ethnic or racial group with a high incidence of heart disease. Blacks have a higher incidence of heart disease than whites. Also, Hungary,

Scotland, Sweden, Ireland, and Italy, among others, have higher incidences of heart disease than the United States.*

Your family medical history is the starting point in determining susceptibility to heart disease (see your family health tree, pages 24–26). Some people are more prone than others to developing heart disease, and this fact can't be ignored. Others may be from a "lucky" family, where everyone smokes and drinks and remains perfectly healthy until the day they die at age 95. Most likely, however, some heart disease lurks in your family.

If you don't know how your grandparents or other close relations died but know they were younger than age 60 when they passed on (age 70 for females), chances are they died of heart disease. This increases your chances of dying before you're 65, especially if their heart attacks were *not* induced by "bad living": smoking, eating unhealthy foods, and not exercising regularly. Also find out about the presence of associated diseases, such as diabetes, obesity, high blood pressure, or high cholesterol.

Below is a list of modifiable risk factors. The tendency to develop some of these factors may be inherited, but these conditions can be controlled and even reversed with walking and lifestyle modifications.

1. High blood pressure

2. Cigarette smoking

3. Sedentary lifestyle

4. High cholesterol levels

5. Being overweight

6. A Type A personality behavior

7. Type II diabetes

The incidence of heart disease in this country has grown over the last 100 years (although in the last 25 years there has been some reduction in the mortality rate, probably because of increased access to medical services and greater emphasis on the prevention of heart disease). The fact that we as a society are less active, eat more fat and processed foods than our ancestors certainly strengthens the argument that lifestyle may be more influential than genetics in causing heart disease. This means that a "couch potato" with no family history of heart disease who smokes two packs of cigarettes a day and eats fatty foods may be at more risk for having a heart

*It is not established whether this is due to lifestyle in those countries or some biological factor that makes these nationalities more prone to heart disease.

attack than someone who lives a more active, healthy lifestyle and whose father died of a heart attack at age 55. Anecdotal evidence bears this out. The Japanese and Chinese are thought to be less genetically susceptible to heart disease than other races, yet Asians who grow up in the United States have the same incidence of heart disease as other Americans. Doctors who have worked with the Amish say that the sons of healthy Amish who have adopted the American lifestyle have more heart attacks than those who remain in the traditional community. The lesson to be learned is that "good" genes can only protect you so much from unhealthy behavior.

Not all risk factors are of equal importance. If you are just starting our cardiowalking program and have several risk factors, you may not be able to eliminate all of them at once. Try to concentrate on the most modifiable and most important ones. The following are listed in order of their contribution to heart disease.

Hypertension (High Blood Pressure)

Hypertension (high blood pressure) is the dominant contributor to cardiovascular disease and strokes. Walking is a proven treatment for high blood pressure (see Chapter 5: Walking to a Lower Blood Pressure). People with hypertension are three to four times more likely to have a heart attack than people with normal blood pressure, and 90 percent of all stroke victims are hypertensive. It's estimated that half of all Americans will develop high blood pressure at some point in their lives, but a third of these people will never know they have it. Reducing your blood pressure by 10 points (measured in millimeters of mercury) reduces your risk of heart disease by 30 percent.

Cigarette Smoking

Cigarette smoking increases your likelihood of having a heart attack by two to three times according to the Centers for Disease Control in Atlanta. It damages your cardiovascular system in several different ways, artificially stimulating the heart to beat faster than normal (and often irregularly) and raising blood pressure by constricting the arteries, a condition that accelerates the buildup of plaque. Cigarette smoking replaces oxygen in the blood with carbon monoxide, suffocating the heart and other organs. Smoking also increases your risk of strokes (by 40 percent in men and 60 percent in women). According to statistics from the Framingham Heart Study, cigarette smoking has a greater negative impact on women than on men. (A woman smoker has a 15 percent higher risk of heart attack than a male smoker.) Women who smoke and take birth control pills are twenty times more at risk for a heart attack and thirteen times more likely to have a stroke than nonsmokers. These risks increases with the length of time the pill is taken and is higher for women who smoke and are over age 35.

It is never too late to quit smoking, and the effects of stopping are dramatic. The risk of having a heart attack is reduced 50 percent after being cigarette-free for one year, and the associated risks are wiped out completely after five years. Smoking is a difficult habit to break both psychologically and physically. Book 5: Walktherapy provides a special walking program for those who want to cut down or quit smoking.

Sedentary Lifestyle

According to a recent study lead by Dr. Steven Blair of the Institute for Aerobics Research in Dallas, a sedentary lifestyle can be as dangerous a risk factor as smoking or high blood pressure in causing heart disease or cancer. But your chances of developing these diseases decrease drastically when a moderate exercise regimen is started. Walking is the easiest way to resume physical activity because it doesn't feel like exercise.

Human beings are designed to be active, and inactivity results in the general deterioration of your body. Specifically, a sedentary lifestyle causes all muscles to atrophy, including the heart, which thus has less ability to deliver nutrients and oxygen to the muscles and other tissues.

Several studies, including one of 16,936 Harvard graduates, have found that those who do not exercise regularly (at least three times a week) had a 55 percent higher rate of heart attacks than those who did. Of the active segment, the exercise of choice was walking.

A sedentary lifestyle also will decrease your chances of surviving a heart attack. A study of 55,000 men in the greater New York area found that inactive participants were almost four times as likely to die from a heart attack as their active counterparts.

High Cholesterol

Cholesterol is a fatlike substance found in all animal products, both meat (including organ meat, which is very high in cholesterol), and by-products such as milk and butter. Our bodies, or more specifically, our livers, manufacture cholesterol, which is used in the metabolism of fat and in the production of hormones. Cholesterol is not found in vegetables or plants, but *saturated fats* that come from some plants, like cocoa oil, coconut oil, palm oil, and palm kernel oil, can raise cholesterol in the bloodstream even more than if you eat foods that contain cholesterol.

There are other kinds of fats, called *monosaturated fats*, that come from olive oil, avocado, rapeseed (canola) oil, peanut oil, and nuts and which do not affect cholesterol levels. Others, called *polyunsaturated oils*, found in safflower oil, corn oil, sunflower oil, soybean oil, and cottonseed oil actually reduce cholesterol. This is the only kind of fat not manufactured in our bodies. Not only should you reduce your fat intake to less than 30 percent of your diet, but you should also replace saturated fats with polyunsaturated fats whenever possible. A good rule of thumb is that foods known to be high in fat are generally high in cholesterol as well.

Our bodies need cholesterol, but having too much in the bloodstream, whether from the liver's overproduction (an inherited trait) or from a diet high in cholesterol and saturated fats, will cause plaque to accumulate on coronary artery walls. Not all people metabolize cholesterol the same way. Some people do not absorb any of the cholesterol they eat. For others, their livers regulate the cholesterol in the bloodstream, so they produce less if they've consumed a high-cholesterol meal. Finally, for approximately one third of the population, a large percentage of dietary cholesterol collects in the arteries. Genetics determine which category you fall into.

Two components of your total cholesterol count that are important in determining your risk of heart disease are HDL (high-density lipoprotein), which removes "bad" cholesterol from the body, and LDL (low-density lipoprotein), which is the cholesterol that forms plaque. All your cholesterol levels need to be in balance in order to reduce your risk of heart disease. Look at the charts on page 153 for the safe cholesterol levels for your age and sex.

Very recent studies suggest that aerobic exercise, such as walking, may decrease LDL in the blood, and it has been proven that walking increases the amount of HDL, the "good" cholesterol that helps to break down plaque buildup. Walking also slims you down, which will further reduce the amount of cholesterol you produce. Another study done at the University of Toronto suggests that eating many small meals can help reduce cholesterol. Although the reasons are not clear, researchers believe that many small meals helps to keep insulin levels in your blood constant, and insulin is a key factor in determining the amount of cholesterol your liver produces.

Overweight

Walking is the easiest and best approach to a lifetime of weight control. Almost everyone begins to put on a few pounds after age 25, when the metabolism begin to wind down, but this tendency to gain weight with age can be slowed down with a regular walking program, because walking not only burns calories, but also acts as a natural appetite suppressant.

Each extra pound of fat places added stress on the heart. In addition, overweight people are three times more likely to have high blood pressure and four times more likely to develop Type II diabetes, and they usually

Safe Serum Cholesterol Counts for Ages 20–39

TOTAL CHOLESTEROL (MG/DL)	IDEAL	MODERATE RISK	HIGH RISK
Male	under 180	180–202	over 202
Female	under 177	177–197	over 197
LDL (mg/dl)			
Male	under 118	118–137	over 137
Female	under 109	109–127	over 127
HDL (mg/dl)			
Male	over 51	37–51	under 37
Female	over 63	45–63	under 45

Safe Serum Cholesterol Counts for Ages 40–59

TOTAL CHOLESTEROL (MG/DL)	IDEAL	MODERATE RISK	HIGH RISK
Male	under 210	210–233	over 233
Female	under 210	210–235	over 235
LDL (mg/dl)			
Male	under 141	141–162	over 162
Female	under 129	129–155	over 155
HDL (mg/dl)			
Male	over 52	37–52	under 37
Female	over 69	49–69	under 49

Safe Serum Cholesterol Counts for Ages 60+

TOTAL CHOLESTEROL (MG/DL)	IDEAL	MODERATE RISK	HIGH RISK
Male	under 214	214–240	over 240
Female	under 228	228–252	over 252
LDL (mg/dl)			
Male	under 144	144–165	over 165
Female	under 150	150–175	over 175
HDL (mg/dl)			
Male	over 60	40–60	under 40
Female	over 74	50–74	under 50

have higher levels of serum cholesterol. Having high blood pressure and being 30 pounds overweight raises your risk of heart attack to five times above normal.

Type A Personality

Stress is often implicated as a risk factor for heart disease, but in fact it is the way one handles stress that determines an increased risk of having a heart attack—a theory that has spawned much research about Type A personalities. Although the original profile was of an irritable, competitive, and aggressive individual, more current research has changed this characterization. Chronic hostility is now thought to be the most destructive emotion. In a 25-year study of 255 medical students, those who scored above the median on a personality test measuring hostility were five times more likely to have heart attacks or heart disease than those who scored below the norm.

The biological reasons for this phenomenon are still under study. A hostile personality may be caused by an overactive sympathetic nervous system (what prepares the body to deal with stress). When this nervous system is activated, two hormones, cortisol and epinephrine, are released. These raise blood pressure and heart rate and release fats into the bloodstream, increasing cholesterol levels in the blood. If these effects are sustained or oft-repeated, damage to the coronary arteries is thought to occur. People with "laid back," Type B personalities are believed to have a stronger parasympathetic nervous system, which calms the body by lowering blood pressure and heart rate.

Walking reduces both the physiological and psychological effects of stress, and according to recent research even a 10-minute walk can reduce the negative effects of stress. Stressful situations create the same physiological reactions as exercise: raising heart rate and blood pressure and increasing blood flow to the muscles. Taking a walk after a stressful encounter will put your increased heart rate and blood flow to its intended purpose. Walking will also help you put your problems into perspective.

Managing stress is extremely important to those who have already suffered a heart attack or have heart disease. Studies done in Finland on heart patients found that those with the highest hostility scores were thirteen times more likely to die or suffer a second heart attack within 3 years. If managing stress is very difficult for you, turn to Book 6: Walk-therapy for a Walking Stress Reduction Program.

Diabetes

Diabetics are twice as likely to have a heart attack or stroke than those without the disease. Although the reasons for this are still unclear, it may be because diabetics are often overweight and are more likely to have high blood pressure. Diabetes may also damage the heart directly.

Although Type II diabetes (which is the most common type of diabetes and is caused by an insensitivity to insulin) has a strong genetic component, it can be controlled in most cases by losing weight, eating a proper diet, and exercising regularly. Walking can be an important tool for diabetics because it increases the body's sensitivity to insulin. (Thus a diabetic who walks would get more benefit from the same amount of insulin than a sedentary individual.)

Combination Risk Factors

Disheartening as it may be, risk factors rarely occur alone. They come in two or threes, which, as the following story illustrates, should alert you to danger.

John Silvani had a family history of high blood pressure (both his parents) and led a very stressful professional life (he is now retired) working 16 hours a day and traveling frequently. As a product engineer for Ford Motor Company, he was required, when things went wrong, to fix them *immediately*. He smoked ten cigars a day for 20 years. Despite his lifestyle and family health history, he never thought he'd have a heart attack, even in middle age, when he began to experience fatigue and intermittent chest pains. Finally, doctors told him his coronary arteries were severely blocked and he had high blood pressure and dangerously high cholesterol levels. A heart attack was imminent if he didn't change his habits. He ignored the diagnosis and went on his merry way—not exercising and maintaining his usual fare of fast food, kosher pickles, and corned beef (all high in fat and sodium).

One day John was doing some carpentry work at his vacation home when he began to feel faint and started to sweat profusely. After a rest, he tried to work again but couldn't. He sat down and looked out at the lake, but everything was in a fog. Still sweating heavily, he took several nitroglycerin pills his doctor had prescribed for chest pains. He only felt worse. A few hours later he was lying in the emergency room of the local hospital. "You're having a heart attack," the doctor told him. John spent 3 weeks in the hospital, where he also had triple bypass surgery (in which veins were taken from his leg and placed around the blockage to provide an alternate route for blood flow).

Over 8 months John slowly increased his stamina and can now walk 5 miles in under an hour. He does so three to five times each week. He also follows a low-fat, low-cholesterol diet. Through exercise and proper diet, he has weaned himself off *all* medication (except an aspirin a day). "The better I felt, the more I believed in walking," he says.

John's experience has so transformed his habits and attitudes that he was named honorable mention in the "Heart Patient of the Year Award," which is given to the heart patient who most changed his or her lifestyle after a heart attack and who has done the most to educate others about preventing heart disease.

3. Testing Your Heart with Your Feet

Whether you are healthy or have signs of heart disease, you'll need to know the right level to start your walking program. Taking a walk test, whether it's self-administered or given by a doctor or other health professional, will help you design a walking schedule that's right for you. You should, however, have a physical examination before beginning *any* exercise program, especially if you're over age 35 and have been inactive for more than 1 year. Show your doctor our tests and exercise prescriptions to ensure that they are appropriate for you.

Measuring Your Workload

For each of the following tests, you'll need to estimate how hard you are working. This is usually done by taking your pulse rate during or immediately after exercise and then comparing that number to your maximum heart rate. To calculate your maximum heart rate, subtract your age from 220. For example, if you are 40, your maximum heart rate is 180. If during exercise your heart rate gets up to 135 beats per minute, then you are exercising at 75 percent of your maximum heart rate. Sports physicians usually tell their healthy patients that to build aerobic capacity (the efficiency with which the body delivers oxygen), they must exercise for at least 20 minutes 3 days a week with their hearts beating at 50 to 85 percent of that maximum number (called the *training zone*). In this range, you will get the most benefit out of your exercise (more than 85 percent is

157

Your Maximum Heart Rate

AGE	MAXIMUM*	TRAINING ZONE (50–85 PERCENT)
25	195	98–166
35	185	93–158
45	175	86–149
55	165	83–140
65	155	78–132
75	145	73–123
85	135	68–115
95	125	63–106

*As you learned in Book 1, the rule of maximum heart rate is only an average, and you may be higher or lower, depending on your fitness level.

unnecessary and may be dangerous, and lower is believed to be ineffective, although this belief is now being questioned).

If taking your pulse before or after exercise is inconvenient, you can define the intensity at which you are exercising, both for the test and for the walking program, by using the relative perceived exertion (RPE) scale. This scale lets you qualitatively describe the intensity of your exercise. The correlation between heart rate and perceived exertion level has proven to be very high. The rule is that if you add a zero to your rating, it equals your heart rate. For example, if you feel your exertion level is a 7, your heart is beating at approximately 70 beats per minute (plus or minus 10 beats). Exercise physiologists recommend the RPE scale to heart patients because some heart medications lower your heart rate, thus making pulse an inaccurate barometer. Heart rate can also be too objective a measure, as factors like how much sleep you got the night before will affect your endurance level, although they will not affect your pulse.

The RPE scale goes from 6 to 20, and odd numbers are labeled from extremely light to extremely hard. Six is the exertion you feel lying in bed, and 20 is the hardest you can imagine working.

Self-Administered Tests

If you have *never* experienced any signs of heart disease while exercising—chest pains or pressure, unwarranted shortness of breath, dizziness, profuse sweating (more than is normal for the activity), or blurred

Relative Perceived Exertion (RPE) Scale

6	No exertion at all
7	Extremely light
8	
9	Very light
10	
11	Light
12	
13	Somewhat hard
14	
15	Hard (heavy)
16	
17	Very hard
18	
19	Extremely hard
20	Maximal exertion

vision—you probably have no risk factors associated with heart disease, and if your doctor has deemed you sufficiently healthy to follow an exercise program, take the following self-administered tests to help you choose your walking level.

The average person can exercise either intensely for short periods of time or mildly for long periods of time, but only the advanced athlete can do both simultaneously. By following the cardiowalking preventive program you can eventually raise both the intensity and duration of your walking workout. However, right now you may be low on the fitness scale, so we've developed a two-tiered group of walking fitness examinations: the walking distance and duration tests and the walking speed and intensity tests. With these two groups of tests, you can be evaluated no matter what your fitness level. This is not true of the walking tests currently used. For example, some tests demand that the participant walk a mile at maximum speed, after which his or her heart rate is measured and compared to a chart to determine at what level he or she should start the walking program. This test, while fine for the healthy (and we included a version of it in Book 1), is not advisable for extremely out-of-shape walkers, those who are sedentary, overweight, or have orthopedic problems, because they may have difficulty walking a mile without stopping. However, our walking distance and duration tests are suitable for anyone. All walkers should take the these tests first. You can then proceed to one of the more strenuous tests if you so desire. If you already exercise 4 or more hours a week, you can begin with the walking speed and intensity tests.

Another drawback of the usual walking tests is that they measure only aerobic endurance levels. Our walking speed and intensity tests measure your *walking capacity—both* your aerobic and muscular endurance. This is so because the level at which you begin the walking program will depend on the strength and endurance of both your heart and your arm and leg muscles. The two are not always equal. For example, the women's team that conquered Anapurna in the Himalayas found that although their cardiovascular performance was extremely high from jogging on level ground, they had difficulty climbing because of leg fatigue.

If you achieve at least a Level II on the distance and duration test and you plan on following a more strenuous exercise routine, such as stair climbing (or marching), or doing a walking workout on an inclined treadmill, take the walking speed and intensity tests.

Take the arm-pumping endurance test to see if your arm fitness is on par with your aerobic and leg fitness levels.

Walking Distance and Duration Tests

We've included two tests in this category.

1. Take the *flat-terrain test* if you plan on doing your walking program on a track, flat roadway, or path, or on a treadmill (little to no incline).

2. Take the *walking-in-place test* if you don't have a treadmill and want to do your walking program in a small place (especially good if you like to exercise while watching television).

Flat-Terrain Test

Begin your walk on a flat treadmill (or on a track or flat terrain) at a self-selected pace, the speed you might use while walking to work or taking a stroll in the park. Walk until you have to stop and rest or until 60 minutes have passed, whichever comes first. Don't push yourself too hard, and stop as soon as you feel fatigued or are out of breath. You shouldn't feel you are working more than somewhat hard (see RPE scale on page 159), and if you can't catch your breath enough to talk (or sing), then you are walking too fast. Measure the distance you walked and compare it with the following chart to determine your fitness level. This is your starting level for the preventive program (see Chapter 4). Feel free to repeat the test on another day if you feel you were unusually tired or energetic when you took the initial test.

Fitness Levels after Flat-Terrain Test

YOUR LEVEL		MILES COVERED
Level I	(poor)	0–1.5
Level II	(fair)	1.6–2.5
Level III	(good)	2.6–3.5
Level IV	(very good)	3.6–4.5
Level V	(excellent)	More than 4.6

Walking-in-Place Test

Start walking in place at your own pace, raising your feet 3 to 6 inches off the ground. Walk until you get tired or until 55 minutes have gone by, whichever comes first. You should not be working more than somewhat hard on the RPE scale, and if you can't catch your breath enough to talk (or sing) to yourself, then you are working too hard. Compare your results to the following chart.

Fitness Levels after Walking-in-Place Test

YOUR LEVEL	NUMBER OF MINUTES WALKED
Level I	Under 10
Level II	11–20
Level III	21–35
Level IV	36–45
Level V	Over 45

Walking Speed and Intensity Tests

These three tests are shorter and more strenuous than the distance and duration tests, and they measure both your leg strength and your aerobic endurance. They will raise your heart rate higher than the previous tests, which is why we ask you to take your pulse. (You can take your pulse at either your wrist, just above the base of your thumb, or at the carotid arteries at the sides of your neck. Place your index and middle fingers on whichever spot you choose, making sure to apply only as much pressure as is necessary to feel your pulse, and count the number of pulses in 10 seconds. Multiply this number by 6 for your pulse rate.)

1. Take the *marching-in-place test* if you plan to march in place as part of your walking program (*marching in place* is lifting your feet from 12 to 24 inches off the ground and is more strenuous than walking in place).

2. Take the *quarter-mile test* if you plan to walk on flat terrain or on a tread mill.

3. Take the *step-up test* if you plan to do stair climbing or walk on an inclined treadmill.

Marching-in-Place Test

As we said, to march, you must lift your feet 12 to 24 inches off the ground. Marching in place is a good way to exercise in a small area (in front of the TV, for instance). Since you will be using your hip flexor muscles (those that help you raise your legs) more than in level walking or walking in place, you will tire sooner than you would walking on a track or level terrain.

March for 15 minutes at a somewhat hard to very hard rate of exertion. (If you get tired before 15 minutes is up, stop). Count the number of steps you take. Compare your results with the following chart to determine your fitness level.

Fitness Levels after Marching-in-Place Test

YOUR LEVEL	TOTAL STEPS
I	251–300
II	301–400
III	401–500
IV	501–750
V	751–1000

Quarter-Mile Test

In this test you'll walk ¼ mile, so you'll need to locate a track or pre-measure a route. (If you live in a city, 5 blocks usually equals ¼ mile.) Walk at a somewhat hard to very hard rate, and note the number of minutes it takes to finish the route. Consult the following chart to find your fitness level.

Fitness Levels after Quarter-Mile Test

YOUR LEVEL		NUMBER OF MINUTES
I	(poor)	Over 5
II	(fair)	3:35–5
III	(good)	3:19–3:44
IV	(very good)	3:00–3:19
V	(excellent)	Under 3

Step-Up Test

This is the fastest of the speed and intensity tests, and it can be done on a staircase or with a kitchen stepstool. Step up with your right foot, followed by your left; then step down with your right, followed by your left. Take two steps up and two steps down in a 5-second period (which means you will take twenty-four steps a minute), and do this for 3 minutes. *Wait 30 seconds* after you have finished and take your pulse *for 30 seconds.* Compare your level with the following age- and sex-graded chart to find your starting level.

Fitness Levels after Step-Up Test: Pulse Rates (in Beats per Minute) for 30 Seconds by Age Group

	AGE (YEARS)			
	20–29	30–39	40–49	50 AND OVER
Men:				
Level 1	50–59	50–59	52–60	52–62
Level II	43–49	44–49	45–51	46–51
Level III	41–42	42–43	43–44	44–45
Level IV	37–40	39–41	40–42	41–43
Level V	34–36	35–38	37–39	37–40
Women:				
Level I	55–66	55–66	57–67	58–68
Level II	47–57	48–55	48–56	50–57
Level III	45–46	46–47	46–47	48–49
Level IV	43–44	43–45	44–45	45–47
Level V	39–42	39–42	41–43	41–44

Arm-Pumping Endurance Test

In order to get the most out of the walking program, you should start pumping your arms as you walk. Arm pumping is different from swinging your arms. To pump, you use all the back and shoulder muscles to control the back and forth movement, which helps you propel forward. Swinging is less athletic and takes only one quarter the effort of pumping. (If you are not familiar with this technique, see page 99 for instructions.) You can take this test concurrently with a leg endurance test or alone while standing in place. Begin pumping your arms, either bending them at a 90-degree angle or holding them straight (see straight arm pumping, page 99). Stop when your arms get tired or when 30 minutes has passed. Then jcompare the number of arms pumps you completed with the following chart.

Fitness Levels after Arm-Pumping Endurance Test

YOUR LEVEL	BENT ARMS	STRAIGHT ARMS
I	30–60	20–50
II	60–120	50–100
III	120–50	100–120
IV	150–300	120–200
V	300–600	200–500

In the beginning your arm-pump level may be lower than your leg endurance level. If this is the case, just walk while pumping your arms until they tire, then drop them for a minute or two, and begin pumping again. Within a few weeks you will be up to par.

Administered Tests

If you've had an anginal episode, have a pulmonary disorder, or have one or more risk factors, your doctor will most likely want to give you a *maximum stress test*.

The maximum stress test is straightforward. You will walk on a treadmill, the pace and incline of which will be increased every 3 minutes until the demand for oxygen of your heart and muscles exceeds the supply. The test will be stopped before this point if you develop any irregular symptoms. The heart rate at which you stopped exercising is considered your "max," and you will exercise at some rate below that. For example, if your maximum heart rate is 130 beats per minute, the doctor might have you exercise at a level that would bring your heart rate to 110 to 120 beats per minute.

Once you know your current fitness level, you are ready to begin walking. If you can take the self-administered tests, come back to this chapter every few weeks to test yourself and gauge your improvement. Over the next few months, you'll undoubtedly make progress, especially if you started out at a very low fitness level.

Getting Motivated

Getting motivated to exercise is never easy. If you are healthy, you may find it hard to truly believe that you *need* to exercise, and if you have heart disease, you may be just plain scared to try to exert yourself.

The best motivational tool is to involve your family and friends in your walking program. Many of the heart patients we interviewed said their children, spouses, friends, or grandchildren accompanied them on their walks. This made the exercise more enjoyable and gave them an opportunity to spend time with the people they love. Your concern about your own health may have a silver lining: You'll get your whole family to develop better health habits, too.

Other motivational tools include:

Choosing varied, interesting routes

Joining a walking group or club

Charting your progress in a walking log

Setting short, intermediate, and long-term walking goals, and rewarding yourself when you reach them (maybe with a new pair of walking shoes or some athletic clothes).

4. The Cardiowalking Prevention Program

This program will help you improve your aerobic capacity and reduce your chances of developing heart disease. It includes a walking workout on level terrain, as well as indoor walking workouts to match the tests you took in the preceding chapter: walking (or marching) in place, stair climbing, and inclined treadmill walking. Level III is considered the average fitness level and a reasonable goal to set for yourself, but remember that whatever level you are walking, you will be improving your health.

The paradigm for fitness standards is slowly changing from the "athlete" to the "average American." Most exercise physiologists used to believe that you had to exercise at 65 to 85 percent of your maximum heart rate for a minimum of 20 minutes at least three times a week in order to improve your cardiovascular stamina or aerobic capacity and your health —which is commonly measured as your ability to resist disease. Recently, the American College of Sports Medicine (which publishes exercise standards) reduced the lower limit of the aerobic training zone, claiming that fitness and health could be improved at a level of 50 percent of maximum heart rate. Dr. Steven Blair, of the Institute of Aerobic Research, in Dallas, Texas, has done studies that suggest that even exercising below 50 percent of your maximum heart rate can improve your fitness level. There is some conjecture that exercising at even lower levels (maybe even as low as 30 percent) may still improve your aerobic capacity and will definitely improve your health. Dr. Blair believes that someone who exercises at 30 percent of his maximum heart rate for most of his life may be as fit as someone who exercises at 85 percent of his maximum heart rate for only

6 months to 1 year. Sustained, regular exercise (regardless of intensity) is most important.

In this book your goal is to build the intensity, duration, and frequency of your walking workouts until you have reached the speed and distance appropriate for your age (see Book 1: Walking and Aging for your age-graded walking prescription). A 2- to 6-week program will get you up to the desired level both in terms of distance and speed. Once you've reached your goal, continue walking the same number of times per week, at the same speed, and for the same distance. If you decide you want to climb to the next level, first increase your distance and then your speed.

Exercise physiologists rate the intensity of an exercise with a unit called METs (which stands for *metabolic equivalent*). One MET is the amount of energy (measured by how much oxygen you use) that a body uses at rest. The MET is a convenient unit to use when discussing exercise because unlike calorie burn or heart rate, it is applicable to all persons. Walking at 2 miles per hour, for example, is *always* valued at an intensity level of 3 METs whether the walker is old or young, heavy or lean. (See the chart on page 168 for walking speeds and their MET equivalents.)

METs are also helpful in comparing walking on a flat terrain with other exercises like stair climbing, incline walking, and walking with weights (see Book 4: Walkshaping and Weight Control).

The Warm-Up and Cool-Down

The warm-up, a brisk 2- to 5-minute walk, increases circulation to the muscles, and prepares them for a walking workout. After warm-up, do a series of stretches, especially for the calf muscles, the thigh muscles (quadriceps), the ankles, the muscles in the backs of your legs (the hamstrings), and your upper arms and back. Stretching your muscles will help you increase walking speed and minimize risk for injury or postexercise soreness (see Book 2, pages 102–103, for stretches).

At the end of your exercise session, never stop suddenly. Always take 10 minutes to gradually slow your peak walking speed to a less intense pace. Walk for 3 to 5 minutes at this cool-down pace before stopping completely.

Building Distance

The first stage of the program will be building distance, so you won't need to time your walking sessions. Start at your walking level and mileage determined by the distance and duration tests, and increase that distance by adding ¼ to ½ mile more to your daily walks each week until you have reached the walking mileage appropriate for your age and level on the chart on page 169. Remember that you should never raise your heart rate

Walking Speeds and Their MET Equivalents

METs	WALKING SPEED (MI/M)	MINUTE-MILES (MM)
1	At rest	
2	1.5	40
3	2	30
4	3	20
5	3.5	17
6	4	15
7	4.25	14
8	5	12
9	5.5	11
10	6	10
11	6.5	9.2
12	7	8.5
13	7.5	8
14	8	7.5
15	9	6.7
16	9.5	6.3
17	10	6

more than 85 percent of its maximum (between hard and very hard on the RPE scale).

For example, if you are a 35-year-old who walked ½ mile in the distance and duration tests, you are at Level I. Start by walking ½ mile per session (walking 6 to 7 days a week) for the first week. The second week, increase your daily walking session to ¾ mile, and by the third week, you will be walking within the Level I weekly mileage range for your age group. As your mileage increases, you can walk fewer days per week (3 days a week is minimum). Find your level on the following chart to determine your weekly mileage.

Level I: Increase your daily mileage ¼ mile above your test level, and walk at the new mileage for 1 week. Every week, increase your daily mileage by ¼ mile until you are walking at the distance appropriate for your age. Walk three to seven times per week.

Age-Graded Weekly Walking Mileage for Five Levels (Flat Terrain)

AGE (YEARS)	LEVEL I	LEVEL II	LEVEL III*	LEVEL IV	LEVEL V†
15–20	8–13	13–18	18–25	25–33	33–46
20–29	8–13	13–18	18–25	25–32	32–40
30–39	8–13	13–18	14–25	25–32	32–39
40–49	7–12	12–17	17–23	23–29	29–35
50–59	7–12	12–17	17–23	23–29	29–35
60–68	3–6	6–10	10–16	16–21	21–26
69–74	2–5	5–8	8–15	15–20	20–25
75–84	2–5	4–7	7–11	11–17	17–21
85 and over	1–2	2–6	6–9	9–12	12–18

*Average fitness level.

†Maximum fitness level.

Level II: Add ¼ mile every week until you are walking at your desired mileage (the average for all ages is roughly 4 miles a walk). Walk three to seven times per week.

Level III: Add ½ mile every week until you are walking at the desired level (the average for all age groups for this level is roughly 4.5 miles per walking session). Walk three to five times per week.

Level IV: Add ½ mile every week until you are walking at the desired level (the average for all ages is roughly 5 miles per session). Walk three to five times per week.

Level V: Add ½ mile every week until you are walking at the desired level (the average for all ages is roughly 5.5 miles per session). Walk three to five times per week.

Building Speed

Once you've reached your distance goal, you can start increasing the intensity of your walking workout by walking faster. As with the distance goals, your time will improve over a 2- to 6-week period by decreasing your daily time per mile (in minute-miles) by 15 seconds each week until you've met the speed goal for your level and age group. The frequency of your walks should remain the same.

Level I: Increase your minute-mile speed by 15 seconds per week until you are walking at least at the Level I speed for your age group (on average 2 miles an hour or 3 METs). Walk one to seven times per week.

Level II: Increase your minute-mile speed by 15 seconds per week until you are walking at least at the Level II speed for your age group (roughly 3 miles an hour or 4 METs). Walk one to seven times per week.

Levels III through V: Increase your minute-mile speed by 15 seconds until you at least walking at the speed prescribed for you level and age group (on average 4 to 5 miles an hour or 6 to 8 METs). Walk three to five times per week.

Exercisewalking Techniques

Use the following techniques to help increase the speed and intensity of your walking:

Proper posture (see page 95).

Stride stretch (see pages 98–99). If you walking speed increases to over 4 miles an hour, you stance will naturally become narrower and shorter.

Arm pumping (see page 99).

Proper breathing. Learning to breath properly will ensure that your walking routine remains an aerobic exercise. Often when working intensely you forget to breathe deeply, and this means you'll tire sooner.

A technique called *breath play*, developed by Olympic trainer Ian Jackson, emphasizes using the stomach muscles to exhale through pursed lips. In this manner, air forcibly leaves the lungs, creating a partial vacuum that naturally draws air back in. This method ensures that you are breathing deeply and providing your cells with oxygen.

According to Betsy Thomason, who teaches the breath play method in workshops, you need to use the diaphragm to force the air out of your lungs. To practice this technique, place your hands on your stomach. As you inhale, make your stomach expand with air. To exhale, collapse your abdomen as if you were trying to touch your stomach to your back. Purse your lips so that the air comes out in a forceful stream. Use this method when your exercisewalking routine becomes intense.

In-Place Walking Programs

The in-place programs are slightly more intense than walking on flat terrain, as you can see from the METs columns in the following charts.

In-Place Walking or Marching Program

Follow the same frequency as the flat terrain program until you reach the desired level. Marching in place (raising your feet 12 to 24 inches off the ground) is a more intense exercise than walking in place (raising your feet 3 to 6 inches off the ground).

In-Place Walking Program

YOUR LEVEL	LENGTH OF EXERCISE SESSION
I	11–15 minutes
II	16–25 minutes
III	26–35 minutes
IV	36–45 minutes
V	46–60 minutes

Increase intensity by building the number of steps you take per minute, as shown on the following chart

Increasing the Number of Marching Steps per Minute

YOUR LEVEL	STEPS PER MINUTE	METs	INCREASE IN STEPS PER WEEK
I	45–90	5	10
II	90–99	6	10
III	100–130	7	10
IV	131–149	8–10	20
V	150–200	10–13	20

The Stair-Climbing Program

Build in the same way as in the level terrain program by adding first the number of steps by increments of twenty-five per week until you are at your desired level and then increasing speed by calculating your step per minute speed and increasing it by 15 seconds each week.

Increasing the Number of Stairs Climbed per Minute

YOUR LEVEL	NUMBER OF STEPS	METs
I	250–299	5
II	300–399	6
III	400–499	7
IV	500–749	8–10
V	750–1000	10–13

Incline Treadmill Walking

As with the basic program, work first on distance and then increase the incline gradation by 2.5 to 5 percent a week, as well as increasing your speed (by 15 to 30 seconds per week).

Increasing the Incline Gradation in Treadmill Walking

YOUR LEVEL	PERCENTAGE OF SLOPE
I	5–10
II	10–15
III	15–20
IV	20–30
V	30–45

In the following chapters we'll discuss specific problems associated with heart disease and describe special applications of the preventive walking programs to these.

5. Walking to a Lower Blood Pressure

Dr. Mort Malkin is a good example of a "doctor heal thyself" story. Dr. Malkin, who suffered from high blood pressure all his adult life, was able to bring it down to normal just by sticking to a 3-day-a-week walking regime.

Both sides of Mort's family were rife with hypertension, and his parents were on medication. His father had had a heart attack. Although Mort himself led a fairly active life, ate healthily, and was not overweight, he continued to have high blood pressure readings. "I thought hypertension was my due," he said.

When Mort was 40 he began walking 4 miles every Sunday morning with an older man of about 60. During the once-a-week trips, "I would keep up for about a mile and then have to stop," he recalls. The friend was doing each mile in 10 to 11 minutes. The sudden death of a colleague from a heart attack induced Mort to join his friend three times a week for the 4-mile trip. After about 3 months, Mort could keep up with the older man's pace, and on good days he even sprinted the last few hundred yards.

Five years later, when he joined the staff of Brooklyn (New York) Hospital, Mort had his first physical examination in many years. His blood pressure was only 117/70 (lower than average). Mort was so shocked that he insisted there had been a mistake. The doctor repeated the test with the same results. According to Mort, the only change in his life was the addition of a walking program.

Now, after 10 years of training, Mort can racewalk 1 mile in under 9 minutes, and he logs 15 miles a week. His blood pressure continues to be normal. "I have defeated my heredity," says Mort.

Anyone with high blood pressure should follow Dr. Malkin's example, because high blood pressure is one of the most dangerous risk factors and one of the easiest to control. Doctors often prescribe medication to control hypertension, but our walking doctors have numerous stories of patients who have been able to throw out or reduce their medication and control their blood pressure by combining a walking program with stress reduction and a healthy diet.

Recently, there have been many articles in the press about the safety of reducing blood pressure after a group of researchers at the Albert Einstein Medical College of Yeshiva University in New York City found an increased risk of heart attacks among those patients who dramatically reduced their blood pressure (although for those who reduced it moderately, the rate of heart attacks decreased). All the patients in the study were being treated with hypertension medication. Some doctors believe the medication may be to blame for the heart attacks, because it causes the blood pressure to drop very quickly over a few days, and this may be harmful to the heart. Lowering your blood pressure slowly with walking and diet (which works over 6 to 12 weeks) is much healthier than taking medication because it permanently improves the health of your heart and arteries. Medication does not.

To understand how walking can help you control blood pressure, you should understand some basic facts about its role in the body. Blood pressure is the force the blood exerts on the arterial walls, and doctors measure it to assess how efficiently your body delivers oxygen and nutrients to your muscles and organs. Your blood pressure is regulated by the kidneys, brain, and nervous system and is dependent on the strength of your heart muscle, the volume of blood it can pump, and the condition of your arteries. Normal blood pressure is anything less than 140/90 (with the average being 120/80). The top number refers to the *systolic* blood pressure—the pressure on the artery walls as the blood is forced out of the heart. The lower number is the *diastolic* pressure—the pressure on the artery walls *between* heartbeats.

These numbers represent average ranges. Blood pressure normally fluctuates throughout the day, depending on the hour or your level of activity. It generally rises with age, but it is best to keep that increase to a minimum.

A good analogy to explain hypertension is a garden hose. Increased blood flow from high blood pressure is akin to the water faucet being

How Doctors Gauge Blood Pressure

NORMAL	MILDLY HIGH	MODERATELY HIGH	SEVERELY HIGH
Under 140/90	140/90 to 159/104	160/105 to 180/115	Over 180/115

turned on high. The higher the pressure, the tighter and more rigid the hose. With continued high pressure, the walls of the hose eventually wear out and the hose ruptures. In the arteries, high blood pressure causes lesions (microscopic fractures) in the delicate lining covering the artery wall. The lesions provide places on the cell wall for plaque to accumulate, and this accumulation leads to atherosclerosis. High diastolic blood pressure (when the denominator of the blood pressure reading is over 115) suggests that you are in danger of a heart attack.

Atherosclerosis can also occur in the arteries of the brain. If a blockage develops, it can decrease or stop blood flow to the brain, causing a stroke. High blood pressure can also weaken the delicate blood vessels in the brain. If one of these bursts, it will also impede blood flow and cause a stroke. A high systolic blood pressure (when the numerator of the blood pressure reading is over 160) usually indicates that you are at risk for a stroke. People with the highest systolic levels (180 and above) are at least seven times more likely to have a stroke (either caused by atherosclerosis or a ruptured blood vessel) than people with blood pressures below 120.

Many people don't know they have high blood pressure because there are essentially no symptoms associated with it—why doctors refer to high blood pressure as the "silent killer." Unfortunately, some people don't take high blood pressure seriously for this reason. Hypertensive people often go off their medication because they "feel fine" or because initial tests after a treatment show that their pressure has come down. Many also falsely believe that hypertension only strikes the aged or the tense. However, anyone, no matter what his or her personality or age, can have hypertension. It cannot be cured, but it is a condition that can be controlled, as is amply illustrated by Dr. Malkin's story.

There are certain risk factors associated with high blood pressure, which are similar to those for heart attacks:

1. *A family history of the condition.* Fifty percent of hypertensives have other family members with high blood pressure. Related familial diseases that can also cause high blood pressure include diabetes, kidney disease, and thyroid conditions.

2. *Age and gender.* Hypertension affects half the population over age 65. There is higher incidence in men before age 50, and more among women after age 50. No one knows why this is true, except that women tend to put on weight after menopause, and weight plays a role in hypertension.

3. *Race.* Blacks are twice as likely as whites to develop hypertension.

4. *Weight.* Approximately 40 percent of all overweight people have hypertension. Each extraneous pound of fat is a circulatory burden, extra tissue that needs to be fed. Studies have shown a direct relationship

between weight reduction and a drop in blood pressure. A 20-pound decrease in weight can result in approximately a 20-point drop in blood pressure. Weight loss may be the only step necessary for mild hypertension, and it is certainly an important factor in reducing severe hypertension. (See Book 4: Walkshaping and Weight Control for more on weight control and diet.)

5. *Salt.* People who are genetically predisposed to hypertension experience a rise in their blood pressure when they eat salty foods because too much sodium (salt is 40 percent sodium) causes water retention, which increases your blood volume and thus the pressure on your artery walls. To decrease the salt in your diet, you need to do more than leave the salt shaker alone. Avoid processed food (including packaged baked goods, snack foods like potato chips and pretzels, and tomato juice). Sodium chloride is often used as a preservative, so even if you don't salt your food, you are probably consuming more than your 5-gram daily limit. Pay close attention to the labels on packaged food, as many foods you'd never suspect—cereal, canned vegetables, and soups, for example—are often heavily salted.

6. *Stress.* Even minor anxiety and stress can raise blood pressure in people with normal blood pressure. For people with moderate to severe high blood pressure, stress can bring them to the stroke danger point.

7. *Cigarette smoking.* Quit! Avoiding nicotine can reduce by half the risks associated with high blood pressure.

Walking reduces high blood pressure indirectly by helping you lose weight, reduce stress, and quit smoking. But it also works on the problem directly by dilating the blood vessels and thus reducing resistance on the walls of the vessels. According to Dr. Norman Kaplan, an endocrinologist who has researched hypertension extensively, aerobic exercise may also decrease the production of insulin, which is known to increase blood pressure. (Hypertensive people have too much insulin in their blood, particularly men, who are more prone to upper body obesity—which increases insulin production.)

In conjunction with your walking program, eating a largely vegetarian diet high in polyunsaturated fats, fiber, and potassium and staying away from processed foods can also help lower your blood pressure.

Walking Regimen for High Blood Pressure

I. Preventive Program

If you do not suffer from hypertension (and are otherwise healthy), follow the cardiowalking preventive program (Chapter 4) to ensure that your blood pressure remains in the normal range. Have your blood pressure checked once a year.

II. For Mild High Blood Pressure

Sixty-six percent of all hypertensive people fall into the borderline or mild hypertension category (140 to 160 over 90 to 104). Despite the name, which suggests that the condition is not serious, your risk of heart attack is double that of people with normal blood pressure. You won't necessarily need medication if you eat a diet low in salt, fat, and cholesterol and exercisewalk four times a week (every other day). Use the guidelines in Chapter 4 to gradually work up to at a level appropriate for your age. Your walking speed need not be more than 3 to 4 miles an hour (a somewhat hard rate of exertion). Although isometric exercises (like weight lifting and using Nautilus machines) are bad for people with hypertension, using hand weights (like Heavy Hands) to help increase the intensity of walking is not dangerous.

III. Moderate and Severe High Blood Pressure

If your diastolic blood pressure is above 104, you should be under the care of a physician, who will likely prescribe medication. Our walking program should not replace your doctor's recommendations and prescriptions. Show him or her the program as a guideline for a walking regimen to work in conjunction with your prescribed diet and medication.

No medication will exclude you from exercise, but you should be aware of any side effects so you can modify your exercisewalking program if necessary. The most frequently dispensed hypertension medications are diuretics. These reduce the salt and fluid in your blood and thus relieve pressure on the arterial walls. Their only effect on exercise is that you will need to drink more water shortly before and while you walk to ensure that you don't become dehydrated. Diuretics can also cause potassium depletion, which can lead to arrhythmias. Low potassium levels have also been linked to high blood pressure. If you are taking diuretics, it is important to eat fruits and vegetables high in potassium (like bananas and sweet potatoes), because you will tend to sweat out potassium when you exercisewalk.

Starting an exercisewalking program may be difficult, especially if you are overweight and haven't exercised in a while. Knowing that others have successfully done it helps. James Chapman, a 50-year-old engineer from Missouri City, Texas, is just one example. He was admitted to the emergency room of his local hospital with a blood pressure of 220/120. He was prescribed three different drugs for hypertension and was told to follow a low-salt, low-fat, and low-cholesterol diet and begin a daily walking regimen.

"I had had no form of exercise in several years, and I weighed 185 pounds on an average 5 foot 10 inch frame," said James. "Initially I walked 2 miles a day in 30 minutes, which was no easy task." But over the next year, James was able to build his walking speed to 2.5 miles in 30 minutes (5 miles an hour). His weight has stabilized at 150 pounds, and his blood pressure is now down to 130/85. "I feel better than I have in years," says James.

6. Walking Through Angina Pain

Angina pectoris, literally "a pain in the chest," is due to a temporary deficiency of oxygen and blood flow to the heart muscle caused by atherosclerosis in the coronary arteries. Angina pectoris (also known simply as *angina*) is not dangerous in itself, but if you have angina, you are twice as likely to have a heart attack as people without the condition. In this chapter we'll teach you how to exercise with angina.

Angina, which affects about 2.5 million people in the United States, usually occurs while you are walking or performing some other activity. It is a signal that your body needs to stop or slow down because the heart's demand for blood is greater than the available supply. Chest pain usually arises only after one or more of the coronary arteries is partially blocked, so angina is *not* just a warning, as some people think, but rather a sign that your heart's blood supply is already compromised. If you begin to experience pain in your chest with exertion, see a doctor. If you do have angina, show your doctor the cardiowalking program for angina to ensure that it is right for you.

The standard treatment for angina is to improve the blood supply/demand relationship of the heart, either with medication or, in some cases, through balloon angioplasty or coronary artery bypass surgery. Recent research, done by Dr. Dean Ornish of the University of California at San Francisco, suggests that for some people, changes in lifestyle may actually reduce the blockages that cause angina and heart attacks. Dr. Ornish found that over a 1-year period, patients who followed a low-fat (10 percent of their diet), low-cholesterol diet, stopped smoking, followed a stress-management course, and exercised a minimum of 3 hours per week decreased the blockages in their arteries by 10 percent on average, with the most severely "blocked" patients making the most progress. Although Dr. Ornish's sample size was relatively small, future research may substantiate the theory that lifestyle is important not only in slowing the progression of angina, but also in reducing blockages.

Walking is a major factor in making these lifestyle changes, as is illustrated from the following story of a woman who learned to walk through, and eventually decrease, her anginal pain.

Dorothea Barnes, at age 72, was more than 30 pounds overweight (140 pounds on a 5-foot frame), somewhat hypertensive, with a history of diabetes. Her cholesterol was very high—about 260 milligrams. She ate what she defined as a "widow's diet" of easy-to-fix junk and fast food and plenty of coffee. What's more, she had a history of heart disease on her mother's side. The unhealthy lifestyle of her own family members reinforced her own behavior: Her husband died of a heart attack, as did her 38-year-old adopted son. She also had a bleeding ulcer, due partially to "nerves," according to her doctor. Dorothea took a different medication for each and every one of these conditions.

Dorothea also suffered very painful angina from normal exertion. "I couldn't walk two blocks. . . . It got so I was afraid to walk," she says. Symptoms included profuse sweating and clammy sensations, nausea, and a "tight choking pain" that made it difficult for her to catch her breath. An exercise stress test supervised by her doctor revealed that Dorothea had moderate to severe angina on exertion, and highlighted the extent of the deterioration of her cardiac health. She felt faint after only 3 minutes on the treadmill.

Dorothea was told to try walking at her own pace. Her first time out she walked half a block and she progressed by increments of half a block, walking as slowly as necessary. In the beginning, she would stop for up to 5 minutes when she began to feel chest pains. Over time, she found that slowing down (rather than stopping) was enough to decrease the sensation of angina. After 9 months of daily walking, Dorothea had worked up to 2 miles a day at a moderate pace. Six months later, she had increased her walking program to 3 miles in 45 minutes.

Dorothea keeps her diet simple and wholesome, eating plenty of fruits and vegetables and cutting out red meat, which she has replaced with chicken and fish. Salt is severely restricted, and she no longer drinks coffee. The result: a cholesterol drop to under 200, a weight loss of 32 pounds, reduced blood pressure, and improved diabetic control. Today, pain-free and drug-free for a year, Dorothea walks the hilly terrain of Tennessee's Lookout Mountain. "Once I start, I don't stop. I only slow down. You can accomplish more that way," she says.

Dorothea's story shows that if you have angina, exercise may be helpful in reducing or even eliminating symptoms. Walking will make the heart work more efficiently and beat slower at all times. Early studies on dogs suggest that regular aerobic exercise, such as walking, may also enhance collateral circulation—blood vessels that naturally grow around a blockage and act as a detour—although research on humans has been inconclusive to date.

Angina falls under the general term *ischemia*, which means an inadequate oxygen supply or delivery to the heart muscle. Sometimes ischemia can cause no pain at all (called *silent ischemia*). In such cases diagnosis is determined with a treadmill test or with a 24-hour *Holter monitoring* (in which a person wears a portable monitor that records heart rate and rhythm).

While angina attacks most commonly occur during exercise or while walking, the pain, pressure, or discomfort can also occur during sleep, at rest, or during a stressful situation. Angina can last anywhere from seconds to minutes, and varies from person to person. It has been described as heaviness or tightness of the chest, an ache, or a burning sensation that is often confused with indigestion. Some people feel pain in their arms, shoulders, jaw, and neck, too.

A similar discomfort can also occur in the calf muscle, where it is called *intermittent claudication*. These symptoms are also a sign of arteriosclerosis. As you get older, the arteries become less elastic, and this combined with gradual narrowing will decrease the blood flow through them. Like angina, intermittent claudication is a temporary pain that occurs during walking or other activities but stops when movement ceases. Intermittent claudication is in itself not dangerous, but it does indicate that arteriosclerosis is advanced and should be evaluated and treated. As in angina, although walking can bring on the pain, it is, along with diet, one of the ways to modify it favorably. If you have intermittent claudication, follow the regimen on pages 182–183.

If your angina has progressed to a severe level and does not respond to medication (the most common of which is nitroglycerin, which transiently opens the arteries) doctors may recommend balloon angioplasty (a tiny balloon catheter is inserted into the blocked artery and then inflated to squash the blockage) or coronary bypass surgery. In the latter case, doctors take the saphenous vein from the leg (the leg has many veins, and removing one causes no problems) or the internal mammary artery in the chest wall, and use it to make a detour around the blockage in the artery, so that blood can flow to the heart. This operation can "rejuvenate" you for many years, although if you do not change some habits (cigarette smoking, high fat diet, etc.) atherosclerosis can begin to develop in the bypasses as well as in native coronary arteries. Walking is vital for rehabilitation from surgery (follow the cardiowalking rehabilitation program in Chapter 9 if you are currently recovering from bypass surgery), and if you can start a walking program *before* surgery, it may help you to rebound more quickly afterward.

Walking Regimen for Angina

If you've been diagnosed with angina, you've probably had a treadmill walking test to determine the extent to which you can walk before experiencing pain. Your goal in walking will be to increase the amount of exercise without inducing an anginal episode. Depending on its severity, you may or may not be able to walk through your pain. (This is also something that can be determined initially during a medically supervised exercise test.)

You may wonder how you can tell the difference between anginal pain and a heart attack. This is fairly easy, because your anginal pain is temporary and generally occurs in the same location (although your pain will undoubtedly be different than that of others). If you experience prolonged chest pain, with or without profuse sweating, and these symptoms do not respond to rest and/or nitroglycerin, stop exercising immediately, as these may be signs of an impending heart attack.

If you have been prescribed nitroglycerin, which generally provides rapid relief, carry it with you at all times. Some doctors even recommend taking it before doing anything likely to cause anginal discomfort, such as exercising or having sex. Nitroglycerin expands or dilates the blood vessels temporarily, thereby reducing the workload of the heart. If you have been prescribed nitroglycerin, discuss with your doctor the times you should take it (during exercise or before exercise).

Warm-up is especially important for the angina patient, and all walking sessions should begin with a 10-minute slow walk to help increase circulation. Then slowly increase your speed to a level just below the point of angina. The idea is not to win a race, but to walk at a comfortable pace, perhaps 2 to 2.5 miles per hour. At first, you may only be able to walk half a block before having to rest. Gradually increase your walking time, adding 5 minutes a week to your daily sessions. For example, if you are walking for 10 minutes per day the first week, walk the next week for 15 minutes each day. If you are unable to add the 5-minute increment, stay at your current level for another week before trying again. Stop or slow down when pain, pressure, or discomfort in the chest begins. This is called *intermittent walking*.

Use the following chart as a gauge of your angina pain:

1+ = barely noticeable (light)

2+ = bothersome (moderate)

$3+$ = very uncomfortable (severe)

$4+$ = Most severe pain ever experienced

If your pain is barely noticeable, you can continue to walk at your current speed, but if your discomfort increases beyond a $2+$ intensity level, *don't exercise through your angina.* Rather, you should slow down or stop your activity until the discomfort subsides. (If in doubt, stop and rest rather than slow down.) Once the pain has diminished—usually after a few minutes—you can increase your speed again. If the pain returns, continue your walking workout at a lower intensity level.

As your endurance increases, usually over a 6- to 12-week period, you probably won't need to stop and rest as often; reducing your walking speed will usually be enough to decrease the anginal pain. Once your angina episodes have become less severe, you can increase your walking speed by a little each week.

Walking Techniques

You can pump your arms when you walk to help strengthen your upper body (see page 99), but this technique is only advisable if it doesn't bring on anginal pain.

A cool-down is also very important for angina patients. Always include at least a 10-minute slow walk at the end of your exercisewalking session. As with all heart disease patients, you should not exercise during extreme cold or heat or wind, since this could bring on chest pains. Mall walking may be a good alternative in inclement, hot, or cold weather.

Garth Russell, a 74-year-old walker from Sun City West, Arizona, has discovered walking's rehabilitative benefits. Garth began walking 5½ years ago after a heart attack. Over the first year he increased his speed to 4 miles an hour, walking 15 miles a week, and he stayed at that level for several years.

A bout of pneumonia last winter decreased Garth's fitness level, and he began to experience anginal pains almost daily. After undergoing a coronary angioplasty, he is now back walking and can go 1 to 2 miles without taking nitroglycerin. Despite this setback, Garth is optimistic that he can strengthen his heart and arteries through walking, and he hopes to eventually get back up to his 4 mile an hour pace.

7. Walking for Stronger Veins

Although the arteries have gotten most of the attention so far, walking is one of the main therapeutic exercises for some of the milder, though still disturbing conditions that can affect the veins: varicose veins, blood clots, and ulcers.

The veins are the vehicles by which blood returns to the heart. There are two types: the superficial system, the small veins you can see under your skin, and the deep system, the veins within muscles that cannot be seen with the naked eye. Blood moves sluggishly through veins, whose walls are far less muscular than those in the arteries. Much of the work of pushing the blood back up to the heart is done by the calf muscles, which squeeze the deep veins and force the blood upward against gravity as they expand and contract. Walking, because it exercises all the leg muscles, plays an important role in increasing circulation, and that's one of the reasons that walking is called the "second heart."

Jane Synovec, a 36-year-old nurse, discovered the benefits of building that second heart. When Jane was pregnant, she developed varicose veins that were so severe that she was forced to stop working after her fifth month. Instead of moping around the house, however, Jane walked 6 miles a day, wrapping Ace bandages around her legs to help aid circulation. Not only did walking improve her varicosities, but it helped pass the time each day when she would normally be working.

Varicose veins are the most common circulatory problem, and it is estimated that 25 percent of women and 10 percent of men are affected. Varicose veins are engorged veins, usually blue or purple, that appear on the legs, causing unsightly bulging rivulets most often located behind the knees or down the backs of the calves. These veins develop over many years and are usually not dangerous. Although often painless, they can cause aching in the feet or legs (especially toward the end of the day), a burning sensation, or a leaden feeling that makes walking difficult. Walking, however, will eventually help decrease the pain.

Heredity is the most common contributor to developing varicose veins. Jobs or situations demanding hours of standing can aggravate any tendency to develop varicose veins, as can arteriosclerosis (which is why varicose veins often develop in older people). Surprisingly, such trauma as landing too hard on your feet or exercising in the wrong shoes will not cause them, although anything that can injure the veins, such as a major fracture of the tibia (large lower leg bone) or twisting an ankle, might bring them on. Other factors known to aggravate varicose veins include pregnancy and weight gain, because these put extra strain on the veins.

Despite this long list of situations that exacerbate varicose veins, no one really understands what causes them. All that is known is that it is a mechanical problem with the valves in the veins (valves are found every 1 or 2 inches in the veins of the legs). For some reason, these valves break down, and blood backs up, causing the portion of vein below the valve failure to bulge. If the pooling is severe enough, it can lead to swollen feet (called *edema*), which can cause skin rashes or even bleeding in the veins. Unfortunately, there is no way to prevent varicose veins, but walking can help ease the pain by improving circulation.

Perhaps the most serious vein condition is a blood clot in a deep vein. As with varicose veins, blood clots also cause a traffic jam in the veins because blood below the clot is trapped and cannot flow upward. This cessation of blood flow will weaken or destroy the valves below the clot, which must endure the extra pressure of the backed-up blood. If a valve breaks down, there is no barrier to keep the blood flowing in one direction, and thus some blood will tend to pool in the foot and edema will occur. This chronic swelling causes the skin above the ankle to become red and thickened. The small vessels may begin to leak blood, and the surrounding cells, now without nourishment, die. The combination of leaking capillaries and thickened skin eventually causes ulcers, or sores, to develop on the skin. Most can be very painful, and they make walking difficult or impossible. Most ulcers will heal in about 2 to 4 weeks with the help of walking and external compression, but a severe condition may take several months to repair.

Blood clots in the deep veins can be life-threatening. If a clot breaks off from the deep veins leading to the heart and lungs, it could cause a heart attack. Clotting requires hospitalization and treatment by a doctor, who prescribes medication to thin the blood. Prompt and proper treatment of deep vein blood clots reduces the future breakdown of vein valves and thus ulcer formation.

Clots can also occur in surface varicose veins, in which case the condition is called *superficial phlebitis*. These clots do not bring on the serious consequences of deep system blood clots, but if untreated, phlebitis can eventually cause external ulcers. Phlebitis happens in about 5 percent of all varicose veins, when the presence of a blood clot causes the vein to bulge even more, so that it becomes red, hard, and hot to the touch. Superficial phlebitis is treated with aspirin and cold packs. If you have this condition, you'll be told to wear support hose and walk. A small incision in the vein can also be made and the clot removed. This combination treatment eventually reopens the vein.

The following story of a 35-year-old Californian illustrates how painful such disorders of the venous system can be and how walking can help reduce the discomfort and get you back on your feet.

Thomas always thought he was healthy until he began developing swelling in his ankles and feet, which caused his skin to break and infections to develop. The pain became so severe that he found a pair of crutches and hobbled off to see his doctor, who diagnosed the problem as blood clots in the deep vein, which may have been dormant for 3 or 4 years before they finally caused the severe swelling.

Thomas's immediate treatment was the application of an isometric dressing (much like an Ace bandage but less elastic) that compresses the area, helps to push blood back up to the heart, and prevents swelling. After 2 days, Thomas could walk again without crutches. He began with a half hour of brisk walking (about 3 miles an hour) and over several weeks built up his regimen to 1 hour a day. After 3 weeks, Thomas could walk without pain or discomfort, and the swelling had been reduced dramatically.

Walking Regimen for Stronger Veins

Most doctors will prescribe an hour's walk a day, which can be broken up into two or three short stints, so that you are continually counteracting the negative affects of standing and sitting. The exact speed will depend on your fitness level. The more briskly and more intensely you can walk (stair climbing is particularly good) the better, although you will not have to walk more than 3 miles an hour to achieve positive results. Normally, within 2 weeks you will begin to experience a lessening of pressure in your legs as your circulation improves. However, doctors report that even after the first day of walking patients can see an improvement. Dr. Forrestal, a walker and doctor at Vein Clinics of America in Beverly Hills, California, says, "We send our patients out the first couple of days to walk, and they're all wrapped up with compression wraps, and they have these big veins which are just starting to heal. But they always come back after their walk to us and tell us how great they feel."

8. *Walking for Better Breathing*

Any lung problem that repeatedly deprives the blood of oxygen will strain the heart and can eventually cause heart failure. This is why we've included pulmonary disorders in the cardiowalking book. The cardiovascular and pulmonary systems are interdependent, so preventing or rehabilitating from pulmonary diseases is part and parcel of maintaining overall cardiac health, and overall cardiac health will increase the efficiency of the lungs. This chapter will explain some common lung disorders and show you how walking, by building a strong heart, will in turn promote improved oxygen delivery to active muscles.

Lung disease impedes the normal exchange of oxygen and carbon dioxide as the blood passes through the lungs. Once a lung has been damaged, it can never be restored, yet the human body has amazing compensatory abilities, and even someone who has lost a lung to cancer or some other disease can achieve the same fitness as a normal person by increasing his or her heart capacity. Walking increases the heart's pumping capacity and thus the efficiency with which oxygen is delivered to the rest of the body. The better the heart functions, the less work the lungs have to do. The name of the game is compensating for weak lungs with a healthy heart.

Walking, besides building aerobic capacity, will also strengthen the body's breathing muscles, like the diaphragm, which stretches across the bottom of the ribs, and the intercostal muscles, which lie beside the rib cage. Walking also helps increase "minute ventilation"—how deeply and steadily you breathe—without straining the lungs. In fact, in many in-

stances walking is the only exercise lung patients can do, as a more strenuous aerobic exercise like running is not within their capabilities.

As with coronary heart disease, pulmonary diseases also have risk factors
associated with them. The main one is cigarette smoking, and the second
is environmental or job-related hazards (like black lung for coal workers).
The major pulmonary disorders associated with these risk factors are bronchitis and emphysema.

Chronic bronchitis is characterized by a cough for 3 months a year for
2 years in a row. It will cause shortness of breath, making activity difficult.
Bronchitis is not necessarily a severe ailment, although if it is left untreated, it can cause heart failure. If severe lung deterioration takes place,
the right ventricle (the chamber that pumps blood into the lungs) becomes
strained because it has to push harder to force the blood into the damaged
lung. The end result can be congestive heart failure, when the weak
ventricle is incapable of pumping blood out of the heart fast enough and
the heart fills with blood (this condition, which often accompanies heart
attacks, can be partially treated with medication).

Emphysema is more serious and can be fatal. Smoking is responsible
for 50 percent of all cases of emphysema, followed by pollution and exposure to toxins. Symptoms include shortness of breath, cough, and extreme intolerance for any type of normal, much less athletic, exertion.

Robert Ross, the truck driver with the bad back you met in Book 2,
has discovered that walking is one of the best treatments for emphysema.
About a year after Robert started walking (for his back injury), he quit
smoking cold turkey. He later noticed an unremittant cough, but he put
that down to his lungs' cleaning themselves out. Then, 6 months after
quitting smoking, he came down with severe pneumonia. X-rays showed
he had emphysema. Robert was put on drugs (Thudor, the standard one
for this disease), which he must now take for the rest of his life. But in
the course of his continued mall workouts, he discovered "the best [treat-
ment] for emphysema was walking!" Breathing was hard at first, but he
kept going back to the mall until it got easier (about 6 months). "Walking
alleviated my hard breathing, . . ." he says, "and when I asked the doctor
[why], he said, 'You're getting oxygen into your lungs.'"

Another common lung disorder is *asthma*, which afflicts about 8 million
Americans and occurs when breathing is inhibited due to spasms and
accumulation of mucus in the breathing tubes connected to the lungs.
There are two main types of asthma, *extrinsic*, which is caused by allergies
to dust, pollen, feathers, and smoke and often improves with age, and
intrinsic, which is usually nonallergenic in origin and is caused by exposure
to pollution, an infection, physical exertion, or stress, among others.

An asthma attack may be brought on by exercise, yet avoiding exercise
is not a healthy solution either. Asthma attacks during exercise can be
reduced by following a less intense aerobic exercise program with a proper

warm-up. If you like to walk briskly and have asthma, you may find that you have to stop during your exercise because of an asthma attack. Practice the breath-play technique in Chapter 4 while you walk. Walking with deep breathing reduces stress (which can bring on an asthma attack), and the breathing techniques you learn while walking will help you during an asthma attack as well.

Walking Regimen for Pulmonary Disorders

Bob, who worked in a factory and sometimes lifted small boxes and crates in his job, came to Dr. Barry Hertz because of a shortness of breath that made him have to rest 5 minutes for every 5 minutes he worked. A stress test showed that he could work to only 3 METs (very low intensity level) before *desaturation* occurred—this is the state when the body demands more oxygen than can be delivered by the lungs.

Bob went on disability from his job, and Dr. Hertz put him on an exercise program to build his capacity up to 6.8 METs. Bob regularly monitored his pulse throughout his walking routine and gradually increased the intensity of his exercise as his heart became stronger and his breathlessness decreased.

Bob began by walking six times per week, covering 2 miles in 30 minutes. Within 3 months of starting this routine, Bob was back at work. His breathing was deeper, and his resting pulse rate had dropped 20 points. Bob has continued to walk three times a week to further reduce his heart rate and increase the delivery of oxygen to his muscles.

If you have bronchitis, emphysema, asthma, or any other shortness of breath, your doctor will put you through an administered stress exercise test to determine the extent of your problem and to help design a walking program for you. During the test, your doctor will measure how much carbon dioxide you produce, how much oxygen you use, and how deeply and rapidly you breathe. You may be put on a bronchodilator, a medication that opens up breathing tubes and makes it easier for oxygen to get through. Side effects can include nausea and tremors, which are unpleasant but should be toughed out during exercise. This medication can, in rare cases, cause arrythmias, which can be fatal. Stimulants such as caffeine will aggravate the arrhythmias, so it is best to avoid coffee. Medication can cause you to feel very "hyper" for some minutes, but this side effect should not prevent exercising.

You will have to monitor your pulse or use the RPE scale to ensure that you are within safe exercise limits (don't exercise more than somewhat hard). Lung patients have been known to even double their exercise capability in a period between 6 weeks and 6 months (depending on their initial condition). However, the general rule at first is to be conservative.

Even walking at a low-intensity level (i.e., for a short time or at a slow speed) can be effective rehabilitation. You may have to stop and rest during your walking routine, although as time goes on this will happen less and less. Ultimately, you will attain a walking regimen of half an hour a day 4 days a week. If you have bronchitis, your exercise regime will be the same, although you will probably be able to exercise more strenuously than an emphysema patient.

Here is a five-level walking schedule to follow to get to the Level III goal of 30 minutes of walking 3 or 4 days a week (of course, if you are able, you can build to a Level IV or V).

Five-Level Walking Schedule

LEVEL	TIME (MINUTES)	SPEED (MPH)	METs	FREQUENCY PER WEEK (DAYS)
I	10	2	3	3
II	20	2.5	3.5	3
III	30	3	4	3–5
IV	35	3.5	5	3–5
V	45	4.0	6	3–5

Increase your walking time by 5 minutes a week. (For example, your walking sessions at Level I would be 10 minutes each the first week and 15 minutes each the second week.) If you are unable to make the 5-minute increase, stay at your current level for another week and try again. Once you've gotten to at least 30 minutes of continuous walking, you can decrease your minute-per-mile speed by 15 seconds a week.

It is important not to walk outside when air pollution is high or, if you have bronchitis, when the weather is damp and cold. Walk indoors instead.

If you've had lung surgery, your rehabilitation will follow the same regimen as the cardiowalking rehabilitation program (see Chapter 9). Although lung surgery patients may be even more debilitated from their experience than heart attack victims (especially because they tend to be older), they can still make amazing progress with walking.

9. Cardiowalking Comeback Program

The following story of a young man who had a heart attack demonstrates both the horror that such a situation creates and what extraordinary results changing lifestyles, walking, and eating right can achieve. If you have some form of heart disease, we hope this story will give you hope and the encouragement to believe you, too, can take control of your life and health.

Stephen Watkinson, age 36, had no history of heart disease in his family, but he smoked heavily (two to three packs a day) and was 100 pounds overweight as a result of a diet chock full of fat and red meat. His cholesterol level was borderline normal, and his blood pressure was mildly elevated, 140/95.

Six to 9 months before his heart attack, Stephen found himself out of breath while climbing stairs. "One flight almost killed me. That should have been a tip-off," he said. Then one evening at bedtime he felt mild chest pains, which he thought were due to indigestion. But the next day, the chest pains were more severe and constricting, and he felt a great pressure on his chest. He checked into a hospital.

At first, doctors were skeptical that he could be having a heart attack —the pain was not radiating down his arm, and his EKG was normal— but they continued to monitor his heart in the emergency room. When the beat changed radically, Stephen was rushed to coronary intensive care. Then and there, he had the heart attack. Stephen's heart stopped, and the team used a defibrillator (electric shock) to revive him. Later, his heart stopped again. The doctors were worried because of the difficulty they had reviving him the second time, and he had severe burns on his chest

191

from the repeated defibrillation. No one thought he would survive. And for several days, Stephen lived in a twilight zone of morphine.

After he had stabilized, his doctors performed an angiogram. (An angiogram involves inserting a catheter into an artery and running dye through the system so that the doctor can ascertain the severity of blockage in the coronary arteries.) Three coronary arteries—one 60 percent, one 80 percent, and one 90 percent—were blocked. Twenty percent of Stephen's heart tissue was dead.

Stephen was discharged from the hospital with a sack of medication, but he returned 2 weeks later complaining of chest pains. The doctors decided on coronary bypass surgery. It took three people to help Stephen get out of bed after his surgery. Stephen's doctor told him he'd have to be able to walk a mile before they would put him in a cardiac rehabilitation program. To Stephen, this seemed an impossibility. When he finally came home from the hospital, Stephen was afraid to sleep because he associated sleep with death. During this time of extreme trauma he decided to drastically alter his life. "I had thought it was the doctor's job to keep me healthy," he says. Now he realized it was time to take responsibility for his own health.

A little more than a year later, Stephen has accomplished just that. He has lost 100 pounds, and he eats a diet low in fat and salt and high in fiber. He regularly walks near his home in Phoenix, including a challenging 2-mile hike up Squaw Peak, on which he often brings along his wife and two children. He is physically fit for the first time in his life, and his resting heart beat is an impressive 54 per minute. "At first, I walked because I didn't want to have another heart attack. Now I do it because I enjoy it."

The Heart Attack

Perhaps what is most painful and frightening for a heart attack patient is the realization that although he or she probably had a family history of heart disease, the attack was in many ways self-imposed and might well have been avoided. After all, 80 percent of all heart attacks are associated with modifiable risk factors. You would think that after undergoing such a traumatic experience, any heart attack patient would be shocked into changing his or her lifestyle. However, 30 percent of all heart attacks are second attacks, which suggests that too many heart attack patients don't change their unhealthy lifestyles after the first attack. If you continue to smoke after a heart attack, your chances of having another are a third greater. Not changing your diet increases your chances even more. And a combination of all risk factors will ensure you a fifty-fifty chance of dying within the next 6 years. While you cannot change heart disease's impact on your past, you can certainly control its effect on your future.

As we've explained before, the main cause of a heart attack is atherosclerosis. A blockage in the coronary artery of more than 50 percent is considered severe, but eventually, the artery can become completely blocked (a *coronary occlusion*) either by plaque or a blood clot (a *coronary thrombosis*), which usually only happens when more than 85 percent of the artery is blocked with plaque. Any total blockage of the artery that lasts for more than 30 minutes will cause a heart attack (called *myocardial infarction*, literally, "heart muscle death").

During a heart attack, the portion of the heart that is fed by the blocked artery receives no oxygen or nutrients, and so it dies. Within 6 weeks, scar tissue will grow over the damaged area, which will never regain its function. The heart, however, is a strong muscle, and other parts of it can take over.

The symptoms of a heart attack include a pressure or pain in the center of the chest or back that lasts for more than 2 minutes; pain in the shoulders, neck, and arms; and dizziness, severe sweating, nausea, or shortness of breath. You may get one or more of these symptoms. Don't be embarrassed to seek help if you aren't sure you are having an attack. It is better to go to the hospital and find out you only had a severe case of indigestion than to die because you did not get help in time. It is crucial to receive medical attention within the first 2 hours of a heart attack.

As you learned from Stephen Watkinson's story, if you rehabilitate properly from a heart attack, you'll be able to live an active life and return to work. You do have to let your heart muscle heal first, and your return to activity will be very gradual. Most people can go back to work in 2 to 6 months, although they will have to adapt a more balanced approach to their work to keep stress at a minimum.

Walking Regimen for Heart Attack Patients

This program is divided into three phases that will lead you back to Level I of the preventive program.

Phase 1: In the Hospital

A normal hospital stay after a heart attack is 8 days. The goal during this time is to exercise at 30 beats over your resting heartbeat (or at about 5 METs). You'll begin by sitting up in a chair five or six times throughout the day (usually starting on day 3). Over the next few days, you'll perform deep breathing exercises, and a physical therapist will prescribe some general exercise to do in bed (mostly moving your shoulders, knees, ankles, and hips around their range of motion—the same type of range of motion exercises outlined in Book 2) to help retain some muscle strength until you can get out of bed and begin to walk. The next day you will be allowed to walk around the room and do standing versions of the same range-of-motion exercises.

In the remaining days of your hospital stay, you will build exercise duration to 20 or 30 minutes per day, done in one or two sessions. Your exertion rate will be a 12 to 13 on the RPE scale (not more than somewhat hard). Upon discharge, you will be given a submaximal exercise test to ensure that your heart is functioning normally.

Phases II and III: At Home

Every walking session should begin with a warm-up session and end with a cool-down, as described in Chapter 3: Cardiowalking Preventive Program.

Typically, when you are discharged from the hospital, you will be exercising at a level of about 5 METs (roughly 65 percent of your maximum heart rate, or less than somewhat hard—12 to 13—on the RPE scale). Take your pulse after 15 minutes of continuous walking to ensure that you are in the correct heart rate range.

The basic at-home program will increase your exercise from 5 to 8 METs. You will walk at least 3 to 4 days per week for approximately 9 to 12 weeks, building the duration of your exercise session to 45 minutes or 1 hour of continuous activity. If at any time you experience chest pain, dizziness, nausea, or extreme fatigue, *stop exercising and call your doctor*.

Do not use the arm-pumping technique until week 3 (if you've had a heart attack) or week 6 (if you've had bypass surgery), as this will place too much strain on the heart. If after each 2-week period you are not able to meet the next gradation, keep at the current pace and time until your endurance increases.

Weeks 1 to 3
Walk 30 minutes total, each exercise day. If you cannot walk continuously for 30 minutes, walk for 10 minutes three times a day. By the third week you should have built to 15 minutes twice a day. Your walking speed will be approximately 2 to 2.5 miles per hour.

Weeks 4 to 6
If you can walk for 15 minutes continually twice a day, you can increase your overall time to 45 or 50 minutes. Again, this is most likely to be done by splitting up sessions throughout the day:

Week 4: Three 15-minute sessions per day

Week 5: Two 20-minute sessions per day

Week 6: Two 25-minute sessions per day

Your walking speed will be 2.5 to 3 miles per hour.

Weeks 7 to 12

If you can walk at least 25 minutes continually, you can increase your walking time. Over these 6 weeks, you should begin to build up to 45 minutes of continuous walking, adding 5 minutes each day to your exercise session. You should be walking at 3 to 3.5 miles per hour.

Week 7: 30 minutes once a day

Week 8: 35 minutes once a day

Week 9: 40 minutes once a day

Week 10: 45 minutes once a day

Week 11: 45 minutes once a day

Week 12: 45 minutes once a day

You are now ready to graduate to the cardiowalking preventive program for your age group (see Chapter 4). Continue at the level that is the closest to your present level in terms of distance and walking speed.

If you are at risk of a heart attack, walking with other people makes good safety sense. Your regular walking partner should know how to revive you in case you have a heart attack (called *cardiopulmonary resuscitation,* or CPR). Classes are available from most local YMCAs and YWCAs or from the American Heart Association. Walk in areas that aren't too remote, so that help is near if needed.

You may be prescribed drugs that can cause side effects. One type of drug many heart patients take is beta blockers. These drugs, part of the sympatholytic drug family, slow both resting and exercise heartbeat and weaken the heart's muscle contraction, thus lowering cardiac output (the amount of blood pumped by the heart in a given period of time). If you're on beta blockers, you may tire more quickly and find that overall they lower your maximum exercise level. If you are taking beta blockers, your heart rate will not be an accurate measure of your exertion, and you should use the RPE scale to monitor your exercise level. Beta blockers (as well as diuretics) have been associated with a decrease in HDL cholesterol levels, so a diet low in saturated fat and cholesterol should accompany the ingestion of beta blockers.

Another drug often prescribed to heart patients is calcium-channel blockers. These widen arteries throughout the body and help the heart pump more efficiently. You may experience leg swelling when taking this drug, which can make walking somewhat difficult, but walking will help reduce the swelling and eventually decrease the discomfort of this side effect.

For the first 6 months after the heart attack, you will be concentrating on regaining stamina and endurance. Once you have built up your walking speed and time (perhaps to levels higher than your pre-heart attack or surgery condition) and you feel better, you may might be tempted to slide a bit in your workout or diet. Don't! Your risk of having a second heart attack will be vastly decreased if you keep exercising, lose weight, stay off cigarettes, and avoid stress. Walking every day for at least 3 miles will help you reach these goals.

If you are overweight, you will be advised to lose the extra pounds. Don't try to take off too much weight at once. One or 2 pounds a week should be your target. If you walk 3.5 miles per hour 6 days a week plus reduce your caloric intake by 400 calories a day, you can loose 30 pounds in 6 months. If being overweight is a major risk factor for you, you should walk longer (an hour or more) at a slower pace, as this will help you shed more pounds.

It is especially important to control your reaction to stress after you've suffered a heart attack. As part of the recovery process, keep a stress journal of what makes you angry. This will help you see how much of your energy is spent being angry. If you are standing in a long line at the bank, do you get angry at those in front of you for not having their deposit slips ready? At a traffic light, do you honk your horn if the car ahead of you doesn't pull out fast enough when the light turns green? If you react in these ways to such situations, you are unnecessarily hostile. At first you will believe your anger is justified, but after you begin analyzing your reactions, you will realize that your anger is often irrational. After several months of modifying your hostility (see Book 5: Walktherapy for details), your stress level should be reduced.

Cardiowalking Caveats

These are certain exercise practices that are especially important for heart patients:

1. Do not take a vigorous walk outside if the temperature is below 32° F or above 80° F (especially if the humidity is high). Extreme temperatures place too much stress on the heart, and cold air especially can harm the arteries. In the warmer months, walking in the morning or evening, when it's cooler, is better for you. In cold weather, walk when the sun is highest, and wear a scarf over your mouth and nose to help warm the air you breathe. Many YMCAs and YWCAs have indoor tracks you can walk on in inclement or severe weather, and many indoor malls open their halls to walkers before the shopping day begins. If you enjoy exercising in the privacy of your own home, invest in a treadmill or march or walk in place. If you do walk outside, choose a pleasant setting

for your walks away from heavy automobile traffic where air and noise pollution is high.

2. Wait 2 hours after eating a full meal before you exercise. Otherwise you may get cramps or be uncomfortable.

3. Wear comfortable, loose clothes that don't bind your movements and comfortable, soft-soled shoes (walking or running shoes are best).

4. Do not drink alcohol or smoke cigarettes immediately before or after exercise, since these reduce blood flow.

5. Avoid taking hot showers or using a steam room both before and immediately after exercise, since these cause blood to flow to your skin and away from your muscles and heart.

6. Do not drink coffee or tea at least 2 hours before exercise (the caffeine raises your heart rate).

The Stroke

A *stroke* is a loss of blood supply to the brain caused by either atherosclerosis (about 80 percent of all cases) or a ruptured blood vessel (about 20 percent). Cardiac patients are at high risk for strokes because the risk factors for the two are the same. Patients who have a heart attack can later have a stroke because blood clots that developed in the heart immediately after an attack can detach and travel to the brain.

The symptoms of a transient ischemic attack (TIA), the precursor of a stroke, include numbness or temporary weakness on one side of your body, temporary blindness (as if a shade were being lowered over your eyes), severe headaches, and nausea. These symptoms may come and go for several weeks before a full-fledged stroke hits. As with heart attack patients, it is better to go to the hospital and find out it's a false alarm than die or be severely debilitated because you did not seek help immediately.

Depending on the severity of the brain damage, the result of a stroke can be permanent or temporary. It can include paralysis of one side of the body, loss of speech, blindness, and memory loss. Two thirds of all stroke survivors are handicapped in one or more of these ways.

Walking Regimen for Stroke Patients

The rehabilitation from a stroke is arduous, taking several years to complete if the stroke is severe and paralysis is involved. The first steps of rehabilitation from a stroke are similar to those outlined in Book 2: Walking for Arthritis, Back and Joints. Passive range-of-motion exercises (when a physical therapist moves a patient's limbs through their range of motion) are begun as soon as the patient stabilizes. Slowly, a patient will begin to regain movement in both his paralyzed side and his undamaged side.

Patients are often taught to crawl, which helps rebuild lost coordination, before they begin walking. After they have regained some coordination, they may start to walk in water (like Arthur, the stroke victim discussed in Book 2) if they have difficulty maintaining balance on land. In the water, they can begin to relearn walking techniques, and water walking will also help them control the muscle spasms that often occur in the legs after a stroke.

If the stroke is not severe and the patient has the necessary balance and coordination to walk, he will begin training in the same way as a cardiac patient, taking a few steps around the hospital room and then later down the hall. However, a stroke patient often uses a walker or four-legged cane and a brace or other orthotic device to help support the weakened leg (most of the time there is some initial paralysis on one side).

After discharge from the hospital, therapy will continue, building in a slower but similar fashion to the heart patient's program. The patient will probably have to stay at each level for 3 weeks to a month (instead of 1 week) before increasing his walking time and speed. After several months, he will use a regular cane and even walk up stairs; eventually, the patient may no longer need to use any walking aids.

Stroke victims are also asked to modify their lifestyle and diet in the same way that heart attack victims must. Robert Littkey is an amazing example of how walking and lifestyle changes helped conquer the disabilities of both heart disease and a stroke. Robert's story is especially inspiring because he lost many mental as well as physical abilities and yet today he has regained 90 to 95 percent of his normal function. His only therapy is walking 2 to 3 miles a day during the week and 6 to 8 miles on weekends and taking a child's aspirin three times a week.

Robert was in his midforties when he had a heart attack and underwent triple bypass surgery. He had no family history of heart disease, but he was a lifelong smoker with a cholesterol level of 300 and was 60 pounds overweight. He also had a stressful job. He changed his ways: began walking, lost weight, and felt great. Unfortunately, his problems were not over.

Four and a half years later (October 1984) he had a stroke completely unrelated to his former lifestyle or high blood pressure. Doctors later determined that he had a slight congenital defect in the blood vessels of his brain that was bound to rupture one day—as his frequent headaches were trying to warn him. He'd been an accident waiting to happen.

On the night Robert suffered the stroke, doctors told his wife and kids, "There's no question, he's going to be dead within minutes. But we have to try. . . ." Neurosurgeons performed a successful craniotomy, an operation in which the skull is opened to repair ruptured blood vessels and stop bleeding into the brain. The next night, another small blood vessel burst. Again, surgeons performed a craniotomy and saved him.

A 12-day coma followed. When Robert came out of it, he was half paralyzed and half blind. Damage to his brain left him mentally disoriented. Over the next 40 days, Robert embarked on physical therapy to restore the use of his limbs and speech. He was also retrained in word and number comprehension. Like many stroke patients, Robert developed, and still has, aphasia, a memory problem.

Robert's physical therapy included endless walking up and down the halls and climbing up and down the stairs, aided and then unaided as he regained total use of his arms, hands, and legs. Without a doubt, the overall health and strength Robert had developed before the stroke helped him to rebound. After 60 days in hospital, Robert came home. He began walking outside for 10 or 15 minutes with his wife, and he slowly built up to his present walking level.

Today Robert's speech is flawless and his mind is acute. Most stroke victims, he says, feel tired all the time, but Robert feels so vital he pops out of bed at 5 A.M. He maintains the healthy lifestyle he developed after his heart attack, and he still aims to become stronger. He boasts that doctors assess his physical condition as that of a man of 40 (he's 54).

Robert maintains that besides giving him a feeling of victory over his stroke, walking also increased circulation, which stimulated his brain and helped him recover both physically and mentally. The stronger his body grew, the sharper his mind became.

Robert regularly visits stroke victims in the hospital to give them advice and pep talks. His favorite words of wisdom: "Get up and walk. I don't care where you are, you can walk." He proclaims, "I'll never stop!"

WALKSHAPING AND WEIGHT CONTROL

Lose Weight and Keep It Off

CONTRIBUTORS

Nikola Boskovski, M.D.

Dr. Boskovski is an assistant professor of anesthesiology at the University of Nebraska in Omaha. He received his M.D. and Ph.D. degrees in his native country of Yugoslavia, the former at the University of Skopje, and the latter, in the subject of anesthesiology, at the University of Belgrade. Dr. Boskovski walks 10 miles per week and lives in Omaha.

Elizabeth Boyce, R.N.

Ms. Boyce is a registered nurse with a diploma from St. Vincent's Hospital School of Nursing. She walks 10 to 15 miles a week and lives in Brooklyn, New York.

Edmund R. Burke, Ph.D.

Dr. Burke is a highly prolific writer and consultant to the fitness industry. His areas of research interest include exercise physiology, cycling safety, injury surveillance systems and helmet standards, cycling physiology, biomechanics, and aerodynamics. Dr. Burke received his doctorate in 1979 from the Ohio State University in Columbus in the area of exercise physiology. A 30-mile-a-week walker, he lives in Colorado Springs, Colorado.

Kathryn Cox, M.D.

Dr. Cox is a gynecologist with a private practice in New York City. A graduate of the University of Michigan Medical School, she walks regularly and lives in New York City.

Charles Eichenberg, Ph.D.

Dr. Eichenberg is the founder of the NewStart Health Center and the NewStart Walking Club in St. Petersburg, Florida. He is a pioneer in introducing walking as part of weight loss and maintenance programs—approximately 70 percent of his practice involves the treatment of obesity—and as a way to deal with such problems as premenstrual syndrome. Dr. Eichenberg is a graduate of Weidener University in Chester, Pennsylvania, and the International University of Nutrition in Concord, California. Dr. Eichenberg is a 36-mile-a-week walker and lives in St. Petersburg.

Peter R. Francis, Ph.D.

Dr. Francis is an associate professor of physical education and adjunct professor of mechanical engineering at San Diego State University. A biomechanics consultant to the U.S. Olympics Committee, Dr. Francis is also on the board of directors of both the International Society of Biomechanics and Sport and the International Dance and Exercise Association (IDEA). He and his wife, Lorna Francis, 1989 recipients of IDEA's Lifetime Achievement Award, lecture worldwide and are the authors of the book, *If It Hurts, Don't Do It*. Dr. Francis received the Ph.D. degree in biomechanics from the University of Oregon in Eugene. He walks 10 to 15 miles a week and lives in San Diego.´

Steven B. Heymsfeld, M.D.

Dr. Heymsfeld is associate professor of internal medicine at Columbia University in New York and director of the Weight Control Unit at St. Luke's Roosevelt Hospital, also in New York City. He received the M.D. degree from Mt. Sinai School of Medicine in New York. Dr. Heymsfeld walks 26 miles a week and lives in New York City.

Frances McBrien, B.S.

Ms. McBrien is a fitness instructor at the Downtown Athletic Club in New York City, and she holds a bachelor's degree in physical education with a concentration in corporate fitness from the University of Tampa in Florida. She lives in Staten Island.

David Roadruck, Ph.D.

Dr. Roadruck is a doctor of health science at Kaiser Permamente in Fontana, California, a branch of the largest HMO in the country, which serves over 34,000 clients every year. Dr. Roadruck instructs all his overweight patients to walk, and he believes that walking is the only way to lose weight permanently. He walks 15 miles a week and lives in Loma Linda, California.

David Toth, M.D.

Dr. Toth practices preventive medicine in San Antonio, Texas. He is one of the founding members and current secretary of the 500,000 member American Volkssport Association, America's largest walking club. Dr. Toth has also completed over 10,000 miles of Volkswalks to date. He brought Volkssporting to America from Germany, where he was stationed with the Armed Forces. He lives in San Antonio.

1. Shaping Your Body

As we grow older, we all begrudge the growth of our girth and gravity's effect on our once firm flesh. We all want to tone up our bodies, to regain our youthful shapes. Yet this goal eludes us. Four of five Americans are overweight, and 34 million are obese (have 20 percent more fat than they should). The number of overweight people has not declined because the success rate for permanent weight control is dismally low. Weight reduction works, but keeping it off remains a constant struggle. The problem is that most of us simply cut calories when we want to lose weight. This does not work over the long run because after we lose the weight, we go back to our old eating habits. What *does* work, however, is increasing the number of calories burned each day over the number taken in; this has been proven both scientifically and anecdotally as the only way to successful long-term weight loss. If you want to lose weight and keep it off, begin an exercise program or increase your current exercise level. Walking has the highest success rate of all exercises prescribed for weight control. It not only promotes weight loss, but with the help of hand weights and special walking techniques, it will help you tone and strengthen your muscles as well.

Being overweight or, more specifically, having too much body fat is life-threatening. Obesity is the disease of diseases, because too much body fat is an important risk factor for such life-threatening ailments as diabetes and heart disease. In fact, virtually every medical problem you'll read about in *Walking Medicine* is complicated by an excess of body fat. Too much fat surrounding the internal organs places undue stress on heart, lungs, and blood vessels, which must then strain to perform their regular functions. Joints in the back, legs, and feet are damaged by carrying around a load they were not designed to bear. The high-fat, high-cholesterol, and low-fiber diets most overweight people eat have been associated with major illnesses like cancer, heart attacks, and strokes. And the damage is not only physical. For many, self-esteem and confidence drop as weight increases.

Walking counteracts every one of the dangers of being overweight. As a moderate aerobic exercise, walking is superior to more intense exercises like running, jogging, and aerobic dancing because it burns more body fat than these more strenuous activities, yet walking still improves the capacity of the heart, lungs, and blood vessels so they work together more efficiently. Because walking is a low-impact exercise, it doesn't cause further strain on the joints the way running and aerobics do. Yet walking does build muscles, which in turn takes further stress off the joints. Walking, like other aerobic exercises, reduces cholesterol levels and improves the body's use of blood sugar. Emotionally, walking raises self-esteem and increases overall energy level.

Most important, walking can save your life. Many of the walkers interviewed for *Walking Medicine* would not be around today had they not lost vast quantities of weight through walking. Walter Stein is one example. He was 100 pounds overweight and suffered from uncontrolled diabetes. He ate all the wrong foods and never exercised. At age 46, he went into a diabetic coma and was told by his doctor that he wouldn't live to his fiftieth birthday.

"I couldn't do a thing about my eating habits. I was so depressed and sick that it was just a matter of time until it was over," says Walter. His doctor had always advised Walter to walk, so after seeing an advertisement for a 1-mile fun walk, Walter decided to enter. He finished the walk, and the first thing he noticed was that he wasn't hungry. That was impetus enough to begin walking every day. He later tried running, but it was too hard on his legs. With his energy higher and his appetite under control, Walter was able to change his diet to one low in fat and high in complex carbohydrates, and although he didn't count calories, he was losing weight quickly.

Within a year, Walter was down to 190 pounds from 290. He has taken up racewalking and is now ranked third in his age group in New Jersey. His diabetes is under control. "I'm not looking back," says Walter. "I've won my race: The race is to live."

Our walkshaping program can help you make permanent changes in how you exercise and the way you eat. Book 4: Walkshaping and Weight Control combines all the latest research on weight control and exercise to provide you with a moderate plan that works and that you can live with. Recent studies have shown that crash diets don't work; that eating fat causes fat; that the most effective exercise programs burn fat, not carbo-hydrates or protein; and that increased activity is the key to losing weight and keeping it off. So in this book you'll find walking programs that get you active again and that are designed to burn fat. You'll even find special applications, such as stair climbing, walking in place, and walking with weights, that will not only burn more calories, but make you trimmer. There's also a walker's diet plan that is nutritious and healthy and teaches you to monitor your fat intake and change bad eating habits. This is not a 2-week fad diet, but a long-term approach to weight control and good health.

Don't expect the quick-fix cures fed to you by a great many diet books, however. What we suggest is not magic, not overnight, and not without effort. You will have to count calories, and you will need some discipline. We aren't going to tell you that losing weight will be easy, because it won't be, especially at the beginning. But once you get into a routine, being fit and staying active *can* become second nature because you *will* feel and look better. The ultimate motivation is positive results, which is exactly what walkshaping produces.

How to Use This Book

In this first chapter you'll learn why walking is central to controlling your weight and why increasing the amount you walk each day is more influ-ential in losing weight than cutting calories. You'll also learn the hard facts about weight gain and what the other diet books are afraid to tell you about the weight-loss struggle.

In Chapter 2, Your Ideal Weight, you'll learn how to evaluate your body type and calculate your percentage of body fat, and from these data, you will pick a weight-loss goal that's reasonable and maintainable.

In Chapter 3, Walking Off the Pounds, you'll learn the five-step method of walking to melt your excess fat and maintain your new physique.

Chapter 4, Powerstepping and Stroking, presents four super calorie-burning and body-toning activities—run to walk (fast-paced walking), high stepping (walking in place), heavy stepping (walking with weights), and stepping up (stair climbing)—that will burn calories even faster than the programs in Chapter 3.

Chapter 5, The Walkshaping Diet Program, complements the walking programs in previous chapters with a healthful low-fat diet developed especially for this book. You'll find a minimum-calorie plan for impatient dieters and a meal plan for those who want to lose weight more slowly and with less effort. Both are nutritious and balanced, and you'll lose fat, not muscle or water.

If you are pregnant, you already know that although doctors tell you to walk, very few of them can provide a specific walking routine for you. Chapter 6, The Pregnant Woman's Walking Guide, does.

The Walking Difference

Cutting calories alone doesn't work. Only 3 percent of all dieters are able to stick with a diet for more than 1 year. This fact speaks volumes about the claims of best-selling diet books that *"You'll never have to diet again"* or *"Throw away your scale forever."* You probably don't believe such claims, and you're right because behind the hype, most of these books prescribe the same general approach: a low-fat, low-calorie diet and aerobic exercise three to four times a week for 20 or 30 minutes. This prescription, however, is based on three faulty assumptions.

The first faulty assumption is that living with a calorie deficit and changing your eating habits are easy to do; the second is that a minimum aerobic exercise level of 20 minutes three times a week is enough to get you down to your optimum weight; and the third is that the average person can and will stick with eating a low-calorie diet and exercising regularly. The perennial success of diet and exercise books indicates that although everyone wants to lose weight, there has yet to be a prescription that works. What makes Walkshaping and Weight Control different?

The fact that walkshaping is a realistic program. Unlike most other diet books, we admit that weight control is not easy and that weight gain is a typical part of aging, so you may never get to your desired "ideal weight." After age 25, your metabolism (the rate at which your body burns calories) begins to slow down. Your weight is going to go up a notch or two every year, even if you eat the same amount of food. You also become less active as you age. There is no longer the pickup basketball game or gym or dance class you joined in college or high school. Family and career responsibilities leave less and less time for exercise. We also depend more on modern conveniences as we get older, opting to drive to the store rather than walk or to ride the elevator or escalator rather than use the stairs. Over several years you can easily gain 10 to 60 pounds.

This minibook shows the way to a fitter, firmer, less fatty body and a healthier lifestyle, but it is realistic about the dedication it will take to lose pounds. The only way to take off weight and keep it off is to raise your overall activity level and begin an exercisewalking program of more than 12 miles a week. In some cases, you may have to walk from 18 to 21 miles a week.

This is so because over time, as you eat approximately the same amount every day and stay at the same activity level, your body adapts to a certain weight, known as your *set point*. This set point is your body's survival mechanism. During a time of decreased food intake, such as a famine or a war, people's metabolism slows down, conserving fuel and fighting against starvation. Even if your current weight is unnaturally high for you, your body will still fight to keep your weight stable. If you suddenly drop your caloric intake far below your normal level, your body will go into starvation mode and you'll end up losing little weight and feeling sluggish as well. This is why cutting calories alone, without the help of exercise, is an ineffective way to lose weight. (And if you suddenly increase your calorie intake, you will probably end up gaining more weight than you lost because your metabolism won't have had a chance to speed up again.)

Walking can help lower your set point and get you down to a lower weight. The secret is that although a reduction in food slows down the metabolism, an increase in fuel use through exercise speeds it up. Walking has a reported success rate of 20 to 30 percent, and it stands on its own two feet (so to speak) because it is the easiest exercise to adapt to your lifestyle and the easiest exercise to stick with month after month.

Walking burns between 65 and 165 calories per mile (depending on your weight and walking speed), with an average of 100 calories per mile. This may not seem like much, but the story doesn't end there. Here's a summary of walking's additional power in the weight-control battle:

1. A walk before a meal suppresses your appetite, so you feel like eating less.

2. Walking keeps your energy high. Diets that just have you cut calories leave you dragging.

3. Walking promotes loss of fat without loss of lean body mass (muscle). You'll lose fat if you walk and diet, but if you just diet, you'll lose muscle, too.

4. Walking builds muscle. This will also increase your basal metabolic rate because muscles burn more calories than fat.

5. Your exercise time takes you away from the kitchen and gives you something to do instead of eating.

6. Walking prevents water retention, which adds weight and makes you feel fat.

7. Walking is a simple and natural exercise that is not embarrassing for overweight people. You need no special equipment nor special clothes.

2. *Your Ideal Weight*

What is your ideal weight? You may have a number in mind, perhaps one you've gotten from a height and weight chart (the most common of which is from the Metropolitan Life Insurance Company). But there is no one average body type and no one average body weight. Every woman who is 5 feet 4 inches tall should not necessarily weigh the same, for example.

This is so because body weight is not just a function of height but is determined by age, bone size and density, muscle mass, and fat, more specifically storage fat (there is fat around the vital organs and in the bone marrow, but normally this accounts for only about 3 percent of total body weight in men and 12 percent in women—a difference related to a woman's childbearing functions), and how fast our bodies burn calories (called the *resting* or *basal metabolic rate*, or *BMR*). We all have different metabolisms, bone densities, and muscle mass, and so the ideal weight for one person could be too low or too high for another.

Here, the term *ideal weight* refers to a healthy weight for *your* age and body type. You might think your ideal weight to be that of your early twenties, a period during which most people are at their lowest adult weight. New research suggests, however, that it may not be healthy (or, at the very least, necessary) to stay at your youthful weight. Some researchers, most notably Dr. Reubin Andres of the Gerontology Research Center in Baltimore, Maryland, have found that in terms of mortality rates (assuming that at age 25 you were of average weight), it is not unhealthy to gain some weight as you age, roughly 10 pounds a decade. In fact, Dr. Andres found that in terms of higher mortality rates, both those people who were extremely underweight and those who were drastically over-weight were at risk. In essence, this means that your mother was wrong when she said, "You can never be too thin or too rich" (half wrong anyway).

Dr. Andres also feels that the Metropolitan Life tables are inaccurate because they don't distinguish between different age groups. He has found that the weights in the table are too low for people over age 45 and too high for people under age 40 (it is also interesting to note that Dr. Andres has factored out gender from the traditional height and weight charts because he found that it made little difference).

"Ideal" Body Weight (in Pounds)

HEIGHT	AGE 25 S→M→L*			AGE 35 S→M→L			AGE 45 S→M→L			AGE 55 S→M→L			AGE 65 S→M→L		
4'10"	84	98	111	92	106	119	99	113	127	107	121	135	115	129	142
4'11"	87	101	115	95	109	123	103	117	131	111	125	139	119	133	147
5'0"	90	105	119	98	113	127	106	121	135	114	129	143	123	138	152
5'1"	93	108	123	101	116	131	110	125	140	118	133	148	127	142	157
5'2"	96	112	127	105	121	136	113	129	144	122	138	153	131	147	163
5'3"	99	113	131	108	124	140	117	133	149	126	142	158	135	152	168
5'4"	102	119	135	112	129	145	121	138	154	130	147	163	140	157	173
5'5"	106	123	140	115	132	149	125	142	159	134	151	168	144	162	179
5'6"	109	127	144	119	136	154	129	147	164	138	156	174	148	166	184
5'7"	112	130	148	122	141	159	133	151	169	143	161	179	153	172	190
5'8"	116	135	153	126	145	163	137	156	174	147	166	184	158	177	196
5'9"	119	138	157	130	149	168	141	160	179	151	171	190	162	182	201
5'10"	122	142	162	134	154	173	145	165	184	156	176	195	167	187	207
5'11"	126	147	167	137	156	178	149	170	190	160	181	201	172	193	213
6'0"	129	150	171	141	162	183	153	174	195	165	186	207	177	198	219
6'1"	133	155	176	145	167	188	157	179	200	169	191	213	182	204	225
6'2"	137	159	181	149	172	194	162	184	206	174	197	219	187	210	232
6'3"	141	164	186	153	176	199	166	189	212	179	202	225	192	215	238
6'4"	144	168	191	157	181	205	171	196	218	184	208	231	197	221	244

*S = Small frame, M = Medium frame, and L = Large frame. The weights corresponding to each age and height represent a range. Smaller frames will tend to fall toward the lower end of the range; medium frames in the middle, and large frames toward the high end of the range.

To Determine Your Build

The quick way to determine your build is by placing your index finger and thumb of one hand around the wrist of the other. If your fingers don't meet, you have a large frame; if your fingers touch or overlap slightly, you have a medium frame, and if they overlap past the nail, you have a small frame.

The chart on page 211 gives you a rough estimate of whether you are at a healthy weight, but whether you are truly overweight depends on your percentage of body fat. For example, a football player who is supposed to weigh 180 pounds for his height may weigh 210 pounds, yet he is not overweight, because the 30 additional pounds is made up of muscle, not fat. Even though his weight might be above the average, his percentage of body fat is probably very much below average. Recent studies have found that even more significant in terms of health threats is the location of your fat. As we age, fat accumulates over different areas of the body. In men, fat tends to gather at the shoulders, the waist, and the abdomen. Too much fat in the upper body is unhealthy. It is metabolized more quickly into the bloodstream than fat elsewhere and is more likely to clog arteries. Upper body fat increases your risk for heart disease, stroke, and diabetes. Women tend to acquire fat at the breasts, hips, and thighs, which is fairly benign from a health standpoint (although you may not like the way it looks). How much fat you accumulate and where you accumulate it also depend on your genetic makeup.

Researchers have found the ratio between your abdomen and buttocks measurements (in lay terms, your "belly-to-butt ratio") is a good indication of your risk of developing diabetes and cardiovascular disease.

Your Waist-to-Hip Ratio

Measure your buttocks at the widest part with a tape measure. The tape should be taut but should not indent the flesh.

Hip measurement: _____

Now measure your waist at the slimmest point. Again, the tape should be taut but should not indent the flesh.

Waist measurement: _____

Now divide your waist measurement by your hip measurement for your ratio.

Waist/hip ratio: _____

Now compare your measurement to the following chart for your age group to see if you are at risk.

Waist-to-Hip Ratios and Risk of Disease

	AGE	LOW RISK	MODERATE RISK	HIGH RISK	VERY HIGH RISK
Women	20–29	0.6–0.72	0.72–0.78	0.78–0.83	0.83 +
Men	20–29	0.6–0.83	0.83–0.88	0.88–0.95	0.95 +
Women	30–39	0.6–0.73	0.73–0.79	0.79–0.85	0.85 +
Men	30–39	0.6–0.84	0.84–0.92	0.92–0.97	0.97 +
Women	40–49	0.6–0.74	0.74–0.8	0.8–0.88	0.88 +
Men	40–49	0.6–0.88	0.88–0.95	0.95–1.1	1.1 +
Women	50–59	0.6–0.75	0.75–0.83	0.83–0.89	0.89 +
Men	50–59	0.6–0.9	0.9 –0.96	0.96–1.2	1.2 +
Women	60–69	0.6–0.78	0.78–0.85	0.85–0.92	0.92 +
Men	60–69	0.6–0.91	0.91–0.98	0.98–1.3	1.3 +

If your waist-to-hip ratio is above the moderate risk zone, you should lose weight. Go back to the height/weight chart on page 211 to calculate how many pounds you need to lose to fall within the safe level for your age, height, and body type. The ranges on charts such as this are rather large. Be realistic in setting your weight goals.

Weight loss goal: _____

Born to Be Fat?

If you are unhappy with your weight, perhaps you can blame it on your parents. If both your parents were overweight, you are more susceptible to being overweight because of inherited physiological differences that make you burn calories more slowly than the average person.

Everyone's basal metabolic rate is not the 50 calories per hour quoted in most diet books, but rather ranges 10 to 15 percent above or below that number. Thus, even among nonobese adults, some people's metabolisms are slower naturally and others are faster. You can determine your metabolic rate by looking at your parents and your own eating habits. If one or both of your parents are overweight and you have always been heavy but don't overeat, then you probably have a slower than normal metabolism. If you've always been able to eat anything in sight without gaining a pound, you have a fast metabolism.

Given that you can't change your metabolic speed, be reasonable about how much you can change the way you look. You must be prepared for the fact that you may have to work harder than other people to lose weight. Don't choose Jane Fonda or Sylvester Stallone as your model unless you are naturally trim and muscular or want to work out 4 to 12 hours a day —as they do. If you plan on eating a normal diet, don't decide that the body you should have is that of a fashion model who only eats lettuce three times a day. Environmental factors may also have increased your likelihood of being overweight. Luckily, these can be changed. If your parents gave you food as a reward, made you eat when you weren't hungry, or taught you to eat when you were under stress, then you may be driven to overeating and gaining unnecessary weight as an adult. (See Chapter 5 for a food attitude quiz.) Or you may come from an ethnic background that specializes in high-fat foods.

The number of fat cells your body produces is to a large extent genetically determined, but if you overeat and the cells become full, then new ones will be created to store the excess fat. Once fat cells are created, they can never be destroyed. They crave fat, and they don't like to give up any of their cargo, which is why dieting can be so frustrating for people with a high percentage of body fat. Becoming more active and modifying your eating habits and attitudes about food will decrease your risk of becoming overweight.

How Many Calories Do You Need?

The number of calories you need to maintain your current weight is dependent on your activity level. Use the following formulas to determine how many calories you burn daily.

1. *You are very inactive.* You don't walk at all and have a very sedentary job. Multiply your weight in pounds by 13 to determine the number of calories you burn daily.

2. *You are somewhat inactive.* You sit at a desk 90 percent of the day and walk 2 miles a week at most. Multiply your weight in pounds by 14 to determine the number of calories you burn daily.

3. *Average activity level.* You walk at least 3 miles a week or your job demands a moderate amount of activity. Multiply your weight in pounds by 15 to determine the number of calories you burn daily.

4. *Above average activity level.* You walk three or more times per week or at least 10 to 12 miles or your job demands physical work 40 percent

of the day. Multiply your weight in pounds by 17 to determine the number of calories you burn daily.

5. *Very active.* You exercise intensely for several hours every day, walking 5 to 10 miles a day, or 70 percent or more of your job is made up of heavy physical labor. Multiply your weight in pounds by 21 to determine the number of calories you burn daily.

Shaping Your Body

Do you think that your buttocks, abdomen, or thighs are too fat? There is no such thing as spot reduction, but walking will firm up the muscles underneath the fat, so that you'll look trimmer even if you haven't lost much body fat. Your clothes will fit better because muscle, although heavier, takes up less space than fat.

In Chapter 4, you'll learn how to shape your body and firm up the fatty portions in your thighs, abdomen, and upper body with the stair-walking and weight-loading programs. The areas most often cited as too flabby are the buttocks, the thighs, the hips, the abdomen, the chest, and the upper arms.

Write your muscle-firming goals here. I want to firm up (list body areas):

Upper arms
Tummy/waist
Butt

You'll match these goals with a walking level in the next chapter and the muscle toning routines in Chapter 4.

Weight-Loss Controls

There are a number of controls you will be under to monitor yourself as you try to reduce your fat and your weight.

Your Scale

Don't weigh yourself every day. Limit this ritual to once a week, since you will only be losing between 1 and 3 pounds a week and won't see progress on a daily basis. If you are losing weight at less than 1 pound a week, weigh yourself every 2 weeks. A final caveat is that as you lose fat, you will be substituting it for muscle (especially if you are using weights when you walk), and muscle weighs more than fat. This is why your scale may not show a dramatic weight loss, even though your clothes are looser and you look trimmer. If you are exercising but not dieting, be prepared for a weight gain during the first few weeks. This weight gain is due to an increase in body fluids brought on by exercise. After the initial weeks, your weight will begin to drop.

Calorie Counting

The calories you ingest must be equal to or less than the calories you expend if you are to lose weight, so you do need to count calories or, if you are following the meal plans in this book, measure serving sizes.

Fat Counting

The conventional wisdom among doctors is now that it is fat, not sugar, that causes fat and that a calorie of sugar is *not* equal to a calorie of fat. This is so because carbohydrates and sugar must be converted into fat and the conversion burns calories. Fats are stored immediately as fat. Keeping track of the amount of fat you eat is imperative, at least until you learn how much of what foods you can eat. Fat should represent no more than 30 percent of your total calorie intake, meaning women should limit themselves to 20 to 40 grams and men, under 80 grams. For purposes of calculations, each gram of fat equals 9 calories.

Mileage Counting

Some diet books de-emphasize the amount of exercise necessary to lose weight, using coy phrases like "Just minutes a day." The fact is that you will have to walk at least 12 miles a week to lose fat, and your weekly mileage will probably be closer to 20 miles in order for you to reach your weight-loss goals. In the next chapter you'll find specific programs to follow.

There are some areas in our program you will not have to control. For one, you don't have to cut out any foods. Just eat the caloric ones in moderation. The second is that a binge once in awhile is expected, whether because you go out to your favorite restaurant or someone gives you a chocolate cake for your birthday. If you've found that you've eaten more than you should, just walk a little more that day. If this routine really is going to be for the rest of your life, realism, not masochism, is the best approach.

Joyce Dearing, a walker from the Red Cross Walking Club in Atlanta, Georgia, has used walking to help her eat in moderation. She started walking 9 months ago after she retired. She found that by walking 3 miles a day five times a week she can eat whatever she wants and not gain weight. She doesn't have to give up her dessert or that occasional glass of wine. She can still "live," as she says, and stay at a reasonable weight.

12 mi/wk = 2 miles × 6 days
2.5 × 5 days   or

3. Walking Off the Pounds

Once you have set your weight-loss goals, you can begin the five-step walkshaping program. *Step 1* is to start a walking program. Don't worry about cutting calories yet. If you only have 5 or 6 pounds to lose, you may find that a walking program by itself, without reducing your food intake, is the least painful way to take it off. Losing weight by exercise alone works, but it will take you longer to lose the weight than if you were to cut calories *and* exercisewalk. Even if you decide not to cut calories, follow the diet analysis instructions in the next chapter to ensure that your fat intake is 30 percent or less of your total calorie input and that the other portions of your diet are balanced as indicated.

Step 2 is to increase your activity level. This is "background exercise," like taking the stairs instead of the elevator, or walking to the corner for the paper rather than driving. Increase your activity level as soon as you begin a walking program. It will take some conscious effort to break such sedentary habits as calling up your coworker instead of walking over to see him or her, but if you sit down and think about all the activities you can add to your life, you'll be surprised how these little bursts of action add up to weight loss.

If after you've been walking for at least 2 weeks you do decide you want to lose weight more quickly, you're ready for *step 3*, cutting calories. In Chapter 5 you'll find a menu plan that cuts down to 1000 calories per day for women and 1200 for men and a slower loss plan that cuts 300 to 500 calories a day from your normal diet.

The most important thing to remember is that you probably gained your weight very slowly, about 1 or 2 pounds a year, which means you ate only 100 or 200 calories a day more than necessary. That's a few cookies or one or two extra tablespoons of mayonnaise. So don't expect to take it off overnight. No matter which diet plan you follow, you should not lose more than 3 pounds a week. This is healthier and promotes permanent weight loss. If you lose more than 3 pounds a week, the loss does not involve fat, but just water or, worse, muscle. (Even if you fasted, you'd only lose 7 or 8 pounds a week, so from that perspective, 3 pounds is acceptable.)

Step 4 occurs after you've mastered a level III walking program. In step 4, you can move on to the weight-loading and stair-climbing programs (see Chapter 4). Not only will you burn more calories in less time, but you will learn to shape your body to the look you want and increase the strength and stamina of your upper body. You can also use the walking in place routine for exercising indoors.

Step 5 is the maintenance program. This is the walking regimen that you'll stay with once you've lost your extra weight and the one that will ensure that you keep it off. If all the walkers we've spoken with are any indication, you'll feel so much better that you'll want to continue walking. However, you'll have to consistently monitor your walking and activity levels, as well as your caloric intake and weight. As you age, you may unconsciously decrease your activity level, and this combined with a decrease in metabolism could cause you to gain too much weight. Decide on an acceptable weight range of roughly 3 to 5 pounds above and below your weight goal. If you start moving out of the range, adjust your activities to address the gain before it gets out of hand.

To understand how our walking program is set up, you'll first need to understand why walking is one of the top calorie- and fat-burning exercises. Not all exercises, even if they burn the same number of calories, are equal fat burners. Strenuous or intense exercises (such as those that involve bursts of energy) burn more carbohydrates than fat. Moderate, constant exercises, like walking, burn more fat than carbohydrates. A more moderate fat-burning exercise will not increase your appetite afterwards as much as a carbohydrate-burning exercise will, because the latter depletes glycogen from the body and glycogen is the body's preferred fuel source. You'll feel hungry when you run low on glycogen. In any exercise, carbohydrates are burned first (for about the first 20 minutes), so that if you want to get the best results out of a fat-burning exercise such as walking, it is best to walk slower for a longer period of time rather than faster for a shorter period of time. Ultimately, the intensity of the exercise should be slightly lower than your optimum (say 55 to 70 percent of maximum heart rate as opposed to 80 percent) to be most efficient at burning fat while still giving you an aerobic workout. You must remember, however, that if you are eating more calories than you are burning, it will make no difference whether your exercise burns more fat or more carbohydrates. For example, if you are eating 2000 calories a day, and only burning 1500 of those calories, the excess fuel will be stored as fat, no matter what kind of exercise you do. In short, behind any long-term weight loss program, *energy in must be less than energy out*. Fortunately, walking helps you eat fewer calories by suppressing your appetite and keeping you away from the refrigerator.

Walkers interviewed for *Walking Medicine* reported a walking threshold of at least 12 miles a week to get positive weight-loss results. Paul Spears of Atlanta, Georgia, for example, lost 20 pounds in 4 months by walking 12 miles a week and cutting out sweets and starches from his diet. He would not have been able to lose that weight had he simply changed his diet. Most other walkers, like John Burns of San Diego, California, found that a minimum of 15 miles a week was needed. Mr. Burns also started doing errands on foot to maintain his 20-pound weight loss. Most walkers got out at least five times a week. If you're just starting out, you'll be more comfortable walking 2 miles a day 6 days a week until you build up your endurance to walk for a longer distance.

The American College of Sports Medicine suggests you burn at least 300 calories per exercise session three to five times per week to lose fat and reduce overall body weight. This is equivalent to walking 3.5 miles a day at 3.5 miles an hour (a moderate pace). The philosophy behind *Walking Medicine* is moderation, both in how much you eat and how much you walk. In fact, for the average person, that 300 calories works out to an hour of walking a day (about a level III on the chart on page 220), an optimal level and one that corresponds to the anecdotal evidence we collected from walkers who lost 20 or more pounds. Remember that as you lose weight, you will be burning fewer calories per mile (a larger body burns more fuel), so after every 10-pound weight loss, adjust your walking program (either by increasing speed, intensity, or distance).

In order to burn more calories per hour, you can decrease your walking time per mile by 5 to 15 seconds every week until you've reached your speed goal. After 4 to 12 weeks (respectively), you will have increased your speed by roughly 1 mile an hour and you will also have experienced a reduction in cardiovascular effort while walking.

The basic walking program follows. The level you begin with depends on your fitness level (which you can test following the instructions in Book 3: Cardiowalking). You might find the weight loss per week column in the following chart depressingly low. Don't fall into the trap of thinking that a third of a pound is not worth the effort of walking almost every day. Even this small amount of walking will give you more energy and suppress your appetite. For example, walking 2.5 miles an hour (which is very slow) will reduce your weight by 9 pounds over a year and improve muscle tone so that your clothes look better on you.

The following chart lists calories burned by a 140-pound person. Look at the next chart for the number of calories burned for someone of your weight.

Calories Burned by a 140-Pound Person

LEVEL	MILES WALKED PER DAY	WALKING SPEED	CALORIES BURNED (PER DAY)*	MILES WALKED PER WEEK	WEIGHT LOSS PER WEEK†	MET
I	2.0	2.0 mph	185	12	1/3 lb.	3.0
II	3.0	3.0 mph	250	18	2/5 lb.	4.0
III	3.5	3.5 mph	290	21	1/2 lb.	5.0
IV	4.5	4.5 mph	435	27	3/4 lb.	7.5
V	5.0	5.0 mph	540	30	1 lb.	8.0

*This is for a 140-pound person. To figure your weight loss per week, use the following calorie chart.

†Based on 6 days of walking each week. This is only an average and will vary depending on how close you are to your weight goal.

Calorie Burn for 1 Hour of Walking

WEIGHT (IN POUNDS)	WALKING SPEED IN MILES PER HOUR						
	2	2.5	3	3.5	4	4.5	5.0
100	130	155	180	205	235	310	385
120	160	185	215	248	280	370	460
140	185	220	250	290	325	435	540
160	210	250	285	330	375	495	615
180	240	280	325	375	420	550	690
200	265	310	360	415	470	620	770
220	290	345	395	455	515	680	845

When to Walk

If you are a social person, you might want to walk in a group. Many people have benefited from joining a walking club or finding other people to walk with as a form of motivation. Many clubs have gatherings in the morning or after work, and if you prefer to walk indoors, some have access to indoor tracks that are open all day.

You'll be more apt to stay with a walking program if it's convenient, so choose your walking time accordingly. Since walking for longer periods of time will lead to greater weight loss, try to pick a time when you can walk uninterrupted for 45 minutes to 1 hour. However, if your only chance is the 30-minute walk to work, for example, and the 30 minutes home, that, too, will certainly burn fat, just not quite as much.

Don't be worried about your appetite increasing with exercise. As long as the walking is moderate (does not raise your heart rate beyond approximately 70 percent of your target heart rate), then you will probably feel less hungry than you would if you did not exercise at all. It is only if you exert yourself beyond your normal activity level or if your activity is anaerobic that your appetite will increase with exercise.

Therefore, use the appetite-suppressing powers of walking to their greatest advantage, and if possible, walk before meals. If you are too hungry in the morning to go out for a walk without anything in your stomach, eat a piece of toast or a small bowl of cereal. This will tide you over without making you feel full or causing cramps. Staying away from fats will help. Walking in the morning will burn more fat because your glycogen sources are low. Going out for a walk after the main course can be a great help in avoiding fatty and high caloric desserts and can keep you from feeling groggy if you've eaten too much (such as after a Thanksgiving or Christmas feast). If you've eaten quite a bit, take a slow, easy walk, since too rigorous exercise will cause cramps as your arm and leg muscles battle with your digestive system for blood.

Activity Level

Researchers at a National Institutes of Health laboratory in Arizona have found that people who fidget can burn up to 800 calories a day more than those who sit still. Therefore, get up to change television channels instead of using the remote or go get a beer from the fridge rather than having your spouse bring it to you. Any movement burns calories, even gardening or housework. Add these daily activities to a basic exercisewalking program and you could double your burn rate. You may only be exercisewalking 15 to 20 miles a week but with all the additional steps added to the formal walking program, you could be burning 25 to 30 miles worth.

The Japanese follow a similar philosophy called *mampo* (which means 10,000 steps). They believe that by taking 10,000 steps every day, two thirds from daily activity (approximately 4.5 miles) and one third from walking for exercise (approximately 2.5 miles), an individual will stay healthy all his or her life. If you are interested in measuring your steps, you can buy a pedometer that records and displays the number of step you take rather than the number of miles you walk.

Here are some hints on changing simple routines in your life so that you too can achieve *mampo*.

Climb stairs (60 calories for a 3-minute climb) instead of taking the elevator or escalator.

Do errands on foot instead of in the car (about 100 calories per mile, more if you are carrying packages)

Push a power mower (210 calories per hour) rather than using a rider mower

Do chores more often. Weeding the garden burns 240 calories per hour, scrubbing floors burns 195 per hour, and ironing burns 160 per hour.

Visit your friends and office colleagues rather than calling them on the phone.

Maintenance Program

Once you've reached a weight that is right for you, you will need to keep at a level of exercise to ensure that your BMR doesn't slow down and that you can continue to eat at your usual level without gaining back the weight you have just worked so hard to lose. Choose the speed and walking time you were exercisewalking at while you were losing weight. Walk at this level at least five times a week (if you are eating the same number of calories). If you have been on a very low calorie program and plan on increasing your caloric intake, determine your caloric maintenance level by slowly increasingly calories (100 calories every 4 days). Continue to walk at the same level. Once you are no longer losing weight, then you have reached your maintenance level. Compute your calorie intake and compare it to your calorie burn based on the formulas on pages 214–215. If you are taking in more calories than you are burning, walk more until you cover the difference. If the distance you would need to walk is too much, reduce calories until you arrive at comfortable eating and walking levels.

Motivation

Jim White, a 47-year-old Californian who has weighed as much as 606 pounds and now weighs 180 pounds (and has for about a year), found some creative ways to motivate himself to walk, mostly by calling up his competitive spirit. Jim was a high school and college All-American in football and wrestling, so he never had a problem starting to exercise, even in a 606-pound body with a 66-inch waist. His problem was that he would approach exercise with such enthusiasm ("Obviously I don't know what moderation is," quips Jim) that he would burn out in 6 to 8 months, after which he would do nothing and gain back any weight he had lost.

A few years ago, at a weight of 495 pounds, Jim started a walking program. He gave himself a goal of once around the block, a distance that initially took him an hour because he had to stop every 20 yards. It now takes him about 7 minutes. Jim also decided that since burnout was such a problem, he would make walking fun. He refused to compute his target heart rate or take his pulse, and the only limit he put on himself was to try to walk 20 minutes or more each day. When he could walk a mile, he slowly upped the distance (about a tenth of a mile a week) until he could walk 3 miles a day. He figured if he could do something every day without killing himself, he might be able to stick with it.

Jim began to walk on a track and soon found that his competitive nature nudged him along. He entered a 5-kilometer walking race and found that having all his friends there to watch made him set a new personal record (approximately 11 minute-miles). He now enters one race a month.

Jim has also found that the buddy system works. He walks every day with his girlfriend, who has lost 200 pounds. Their goal is 3 miles a day, although they usually egg each other on to do 6 to 8 miles. Jim also varies his routine to prevent boredom. "I've mapped out a number of routes around my neighborhood. On the weekends my girlfriend and I go on longer walks, making a day's outing out of our walking routine."

If competition is not for you, you can join group walks, like the walk-a-thons put on by non-profit organizations, or walking events sponsored by associations like the American Volkssport Association, a national group with 641 local clubs that holds 10-kilometer walks at locations across the country.*

*To find the AVA chapter near you, contact: AVA—National Office, 1001 Pat Booker Road, Universal City, TX 78148, (512) 659–2112.

4. Powerstepping and Stroking

Powerstepping and stroking are designed for walkers who not only need to burn more calories than regular walking to fulfill their weight loss goal but who also want to build muscles and tone their entire body at the same time. The arm and leg movements in this chapter are referred to as *powersteps* and *strokes* because in the four routines described, the arm and legs move over longer distances (you raise your legs farther off the ground and move your arms more than you do in a regular exercisewalking workout). The powerstepping arm strokes are always synchronized with the powersteps (opposite arm and leg move together).

This chapter presents four routines: *run-to-walk*, which combines the safety of walking with the intensity of jogging; *high stepping*, a series of marching and walking in place exercises that can be done in small spaces (with or without hand or ankle weights); *heavy stepping and stroking*, a walking routine done with hand weights, ankle weights, and weighted backpacks; and *step-ups*, routines for stairs and inclines. All these routines burn two to six times more calories than regular walking and tone both the upper and lower body faster and more dramatically than walking on level ground without weights. Although some of these programs may appear complex at first, you'll find that the benefits of a stronger and shapelier body are worth the effort of learning them.

Which program you choose depends on which you find most enjoyable and which fits best into your daily schedule. You'll need to be in good shape to start one or more of the powerstepping programs, so make sure you can walk at Level III for at least a month before trying these programs out. *

Think of the four powerstepping routines as a new form of walking calisthenics that is safe because it uses rhythmic, continuous, and non-ballistic (no jerking, kicking, or throwing) motions that don't strain the joints when proper posture and walking techniques are used. Even if your percentage of body fat is high, toning your muscles will make you look trimmer and will increase the number of calories you burn at rest. With this program, there is no need to follow a separate weight-training workout, even for typical problem areas such as the abdominals and the lower back.

In addition, powerstepping does strengthen and tone all the major muscle groups in your body, including your shoulders and arms, your back and stomach, and your legs and buttocks. Strengthening these areas as you grow older is especially important because after age 30 adults begin to lose muscle mass. The added strength you'll build with powerstepping will help you avoid injuries from accidents or other sports.

As with your weight-loss goals, you must be realistic about how much you can tone and shape your body. We can't promise that you will be able to flatten your stomach completely or tone your thighs until they replicate those of your teenage years unless you are willing to work out 4 to 8 hours a day, and even then, genetics has some control over how trim and muscular you can become. Just remember that the walking philosophy is not to strive for *the* paradigms of the youthful fitness god and goddess, but rather to make you look as fit and trim and healthy as possible for you given the restraints of your lifestyle, age, genetic makeup, and determination.

In the powerstepping program, you can alternate your walking sessions between the basic exercisewalking program outlined in Chapter 3 and one or more of the four routines to vary your workouts or increase your calorie burn. Or, you can mix and match the programs. For example, you can add weights to the high-stepping routine or use them when climbing stairs to burn even more calories.

In Chapter 2 you identified the body areas you want to tone and shape. The following chart shows which programs shape which parts of the body. All the programs work on all parts of the body, but the first two slim down and tone and the latter two build up muscle, especially in the legs. Although all programs are effective body toners, the step-up program will give you the most dramatic results and the walk-to-run program will give you the least dramatic results.

*The routines in this chapter are a variation on the weight walk, climb walk, and dancewalk routines introduced in Gary Yanker's *Walking Workouts*. We've tried to avoid duplication of these routines by creating new steps and arm pumps (called *strokes*).

Shaping and Strengthening Techniques Where You Want Them

PROGRAM	PARTS OF BODY SHAPED
1. Walk to run 2. High stepping	Slims thighs, firms buttocks, shapes calves, strengthens shoulders and upper back, strengthens chest, strengthens lower back, flattens stomach, improves posture
3. Heavy stepping 4. Step-ups	Build up thighs, firms buttocks, shapes calves, strengthens shoulders and upper back, strengthens chest, strengthens lower back, flattens stomach, tones upper arms

For all these routines, use the breath-play technique discussed in Book 3: Cardiowalking (see page 170). Breathing properly will ensure that your walking routine remains an aerobic exercise and thus burns fat (fat cannot be burned without the presence of oxygen). You should also concentrate on holding proper posture (see page 95).

Run to Walk

This technique, which turns the adage "Walk before you run" on its head, is designed for the very fit walker who needs to increase his or her pace to get aerobic conditioning from walking or for the jogger who wants to change over to injury-free walking but still wants to reach the same intense aerobic levels of running. Run-to-walk uses jogging to ease you into the natural movements of walking at a fast pace, complete with hip extension, the heel strike, and a brisk arm stroke.

Begin by jogging. Notice that you land flat-footed when you run and that you push off for each new step with the ball of your foot. Once you're moving at a good pace, pull your toes up so that you land on your heel in a classic heel strike (see Book 2, page 98 for instructions). This "forefoot up" landing is much less damaging to the body. It is a smoother motion, analogous to the way a pilot lands an airplane, touching down on the back wheels first. Your arms should be bent at a 90-degree angle, moving straight forward and back, not across your body.

After you've mastered the first two techniques, concentrate on the hip extension you learned as part of the stride stretch (see page 99). Let the left hip rise as you take a step forward with your right leg (and vice versa). Because you are moving fast, do not use a long stride, but instead mimic the quick step of a jogger. You will tend to place one foot in front of the other rather than using the hip- to shoulder-width stance most walkers use. (If you have arthritis in your hip, don't use the hip extension.) The hip extension will tone and strengthen the buttocks, as well as the muscles on the sides of your stomach (called the *oblique muscles*) and may help reduce your "love handles."

Once you are doing all three, you are in the realm of the fast-paced walk. This is similar to racewalking, although you may bob up and down as you walk—a violation of racewalking technique.

If you lose control over the heel strike, the arm stroke, or the hip extension, break into a jog and start from the beginning. In 3 or 4 days you should have weaned yourself from jogging completely. Once you have mastered the technique, build a progression according to the guidelines set down in Chapter 3.

High Stepping

You may think of walking in place as the ultimate bore. But at times walking in place can come in handy, for instance, late at night when you want to get some exercise but don't want to go out. The nonstrenuous portions of this program can even be done next to your hospital bed as part of rehabilitation. Outdoors you may want to walk in place as part of your warm-up.

Below is a choreographed routine for you to follow. Just put on some marching or dance music and you're ready to go. We've pared this program down to ten steps that make up the core of the routine (both the warm-up and the aerobic section). The intensity of each exercise and the number of times the routine is repeated depend on your fitness level (see the chart on page 237). For some exercises, duration is measured in counts (each time your left foot hits the ground is one count). The main unit of exercise is eight counts, and you will be asked to do most exercises twice, for a total of sixteen counts. Once you've tried the routine a few times and you've gotten to know the moves, add ankle and hand weights to increase the intensity of the exercise (see the Heavy Stepping and Stroking section for more information on using weights).

The basic steps are the *quick step, walking in place,* and *marching in place.* They are combined with the arm strokes listed on page 228. The number of calories you burn will depend on how high you step and how much you pump your arms.

The *quick step* is the fastest step; the feet lift off the ground an inch or less. *Walking in place* is a fast- to normal-paced step, legs coming off the ground 1 to 6 inches. *Marching in place* is the slowest of the steps because you raise your feet highest off the ground (from 6 to 24 inches). In marching in place (or "marking time" as it is known by marching bands), the higher you raise your knees, the more calories you burn. Lift your knees to the desired height, depending on your fitness level (take the in-place walking test in Book 3, Chapter 3). Your toes should be pointed down as your feet lift off the ground, and your toes are the first part of the foot to touch the ground before you roll back to the heel.

The arm-stroking techniques in this program are an expansion of the basic arm-pumping technique you learned in Book 2 (see page 99). The basic technique, the *medium arm stroke*, is done as follows: With your fists loosely clenched and your arms at a 90-degree angle, move your arms straight forward and back (not across your chest), brushing your sides as your arms move. Your fists should reach shoulder height in the front swing, and your elbow should reach shoulder blade height in the back swing.

Low Strokes: Straight Arm Strokes and Waist-High Arm Strokes

The lowest stroke is done with the arms straight, brushing along the sides of the body. Waist-high strokes are similar to medium arm strokes, except that the fist does not move much above the waist.

High Arm Strokes: Head-Height and Overhead Arm Strokes

Again, these strokes are similar to the medium stroke, except in the front the fist comes to head height (for the head-high stroke) and over head (for the overhead stroke).

In the warm-up portion of the routine, use the straight arm or waist-high arm stroke. For the aerobic portion, pick an arm-stroke level to match your marching fitness level from the following charts, which indicate the

Choosing a Arm-Stroke Level to Match Your Marching Fitness Level

STEP LEVEL		METs
I	Quick step and walk in place (1 to 3 inches off the ground)	2
II	Low march step (3 to 6 inches off ground)	3–8
III	Medium march step (7 to 12 inches)	9–12
IV	High march step (12 to 24 inches; thigh is parallel to ground)	13–15
V	Knee to chest march step (24 or more inches)	16–20
ARM-STROKE LEVEL		METs
I	Straight arm strokes	2
II	Waist-high arm strokes	3
III	Medium arm strokes	4
IV	Head-high arm strokes	5
V	Overhead arm strokes	7

the intensity of each march level and each arm stroke (expressed in METs). As you can see, using the arm stroke and march steps together can be a powerful calorie-burning weapon. (METs are multiples of how many calories you burn at rest. For example, an exercise with a value of 2 METs means that you will burn twice the number of calories doing that exercise than you would doing nothing.)

If at any time during this routine you become dizzy or out of breath, *stop*; then walk slowly until you have recovered. Don't worry if you cannot complete the whole routine. Build up slowly over several weeks if you are out of shape.

Stretches and Warm-Ups (10 Minutes)

Stretching is an important starting point for any exercise routine. The safest way to stretch is to hold a static pose (don't bounce).

All marching steps and arm pumps should be Level I or II (your choice) unless otherwise noted.

1. *Neck.* Standing straight with proper posture, look to your right as far as you can and feel the stretch in your neck. Move your head slowly until you are looking straight ahead. Then turn to the left, trying to look over your left shoulder. Repeat four times—each time you look to the right is a count.

   Now bend your head to the right and try to touch your right ear

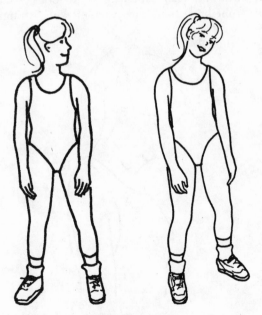

Neck Exercises

to your right shoulder. Keep your shoulders down and relaxed. Repeat on left side. Repeat four times—each time you move your head to the right is a count.

2. *Chin touch.* Looking straight ahead, tuck your chin into your chest. Repeat four times.

3. *Shoulder shrugs.* Shrug first your right shoulder, keeping your left one down, and then switch. Do this for four counts (each time your right shoulder shrugs is one count). Then shrug both shoulders together for four counts.

4. *Pelvic tilt.* With your knees slightly bent, bend forward at the waist, supporting your upper body by placing your hands on your thighs. Round the lower back by sucking in your abdominals as if you were trying to pull your belly button to your back bone. Exhale as you suck your belly in. Hold your abdominals in for four counts, then inhale and release abdominals. Repeat eight times.

5. *Quick step.* Do the quick step with chest-high arm strokes. Repeat for sixteen counts.

6. *March.* March with a low marching step and chest-high arm strokes, stepping forward two steps and then backward two steps for sixteen counts.

7. *Leg stretch.* Step forward with your right foot so that you are in a lunge (your front knee bent and your left knee straight). Your right

Chin Touch

Shoulder Shrugs

Pelvic Tilt

Leg Stretches

knee should be directly over your right ankle, and the heel of your left foot should be on the ground. Start counting to sixteen. After the first two counts, raise the heel of your back leg off the floor. After two more counts, lower the heel to the floor. Continue to raise and lower your heel every two counts. Once you've completed the first sixteen counts, start counting to sixteen again, this time raising the toes of your right foot for two counts and lowering them for two counts. Repeat this exercise with the left leg forward and your right leg back.

8. *Heel-toe rolls.* Stand on the heels of your feet and roll on the outer edge of your feet to your toes. Roll back to the starting position. Repeat this for eight counts. Try not to bend at the waist when you do this exercise. (You may find that swinging your arms straight forward and back helps you to keep your balance.)

9. *Quick step.* Do the quick step with chest-high arm strokes. Repeat for sixteen counts.

10. *March.* March with a low marching step and waist-high arm strokes, stepping forward two steps and then backward two steps for sixteen counts.

11. *Crossovers with cradle.* Stand with your legs shoulder-width apart. Lift your left leg up (lifting your hip along with the leg) and cross it over the right foot. Try to place your left foot as far away from your right foot as possible for added stretch in the hip. Then move your right foot to the left so that you are again standing with your legs shoulder-width apart. At the same time you are doing the crossover step to the left, do the cradle arm pump, which will teach you to keep your arms close to your body when you do the various arm pumps. Place your hands on your hips. Then, keeping your elbows in the

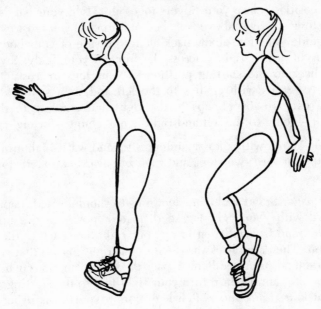

Heel-Toe Rolls

Crossover with Cradle

same position, clasp your fingers together. Hold your hands close to your stomach, right above your belly button. As you cross over to the left, guide your left elbow back along the side of your body so that your right arm is pulled across the front of your body. Swing your arms back to the starting position as your legs uncross. Take two crossover steps with cradles to the left and then switch direction, taking two crossover steps to the right and cradling to the right. Repeat—going to the left and right is one count—for eight counts.

12. *March.* March with a low marching step and waist-high arm strokes, stepping forward two steps and then backward two steps for sixteen counts.

13. *Robot walk.* Stand with your feet hip- to shoulder-width apart. Step forward with your right leg so that your foot is in the heel-strike position, and freeze. Then bring your right foot back to the starting position. Then step backwards with your right foot so that you are in the toe-off position (see Book 2, page 98, for explanations of heel strike and toe off), and again return your right foot to the starting position. Repeat four times and switch legs. Pump your arms using a waist-high arm pump.

14. *Charleston.* Start with your feet hip- to shoulder-width apart. This is similar to the robot walk. Step forward with the left leg to the heel-

Robot Walk

strike position and return to the starting position. Then step backwards with the right foot to the toe-off position. Repeat eight times, pumping your arms with a waist-high pump.

15. *Side bends*. Using a low marching step and pumping your arms at waist height, bend to your left side every time you raise your left leg. Do this for eight counts and then switch, bending to the right every time your right leg comes up (also for eight counts). Bend to each side twice.

16. *One-legged marching*. Step forward with your left leg, so that you are in a minilunge, your left knee slightly bent. This leg will stay static. Now pull your right leg forward until your right thigh is in front of your body about waist height and perpendicular to the floor. Return the right leg to its starting position and repeat eight times. Pull both arms back with each step as if you were rowing a boat. Repeat the exercise, lunging with your right leg forward. Repeat so that you have marched on each leg twice.

17. *Ankling*. Rise up on the toes of the right foot, keeping the left foot flat on the ground. Then switch, rising up on the toes of the left foot with the right foot flat on the ground. Your hips will rise slightly as

Side Bends

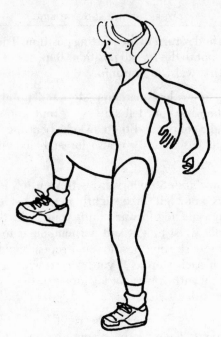

One-Legged Marching

Ankling and Pulse-Check

you do this. Repeat for sixteen counts. (You can take your pulse during this exercise. Your heart rate should be in the bottom part of your training zone—roughly 60 percent of your target heart rate. See pages 157–158 for discussion of setting your training zone.)

Aerobic Portion (10 to 50 Minutes)

Now you are ready for the aerobic portion of the exercise. Just repeat exercises 9 through 17, this time with higher arm and leg pumps (the height you choose is based on your fitness level). How many times you repeat the routine also depends on your fitness level (see chart below). Every time you come to ankling, take your pulse to ensure that you are working hard enough without overextending yourself.

There is one change in the aerobic portion of the routine. During the crossover step (exercise), circle your arms (clockwise when you step to the right and counterclockwise when you step to left) as you cross over instead of doing the cradle pump.

If you are at Level III and want to progress to Level IV, first do the routine three times with the Level IV arm strokes and marching heights. Once you have mastered the routine with the new arm strokes and steps, then increase the number of routine repetitions to four times. Follow this same logic for advancing from Level IV to Level V. You should take 2 weeks to move from one level to the next (one week to get used to the higher arm strokes and steps and another to increase the duration of the aerobic portion of the routine).

There is one change in the aerobic portion of the routine. During the crossover step (exercise), circle your arms (clockwise when you step to the right and counterclockwise when you step to left) as you cross over instead of doing the cradle pump.

If you are at Level IV or V, you can do this routine with hand and ankle weights. All the steps are the same, except for two arm-stroke modifica-

Repetitions for Aerobic Portion of Routine

YOUR FITNESS LEVEL	NUMBER OF TIMES TO REPEAT AEROBIC PORTION OF ROUTINE	APPROXIMATE DURATION OF AEROBIC PORTION (IN MINUTES)
I	1	10
II	2	20
III	3	30
IV	4	40
V	5	50

Crossover Step   *Quick Step*   *Crossover Step with*
Nautilus Pump

of your face. Return to the starting position. This move should be done
once per crossover step.)

Cool-Down (3 Minutes)

March at your current height for sixteen counts. Then slowly decrease the
height of your legs and arms, going through each level below yours (sixteen
counts of each) until you are walking in place with a straight arm pump.
If you are still breathing heavily, walk around the room for as long as it
takes you to get your heart rate under 100 beats per minute.

Heavy Stepping and Stroking

Heavy stepping and stroking, like high stepping, revolves around a series
of steps and strokes, but it provides an even greater calorie burn because
you wear weights on the hands, ankles, and torso while doing the routines.
Heavy stepping is a weight-lifting and aerobics exercise wrapped into one.
By following this program, you can tone your muscles while increasing

your aerobic capacity and burning lots of fat and calories. Weight training alone can't claim these benefits.

Anyone who has ever lifted weights knows that lifting a low weight many times (called *repetitions*) is the way to develop good muscle definition without bulk. In the heavy-stepping program, pumping your arms with anywhere from ½- to 10-pound weights attached, you might carry out more than 100 repetitions a minute, many more than you would do in a minute of weight training with machines or free weights. Thus heavy stepping will increase your stamina and tone your body better than weight lifting, and it's less boring because you are outside walking around instead of trapped inside a gym.

The most effective place to wear weights is on your extremities, especially your hands. In a study done at the Human Energy Resource Laboratory at the University of Pittsburgh, Tom Auble (who does research for Dr. Schwartz, the developer of Heavy Hands—an exercise routine using hand weights) found that walking with hand weights increased the caloric burn by 20 to 155 percent over walking without weights (this wide range was because of varying weight size and amount of arm movement. The 20 percent increase was obtained using a vertical arm stroke to shoulder height, and the 155 percent increase in caloric burn was from a vertical arm stroke to overhead—description of the vertical arm stroke is below).

According to Dr. Schwartz, walking with hand weights is effective because you use a wide variety of muscles in your arms and back to pump the weights and you move the weights over a long vertical distance against gravity, especially if you pump your arms from a dead hang to above your head. You can also carry weight in a backpack or across your body in a bandolier fashion, but 1 pound of weight in the hand is worth 3 to 5 pounds on the body in terms of caloric burn, so hand weights are more of a caloric bang per pound. If you want a more intense exercise, you might use body or ankle weights in addition to your hand weights (see chart on page 243).

Although there has been much controversy about the safety of hand weights (some studies have found that they raise blood pressure slightly), Dr. Schwartz and other researchers have done studies proving that the use of such weights is not dangerous. There are even Heavy Hands classes for heart patients at the University of Pittsburgh.

Using Ankle Weights

You can also use ankle weights while walking, although improper use could cause damage your knee or ankle joints. Some exercise physiologists believe that the extra weight on the ankle as the leg swings through the walking motions causes overextension of the leg joints, which could lead to injury. For this reason, take shorter, slower strides than you normally would. Keep your walking speed under 3.5 miles an hour for optimum control, and make a conscious effort to use your muscles to control the swing of your leg.

Try ankle weights first while practicing the high-step routine. Because you move your legs vertically when you walk in place, the weights will not put extra strain on the joints and will be effective at shaping your calves, thighs, and buttocks. Take a few high steps forward and back, and step from side to side as well. The crossover step is especially good for firming up the inner thighs. Once you feel comfortable with the ankle weights, you can start walking with them. Woman should not wear more than 3 pounds total (1.5 pounds on each ankle), and men should wear no more than 5 pounds total. Start out with ½ pound, building up over several weeks if you want to work at higher levels of weight.

How to Use Hand Weights

To get used to the weights, start with a low arm stroke (see description of the waist-high arm stroke on page 228). As you become more comfortable with the weights, you can pump your arms more vigorously using the basic arm pump you learned in Chapter 2. For a real upper body workout, try vertical arm strokes. To do these, begin with your arms hanging at your sides (palms facing your body), and lift the weight to shoulder height. This pump can also be done to head height or overhead (so your arm is extended above your head).

The first time out, try the various arm pumps standing still with the smallest weights you have. Then you can begin walking, alternating among the various arm pumps (the vertical pumps will be hard to sustain for long periods of time at first).

Trunk Weights

The easiest way to carry weight on the trunk of the body is with a backpack, a weight belt, or a fanny pack. These are all safer than a weighted vest because the former allow you to carry the extra weight on your hips (a very strong part of your body) rather than placing the burden of the weight on your shoulders or back. Anything can be used to weigh down a backpack. Plastic bags filled with sand make good weights. Maybe you already do a version of weight-loaded walking when you walk to school or the office with a pile of books or papers slung on your back.

Wear a backpack that has a belt at the waist. This allows you to pull the weight into your hips and will keep you from straining your back. When you put the pack on, adjust the shoulder straps so that the pack reaches your hips. Then fasten the belt so that it is snug but not uncomfortable. You can also weight down a fanny pack, but make sure not to wear the weighted portion at the front of your body, since this strains the back.

Waist-High Arm Stroke   *Chest-High Arm Stroke*

Head-High Arm Stroke

Special Weight-Walking Steps

All the following steps can be done with a weighted backpack or a belt (the walk and bend will be more comfortable with a belt or fanny pack). These steps will strengthen your thighs, back, and stomach muscles. You may feel self-conscious at first doing these steps in public. If this bothers you, convert these exercises into a walking-in-place routine that can be done in the privacy of your own home.

1. *Two-step.* While using a medium arm pump, take two steps with your knees bent, dipping down about 4 inches. Then follow with two normal steps. Alternate two bent, two normal. Once you get comfortable with this step, you can try it with vertical arm pumps.

2. *Side-bend walk.* Bend your torso to the right for two steps, letting your right arm hang straight down. Then bend to the left for two steps.

3. *Marching.* As with marching in place, you can march on the move, picking a leg height and arm stroke level to match your fitness level. When you lift your leg, point your toes. As your foot comes down to the ground, you will hit with the ball of your foot and roll back to your heel. Make sure your back is straight and your pelvis is tilted under as you march.

Two-Step and Side-Bend Walk

Weight Loads for Different Levels

Build up your weight loads over 6 weeks. Look at the chart for your walking level in the regular exercisewalking program. Then follow the prescribed program for 6 weeks. Don't try and do too much at once. You'll be amazed how much of a workout you get even with ½-pound weights.

Six-Week Program: Weight Loads and Fitness Levels

Week:	1	2	3	4	5	6
Speed (mph)	1.0–2.0	1.5–2.5	1.5–3.0	2.0–3.5	2.5–3.5	2.5–3.5
Distance (miles)	0.5	0.5–1.0	0.75–1.25	1.0–2.0	1.5–2.5	2.0–3.0
Level III (pounds)						
Men:						
Hand	1.0	1.0	1.0	1.0	1.0	2.0
Trunk*			5.0	5.0	5.0	6.0
Ankle			1.0	1.0	1.0	1.25
Women:						
Hand	0.5	0.5	1.0	1.0	1.0	2.0
Trunk*				5.0	5.0	5.0
Ankle			0.5	0.5	0.75	0.75
Level IV (pounds)						
Men:						
Hand	1.0	2.0	2.0	2.0	2.0	3.0
Trunk*			5.0	5.0	5.0	8.0
Ankle			1.0	1.0	1.5	2.0
Women:						
Hand	0.5	1.0	1.0	1.0	2.0	3.0
Trunk*				5.0	5.0	6.0
Ankle			0.5	0.75	1.0	1.0
Level V (pounds)						
Men:						
Hand	3.0	3.0	3.0	3.0	3.0	4.0
Trunk*			5.0	5.0	5.0	10.0
Ankle			1.0	1.5	2.0	2.5
Women:						
Hand	1.0	1.0	1.0	2.0	2.0	3.0
Trunk*			5.0	5.0	5.0	7.0
Ankle			0.5	1.0	1.5	1.75

*Weight on trunk includes hand weights.

After the first 6-week period, you can build weights up by 1 pound every 2 weeks if you want to increase intensity and upper body stamina. After a few weeks you will also find that you are walking faster and farther as you become stronger, until you are walking for 45 minutes to an hour. Women shouldn't carry more than 10 pounds in their hands and 15 pounds on their trunks. Men should not try more than 15 pounds on their hands and 25 pounds on their trunks.

You may want to give heavy stepping a try before you invest in weights. Try the steps outlined above while holding a small can of soup in each hand. If you like the results, you can buy small dumbbells of various weights, or special heavy hand weights with built-in handles.

Step-Ups

Step-ups, a routine centered around climbing stairs, is the most vigorous of the four powerstepping programs. With each step, you are moving your body forward as well as upward. Stepping up burns about 500 to 1500 calories an hour (depending on your weight), so it is a great exercise to do in conjunction with a weight-loss program. This routine also firms up thighs, stomach, and buttocks. You can make the exercise even more intense by adding hand and/or ankle weights. Do some back of leg stretches (see Book 2, pages 102–103) before you begin to prevent your legs and buttocks from being sore the next day.

This walking routine can be done either climbing multiple staircases (as in a sports stadium or an apartment or office building), with a stepping machine, on a stoop or short flight of stairs, or even stepping up and down on a step stool. If you choose the latter method, make sure you pick a sturdy stool with rubber on the bottom of the legs for traction. Place it near a counter or wall so you can brace yourself against it in case you lose your balance.

No matter what kind of stairs you are climbing, use the following technique. Take a step up the stair and land on the heel of your foot, just the way you do on when walking on level ground. This puts less strain on the ankle.

If you live or work in a high-rise building or near a stadium, then you will probably want to do a continuous climbing workout. This is quite tiring, so don't expect you will be able to walk as long as you do on flat ground (there are approximately 2600 stair steps per mile).

Use the following chart for a step-up routine for your fitness level (take the stair-climbing test in Book 3, page 163).

Try some of the following steps to add variety to your stair-climbing routine, especially if you are using a step stool or short flight of stairs.

Choosing a Step-Up Routine for Your Fitness Level

LEVEL	MILES PER HOUR	EXERCISE TIME (MINUTES)	STEPS PER WORKOUT*	METs
I	1.0	30	1300	5
II	1.5–2.5	30	1950–3250	6–8
III	2.5–3.5	45	4875–6825	9–12
IV	3.5–4.0	45	6825–7800	13–15
V	4.5	60	11,700	16

*Steps per mile equals 2600.

Step-Up Steps

1. *Traditional step-up.* Step up the left foot onto a step or low bench. Bring the right foot to meet the left so you are standing on top of the bench or step (don't push off the ground with the back leg, rather use the lead leg to pull the back leg off the ground). Step down with the right leg first. When you are back at the starting position, step up with the right leg first (keep alternating leading with the left and right legs).

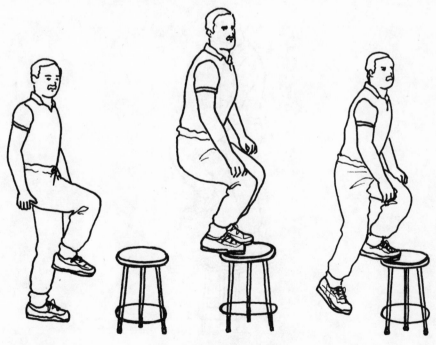

Traditional Step-Up

2. *Lift-up.* Step up with the left leg. Pull the right leg up until your knee is at least waist high. Step down and repeat ten times. Then switch legs. (You can increase the number of lift-ups you do as you get stronger.)

3. *Crossover steps.* These are similar to crossover steps on the floor, except that they are even more effective for firming the inner and outer thigh when done on stairs. Adding weights to your ankles is even better conditioning. Make sure to walk both up and down stairs, crossing both in front of and behind the lead foot.

4. *Side step-ups.* Side step-ups are similar to crossovers, except that the same foot always leads the climb (meaning that the back foot never crosses over the lead foot).

5. *Step-backs.* Climb the stairs backwards, using the stair-walking technique in reverses: land on your toes and roll back to your heel.

6. *Two-at-a-time steps.* Taking steps two at a time (or even three at a time) builds buttocks and thigh muscles even more than regular climbing.

Lift-Up

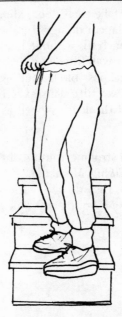

Crossover Steps

Ballet Climbing

7. *Ballet climbing.* As you take each step, extend the back leg completely, as if you were a ballet dancer doing an arabesque. Lift your leg as high as is comfortable in the back without bending forward at the waist. Hold onto the railing or wall (if you are using a step stool) for balance. Keep your back as flat as possible by pulling your stomach in (as if you were practicing the pelvic tilt). This exercise works the buttocks and muscles at the backs of the legs, as well as the abdomen. It will also increase leg flexibility.

The powerstepping and stroking routines in this chapter are the most advanced exercises in *Walking Medicine*. Even if you don't use these exercises on a regular basis, they do offer variety when you feel like trying something new, want to tone your body quickly, or want an extra challenge.

5. Walkshaping Diet Program

America has one of the highest obesity rates of any country in the world. One of the reasons is our overconsumption of fat, which has grown from roughly 30 percent of our diet in the early 1900s to over 40 percent today. Changes in food manufacturing, especially the introduction of refined sugars and processed foods, have turned us against natural alternatives. Our diets are also low in complex carbohydrates and fiber, which puts us at a greater risk for heart disease, diabetes, and perhaps even cancer.

The menu plans in this book, designed by Dr. Charles Eichenberg, director of NewStart Health Center in St. Petersburg, Florida, will provide you with a balanced diet, low in fat (less than 30 percent of your total calories) and cholesterol and high in fiber.

Most of us have also acquired bad food habits. We often eat when we aren't hungry and look to food for comfort and for the relief of boredom and stress. We need to modify our eating *behavior* as well as our diets if we are to lose weight.

Food Attitude Test

Answer the following questions for an insight into your relationship to food.

1. Do you eat when you are under stress or are bored?
2. Do you regularly indulge in a late-night snack?

3. Do you feel compelled to finish all the food on your plate, even if you are no longer hungry?

4. Do you do a lot of snacking in front of the television?

5. Do you eat as a reward or consolation prize?

6. Do you often feel uncomfortable after a meal or snack because you've eaten too much?

7. Do you tend to eat in binges?

The point of these questions is that if you answered yes to even one of them, you have an unconscious habit that drives you to eat when you aren't hungry. Cutting out these habits will take you a long way toward cutting calories.

Look at the preceding questions that you responded yes to, and find the corresponding suggestions below to help you break your habit.

1. If you tend to eat when you are under stress or bored, go for a walk (away from the fridge) instead. Walking will give you energy, relax you, and help you face whatever situation is causing you difficulties (see Book 5: Walktherapy for more details).

2. If you're a late-night snacker, go to bed earlier or take a slow walk at the time you would normally eat. If you don't want to go outside, you can walk in place. As long as the exertion is moderate, the activity will relax you and help you sleep better (too vigorous a workout before bedtime will keep you awake).

3. Finishing the food on your plate when you are no longer hungry is an easy trap to fall into, especially if as a child your mother constantly reminded you of starving children in other parts of the world. Cleaning your plate, however, will do nothing for those children or for you. Don't eat if you aren't hungry, and don't feel guilty about throwing food away. If what's left over is substantial, store it for use as part of another meal. If it's tiny, throw it out; two mouthfuls aren't worth saving, and you know it will just sit in your refrigerator rotting. If you often find you have extra food on your plate, you're giving yourself portions that are too big.

   If you do have food left on your plate, clear your place as soon as you're done eating so you don't nibble unconsciously. If you're in a restaurant, signal to the waitperson so he or she can take your plate away before you begin to finish what you don't really feel like eating.

4. Instead of snacking in front of the television, try another activity: Read the paper, do crossword puzzles, or iron clothes for the next day while you watch the tube.

5. If you've done something spectacular, don't celebrate with your favorite dessert. Buy yourself a book, go see a movie, or splurge on an article of clothing you've been wanting instead.

6. If you always feel stuffed after a meal, then you haven't learned when to stop eating. Learning to stop before we are full becomes more difficult as we age because signals that tell us when our appetite is sated slow down. Eat slowly so that your brain has time to warn you when your stomach has had enough. There are several tricks you can use, including chewing each bite ten times, waiting 10 to 20 seconds between bites, or putting your utensils down after each bite.

   Many diet books will tell you not to do other things when you eat, so that you concentrate on your food and don't continue to eat when you aren't hungry. This approach is unrealistic. Although studies have found that people who eat while watching television usually consume more calories than those who don't, it is okay to read or listen to music while you eat. Just pay enough attention to your meal so that you eat slowly, serve yourself a reasonable portion, and register when you've had enough.

   If you're snacking on a food that comes in a package, such as crackers, pretzels, or cookies, remove the appropriate serving size from the package and return it to the cupboard. Don't eat directly from the box or bag (you'll end up eating more if you do).

7. If you often eat in binges, fasting during the day and eating a huge dinner at night, you may have a compulsive attitude toward food and weight gain. It is much better for your physical and mental well-being to eat moderately throughout the day rather than starving in the morning and feeling bloated at bedtime. Get in the habit of eating at least three balanced meals throughout the day, with the only caveat being that you are hungry when you eat them.

Cravings

Cravings for salt, fat, and carbohydrates have a physiological and psychological basis. Your body is asking for a specific kind of food. Yet if you give into these cravings, you will undoubtedly be eating too much salt, fat, or carbohydrates, since the amount the body needs is present in adequate proportions in a balanced diet. Follow the advice below to help stave off the urge to eat.

Everyone experiences cravings for ice cream, chocolate, or french fries. These are fat cravings, and what degree you experience them depends on your genetic and cultural background. No matter their intensity, these yens can be controlled. The best approach is with carbohydrate preloading. Eat a starch or complex carbohydrate at the beginning of each meal. This will help to turn off your craving for fat.

Do you crave *salt?* This can be caused by sweating a lot after exercise and or by stress. Vitamin C is thought to reduce salt cravings, which lead to the retention of water and a bloated, uncomfortable feeling. Spice up your foods with lemon juice and herbs, and eat citrus fruits as part of your diet.

If you crave crackers or potato chips, your body is asking for *carbohydrates.* This is caused by low blood sugar, which is in turn brought on by not eating for several hours or, in women, by the hormonal changes that occur prior to the menstrual period. Make sure your diet consists of complex carbohydrates rather than junk food high in fat and salt.

Now that you are aware of the dieter's pitfalls, what your attitudes are toward food, and its place in your life, you are ready to change your behavior toward food and eating, what the experts call *behavior modification.* The key behind behavior modification is to keep track of the behavior you are trying to change. This is the only way you will be conscious enough of your actions to change them, and this is why you should keep a diary each day of what you ate and drank, including the amount, the time of consumption, and how you felt at the time (hungry, bored, angry, etc.).

Keep this food diary for 1 week before you go on any diet (see the diary format at the end of this chapter). Make sure it is a typical week for eating (for example, not the week you go on vacation or the week you have an unusual number of dinner appointments at restaurants). After a week, go back and analyze your eating habits. Do you eat when you are bored or under stress? Calculate your average daily calorie consumption, as well as the percentage of fat, carbohydrates, and protein, to see if you are in the proper dietary limits. For calculation purposes, 1 gram of fat is 9 calories, 1 gram of carbohydrates and protein are 4 calories each. Fat should be no more than 30 percent of your diet, carbohydrates should be at least 50 percent, and protein should be 20 percent. If you can get your fat intake down to 20 percent, you can boost carbohydrates to 60 percent of your diet, keeping protein the same.*

Menu Planning

Planning ahead is another important tool in behavior modification. It works because if you're prepared, armed with nutritious food, then you will be less likely to eat some high-fat alternative. If you know when you go to the supermarket that Monday you plan on eating fish and Tuesday you plan on eating a lean cut of beef, then those items will be in your refrigerator when you come home starving for dinner. This will avoid the "I'm too tired to shop and there's no food in the house, let's go to Burger King"

*Calorie and food composition charts are available free from the Department of Agriculture (201-783-3238).

syndrome. Also keep salad and sandwich items on hand for those nights when you don't feel like cooking (this is especially important in the summer when the heat and humidity depress your appetite).

The Walkshape Diets

Health experts say you should not reduce your calorie intake below 1000 calories for women and 1200 calories for men without medical supervision. Our minimum-calorie diets take you down to these limits. The best way to lose weight is with a small cut in calories teamed up with exercise-walking. If you don't have much weight to lose, this is a more comfortable approach, especially because you will probably feel hungry if you drastically cut your calorie consumption.

However, we include the minimum-calorie diet because the only way some people will be motivated to lose weight is if they see results quickly. Not even this diet, however, promises more than 2 to 3 pounds per week over the long run (if you are 50 pounds or more overweight, you might lose more weight in the first few weeks as a result of water loss). The only other rule if you currently consume more than 1800 calories for women or 2100 for men is not to cut down all at once to the lowest limit. Do it in stages. Cut your diet by 500 calories the first week or two; then cut another 500 calories or part thereof.

The following chart will tell you how much to cut depending on your ultimate weight-loss goal. The more weight you have to lose, the more you can cut out of your diet without being hungry.

As you can see, by cutting your diet by 200 calories a day (equal to one fruit yogurt or one and one-half 12-ounce glasses of cola), you can lose 1 pound in about 2½ weeks. By cutting 500 calories, equivalent to the preceding plus four chocolate chip cookies and a piece of bread with butter, you will lose a pound a week, or 52 pounds a year. Of course, you'll be

Matching Calorie Cuts to Weight-Loss Goals

LEVEL	CALORIES TO CUT PER DAY	DAYS NEEDED TO LOSE ONE POUND	POUND LOSS PER YEAR
I	50–200	70–18	5–20
II	200–300	18–11	20–34
III	300–500	11–7	34–50
IV	500–1000 (in two stages)	7–4	50–90
V	1000–1500 (in three stages)	4–2	90–150

combining this calorie reduction with the basic walking program in Chapter 3 or the powerstepping program in Chapter 4, so you'll lose at least twice this amount (approximately) at every level. Remember not to skimp on exercise. If you do, your metabolism will slow down and you'll lose less weight, feel miserable, and gain back more fat if you go off your diet.

Minimum-Calorie Program

At the end of this chapter you'll find a 1200-calorie diet (for men) and a 1000-calorie diet (for women). These diets have been designed using the exchange system, which is used by many diet programs with a good deal of success (see the exchange template below). With this plan, the calorie counting is already done for you—all you have to keep track of is amounts and portion sizes.

Your food choices are listed by food group; for example, breakfast is 1 bread, 1 fruit, 1 milk, and 1 fat. This means that you could eat a shredded wheat with a peach and milk or a slice of bread with butter and an apple. As long as you stay within the ranges for each day—4.5 breads, 5.5 fats (4 fats for 1000-calorie diet), 2 vegetables, 3 fruits, 2 milks (1.5 milks for 1000-calorie diet), and 4 meats, you can eat these foods in the suggested arrangement or in any other way you like. For example, you can eat two slices of toast at breakfast instead of one; you will just cut out a bread from

The Template for the Exchange System

BREAKFAST *1500*		MORNING SNACK	
1 bread *2 bread*		1 fruit *2 fruit*	
1 fat *1 fruit*		*2 veg*	
1 fruit *1 milk*			
1 milk			

LUNCH		AFTERNOON SNACK	
1.5 meat *3 meat*		0.5 bread	
1.5 bread *2 bread*		*1 milk*	
0.5 vegetable *2 fat*		*or*	
2.5 fat (1 fat for 1000- *1 fruit*		*1 bread*	
calorie diet)			
1.0 fruit			

DINNER		EVENING SNACK	
2.5 meat		1 milk (½ milk	
1.5 bread		for 1000-calorie diet)	
1.5 vegetables			
2.0 fat			

a later meal. You'll find food-substitute lists (starting on page 268) that give food amounts for 1 exchange, as well as seven suggested menu plans to get you started.

Even if you don't plan on cutting calories all the way, use this plan as a guide. Double the portions if you want a 2400-calorie diet rather than a 1200-calorie diet. Or follow the breakfast or dinner menu, but eat a larger lunch. Note that you are asked to eat five to six times during the day (three main meals and two or three snacks). Your dieting will be easier if your blood sugar level is fairly constant, so don't skip meals. Doing so will only lead to binges. Also, it is better to eat a larger breakfast or lunch than a large dinner. Studies have shown that people who eat more of their calories in the morning lose more weight than people who eat more of them at night.

Beverages

Diet Sodas and Artificial Sweeteners
Diet soda is not the dieter's savior. In fact, several studies have shown that people who consume food or drink with artificial sweeteners tend to gain more weight than those who do not. Whether the reason is psychological (I'm drinking diet soda so I can eat three pieces of pie) or physical (some researchers believe that artificial sweeteners create a craving for sweet foods), it is best to avoid or at least not depend on drinks and food made with artificial sweeteners.

Alcoholic Beverages
Since this book presents a realistic solution to weight loss, it would be silly to say, "*No alcohol allowed*," because most people don't want to cut out their occasional cocktail. Our goal is for you to change your habits so that you can permanently control your weight. Therefore, you need to learn to modify your habits so that you can still enjoy a drink without blowing your weight-loss efforts.

Alcohol is often touted as a dieter's no-no because of its caloric punch of 7 calories per gram. A 12-ounce beer, for instance, has anywhere from 100 calories (for a light beer) to 190 calories for some dark beers. The average is about 150 calories. White table wine has about 80 calories per 3.5 ounces. For hard liquor, 1.5 ounces is roughly 125 calories, plus calories for any mixers. Sweetened soda, such as Coca-Cola, has 144 calories for a 12-ounce can, which is bad diet news if you use such mixers in your drinks. The high calorie count of soda also means you are no better off with such nonalcoholic drinks, calorically speaking.

Although overconsumption of alcohol is a health risk, alcohol in moderation is not unhealthy for most people, and some studies have found that one serving of alcohol a day promotes better circulation. To keep the calories down, change your drink of choice. For example, switch from regular beer to light beer. Drink wine spritzers (half seltzer and half the calories) instead of wine. If you like mixed drinks, mix them with fruit juice and seltzer mixture or plain seltzer or water rather than sweetened soda. If you switch to unmixed drinks, you'll probably end up drinking less, since you'll sip them more slowly than mixed drinks. (See Book 5: Walktherapy for more advice on cutting down alcohol consumption.)

You can also increase your walking time to make up for the extra calories you might drink. For example, if you average three light beers a week, that's 300 calories. You can counteract these calories by walking about 20 minutes more daily.

The Caffeine Controversy

The debate among nutritionists is whether dieters should drink coffee and other caffeinated beverages. Caffeine increases muscle stamina and speeds up the metabolism, but it also reduces blood sugar level, which can cause an urge for sweets. Although drinking too much coffee can cause acid stomach and jitters, in moderation (no more than 2.5 cups of coffee a day or 5 cups of tea), caffeinated beverages will probably not harm the dieter.

If your usual dose of coffee exceeds this moderate level, try switching to other hot beverages without caffeine: herbal teas, hot water and lemon, or broth. (For details on caffeine addiction, see Book 5: Walktherapy.)

Other Beverages

- Drink skim milk rather than whole milk.

- Water is the best diet drink. You can add a slice of lemon or lime to spice it up. If the water in your town or city is not to your liking, try bottled water.

- If you like carbonated drinks, seltzer is the answer. This now comes in a variety of fruit flavors.

- Cut down the calories in fruit juice by mixing two parts seltzer with one part juice. It makes for a less sweet drink, but it quenches your thirst better than plain juice.

Fiber

Fiber or *roughage* refers to that portion of plants such as wheat, vegetables, and fruit that cannot be digested by the body. You may wonder why something not absorbed by the body is so important to your health. The answer is that fiber (specifically insoluble fiber found in whole grains, legumes, nuts, and some vegetables and fruits) helps stools pass through the large intestines more easily by preventing the overabsorption of water by the intestine. Soluble fiber (found in some fruits, vegetables, beans, and seeds) also impedes the absorption of cholesterol and bile acids by binding to these substances and carrying them out of the body.

Fiber has long been recognized as an important part of one's diet, but it is also a good dieting food. According to research, eating a moderate amount of fiber reduces the number of calories you absorb from food. (One study done at the University of Maryland and the U.S. Department of Agriculture found that men on an average fiber diet—fruits and vegetables and white bread—absorbed almost 5 percent fewer calories than those on a low-fiber diet.) Fiber also improves digestion and is thought to lower blood pressure, and fiber fills you up. You'll feel less hungry after a breakfast of a bowl of oatmeal, for example, than an egg.

Fiber is considered key to preventing constipation, which can lead to hiatal hernias and hemorrhoids. It is also thought to reduce the likelihood of developing colon cancer by reducing the absorption of bile acids in the intestines.

You can have too much of a good thing, and dietary fiber should be limited to 20 grams or less per day. Most Americans eat less than half this amount, and you should increase your intake of fiber slowly, since too much of it can cause flatulence, mineral deficiencies, or blockages in the intestines.

Smart Cheating

It would be crazy to suggest that dieters don't cheat. Most of us have a weakness for high-calorie, high-fat foods, whether cookies, cheesecake, ice cream, butter, or cheeses. Below you'll find some hints to help you cheat without too much damage.

For Sweet Freaks

If you like baked goods like muffins, quick breads (made without yeast), or cookies, become a home baker. You can make low-fat, low-sugar substitutes to commercial brands. Try adding buttermilk (made from skim milk) rather than regular milk to cake and muffin recipes to give them more flavor without additional fat.

If you don't have the time or inclination to bake, eat fig cookies (such as Fig Newtons), ginger snaps, vanilla wafers, and animal crackers, which all have less fat than most cookies. Angel food cake is the least fatty dessert cake around.

If you crave ice cream, try ice milk, sherbet, or sorbet instead. If you can't bear these substitutes, try changing from a high-fat ice cream to a lower-fat ice cream. (Among the major brands there are fairly significant differences in fat content.)

For Butter Lovers
Whipped butter and margarine have fewer calories than stick butter and margarine. Margarine, although it has almost the same number of grams of fat as butter, is lower in cholesterol.

For Cheese Fanatics
Most cheeses have 7 to 9 grams of fat per 1-ounce serving. If you like cheese but want to avoid extra fat, stick with cottage cheese (to which you can add vegetables or spicy sauces), part-skim mozzarella cheese, and Monterey Jack.

Away from Home

You may not find dieting difficult at home, but once you leave your own kitchen, it's difficult to find a good selection of low-calorie, low-fat foods. Even going to work can pose problems because you are at the mercy of restaurants and delis for lunch. Vacations are even harder. In order to be successful in controlling your weight away from home, you have to learn to carry "good" food with you and/or to pick restaurant meals with care.

The Walker's Picnic Basket

The "walker's picnic basket" was first conceived as a list of nutritious, easily transportable foods that can be brought along on a walk or hike without much hassle. However, you can follow the same strategy to fight hunger pangs whenever you are away from home by carrying some of these low-calorie foods in your purse or briefcase.

Walker's Picnic Basket Food List

- **Dried fruit** (You don't have to worry about bruising it, and it keeps for a long time; however, it is more caloric than fresh fruit.)
- **Fresh fruit** (Bananas, oranges, apples, pears, peaches, and plums are especially good. Berries don't travel well.)
- **Cereal** (A bag of bite-sized shredded wheat or other low-fat cereal makes a good snack. Although granola has long been thought of as an optimum travel snack, it is very high in fat.)
- **Pretzels** (These are low in fat and come in low-sodium versions if you prefer.)
- **Rice cakes** (These are low in fat and sodium.)
- **Pita bread sandwiches** (These make good traveling companions because this low-fat bread, which is shaped like a pocket, can hold many nontraditional sandwich items, such as salad, without falling apart.)

Restaurants

Restaurants are the dieter's downfall. You have no control over the ingredients used in preparing the meal. But you can dine out with diet savvy. Many new restaurants (especially on the West Coast) cater to low-calorie eating, and you can learn to scout menus in all sorts of restaurants, even steak houses, for less fattening foods. If you are in a bind and fast food is your only option, try a pizza parlor (at many pizza places you can get vegetarian pizza, which has less cheese and thus less fat). McDonald's hamburgers are the lowest in fat and calories of all the burger joints. Most fast-food restaurants also have salad bars now (but go easy on the dressing).

Breakfast is probably the easiest meal to eat out. Most restaurants carry some sort of cereal, and you can usually request low-fat or skim milk. Fresh fruit is also a good choice, as are various breads (opt for whole-grain bread if available). Stay away from the eggs and bacon route, which is loaded with fat.

For lunch, your best bet is to eat soups and salads and steamed vegetables. Ask how the soups are made if you suspect they have bacon fat or other ingredients that might make them overly caloric. Salad can be eaten with lemon juice or low-cal dressing, or if none is available, ask for dressing on the side. Dipping your fork into the dressing and then eating several mouthfuls of salad will give you the taste of the dressing without many of the calories.

For entrees, any of the lean meats or fish advocated in the regular menu are good choices, as are pasta and rice (especially brown or wild rice) and all vegetarian dishes. Stay away from cream-based sauces, but wine or tomato sauces are fine. If you feel that the portions are bigger than what you would normally eat on the exchange diet, ask for a doggy bag for the remaining portion. If you do end up cleaning your plate, then eat less for the rest of the day or (if it was dinner) walk more over the next few days.

Vacations

Vacations are notorious for weight gain. The next time you plan a vacation, think walking. For every destination, whether a city, a beach, or a mountain setting, you can plan walking excursions. You'll be surprised how much more you'll see and notice exploring on foot and how many more people you'll meet.

Walking also makes a great weekend getaway activity. Within an hour's drive of your home there is undoubtedly a place to walk, whether it's a park, a forest, a country road, or a city street.

1000- or 1200-Calorie Diet—Sample 7-Day Meal Plan

Substitution lists follow so you can create your own menus. Here's some information to help you with the portions:

- Four ounces of raw meat cooks to 3 ounces of cooked meat.

- Three ounces of meat or poultry is about 3 inches across by 4 inches long. Thickness is about ½ inch.

- Three ounces of fish is slightly smaller than 3 ounces of meat or poultry.

- Three ounces of shellfish is equivalent to ten oysters, ten scallops, twelve shrimp, or twelve clams.

- One-sixth cup of rice cooks to a ½-cup serving

If you must buy meat or cheese in larger proportions than those suggested above, you can plan a few meals in a week that use the meat or cheese so the food won't go to waste. You also can, for example, eat your daily allotment of a category in one meal and then not eat any more of that category that day (for example, you can eat 4 ounces of fish for lunch and no other protein for the rest of the day). Remember, the advantage of the exchange diet is that it is flexible.

Note: Salads should be consumed first because they provide bulk. You should drink 64 ounces of water daily, because water helps in fat metabolism and prevents fluid retention.

Day 1*

Breakfast

½ cup All Bran cereal
½ banana
1 cup skim milk
6 oz. coffee or tea

Midmorning Snack

1 apple

Lunch

1 oz. cheddar cheese
2 slices cracked wheat bread
1 tsp. whipped margarine
⅔ cup steamed broccoli
large tossed salad with basic greens and raw veggies
1 tbsp. low-cal salad dressing
12 fresh cherries

Midafternoon Snack

2 cups plain popcorn

Dinner

3 oz. lean (10% fat) hamburger
1 roll
large tossed salad with basic greens and raw veggies
1 tbsp. low-cal salad dressing

Evening Snack

1 cup nonfat yogurt

*For approximately 1000 calories, delete margarine and ½ cup yogurt.

Day 2*

Breakfast

1 water bagel
1 tsp. whipped margarine
1 cup skim milk
1 tsp. low-cal jam
6 oz. coffee

Midmorning Snack

1 apple

Lunch

1 cup spaghetti with meat and tomato sauce
large tossed salad with basic greens and raw veggies
1 tbsp. low-cal salad dressing

Midafternoon Snack

3 low-sodium crackers

Dinner

2 oz. lean roasted pork
1 slice French bread
1 cup steamed asparagus
large tossed salad with basic greens and raw veggies
1 tbsp. low-cal salad dressing

Evening Snack

1 cup nonfat yogurt

*For approximately 1000 calories, delete ½ cup yogurt.

Day 3*

Breakfast

1 slice cracked wheat toast
1 tsp. whipped margarine
¾ cup fruit cocktail in water or juice (not syrup)
1 cup skim milk
6 oz. coffee or tea

Midmorning Snack

1 orange

Lunch

1 oz. lean roast beef
1 cup brown rice
large tossed salad with basic greens and raw veggies
1 tbsp. low-cal ranch dressing
1 grapefruit

Midafternoon Snack

1 bran muffin

Dinner

3 oz. any whitefish
1 baked potato
¾ cup steamed spinach
1 tsp. whipped margarine
large tossed salad with basic greens and raw veggies
1 tbsp. low-cal salad dressing

Evening Snack

1 cup nonfat yogurt

*For approximately 1000 calories, delete ½ muffin and ½ cup yogurt.

Day 4*

Breakfast

½ cup oatmeal
½ grapefruit
1 cup skim milk
6 oz. coffee or tea

Midmorning Snack

1 cup fruit cocktail in
juice or water

Lunch

2 oz. turkey breast
1 roll
⅔ cup steamed cauliflower
large tossed salad with basic greens and raw veggies
1 tbsp. low-cal salad dressing
1 cup white grapes

Midafternoon Snack

3 large pretzels

Dinner

2 oz. lean pork chop
¾ cup steamed green snap beans
large tossed salad with basic greens and raw veggies
1 tbsp. low-cal salad dressing

Evening Snack

1 cup nonfat yogurt

*For approximately 1000 calories, delete ½ cup fruit cocktail and ½ cup yogurt.

Day 5*

Breakfast

1 poached egg
1 slice cracked wheat bread toasted
1 tsp. whipped margarine
1 cup skim milk
6 oz. coffee or tea

Midmorning Snack

½ banana

Lunch

2 oz. tuna, water packed
2 slices whole wheat bread
1 tomato
1 tbsp. low-cal mayonnaise
1 orange

Midafternoon Snack

3 low-sodium crackers

Dinner

3 oz. chicken breast
1 cup brown rice
1 cup steamed brussels sprouts
large tossed salad with basic greens and raw veggies
1 tsp. low-cal salad dressing

Evening Snack

1 cup nonfat yogurt

*For approximately 1000 calories, delete ½ cup brown rice and ½ cup yogurt.

*Day 6**

Breakfast

1 cup Nutri Grain cereal
½ banana
1 cup skim milk
6 oz. coffee or tea

Midmorning Snack

1 cup strawberries

Lunch

1 oz. lean ham
1 slice French bread
large tossed salad with basic greens and raw veggies
1 tbsp. low-cal salad dressing
1 apple

Midafternoon Snack

1 cup plain popcorn

Dinner

4 oz. any whitefish
⅔ cup mashed potatoes
⅔ cup steamed carrots
large tossed salad with basic greens and raw veggies
1 tbsp. low-cal salad dressing

Evening Snack

1 cup nonfat yogurt

*For approximately 1000 calories, delete ½ cup yogurt.

Day 7*

Breakfast

½ cup oatmeal
1 cup skim milk
1 apple
6 oz. coffee or tea

Midmorning Snack

½ cup grape juice

Lunch

3 oz. tuna, water packed
½ cup cooked noodles
1 cup V-8 juice, low sodium
large tossed salad with basic greens and raw veggies
1 tbsp. low-cal salad dressing
½ grapefruit

Midafternoon Snack

2 rice cakes

Dinner

4 oz. turkey breast
2 slices mixed grain bread
1 tsp. whipped margarine
1 cup steamed asparagus
large tossed salad with basic greens and raw veggies
1 tbsp. low-cal salad dressing

Evening Snack

1 cup nonfat yogurt

*For approximately 1000 calories, delete 1 oz. turkey and ½ cup yogurt.

Vegetable Exchange List

One exchange equals ½-cup serving
Note: The following raw vegetables can be eaten as desired: chicory, Chinese cabbage, endive, escarole, lettuce, parsley, radishes, and watercress.

Asparagus	Collard greens	Rutabaga
Bean sprouts	Dandelion greens	Sauerkraut
Beet greens	Cucumber	Spinach
Beets	Eggplant	String beans
Broccoli	Green pepper	Summer squash
Brussels sprouts	Greens	Tomatoes
Cabbage	Kale	Tomato juice
Carrot (raw)	Mushrooms	Turnip greens
Carrots (boiled)	Mustard greens	Turnips
Cauliflower	Okra	Vegetable juice
Celery	Onions	Zucchini
Chard	Rhubarb	

Source: American Diabetes Association and the American Dietetic Association

Fruit Exchange List

(equals one fruit exchange)

Apple juice	½ cup	Melon	
Apple	1 sm.	Cantaloupe	¼ sm.
Applesauce	½ cup (unsweetened)	Honeydew	⅛ med.
Apricots, fresh	2 med.	Watermelon	1 cup
Apricots, dried	4 halves	Nectarine	1 sm.
Banana	½ sm.	Orange	1 sm.
Blackberries	½ cup	Orange juice	½ cup
Blueberries	½ cup	Peach	2 sm.
Cherries	12	Papaya	¾ cup
Cider	⅓ cup	Peach	1 sm.
Dates	2	Pear	1 sm.
Figs	1 (dried or fresh)	Persimmon, native	1 med.
Fruit cocktail	1 cup (in water)	Pineapple	½ cup
Grapefruit	½	Plums	2 med.
Grapefruit juice	½ cup	Prunes	2 med.
Grapes	1 cup	Prune juice	¼ cup
Grape juice	⅓ cup	Raisins	2 tbsp.
		Tangerine	1 med.

Source: American Diabetes Association and the American Dietetic Association

Bread and Starchy Vegetable Exchange List

(equals one bread exchange)

Breads		**Dried beans, peas, lentils**	
Bagel	½	Beans, peas, lentils	½ cup (cooked)
Bread	1 slice	Baked beans (canned,	
English muffin	½	no pork)	¼ cup
Roll, sandwich	½	**Starchy vegetables**	
Cereal		Corn on the cob	1 sm. ear
Bran flakes	½ cup	Corn	⅓ cup
Other unsweetened	¾ cup	Lima beans	½ cup
Puffed cereal	1 cup	Parsnips	⅔ cup
Cooked cereal	½ cup	Potato	1 sm.
Grits	½ cup	Potato (mashed)	½ cup
Rice or barley	½ cup (cooked)	Pumpkin	⅔ cup
		Winter squash, yams,	
Pasta (includes spaghetti,	½ cup	or sweet potato	¼ cup
noodles, and macaroni)	(cooked)	**Prepared foods**	
Popcorn (air popped)	3 cups	Biscuit, 2-inch	
Cornmeal (dry)	2 tbsp.	diameter	1 plus 1 fat ex.
Flour	2½ tbsp.	Corn bread, 2 × 2	
Wheat germ	¼ cup	× 1 inches	1 plus 1 fat ex.
Crackers		Crackers, round	
Arrowroot	3	butter	5 plus 1 fat ex.
Graham, 2½-inch		French fries, 3½	
square	2	inches	8 plus 1 fat ex.
Matzoth, 4 × 6 inches		Muffins	1 (low-fat,
Oyster	20		homemade)
Pretzels, 3⅛-inch long,		Muffin (store-bought)	1 plus 1 fat ex.
⅛-inch diameter	25	Potato or corn chips	15 plus 1 fat ex.
Rye wafers, 2 × 3½			
inches	3	Pancake, 5 × ½	
Saltines	6	inches	1 plus 1 fat ex.
Soda, 2½-inch square	4	Waffle, 5 × ½ inches	1 plus 1 fat ex.

Source: American Diabetes Association and the American Dietetic Association

Protein Exchange List (Meat, Cheese, Fish)

Lean Meat

Beef: Baby beef, chipped beef, chuck, flank steak, tenderloin, plate ribs, plate skirt steak, round (bottom, top)	1 oz.
Lamb: Leg, rib, sirloin, loin (roast and chops), shank, shoulder	1 oz.
Veal: Leg, loin, rib, shank, shoulder, cutlets	1 oz.
Poultry: Chicken, turkey, cornish hen, guinea hen, pheasant	1 oz.
Fish: Any fresh or frozen canned salmon, tuna, mackerel, crab, or lobster (packed in water)	1 oz. ¼ cup
clams, oysters, scallops, shrimp	5, or 1 oz.
sardines, drained	3
Tofu	1 oz.
Cheese with less than 5% butterfat	1 oz.
Cheese, cottage (1% fat)	⅓ cup
Cheese, cottage (2% fat)	¼ cup

Medium-Fat Meat (add ½ fat exchange)

Beef: Ground (15% fat), corned beef (canned), rib eye, round (ground commercial)	1 oz.
Pork: Loin (all cuts tenderloin), shoulder, arm, shoulder blade, Boston butt, Canadian bacon, boiled ham	1 oz.
Organ meat: Liver, heart, kidney, and sweetbreads (all high in cholesterol)	1 oz.
Creamed cottage cheese	¼ cup
Cheese: Mozzarella, ricotta, farmer's cheese, neufchatel	1 oz.
Parmesan	3 tbsp.
Egg, poached	1

High-Fat Meats (add 1 fat exchange)

Beef: Brisket, ground beef (more than 20 percent fat), roasts (rib), steaks (club and rib)	1 oz.
Lamb: Breast	1 oz.
Pork: Spare ribs, back ribs, ground pork, country-style ham, deviled ham	1 oz.
Poultry: Duck, goose	1 oz.
Veal: Breast	1 oz.
Cheese, Cheddar types	1 oz.
Cold cuts	1 slice
Egg, scrambled or fried	1
Frankfurter	1 small
Liverwurst	1 oz.
Peanut butter	1 tbsp. plus 2 fat ex.

Source: American Diabetes Association and the American Dietetic Association

Fat Exchange List

Avocado (4-inch diameter	⅛	Oils:	1 tsp.
		Corn, cottonseed, safflower,	
Bacon	1 strip	soy, sunflower, olive,	
Bacon fat	1 tsp.	peanut (these last two are	
Butter	1 tsp.	mostly monounsaturated)	
Cream, light	2 tbsp.	Nuts:	
Cream, sour	2 tbsp.	Almonds	10 wh.
Cream, heavy	1 tbsp.	Pecans	2 large wh.
Cream cheese	½ oz.	Peanuts, Spanish	20 wh.
Mayonnaise (low-cal)	1 tsp.	Peanuts, Virginia	10 wh.
Margarine	1 tsp.	Walnuts	6 sm.
		Others	6 sm.
		Salad dressing (low-cal)	⅔ tsp.

Source: American Diabetes Association and the American Dietetic Association

Milk Exchange List

Buttermilk (from skim milk)	1 cup	Canned, evaporated skim milk	½ cup
Milk, no fat	1 cup	Powdered milk, nonfat (before adding liquid)	⅓ cup
Milk, 1% fat	1 cup plus ½ fat ex.	Yogurt, plain nonfat	1 cup
Milk, 2% fat	1 cup plus 1 fat ex.	Yogurt, plain 2% fat	1 cup plus 1 fat ex.
Milk, whole	1 cup plus 2 fat ex.	Yogurt made from whole milk	1 cup plus 2 fat ex.

Source: American Diabetes Association and the American Dietetic Association

Food Journal

After each item or meal, please list the time you ate it and the fat, carbohydrate, protein, and calorie counts. Under the Comments column, note your feelings and what prompted you to eat (hunger, depression, boredom, etc.).

FOOD	TIME EATEN	FAT (GRAMS)	CARBOHYDRATES (GRAMS)	PROTEIN (GRAMS)	CALORIES	COMMENTS

6. The Pregnant Woman's Walking Guide

Chris Oehler, age 24, was overweight before her pregnancy and had never done any sort of regular exercise program. But once she found out she was going to have a child, she decided to make some changes in her life. She began by walking around the block every night. Slowly, she built up her stamina and finally settled in to walking 2 to 4 miles a day (averaging 6 days a week), either in the morning or evening, a routine she continued until she delivered, even though her third trimester was during a terrible heat wave. "I had five friends who all got pregnant about the same time, but I was the only one who started exercising. My friends sat around saying 'Aren't you tired?' But I found if I got up in the morning to walk, my energy would be up all day.

Chris also reached her goal of keeping her weight down. She gained 24 pounds (the average is 20 to 30 pounds), and she is sure she would have gained much more if she had not walked during her pregnancy. Her aerobic capacity also increased. When she started, her heart rate would shoot up to 180 beats per minute after just four blocks. She was told by her doctor that her heart rate should not go over 140 beats per minute. After walking for 9 months, Chris's heart rate was only 120 beats per minute after her walking workout, even in her third trimester.

Anne Kashiwa, an aerobics instructor and racewalker who first started walking for exercise during her pregnancy, said she began a walking routine not only to keep her weight gain to a minimum, but also because she noticed her calves getting weak and sore during her first trimester. She felt walking would help strengthen them and ease the pain. Anne, who

273

gained 30 pounds during her pregnancy, feels walking during pregnancy boosts self-esteem at a time when it's needed most and also makes for an easy recovery after giving birth. Anne had a cesarean section but was able to exercisewalk 2½ weeks later.

Most obstetricians recommend walking to their pregnant patients over all other exercises because it does not jar the body. Many women involved in other sports or strenuous activities are usually urged to change to walking during their pregnancy. This is so because the hormonal changes in the body tend to loosen the joints, making them susceptible to injury, especially from the bouncing movements in tennis or jogging. Walking, because it is a low-impact exercise, does not place stress on the joints and is therefore safe. While women should not try to lose weight during pregnancy, walking will help keep them within healthy limits if they tend to overeat. Walking can also help prevent varicose veins and the swelling of the legs and ankles (called *edema*) that often occurs in the third trimester. Although walking regularly during pregnancy has not been found to decrease the length of labor, it does build stamina so that delivery is easier. Walking is perhaps most helpful because pregnant women feel in control of their bodies, a feeling they often lose as the fetus grows.

Despite the high marks that walking has received from the medical profession, few doctors prescribe a specific walking program. Most women, including Anne Kashiwa and Chris Oehler, make up their own routines. The exercise standards for pregnant women, set up by the American College of Obstetricians and Gynecologists (ACOG), are quite stringent, probably because little research has been done on pregnant women and exercise. These standards, however, are the only ones that exist, so our pregnancy exercisewalking program falls within their limits. Show your doctor our exercisewalking recommendations before starting, especially if you have any of the following complications: high blood pressure, anemia, thyroid disease, diabetes, heart palpitations, breech position in the last trimester, excessive obesity, history of extremely sedentary lifestyle, history of bleeding during pregnancy, placenta previa, a twin pregnancy, or history of premature labor.

If you have already been active, don't look at pregnancy as a time for all-out training or a time to drastically improve your physical condition, but rather as a time to maintain your present fitness state. If you've never exercised before, you will be increasing your aerobic capacity, and thus your fitness level, reasonably and slowly. Be careful not to overextend yourself. Most doctors agree that you should not exercise at more than 70 percent of your target heart rate (which is 220 heart beats minus your age) during pregnancy. For example, if you're 30 years old, your target heart rate is 190 beats per minute, and the upper limit that your heart should beat during exercise is therefore 133 beats per minute. The American College of Obstetricians and Gynecologists says that your heart rate should not increase over 140 beats per minute; more intense exercise will divert blood away from the fetus.

Your body temperature rises slightly during pregnancy, so it is easy to get overheated. If you are pregnant during the summer, it is best to walk in the cooler hours of the day, either early morning or evening. Carry water with you and drink it throughout your exercise period to avoid dehydration. During hot weather, women are advised to drink 12 ounces of water for every 10 to 15 minutes of exercise. Wait 2 hours after eating before you walk, since food takes longer to digest during pregnancy. Stop exercising if you experience any of the following signs: pain, bleeding, dizziness, shortness of breath, palpitations, faintness, back pain, pubic pain, or difficulty walking.

The Pregnancy Program

Try to walk at least three times a week. If you don't feel well on a day you are supposed to walk, don't walk. It is best to pamper yourself during these 9 months, so this program should be flexible. Keep in mind, however, that sticking with a regular walking program will be better for you than exercising sporadically. The following chart will give you an idea of a suitably moderate exercisewalking routine.

Note: These exercise routines should be preceded by a 5-minute warm-up of slow walking and 5 to 10 minutes of cool-down.

Moderate Exercise Program During Pregnancy

WEEKS	LEVEL I	LEVEL II	LEVEL III	LEVEL IV	LEVEL V*
1–4	20 minutes 55% MHR†	30 minutes 60% MHR	30 minutes 65% MHR	45 minutes 65% MHR	60 minutes 65% MHR
5–8	25 minutes 60% MHR	30 minutes 65% MHR	30 minutes 65% MHR	45 minutes 65% MHR	60 minutes 65% MHR
9–36	30 minutes 65% MHR	30 minutes 65% MHR	30 minutes 65% MHR	45 minutes 65% MHR	60 minutes 65% MHR

*Level I is for those who have led a very sedentary life, and level V is for those who are most active. If you are in doubt as to your fitness level, start at Level II.

†MHR = maximum heart rate.

Walking in Your First and Second Trimesters

Start slowly and increase your walking time gradually over 4 or 5 weeks. In your first trimester, you will most likely experience nausea and fatigue. In your second or third month, you may also experience violent mood swings. These are thought to be caused by an increased hormonal levels.

Estrogen production rises dramatically; it would take an ovulating woman 150 years to produce the same amount of estrogen that a pregnant woman produces in 9 months. Progesterone, which also increases during pregnancy, is thought to be primarily responsible for the depression pregnant women encounter.

You need to walk at least three times a week to experience any sort of energy-boosting, antidepressant result, as well to maintain your fitness level. When you feel particularly irritable or depressed, a brisk 10-minute walk can help calm you down and put your emotions back in order. During your second trimester, you will probably feel less sick, which will be a help in sticking with your program.

Third Trimester

In your seventh or eighth month you may experience edema (swelling in the legs); walking has been proven to dissipate this accumulation of fluids. Even a 10-minute walk helps, and pregnant women with desk jobs should get up for a brisk 5- to 10-minute walk every hour. Leg swelling tends to be the worst in the evening, so you may choose to walk at that time. If you do have mild leg swelling, wear pregnancy support hose, which will help circulate the blood back up to the heart. You may also experience leg cramps and back aches, which walking will help by increasing circulation and exercising the muscles, which alleviates muscle spasms.

At this point, if you've been walking regularly, you may not notice a significant decrease in your walking speed, surprising as that may seem. Don't be ashamed to take rests, especially if it is hot. If you do experience leg swelling, elevate your feet during these rests. A rest of 5 to 10 minutes should be sufficient, although you are the only person who can judge when you are ready to resume. During the latter stages of pregnancy, it is a good idea to walk with someone and stay on well-traveled roads in case you need help.

Many women experience the "nesting instinct" during their last month of pregnancy: They have a burst of energy and begin to prepare their homes for the baby's imminent arrival. This energy burst is probably psychological and physical, brought on both by the knowledge that the child will be arriving shortly and by the body's increase in hormonal activity in preparation for delivery. Don't be tempted to increase your walking activity just because you feel more energetic. Stick with the same program.

Labor

Often women are tempted to become inactive during the initial stages of labor, which often slows down the process. Walking a half a mile or so at this time can help speed up delivery. This is because standing and walking allow gravity to pull the child down, putting pressure on the cervix. Walking will also pass the time and calm you down.

Walking Techniques for Pregnancy

By far the most important technique to practice during pregnancy is the pelvic tilt. This position, in which the hips are tucked under the upper body, is important for all walkers, but for pregnant women it is the only way to ensure comfort in motion. This is so because you have a rather large weight in the front of your body pulling you forward. Pregnant women often complain of lower back pains because it is difficult to do the pelvic tilt as their stomachs grow larger. Instead, they are forced to arch their backs, which causes lower back strain and pain.

When Gary's wife was pregnant, he saw how difficult it became for her to walk, and he started experimenting with different stances that might help balance the weight more evenly. The result is what he calls the "Groucho Marx walk." Walking with your knees slightly bent at all times helps you to tilt your pelvis under your body and ease the weight off your lower back. Other women said they did not have to alter their walking styles and simply concentrated on keeping their backs straight. Try different stances to see which feels right for you. You may want to widen your stance, since your center of gravity has changed. You should also practice pelvic tucks by standing against a wall and trying to flatten your lower back against it. Walking also seems to be its own best medicine. Women who walk during pregnancy report that they tend to waddle less than those who don't.

Although arm pumping is usually an important part of exercisewalking, some women found that it raised their heart rate too much during the last trimester. However, if you experience swelling in your arms when you don't swing them, try shaking them out every 15 minutes to increase the circulation. You can also shake out your ankles every so often to prevent swelling.

Diet

The dietary needs of pregnant women have not always been well understood. In the beginning of this century, for example, doctors told women to cut down on calories so that the baby would be small and easy to deliver. Now we know that a woman must eat more and eat well for the baby to be healthy. A woman's BMR rises during pregnancy because of the increase in size of the uterus, breasts, fetus, and placenta, plus the increased cardiac and respiratory rates. This equals about a 20 to 25 percent increase in the metabolic rate, or about 300 extra calories per day. If you weren't walking before your pregnancy, add another extra 100 calories to your diet for every mile you walk. Using this formula, you will maintain the proper intake of calories. Lactation also boosts the BMR heavily, increasing it about 60 percent, because of the increased energy needed to produce the daily average of 30 ounces of milk.

Women should gain roughly 20 to 30 pounds during pregnancy, which includes the weight of the fetus and added approximate weights of the placenta (1 pound), amniotic fluid (2 pounds), increase in weight of the uterus and breasts (5.5 pounds), increased blood volume (4 pounds), and maternal stores of fat (4 to 8 pounds). Women will usually gain about 2 to 4 pounds during the first trimester and a pound a week thereafter.

Hormonal changes often cause morning sickness in early pregnancy. Eating small meals of carbohydrates (which are easy to digest) and drinking liquids between rather than with meals will help reduce nausea.

Constipation is also sometimes a result of pregnancy. Eating whole grains and fruits and drinking lots of liquids will dispel any problems that arise. Laxatives should be avoided. And as we all know, pregnant women should avoid cigarettes, alcohol, drugs, and caffeine during pregnancy.

After the Baby's Born

Unless you have had complications or have had a cesarean section, you can resume your walking program within 4 or 5 days. You can even take your baby with you in a chestpack. Some doctors have found that walking helps relieve postpartum depression; it also exercises and strengthens your back muscles, which will protect them from the added strain of carrying a child and his or her belongings for the next 3 to 5 years.

A study done in an Eskimo community found that children taken out for walks in backpacks or chestpacks were better adjusted than those who were not. Carrying your child with you as you walk has the additional benefit of increasing your aerobic workout (another form of weight-loaded walking). When your child grows heavier, or if he or she is a large baby, use a stroller (sports models are available for fast walkers) instead of a backpack. (see Book 1: Walking and Aging for information on walking and children).

Finally, walking is a great way for new mothers to lose weight and get back into shape. Lori Rogers, a 32-year-old walker from Oberlin, Ohio, lost all the 30 pounds she had gained during her pregnancy in 5 months.

Walking for weight control is among the most potent applications of an exercisewalking program. No matter what the reasons walkers we interviewed started walking, almost everyone mentioned the body-toning and weight-loss benefits of exercisewalking. Even younger, fit adults like Jo Ann Taylor, age 32, who thought that "walking was only for the aged and overweight," reported that walking has helped tone her body. Many walkers, including some of the doctors listed in the directory in Book 7, reported significant weight losses of 50, 60, and 80 pounds. Edmond Joseph Rivet, age 43, who walks 15 to 20 miles a week, has maintained an 80-pound weight loss over 7 to 8 years. Others, like Georgette Maffei, a registered nurse in Sonoma, California, have been able to get off the yo-yo diet syndrome by walking 30 miles a week. These significant and maintainable weight losses just don't happen for people who try to diet without exercising. Walking is the key.

Become Stress Hardy and Gain Control of Your Life

CONTRIBUTORS

Deena and David Balboa, M.S.W., M.B.A.

David and Deena Balboa are codirectors of The Walking Center in New York City and coauthors of the book *Walk for Life*. Mr. Balboa, a sports psychotherapist, and Ms. Balboa, a lay psychotherapist, treat patients with a unique combination of traditional therapy and walking. Mr. Balboa is a certified clinical social worker with a master's degree in social work from Hunter College in New York City and an M.B.A. in public health care administration from Baruch College in New York City. Mr. Balboa racewalks 28 miles a week, and Ms. Balboa walks 25 miles a week. They live in New York City.

Sheldon B. Cohen, M.D.

Dr. Cohen is clinical assistant professor of psychiatry at Tulane University in New Orleans. He is a fellow of the American Academy of Psychoanalysis. Other major professional interests are group therapy (master instructor of the American Group Psychotherapy Society and past president of the Atlanta Group Psychotherapy Society), hypnosis (past vice president of the American Society of Clinical Hypnosis and past editor of the *American Journal of Clinical Hypnosis*), and forensic psychiatry. Dr. Cohen received his psychiatric training at Tulane University. Dr. Cohen walks 6 to 10 miles a week and lives in Atlanta, Georgia.

Ruth Lerner, Ph.D.

Dr. Lerner is a licensed clinical psychologist based in California, working primarily in private practice and doing some consulting work. In the past she worked as a sports psychologist with the UCLA women's track and field team teaching Olympic-bound athletes the arts of positive affirmation, visual imaging, and autogenic training. A practitioner of holistic health, Dr. Lerner incorporates walking into her therapy sessions, and finds that exercise is especially helpful for depressed patients. Dr. Lerner was awarded a Ph.D. in clinical psychology from the California School of Professional Psychology in Los Angeles. Dr. Lerner walks 4 days a week and lives in Los Angeles.

Claude Miller, M.D.

Dr. Miller is a psychiatrist with a private practice in New York City and a life fellow of the New York Academy of Medicine. In 1945, Dr. Miller received the M.D. degree from Creighton University in Omaha, Nebraska. Dr. Miller walks 2½ miles a day and lives in New York City.

Howard L. Millman, Ph.D.

Dr. Millman is a clinical psychologist working in New York City who prescribes walking for depression, drug dependency, obesity, anxiety, hyperactive children, and as a preventive measure. In his book, *How to Help Children with Common Problems*, he recommends walking for obese, hyperactive children, and in *Therapy for Adults*, he recommends walking for people with depression. Dr. Millman received the Ph.D. degree from Adelphi University. He walks 25 miles a week and lives in Westchester County, New York.

Keith Sedlacek, M.D.

Dr. Sedlacek, an expert in stress-management and biofeedback techniques, is president of the Biofeedback Society of New York, medical director of the Stress Regulation Institute of New York, an adjunct professor at City University of New York, and faculty member in clinical psychiatry at Columbia University in New York City, where he received the M.D. degree in 1972. Dr. Sedlacek is the author of the book, *The Sedlacek Technique: Finding the Calm Within You*. He walks 3 miles a day, 6 days a week and lives in New York City.

John C. Simpson, III, Ph.D.

Dr. Simpson is in private practice with the Eastover Psychological and Psychiatric Group in Charlotte, North Carolina. He is a partner in Psychsport Consultants, also in Charlotte, which focuses on sports psychology. Dr. Simpson received the Ph.D. degree in psychology from the University of Tennessee in 1978. Dr. Simpson walks 30 miles a week and lives in Charlotte, North Carolina.

Kathryn Welds, Ph.D.

Dr. Welds is a psychologist with a private practice in Los Angeles. She is also a consultant whose special field is employee assistance and organizational development. Dr. Welds has directed continuing education in personal/career development, professional psychology, and women's programs for the UCLA Extension in Los Angeles. She has taught at Harvard University, the University of California, and the University of San Francisco. Dr. Welds was awarded the Ph.D. degree from Harvard University and has completed postdoctoral fellowships at Cornell Medical College/New York Hospital and Westside Community Mental Health Center/Pacific Medical Center, San Francisco. She walks daily and lives in Los Angeles.

Robert Thayer, Ph.D.

Dr. Thayer is a professor of psychology at California State University at Long Beach and has done extensive research on the effects of walking on mood and energy levels and its use in behavior modification. He is the author of *The Biopsychology of Mood and Arousal*. Dr. Thayer walks daily and lives in Long Beach, California.

1. *Therapeutic Walking*

In many ways this book is the closest to Gary Yanker's heart because it is in the area of reducing stress, learning to relax, and becoming less of a "Type A" person that walking has had the greatest impact on his life. From age 12, when he founded his own lawn and garden service business, Gary manifested quintessential "Type A" behavior. Even then he was a workaholic, and this pattern continued through college and graduate school (where he got both an M.B.A. and a J.D.—law—degree in 4 years while simultaneously running his own book packaging business) and into his first years of law practice at a large Wall Street firm. At this point his time was so tightly budgeted that he allowed himself only 1 hour to eat and 6 hours to sleep each day, devoting the other 17 hours to work. He was in the office every weekend, never dreamed of going on vacation, and took Christmas Day as his only holiday.

This schedule was taking its toll on Gary. He was 60 pounds overweight, smoked two packs of cigarettes a day, and had, at one time or another, a whole battery of stress-induced illnesses, including colitis, muscle spasms, back pain, and even trench mouth.

One good friend and a 100-mile weekend walk turned Gary's life around. His friend nagged him to take a weekend off and get away from the city. They planned a 50-mile walk from Manhattan to Dutchess Country in upstate New York. This weekend relaxed Gary so much that the two friends planned another. After his trip, Gary started walking more during the work week, squeezing in walks between meetings and before meals. He began substituting walks for cigarettes, and the extra pounds started to melt away. He felt less stressed at work and was more productive.

This was the beginning of a career dedicated to spreading the walking word. "I'm a Type B + now," Gary quips. Although still given to overwork and, at times, susceptible to stress-related muscle spasms (especially with the deadline of this book fast approaching), he now has learned to seek balance in his life. His work is no longer all-encompassing, and he spends much more time with family and friends. He is trim, has been off cigarettes for 8 years, and has cut down his coffee consumption. He can barely believe that he was once so "stressed out."

This minibook will teach you how walking can make a difference in your life, too, whether it's in dealing with everyday stress, overcoming addictions—including caffeine and cigarettes—modifying "Type A" behavior and other unhealthy personality traits, or coping with major life changes. The theme of this minibook is that *walking can help you take control*—over your life, your habits, and your emotions.

Throughout this minibook you'll learn how and why walking is such a powerful therapeutic tool and in what areas it can best help you. In summary, walking can *improve* or *increase* your

Sociability

Creative energy

Relaxation

Optimism

Awareness of details

Intimacy with family and friends

Sexual satisfaction

Self-image

Self-confidence

Concentration

Assertiveness

Feelings of independence

Control over your life

Memory

Immune system

Walking can *reduce*

Depression

Addictive behavior

Headaches, back aches, and muscle tension

Phobias

Mood swings

Emotional fatigue

"Type A" behavior

Egocentricity

Boredom

How to Use This Book

In this first chapter, Therapeutic Walking, you'll learn how to analyze the amount of stress in your life and find out why walking is the best exercise to help you cope with it.

In Chapter 2, Walking for Everyday Problems, you'll find walking intervention techniques to help control your stress and keep you fit, whether you are bored, tired, under a lot of pressure at work, or have family problems.

Chapter 3, Walking, the Positive Addiction, will show you how walking can be your key to quitting smoking, coffee, sugar, alcohol, drugs, or other bad habits or addictions.

Chapter 4, Walking for Life's Major Traumas, will provide a walking program to follow in the face of life's major stresses. Whether you've just experienced the death of a spouse or close friend, have lost your job, are entering retirement, or have been diagnosed with a major illness or disease, walking can increase your optimism, reduce your depression, and help you on the road to recovery.

In Chapter 5, Walking for Personality Changes, you'll learn that how you walk is a window to your personality and how walking can help you change your behavior, whether you're a "Type A" who wants to calm down or a "Type C" who wants to boost assertiveness or improve self-confidence.

Chapter 6, The Walktherapy Program, will supplement the short-term techniques found in Chapters 2 and 3 and provide a long-term maintenance program to follow throughout your life.

The Walking Way

Throughout *Walking Medicine* we've tried to represent walking not just as an exercise, but as a philosophy of balance and moderation. Walking symbolizes the noncompetitive paradigm of life, a response for the "reasonable person" to the rough and tough sports game where you fight and scratch your way to the top. If you are a walker, you'll tend to look at life as a journey, with ups and downs and points of interest along the way.

Walking is the nonathletic everyman's sport. It fits people's need for a pleasurable activity that also happens to be good for them. Although the "fitness revolution" has been around for 25 years, less than 10 percent of the adult population is exercising at recommended levels. This suggests that most people want an accessible, safe, and moderate activity that doesn't seem like a chore. That activity is walking.

Many people have already made this discovery. In a recent survey of the National Sporting Goods Association, 65 million Americans named walking their primary exercise, meaning walkers outnumber swimmers and runners. This is so because, both physically and mentally, walking fits the human makeup. Walking is our means of mobility and what we were designed to do, and by making an effort to walk more, you will improve both your physical and psychological well-being.

While walking is the natural exercise choice, however, you still might wonder why you should incorporate it into your life. The answer is *stress*. Every change you experience, both good and bad, big and small, is stressful and demands a response. Stress comes in two forms: physical stress, such as changes in temperature, and emotional stress, such as a speaking engagement or an examination. The effects of stress can surface in physiological, emotional, and cognitive symptoms. Physiological effects include raised heart rate, blood pressure, muscle tension, and over the long term, psychosomatic symptoms such as chronic headaches, back aches, and even heart disease. Emotional symptoms include fear, anxiety, and depression, and cognitive changes include a decrease in productivity, learning, and creativity.

Too much stress can lead to illness, since all the effects of stress weaken the body, including the immune system. To determine the amount of stress in your life and how it can affect your health, we've developed a test based on the Holmes-Rahe Social Adjustment Rating Scale. This is a widely used scale created in the late sixties to quantify the probability of having a health "breakdown" due to stressful events. Everyone copes with stress differently, and some people handle stress better than others. Where this test falls short is that it cannot account for your *ability* to cope with stress, so that even if you have a high stress score, you may not be in danger of becoming sick. Our walking program, however, can teach you to handle stress more effectively, whatever the level, so that any risk of illness is greatly reduced. We have intertwined events discussed in *Walking Medicine* with those of Holmes and Rahe. The events are also segmented into five levels that correspond to the walking levels found in the walktherapy maintenance program in Chapter 6.

Now look at the stress scale that follows and mark all the incidents which you have experienced within the last year. If any have happened more than once, multiply the score by the number of times it has happened.

In general, a score of 150 to 300 is considered moderate, and a score above 300 is high. If your score is under 100, you may feel bored because you don't experience enough change. This can also be a source of stress, and in Chapter 2, you'll learn how walking can add a new dimension to your life.

Two kinds of therapeutic walking are prescribed in walktherapy: brisk, short walks (or short, intense superstepping routines) as an antidote to the physical and cognitive symptoms of stress such as muscle tension, fatigue, and lack of concentration (generally for the events in Levels I through III on the stress scale) and slow, longer, meditative walks for emotional symptoms such as depression, fears, or worries (generally Levels IV and V). In the following chapters you'll find why and how these two kinds of therapeutic walks work.

A Word about Motivation

Motivation is not only the key to starting and staying with an exercise program, it is also the stimulant to coping with any of life's changes and stresses. You have to be motivated to overcome your problems.

The greatest motivator is the knowledge that what you are doing works and works quickly. Instant gratification is the name of the game. Long-term benefits rarely motivate people to do anything.

Walking's biggest advantage is that it is easy to do, doesn't cost any money, can be done anywhere, and makes you feel good almost immediately. If you can get yourself to try walking just once or twice, it should sell itself, unless you approach walking as another thing for your "to do" list. Nothing is more of a turn-off than an obligation.

Probably the easiest way to work walking into your life, at least until you are won over by its benefits, is to trick yourself into taking walks. Here are some examples:

1. If you drive to work, park as far away as possible so you can get in a walk both on arrival and departure.

2. If you take public transportation, get off a stop earlier and walk the rest of the way (or walk part of the way before getting on public transportation).

3. Visit friends who live nearby on foot instead of driving or taking public transportation.

4. Suggest a walk with a friend rather than coffee and a snack at a restaurant.

5. Take the stairs instead of the elevator.

6. Walk your dog (or someone else's) or accompany a friend on his or her dog-walking detail.

Once you see how much better walking makes you feel, you'll want to walk, and this walking will help you feel in control, which will motivate you to take other positive steps in your life.

The Stress Scale

LIFE EVENT	MEAN VALUE
Level V	
1. Death of spouse	100
2. Diagnosis of cancer, AIDS, or other fatal disease	95
3. Unwed pregnancy (for woman)	92
4. Divorce	73
5. Marital separation	65
6. Detention in jail or other institution	63
7. Death of close family member	63
8. Stroke or heart attack	53
9. Diagnosis of rheumatoid arthritis	53
10. Diagnosis of multiple sclerosis	53
11. Diagnosis of angina pectoris	53
Level IV	
12. Getting married	50
13. Being fired from a job	47
14. Marital reconciliation with mate	45
15. Retirement	45
16. Major change in health or behavior of family member	44 x2
17. Pregnancy	40
18. Quitting an addiction to cigarettes, drugs, or alcohol	40
19. Changing "Type A" to "Type C" behavior	40
20. Sexual difficulties	39
21. Gaining a new family member (e.g., through birth, adoption, relative moving in, etc.)	39
22. Major business readjustment (e.g., merger, bankruptcy, etc.)	39
23. Major change in financial state (e.g., a lot better off or worse off)	38
24. Death of a close friend	37
25. Changing to a different line of work	36

LIFE EVENT	MEAN VALUE
Level III	
26. Major change in the number of arguments with spouse (either more or less)	35
27. Taking on a mortgage greater than $10,000	31
28. Foreclosure on a mortgage or loan	30
29. Major change in responsibilities at work (either promotion, demotion, or a lateral move)	29
30. Son or daughter leaving home	29
31. In-law troubles	28
32. Outstanding personal achievement	(28)
33. Spouse beginning or ceasing work	26
34. Beginning or ceasing formal schooling	26
35. Major change in living conditions (building a home, remodeling, deterioration of home or neighborhood)	25
Level II	
36. Revision of personal habits (e.g., dress, manners, association)	(24)
37. Troubles with the boss	(23) ×2
38. Major change in working hours or conditions	20
39. Change in residence	20
40. Changing to a new school	20
41. Major change in usual type/amount of recreation	19
42. Major change in church activities (more or less)	19
43. Major change in social activities (clubs, dancing, movies, etc.)	18
44. Taking on a mortgage or loan of less than $10,000 (purchasing a car, TV, etc.)	17
45. Major change in sleeping habits (insomnia, sleeping more, or change in part of day you are asleep)	16
46. Major change in number of family get-togethers (more or less)	(15)
47. Major change in eating habits (dieting, eating more, or very different meal hours or surroundings)	(15)
Level I	
48. Business travel	13
49. Vacation	(13)
50. Christmas	(12)
51. Minor violations of the law (traffic tickets, jaywalking, etc.)	11
52. Car trouble	(11) ×2
53. Commuting	11
Your score:	301

2. Walking for Everyday Problems

Everyday problems, from getting a parking ticket to having a fight with your spouse, or just being bored are on the lower end of the stress scale discussed in Chapter 1. By taking 5- to 15-minute pressure-valve walks when the tension gets too much and following a regular walking program of 30 to 60 minutes daily, you can greatly reduce the stress you must face every day—what Dr. Claude Miller, a psychiatrist practicing in New York City, calls the two quarts of aggression that are delivered to our doorstep each morning. If you don't get rid of them, they turn sour and make you sick, says Miller, who walks 2½ miles every morning to get rid of his.

Life is full of change, and it is the demands of change that cause stress. Stress sparks our sympathetic nervous system, "our fight-or-flight responses," into action. A leftover from our distant past when we had to fight animals for survival, our sympathetic nervous system increases blood flow to the large muscles of the body and the brain (to prepare us to fight or to run away) and raises our heart rate and blood pressure.

It was Dr. Hans Selye, a Czechoslovakian-born endocrinologist, who first addressed the issue of our stress response by studying animals' reactions to various situations—cold, fatigue, infection. Dr. Selye found that an animal's reaction was the same to all of them, whether the stimulus was psychological or physical. The heart raced, the blood pressure rose, and the pupils dilated. We know that stress produces these physical results in humans, but it also can cause other reactions. Stress can make us anxious, fearful, depressed, lethargic, or moody. Stress can make us blow up at our loved ones or retreat into our own world. It can cause headaches, insomnia, back pain, muscle spasms, heart disease, and perhaps even speed up the aging process.

Of course, *how* we perceive a situation will have much to do with how much stress we feel. If your boss comes in with a project that you have confidence you can master, you will not feel stress. If you perceive that you are not capable of the job, you will experience stress. Again, the idea of control comes into play. You can learn to use the physical responses of the sympathetic nervous system to good ends, to "rise to an occasion." But the body can't tolerate these reactions for too long, so you must learn to relax. A brisk walk can help you to do that. To cope effectively, you must develop stress hardiness, a package of skills and a level of fitness to deal with everyday stress.

You may find it difficult to believe that walking, such a seemingly simple solution, can help you conquer dire situations, but research and anecdotal evidence alike have proven that walking alleviates both the physical and psychological effects of stress. Exercise is a "eustress" (a good stress) and increases your resistance to the "distresses" of life. The energizing and soothing effects of walking will better enable your mind and body to handle unexpected stressors.

According to Robert E. Thayer, Ph.D., of California State University at Long Beach, who has done extensive research on the psychological benefits of walking and is the originator of the brisk 10-minute-walk concept for stress reduction, a short walk can help you control the physical reactions to stress. Your hair-trigger adrenaline "fight-or-flight" mechanism will react with less intensity and you'll be putting your stress response to its natural use by using your muscles to go for a walk.

For example, a student came to Dr. Thayer suffering from test anxiety. She was afraid of "freezing" on an important exam. Dr. Thayer recommended a brisk 10-minute walk before the test. She followed his advice and came back to him with the news that she had "aced" it.

If you have just had a fight with your spouse or are worried about something, a short walk will remove you from the stressful situation. If your goal is to relax, don't think about the problem. As your body loosens up, however, you may want to begin to work through your dilemma and may even come up with a solution.

Walking primarily works on stress by increasing your arousal and energy levels and secondarily by reducing tension. The energy boost is immediate, while the tension reduction reveals itself later and over time. The *enhanced energy enables you to better cope with stress*, so that you are less likely to become tense in the first place.

Walking prevents tension from accumulating because, by its nature, tension builds slowly. Tension itself is designed to help you—it's an adaptive reaction that prepares you to take arms against misfortunes. As the sympathetic nervous system increases signals to prepare your muscles for action, your body tightens. If your muscles are weak from lack of exercise, this tension will place a heavy strain on them and they will eventually go into a spasm (permanent contraction), which produces pain. An exercised muscle can bounce back and is able to relax after a strain has been placed on it. However, if like most of us you don't take action (chew out your boss, find the money to avert the foreclosure), the tension gets stored and winds up disabling you. But if you are walking—*regularly*—those tensions never get a chance to accumulate. *Therefore, you should regularly walk to prevent storing tension, and take extra therapeutic walks for their cope-enhancing effect—10 brisk minutes each.*

Depending on your problem, *when* you choose to exercise can enhance or dampen the effects of your therapy walk. The best time to walk depends on your energy cycle, which varies from person to person but on average follows the following pattern: low in early morning, peaking in the late morning, bottoming out in the late afternoon before rising to a smaller peak in the evening, and finally dipping again before bedtime. Dr. Thayer has found through various studies that these energy levels coincide with moods. He asked study subjects to rate the seriousness of their problems at different times throughout the day and found that subjects were most glum during late afternoon—about 4:30 P.M., when energy is generally at its lowest—and that they felt the most energetic and rated their problems as least bothersome in late morning when energy is highest. As Thayer says, "Issues don't change; mood changes."

What this means for walking is that *you should take therapeutic walk breaks at the times of day when you feel worst.* While some people can predict when they experience lows and highs throughout the day, others will have to plot a mood/energy curve to ascertain when a walk can do them the most good. The effect of the walk is that you will feel the same positive energy you would at the best time of day, the late morning! The less active or more lethargic or depressed you are, the greater will be the effectiveness of the 10-minute walk. If you are athletic, you'll need more of a boost to knock out the stress, and a slow walk will not be useful for you. However, if you are physically exhausted, have the flu, or are coming down with a cold, walking will not make you feel better. Rest up and begin to walk slowly once you recover.

Walking Out the Stress

Work-Related Stress

Many studies show that those who walk and stay physically active on the job tend to be both physically and psychologically healthier. The following examples illustrate how to walk through the stress "mine field" of the workplace.

Every Monday morning at 7:00 A.M., John, the chairman of a large

Fortune 500 company, has a "butt kicking" meeting with his top people. By 8:00 A.M., when John rolls into the gym for his workout, his face and body are stress personified. Everyone in the gym knows not even to talk to John when he first arrives. But after 10 or 15 minutes of walking on the treadmill, the tension leaves John's face and he might even say hello.

Work-related stress is probably the most prevalent form of anxiety in our society. If you are often upset, tense, and irritable or suffer from headaches or backaches that seem to all but disappear on the weekends, you are probably experiencing work-related stress. Another, more serious tip-off (although one you won't be cognizant of unless you have a portable blood pressure kit) is elevated blood pressure, *the* short-term sign of being overstressed. Blood pressure shoots up directly in proportion to how tense you are over, say, a speaking engagement or how badly your latest board meeting went. If you chronically suffer from high blood pressure, these short-term increases can be dangerous.

To combat job-related stress, you'll need to take the bilevel approach mentioned earlier: a regular walking program to build stress hardiness and quick walks as pressure release valves.

The timing of your walk is very important. You want to use the mind-sharpening, mood-enhancing benefits of walking right before the time you need most to be on your toes. If you must make an important presentation at 2:00 P.M., exercise during your 1 o'clock lunch hour. If you know you tend to droop after that business lunch, walk before you eat (the walk will also help to depress your appetite). Use your time in an airport during a layover to walk around and energize yourself for your next meeting (or to calm down if airplane travel makes you nervous). Even if you're trying to meet a deadline, taking a quick 5-minute walk will help you keep your cool and will in the long run help you work faster.

Walking will not only reduce the stress of a bad meeting with your boss, bad news about an account, or a run-in with a fellow employee, but will also keep you from losing your temper or acting in some other un-professional way. Whether you just take a walk down the hall or leave the building for 10 minutes for a quick spin around the block, removing your-self from the stressful environment will immediately calm you down.

You may be saying to yourself, "My schedule is full. I don't have time to walk." But if you give it a try, the positive effects will encourage you to rethink your priorities. Meet with fellow workers while you walk. After all, Peter G. Diamondis got offered his job as head of CBS magazines while on a stroll with CBS President William S. Paley. If the executives of the world's biggest corporations can find the time to walk, so can you.

Jennifer Pulsifer, the personal assistant to the head of a large public relations agency in Boston, has a demanding day that starts at 7:00 A.M and ends at 8:00 P.M. Jennifer, age 46, has found that walking helps her to reduce stress, put her problems in perspective, and clarify her thoughts.

She walks in the morning or in the evening, 4½ miles around a lake near her home. In the morning her walk helps her plan her day. In the evening it is a time to forget about work-related responsibilities. Jennifer feels that taking care of yourself by exercising regularly not only makes you feel better, but also makes you more productive.

Boredom and the Dead-End Job

Lack of change, excitement, and responsibility can be just as stressful as too much action and can lead to the same physical and emotional problems. A dead-end job is demoralizing not only because it undermines self-confidence, but also because it creates the feeling that you have no power over your destiny.

One way to feel *in* control is to cultivate outside interests and activities that are important to you. Try starting a walking program during your lunch hour. Getting others involved will make it a social event and a great break from the boredom of your job. You also will rack up points with your superiors as a "doer," which may help you get placed in a more challenging position.

Or it may be time to look for another job. The expression "pounding the pavement" symbolizes how you can use walking to help meet your new career goals. Do a substantial part of your new job search on foot, being sure to take the extra time (and steps) when visiting a potential employer to walk around the building and area and survey the community. Who knows, the company you end up working for may be next door to the one you went to visit. A walk opens up your vistas and creates new opportunities.

Taking time out during your job search for a reflective walk will keep you calm and give you a chance to put your troubles in perspective. It may also give you the opportunity to figure out what exactly it is you want to do. Walking will elevate your mood, and you'll feel more optimistic about your future.

Another plus is that a daily walk will trim you down and keep you looking fit (walking increases blood flow to your skin, creating a healthy glow) and feeling energetic, which will give you greater confidence for job interviews.

Family-Related Stress

The relaxing effects of a walk can calm you down even after the bitterest argument, and walking is a great way to bring the entire family together in a healthful and fun activity that everyone can and will enjoy. And walking is bound to get everyone talking together.

Fights

Gary Yanker challenges anybody having an argument with his or her spouse, family member, friend, or even boss or coworker to take the sparring partner on a walk. Within 10 minutes your anger should be under control. This is so because the natural rhythms of walking are relaxing and immediately lower your defenses. You are more open to constructive criticism and advice when you walk, and many people, including our contributing doctors, have told us about family disputes that were settled through walking. The energy used in walking will dissipate your anger (you'll notice that if an argument really gets heated, you'll automatically stop, so try to keep moving).

Holidays and Family Gatherings

It's Thanksgiving, and the entire family is gathered together in Grandmother's house. You've traveled many miles to be with your family, but after 2 hours, you begin to wonder why. You still aren't speaking to your eldest brother because of a fight 3 years ago. None of the children will talk with their grandparents, preferring to cluster around the TV until dinnertime, and you are too tired from traveling and cooking to really enjoy yourself. Family gatherings can be wonderful experiences, but they are rarely without stress. Old grudges can surface and tempers can fly. The pressure that holidays are "supposed" to be fun, added to the amount of work needed to prepare for them, can be enough to tense up even the most relaxed person.

The best antidote: Organize a family walk. Everyone from infants, who can be placed in strollers or backpacks, to the octogenarians can participate in a walk, and it's a great way to bring people of all ages together—certainly a much greater unifier than the television set. A walk will also wake everyone up after a heavy meal and get rid of that overstuffed feeling.

Usually, if you can persuade at least two people to go on a walk, others will follow. And because the pace is slow, conversation is easy. You can eventually visit with everyone in a small group of walkers by moving from the front to the back of the group.

Balancing Work and Family

Dr. George Monroe walks regularly with his wife and children, a 12-year-old son, a 10-year-old daughter, and a 14-month-old baby. His wife started walking with the baby in a frontpack, after she gave birth, to lose weight, and soon she had convinced the whole family to walk together. Dr. Monroe is aware of the health benefits of walking, but the primary reason for these outings is to draw the family closer together. It is the one time of day that everyone is together and can forget about their jobs and schoolwork and concentrate on each other (headphones are banned during the walks). Monroe's children are proud that their 49-year-old dad keeps in shape, and they are proud to be part of the process. "When my son got back from camp [this summer], he was champing at the bit to walk with his pa again," Monroe says.

Walking is the perfect family activity because it's spontaneous, you can talk while you walk, persons of any age can walk, and for those on a budget, it's cheaper than taking everybody out for ice cream or a movie.

Physical Symptoms of Stress

If you do nothing to remove the stress-induced tension from your body, it can, over time, strain your heart, arteries, and muscles and weaken them, causing high blood pressure, heart disease, and digestive tract disorders. Below are some common physical symptoms of stress, along with their walking solutions.

Muscle Tension

The back aches and headaches you may experience after a stressful day are directly related to muscle tension. If you sit at a desk all day, your back muscles are probably weak. Since they are not resilient, any tension at all will cause them to go into a spasm after only a short amount of time. Regular walking will gently exercise all the back muscles and thus reduce built-up tension, making your muscles stress hardy. The same goes for tight neck or facial muscles, which bring on headaches by constricting blood vessels leading to the brain. Again, walking will relax the body and release the tension, which will increase circulation to the brain and stop the pain.

Insomnia

If you've ever experienced insomnia, you know that the dread of going to bed and then lying awake, coupled with the worry of being too tired to face the following day's challenges, just increases your anxiety. Sleeping pills can be dangerous and addictive and are not a long-term solution. Walking can help to relax you and physically tire you out so you'll fall and stay asleep.

Try taking a vigorous walk (either outside or by walking in place) 2 to 3 hours before bedtime. Initially this may make you feel more awake, but if the walk was fast enough and long enough, you will begin to feel tired within a few hours and will fall asleep more quickly and sleep longer. A rule of thumb is to increase your walking mileage 25 to 50 percent per day when you experience insomnia. (Gary Yanker follows this rule whenever he can't sleep, and he not only sleeps through the night but can usually sleep an hour more than usual). If you must walk closer to bedtime, try a slower pace (a brisk walk may keep you awake too long) to relax you.

Illnesses

The long-term effects of stress can make you more susceptible to colitis, ulcers, and heart disease, although stress alone will probably not cause these conditions or diseases. Again, the adoption of a regular long-term walking program will help keep you free of these problems.

Probably the three most discussed intestinal disorders associated with stress are colitis, irritable bowel syndrome, and ulcers. Colitis is an inflammatory disorder of the colon that causes severe diarrhea, cramps, and many other symptoms. Two million people suffer from colitis and related diseases. Colitis is thought in some instances to be inherited, but an episode can be brought on by stress. Another, more common digestive tract disorder is irritable bowel syndrome (IBS), which strikes 50 to 75 percent of us at some time. IBS causes diarrhea or constipation (or alternating bouts of both) as well as stomach pains. Doctors do not know the cause of the condition, although studies have shown that stress brings on attacks of IBS. Although ulcers are not caused by stress, people with a tendency to develop ulcers also produce an increased amount of stomach acid when under stress. This excess acid in turn causes or aggravates ulcers.

To understand the effects of stress on the heart, refer to Book 3: Cardiowalking.

Walking Intervention Techniques

The intervention techniques described here are for alleviating stress and boredom when they occur (the walktherapy maintenance program in Chapter 6 is intended to help you reduce overall stress and anxiety over the long term by making your mind and body resilient to stressful episodes). These pressure-valve techniques will become increasingly unnecessary as you train your body to bounce back from stress.

The key is to use walking as an intervention therapy, by taking a walk break right before or right after a stressful situation or as soon as you become bored or lethargic. Your first step is to keep a stress, energy, and boredom log for 1 week (see sample on page 302). Pick a week that is representative of your normal schedule (i.e., not the week you go to the Bahamas on vacation, nor the week your annual budget is due). For each day, record the time and situations in which you felt bored or when your energy level hit a trough. Also record those times when you were under stress, felt tense or uneasy, fidgeted, or overate because you were nervous or bored.

This log will show you the best times to walk each day. Maybe its before or after your 10 o'clock business meeting, or perhaps at 4 o'clock when you begin to feel tired and unproductive. Some days you may have a more stressful schedule than others, so you should walk more on those days. Over time, you will see a pattern emerge. If you can anticipate stress, you can design a program that takes it into account. You'll also discover which works best for you—exercising before or after the stressful episode.

Add up all the times you made notations during the week and compare that number with the following chart. These levels will correspond to how long each miniwalk lasts, as well as the levels you will follow in the maintenance program. As you become less stress prone, you may be able to lessen both the duration and frequency of your short walks, and your maintenance program should eventually be enough on a daily basis (or at least 5 days a week) to keep stress at a minimum. Of course, situations will undoubtedly arise when an unscheduled walk break will do wonders. Keep a stress log for 1 week a month to monitor how well the techniques and program are working.

For every time you noted feeling bored, under stress, or lethargic, go out and walk for the prescribed length of time (if you are at level IV or V but only have time for a 5-minute walk, take it anyway—every little bit helps, although 15 minutes would be best). *Don't* skip the walk because you "don't have enough time." Any break will make you more productive and save you time in the end. If you absolutely can't leave your home or desk, walking in place for 5 to 10 minutes will provide the same result.

Exercisewalking Techniques

Choose a speed or intensity within the prescribed level at which you can exercise without becoming exhausted. Use the following techniques to

Walking Intervention Prescriptions

	LEVEL I	LEVEL II	LEVEL III	LEVEL IV	LEVEL V
Stress Episodes per week	Under 7	8–15	16–28	29–35	Over 35
Walking prescription	5 minutes	10 minutes	10 minutes	15 minutes	15 minutes
Speed (mph)*	3.5–4.5	3.5–4.5	3.5–4.5	3.5–4.5	3.5–4.5
METs†	5–15	5–15	5–15	5–15	5–15
Approximate number of walks per day	1	1–2	2–4	4–5	5–6

*If you are comfortable walking faster, do so. But the goal is to walk briskly, not as fast as you possibly can.

†METs are included in this chart for those who want to replace a traditional walk with one of the superstepping programs in Book 4.

help you reach the desired walking intensity and to make your walking effective.

Hold proper posture. Keep your back straight and your head up (see page 195 for full instructions).

Use breath play. Breathe deeply from your diaphragm (the muscle at the bottom of the lungs, behind the abdominal wall), feeling your chest and stomach expand with every breath (see page 170 for a full description).

Pump your arms. This will release tension that tends to accumulate in the neck and shoulders (think of the expression, "He's got his back up"). Pumping your arms can be almost as effective as a massage for dissipating muscle tightness (see page 99 for a full description).

You should not be winded or feel that you are exercising more than somewhat hard (see RPE scale on page 159). Take the talk test: If you can't talk or sing as you walk, then you are overexerting yourself.

Stress/Fatigue/Boredom Log

Write down the times and situations in which you felt stress, fatigue, or were bored (denoted by *s*, *f*, and *b*). Make a copy of this form for each day, and keep a log for 1 week.

Date: _____

TIME	S/F/B	SITUATION
____	____	_____
____	____	_____
____	____	_____
____	____	_____
____	____	_____
____	____	_____
____	____	_____
____	____	_____
____	____	_____
____	____	_____
____	____	_____
____	____	_____
____	____	_____
____	____	_____
____	____	_____
____	____	_____
____	____	_____
____	____	_____

Total number of episodes: _____

3. *Walking, the Positive Addiction*

All of us have some habit we'd like to break. Maybe you smoke and want to quit but don't know how, or maybe you'd like to cut down on your before-dinner drinks. Whether you've got a bad habit of overconsuming cigarettes or alcohol or a full-fledged addiction, you can cut back or cut out the problem by following the walktherapy program, *and* you'll be taking the first positive step toward improving your health and lifestyle.

All addictions and bad habits are responses to the challenges of life. Whether we need a cup of coffee to wake up, a cigarette to calm down, or sugar for a boost of energy, we are drawn to these substances because we believe they help us. Our careers, family, and social lives put us under much strain and pressure, and we are always looking for ways to handle what life throws at us. But these substances also can rob us of time and money and, in some cases, our health, and are not at all our best allies. However, if we are going to stop these bad habits, we need a substitute: something that works just as well or better. Otherwise there is no motivation to quit.

We cannot honestly tell you that being healthy and fit in general or that walking in particular will give you a short-term high equivalent to the kind you may find in alcohol or drugs, but we can promise that over the long run you will have a greater sense of well-being, which in the end will make you far happier and healthier than the effects of drugs or alcohol ever can.

The substances we discuss in this chapter—sugar, cigarettes, caffeine, alcohol, marijuana, sleeping pills, tranquilizers, cocaine, and other hard drugs—act as either stimulants or depressants. Stimulants like caffeine, sugar, and nicotine boost our energy to face problems; depressants like alcohol and sleeping pills relax us. Walking is the substitute for both: A brisk walk will energize you, and a slow walk will relax you. And walking has no negative effects associated with it, which is why we call walking the "positive addiction."

In this chapter you'll also find information about activity addictions, like compulsive gambling, workaholism, and overexercise. Walking and the moderate, balanced philosophy it exemplifies can help break these addictions as well, because it discourages obsessive or compulsive behavior.

First, we need to explain the difference between an addiction and a bad habit, although our exercisewalking techniques for stopping either are basically the same. If you can quit or reduce your consumption of a substance without experiencing any physical or mental discomfort, then you had a *habit*. If, however, you are *addicted* to a substance (and all the substances covered in this chapter can be addictive), cessation or reduction of intake will cause withdrawal symptoms like insomnia, headaches, and restlessness. The withdrawal symptoms associated with harder drugs like cocaine and heroin can be severe and include paranoia, depression, and even suicidal tendencies. A doctor's supervision is strongly recommended if you are contemplating quitting these drugs. No one really understands the cause of withdrawal symptoms, but doctors do know that when the harmful substances, whether nicotine, alcohol, or caffeine, leave your body, it is in a weakened state. Walking can help battle the depression that usually accompanies the breaking of a habit. Continuing a regular exercisewalking program will reduce the chances of a relapse.

Doctors, researchers, and psychiatrists believe that an addiction is a metabolic disorder that affects the central nervous system, specifically the hormonal-producing adrenal, hypothalamus, and pituitary glands. Some studies have also linked addiction to depression, a sadness or despair that in its clinical form is caused by a chemical imbalance in the brain and that researchers find drives some people to drug and alcohol abuse.* Like the tendency to have heart disease or hypertension, an addictive personality can be inherited, and depression runs in families, too. Having an alcoholic parent or a close relative who has been diagnosed with clinical depression is a clue that you may be prone to addictive behavior.

The walktherapy program is graded in terms of consumption. You can use the program to help you quit the more serious addictions cold turkey (under the supervision of a doctor or group program), or you can reduce

---

*Dr. Edward V. Nunes, who heads a drug study at the New York State Psychiatric Institute and Columbia Medical Center, has been doing studies that suggest that depression causes rather than is a result of drug addiction.

consumption, which is perhaps a more realistic option, especially for substances such as caffeine and sugar, which in moderate amounts are not dangerous. Of course, habits such as cigarette smoking are best dropped all together, but if you can reduce your consumption, you have already taken the first step to controlling your habit and reducing the health risks associated with it.

Why control your habit or addiction at all? The answer lies in questions like the following: Do you have to leave movies or meetings to go sneak a cigarette? Do people at the office know to avoid you until you've drunk at least one cup of coffee? Is your urge for sweets resulting in a larger dress or pant size? Does your workaholic nature anger your spouse or friends? Even if these don't seem like serious problems, they are signs that these substances and activities rule your life. If this lack of control bothers you, that is a reason to cut down or quit.

Take the following consumption test, which will signal if you are an overconsumer of any substance and if you are at risk for developing an addiction.

The Consumption Test

Sugar

1. Do you eat foods high in sugar or simple carbohydrates (for example, cakes, cookies, pies, jams, jellies, ice cream, bread or pasta made with white flour, or soft drinks) more than three times a day?

2. Do you have distracting cravings for foods high in sugar or simple carbohydrates more than twice a day?

3. Do you regularly (at least once a week) experience unexplained headaches, tenseness, mild depression, trouble sleeping, fatigue, anger, or shakiness? Does eating sweets cure these symptoms?

Alcohol

4. Do you have problems controlling the amount of alcohol you drink?

5. Do you have blackouts when you drink?

6. Do you pass out when you drink?

7. Do you drink three or more glasses of hard liquor, three or more beers, or three or more glasses of wine daily (or do you average more than 21 drinks, beers, or glasses of wine a week)?

8. Have you ever been treated for alcohol abuse?

9. Have you ever felt you should cut down on your drinking?

10. Have friends or family ever told you to cut down on your drinking?

11. Do you ever feel bad about your drinking?

Drugs

12. Do you ever use "recreational" drugs (marijuana, speed, acid, cocaine)?

13. Do you take prescription diet pills, tranquilizers, sleeping pills, or pain relievers on a regular basis and for more than 2 weeks at a time?

14. Have you ever been treated for drug abuse?

15. Do you smoke more than one pack of cigarettes a day?

16. Do you drink more than three cups of coffee a day (or five cans of soda with caffeine)?

17. Do you ever worry about the amount of drugs you take (or the amount you smoke)?

18. Do your friends and family worry about the amount of drugs you take (or the amount you smoke)?

Depression

19. Have you ever been treated for depression?

20. Do you consistently feel tired, lethargic, and without motivation?

Heredity

The following questions on your blood relatives' medical histories will shed light on your risk of having a chemical or metabolic disorder that could lead to addictive behavior.

21. Have any of your blood relatives consumed large quantities of sugar or simple carbohydrates on a regular basis (more than three times a day) and are thought of as having the "sweet tooth" in the family? If so, how many?

22. Have any of your blood relatives been diagnosed as alcoholics, or do you suspect any of your blood relatives of being alcoholics? If so, how many?

23. Have any of your blood relatives been addicted to drugs (marijuana, sleeping pills, tranquilizers, cocaine, other hard drugs)? If so, how many?

24. Have any blood relatives been heavy smokers (more than two packs a day)? If so, how many?

25. Have any blood relatives been treated by a doctor for severe depression? If so, how many?

The more immediate blood relatives (parents and siblings) you have who have manifested signs of addiction, the higher your chances of having inherited those tendencies. (If you have only one relative with any given addiction, your chances are probably less than 50 percent.) However, as with risk factors associated with heart disease, even if others in your family have had difficulties with substance abuse, it does not mean you are fated to become an addict. Even if you have the chemical errors that cause addiction, you can avoid it by abstaining from such substances as sugar, alcohol, drugs, and cigarettes.

If you answered yes to more than half the first twenty questions, then you can be considered an overconsumer. Also look at your answers within each category. If you answered yes to a majority of the questions in any area, you may have a problem with that substance. And you may find that some addictions feed on others; for example, high cigarette consumption often goes hand in hand with high alcohol or coffee consumption.

For a more specific view of exactly how much you consume, look at the following chart. At the end of the chapter you'll be asked to make a consumption log for 1 week to determine your level of usage, but for now just make a quick estimate to come up with a general idea of where you stand.

Levels I and II represent those who abstain or are very light users. Level III is a moderate user and represents the border between safe consumption and overconsumption. You may want to consider cutting down if you're at Level III. Levels IV and V are definite overconsumers and should try to cut down or quit their habits. Consuming at this level will almost certainly lead to future health problems.

If you feel your overconsumption is getting in the way of your life and goals, or if you believe you are addicted, follow the intermittent walking techniques at the end of this chapter to help you substitute a 5- to 15-minute walk break for your cigarette, cup of coffee, or any other habit. Follow the walktherapy maintenance program in Chapter 6 once you've gotten your habit under control.

Consumption of Sugar, Caffeine, Cigarettes, and Alcohol

LEVEL:	I	II	III	IV	V
Amount of sugar per day (in teaspoons)*	0–10	11–20	21–25	25–35	35+
Milligrams of caffeine per day†	0–300	300–600	600–750	750–1500	1500+
	0–2	2–4	4–6	6–10	10+
Cigarettes per day:	0–5	6–10	11–20	20–40	40+
Alcoholic drinks per day‡	0–1	1–2	2–3	3–5	5+
Alcoholic drinks per week:‡	0–5	5–9	9–14	14–21	21+

*See chart on page 309 for sugar content of selected foods.

†See chart on page 311 for caffeine content of selected foods.

‡One drink equals 2 ounces of hard liquor, 4 ounces of wine, or 8 ounces of beer.

Below you'll find general descriptions of sugar, cigarette, caffeine, alcohol, and drug habits, as well as compulsive behaviors such as chronic
gambling, overworking, and overexercising. Here you'll learn why you
are driven to these habits and why walking is a superior substitute.

Sugar

Yes, sugar is a drug, and according to some doctors, an addiction to sugar
may be the addiction that is the basis for all others. In chemical makeup,
alcohol and sugar are similar, and they are metabolized in similar ways
because they both immediately enter the bloodstream without the delay
of digestion. Sugar includes refined sugars (sugar, corn syrup, and honey)
and *refined* carbohydrates (as opposed to *complex* carbohydrates) made of
white flour.

Many people turn to sugar in times of depression or anxiety because it
offers a quick burst of energy. Chocolate, especially, is thought to release
hormones in the brain that create a mild state of euphoria. Unfortunately,
sugar's effects are short-lived. Within an hour of eating a candy bar, you
will "crash," i.e., become tired and tense. This drop in energy is thought
to be caused by an increase of serotonin, a neurotransmitter in the brain
that is a natural sedative. The tension may be a by-product of the fatigue.
You want to sleep, but you can't because it's the middle of the day, so
you end up feeling tense. However predicable the results of eating sugar,
we rarely learn that sugar is not a good pick-me-up. Instead, we may
repeatedly go back to sugar because we only remember the positive,
immediate results of eating it.

Walking can replace the good effects of sugar. A 10-minute walk will
give an energy boost comparable to that of a 2-ounce candy bar, without
the ensuing fatigue, and walking boosts your mood and therefore fights
depression.

Other Hints

Try substituting fruit for your candy or cakes. Fruit's natural sugar and
sweet taste will satisfy you and will reduce your hunger. Use wheat flour
products instead of bread and pasta made with white flour. Eat at regular
intervals, and carry appropriate snacks, such as fruit or whole wheat crackers, with you in case you get hungry and are away from home and your
supply of sugar-free foods.

The following is a list of foods and their sugar content. This will be used
with the analysis at the end of this chapter to determine how much sugar
you eat.

Sugar Content of Selected Foods

FOOD	SUGAR (IN TEASPOONS)
12-ounce sugared cola drink	8
12-ounce ginger ale	6
12-ounce milk shake	18
1 cinnamon roll	8
1 plain donut	4½
1 brownie	4
1 Fig Newton	3
1 cup vanilla ice cream	7½
1 slice apple pie	15
2-ounce candy bar	9
2-ounce milk chocolate bar	8
1 tbsp. jam	3½
1 cup sugar-coated cereal	8
1 slice white bread	3
1 cup pasta (made with white flour)	10

Caffeine

Caffeine is a ubiquitous drug, found in coffee, soft drinks, tea, over-the-counter pain killers and stimulants, and diet pills. Caffeine has a number of benefits, which is why 100 million Americans start their day with one or more cups of coffee. It stimulates the body and the mind, increases blood pressure and heart rate, boosts your mood, makes you feel alert, and helps you think more clearly. It is also thought to improve hand-to-eye coordination and prolong muscular stamina. Caffeine also increases your metabolic rate, meaning that one cup of coffee will make your body burn 3 to 4 percent more calories per hour.

You may be surprised to learn that caffeine is addictive, but if you currently drink six or more cups a day, you have probably experienced withdrawal symptoms without knowing it, in the form of headaches, tension, or fatigue. These reactions can begin after *only* 2 hours of abstinence from caffeine.

You may think that an occasional headache is a small price to pay for the benefits of caffeine, but studies have shown that more than two cups of coffee a day (between 200 and 300 milligrams depending on the way it's made) can cause serious problems, especially if you are pregnant, have heart disease, or have an ulcer or hiatal hernia. Caffeine is known to cause arrhythmias (irregular heart beats) and, for women who drink four or five cups of coffee a day, fibrocystic breast disease (benign cysts in the breast). Caffeine can also give you the jitters, keep you from sleeping at night, and increase your craving for sweets by lowering blood sugar levels. Caffeine has also been indicted in osteoporosis, because it is thought to impede the body's absorption of calcium. Other studies have shown that high caffeine intake in pregnant women can lead to low birth weights, and it may negatively affect fertility. Some researchers also believe those who drink more than two and a half cups of coffee experience more anxiety and depression than those who drink less than one cup a day.

Caffeine stays in smokers' systems only half as long as it does in the systems of nonsmokers. Therefore, if you quit smoking, decrease your caffeine consumption (if it is more than two and a half cups per day), because without the nicotine in your system, caffeine will have a much stronger effect on you.

Walking has all the positive effects of caffeine but none of the negative effects. A 10-minute walk break will make you more alert and help you think clearly, without artificially raising your blood pressure or heart rate. And the effects of walking last 1 to 2 hours, while caffeine lasts only about ½ hour. A few walks a day will help you sleep better, so you won't need that cup of coffee to get you going in the morning. A walk in the morning rather than a cup of coffee will prepare you for the day. Our bodies do not normally become fully alert until late morning, but you can help your body get up to speed with a walk before your day begins. Start out slowly, and work up to a brisk pace.

If you want to reduce your level of caffeine intake, your goal should be to drink only one to two and a half cups of coffee per day (a level I or II in our chart at the end of this chapter). If you have some of the health conditions mentioned earlier and want to quit totally, decaffeinated beverages, although they have approximately 3 milligrams of caffeine, are safe for you.

Other Hints

Switch to tea. A cup of tea has a third of the caffeine of a cup of "dripolated" coffee. Other beverages you may want to try are hot water with lemon, fruit juices, and milk.

The following chart will help you figure out how much caffeine you are ingesting. Use it when you do your consumption analysis at the end of this chapter.

Smoking

You know the hazards of smoking and you want to quit, but you don't know how. Walking is one of the best tools to help you break free of the smoking habit because it replaces the good effects of nicotine while *increasing* your level of health and fitness and helps you avoid the weight gain that often comes with quitting. *And walking can give you the same psychological benefits of smoking without any of the negative side effects.*

Caffeine Content of Selected Substances

SUBSTANCE	CAFFEINE (IN MILLIGRAMS)
Coffee (6-ounce cup, drip method)	150
Instant coffee (6 ounces)	60
Decaffeinated coffee (6 ounces)	3
Tea (6 ounces)	46
Hot cocoa (6 ounces)	13
Chocolate (1 ounce)	15
Cola drinks (12 ounces)	45
No-Doz (1 tablet)	100
Vivarin (1 tablet)	200
Anacin (1 tablet)	32
Exedrin (1 tablet)	65
Dexatrim (1 capsule)	200

All this means that you'll feel even better as a walking nonsmoker than you did as a sedentary smoker.

The reduction in the number of Americans who smoke over the last 20 years is the self-help, behavior modification success story of the century. In 1965, 40 percent of all adults smoked, but in 1987, that number had fallen to 29 percent, and most of those people quit without the aid of support groups or formal programs. Such a dramatic decrease is encouraging news for anyone who wants to change or break a habit.

We know the negative physical effects of smoking: heart disease, emphysema, strokes, cancer, and increased sickness, among others. Despite the reduction of smokers in the United States, there are still 50 million Americans each taking 1 million drags a year. The continued presence of smokers indicates that the threats of prolonged sickness, becoming a burden on one's family, and early death are *not enough* to get people to quit.

So why do smokers smoke? The act of smoking, occupying both the hands and the mouth, is habit forming. It gives you something to do, especially in uncomfortable social situations.

In addition, nicotine, the addictive ingredient in tobacco, is a very powerful drug with many positive qualities. It reduces stress and tension, increases energy, improves concentration, produces a mild euphoric state, and promotes weight loss. Nicotine acts quickly on the body. Within seconds it begins working on the brain, increasing the chemicals (called *neurotransmitters*) that make us more alert, reduce pain and anxiety, and enhance our feelings of well-being. This versatile drug is both a stimulant and a relaxant, and smokers can control the effects by taking quick puffs to wake up and deep long drags to relax.

Clearly, part of smoking's charm is its ability to deliver instant gratification to the smoker, which psychologically overpowers the knowledge that 20 years down the road smoking will almost inevitably cause health problems. The younger you are, the less you worry about your mortality, which is why teenagers continue to begin smoking each year. Yet the fact remains that cigarette smoking kills an estimated 540,000 Americans every year and that *each cigarette* costs the smoker up to 20 minutes of his or her life by substantially increasing the risk of developing heart disease, lung cancer, Alzheimer's disease, and other illnesses. Nicotine also destroys lung tissue, suppresses the immune system, and decreases the amount of oxygen that reaches the brain.

Your risk of sickness and death increases with the number of cigarettes you smoke per day, the number and deepness of your puffs, and whether you smoke low- or high-tar cigarettes. People who are at high risk for complications due to smoking include pregnant women, women who take birth control pills (especially if they are over age 35), people who come from families at high risk for heart disease, and people who already have such diseases as diabetes, osteoporosis, ulcers, blood clots, lung diseases, and glaucoma.

Walking has a higher payoff than smoking, and its effects are almost as instantaneous as smoking's. A 10-minute walk replaces, one for one, all the benefits of nicotine, and research shows that these effects will last up to 2 hours, while a cigarette may only appease you for 10 to 20 minutes.

The secret to quitting is to replace your cigarette addiction with walking.

Comparison of the Benefits of Walking and Nicotine

Walking	Nicotine
1. Increases alertness and gives you a sense of well-being	1. Increases energy
2. Provides a "retreat" from stress	2. Reduces stress
3. Relaxes you physically and mentally	3. Reduces tension
4. Decreases anxiety and depression and boosts your mood	4. Produces a mild euphoric state
5. Improves the quality of your work	5. Improves concentration
6. Reduces weight	6. Promotes weight loss

In addition, walking:

7. Improves your self-image

8. Helps you sleep better

9. Reduces risk factors associated with heart disease

Every time you have the urge for a cigarette, take a 10-minute walk break instead. Even if you quit by reducing the number of cigarettes you smoke over time rather than stopping cold turkey, walking will help keep you healthier. Longevity studies have shown that smokers who exercise are less likely to die prematurely than those who smoke and are inactive.

Studies have also shown that smokers involved in regular aerobic exercise are more likely to quit than those who are sedentary. Most likely, this is so because walking, and other exercise, reduces the withdrawal symptoms that often keep people from quitting.

Dorothy Chester, a 61-year-old from Cedar Rapids, Iowa, is a prime example. At age 59, after being diagnosed with high cholesterol, Dorothy decided to quit her 40-year-old 1½-pack-a-day smoking habit.

Dorothy felt fine for the first 6 weeks, probably owing to her daily 4-mile walk at her local mall. Yet at about the 2-month mark, Dorothy began to note some disturbing differences in her personality. "I'm usually a very even-tempered person," she says, "but I became very irritable and restless. I fidgeted all day long, and I'd wake up two or three times during the night." Her husband had recently gone into retirement, and these withdrawal symptoms, as well as the added stress of having him at home all day, made her fuse very short.

Dorothy decided she needed some way to diffuse this stress, so she added an extra 2-mile evening walk to her daily schedule. After about a month, she noticed that her irritability and hot temper were subsiding. "It took my mind off the urge to smoke and I found the natural, rhythmic motion of walking relaxing."

Dorothy has been off cigarettes for more than a year now and has not experienced withdrawal symptoms for 4 months. (Her friend at the Cancer Society said you can experience withdrawal symptoms for up to 2 years if, like Dorothy, you have smoked for a large percentage of your life.) "I can't tell you how much better walking has made me feel," Dorothy says.

Other Hints

If you are planning to cut down your habit rather than quit all at once, you can take a threefold approach: (1) use the walking intervention techniques and maintenance walktherapy program, (2) smoke cigarettes with lower tar and nicotine than your current brand, and (3) smoke less of each cigarette, take shallower drags, and take them less often.

Here's a schedule to help you smoke less of each cigarette: Smoke a cigarette, counting how many drags you take and how far you smoke the cigarette down. If, for example, you take ten drags on a cigarette and smoke it right down to the filter, you can begin your reduction program by cutting your puffs down to five and stubbing out the cigarette ¼ inch from the filter. Make a goal to decrease not only the number of cigarettes you smoke each day, but also how much of each cigarette you smoke. You can decrease the amount of smoke taken into your lungs by taking a drag, holding the smoke in your mouth, and then sucking it into your lungs with air (which will cut the concentration of pollutants traveling into your lungs).

The American Heart Association has recently announced that easing out of the nicotine habit, especially with the use of nicotine gum, is more successful than quitting smoking cold turkey. Nicotine gum is available with a doctor's prescription.

Alcohol

Alcohol can be a life-threatening drug for alcoholics (about 10 percent of the population). However, even if have your alcohol intake under control, you may wish to cut down because the few beers or glasses of wine you have each week are increasing your waistline or making you less productive (either because you fall asleep earlier after a few before-dinner drinks or you are groggy the morning after a lively party). Walking can help you reduce your consumption by replacing a drink with a walk.

For example, one couple, both high-powered executives, quit alcohol by taking a walk before dinner, the time they would normally drink to unwind after work. The walk helped them relax so much that they no longer had the urge to drink. Walking can also help by getting you away from other alcoholics or heavy drinkers, who may tempt you to take a drink. Try a walking club in your area. Here you'll meet people who have other ideas of entertainment than a glass of beer or a highball and in a setting devoid of alcohol.

A moderate level of drinking is no more than two drinks a day: two 1½-ounce drinks of hard liquor, two 4-ounce glasses of wine, or two 8-ounce glasses of beer every day or the same amount averaged over the course of 1 week. If you drink more than this each week, then you may be an alcoholic. Remember that this is just a guideline. Alcoholism is perhaps better defined as your compulsiveness about alcohol and how well you can control the amount you drink.

Signs of alcoholism include having memory blackouts and developing an increased tolerance for alcohol over time. If this describes your relationship with alcohol, and if you have suffered withdrawal symptoms, including depression and nervousness when you can't have a drink, then you may be an alcoholic.

If you are and decide it is time to stop drinking, you will want to quit cold turkey, and the intervention techniques and maintenance programs herein can help you do this (along with a visit to Alcoholics Anonymous or another support group). If you are a social drinker who wants to cut down, you can use our program to reduce your consumption to the desired level.

What if you are trying to quit but run into stumbling blocks like business or social gatherings where drinking is expected? It is true that alcohol is an integral part of some people's jobs. Salespeople especially complain that if they have hard-drinking clients, they are obliged to drink with them. If you are faced with such a situation, gracefully refrain from joining in a drink by explaining that you have work to do back at the office (thereby impressing your client with your professionalism).

Cocktail parties may also present problems for someone trying to avoid alcohol. Try going for a brief walk before you go to such a party. Nervousness is one reason you might take a drink as soon as you get to a party, and the walk will relax you. If you are in a bar or at a party, go for a walk (maybe with a friend) instead of sticking around for another drink. Hints for cutting down your alcohol consumption include mixing your drink with seltzer, water, or juice or switching on and off throughout the evening between alcoholic and nonalcoholic beverages. Drinking a glass of water before the party and one when you first get there will quench your thirst and make a drink less desirable.

Other Drugs

Some people turn to illegal substances, both stimulants and depressants, to give them energy, create positive moods, combat depression, and fit into certain social situations. Walking can give you all these positive benefits without any of the drawbacks of drug use.

The most popular stimulants are cocaine, amphetamines, and methamphetamines. These drugs all work on the central nervous system by raising levels of norepinephrine (adrenaline) in the brain. Norepinephrine increases heart rate, blood pressure, and respiration. In low doses, stimulants enhance positive moods and relieve tension.

Depressants, such as sleeping pills and tranquilizers, and hallucinogens, such as marijuana, are generally taken as relaxants or as a means of escape. Walking is the healthy alternative to these drugs because it is both a known relaxant and a great means of both physical and psychological escape. Walking at a comfortable pace provides what many psychologists refer to as an "island of peace" in your day. It is the action of walking rather than the setting that calms the mind, so even if you walk in a stark white room with no windows, you will feel less tense after your walk.

Walking's versatility as both a stimulant and a relaxant is why more and more substance abuse programs, such as the Benjamin Rush Center in Syracuse, New York, use walking to help their clients after detoxification. Walking gives them something to fill their time, provides a sense of satisfaction for completing a task, and increases self-esteem—all qualities that can help people stay off drugs.

If you are addicted to any drugs and want to quit, doctors recommend going cold turkey. Reducing intake over a long time from severely addictive substances does not work. If you are in need of support, look in the directory (Book 7) for walking doctors in your area who treat addiction or contact Narcotics Anonymous or your family doctor, who can help you find a drug rehabilitation program. You should also turn to the walktherapy maintenance program (Chapter 6) and begin a daily walking program before you start to quit so that it is already in place when you need it. After about 12 weeks, you will have a higher energy level, have lost weight, breathe easier, and look better. You do not need to follow the walking intervention techniques, although you may find that brief walks throughout the day will help you relieve stress.

Nonsubstance Addictions

Doctors indicate that people who are susceptible to substance addiction are also often compulsive gamblers, workaholics, or exercise addicts. Such people may also be more prone to compulsive eating disorders such as bulimia or anorexia nervosa. Let's examine these addictions.

Gambling

Gambling has been called the latest "social" addiction. There are twice as many pathological gamblers now as in 1974, and there is thought to be 5 million compulsive gamblers in America today, including a growing number of teenagers. Stories abound of people turning to crime to support their gambling habit and marriages breaking up because of one spouse's addiction to gambling. Police in Maryland even note that traffic accidents are up in their state because some gamblers are so eager to reach the Atlantic City casinos that they drive 100 miles an hour to get there.

A recent study done by Dr. Alec Roy, formerly of the National Center of Alcohol Abuse and Alcoholism, found a chemical imbalance in compulsive gamblers that may be responsible for their behavior. They are thought to lack neurochemicals that regulate arousal, thrill, and excitement and thus seek external stimulants, like gambling, to boost these neurochemicals. This theory is supported by gamblers' admissions that they gamble for the excitement, not for money.

Walking can help the compulsive gambler because walking also stimulates the arousal of the brain. If a simple walk doesn't seem to do the trick, you may want to take up wilderness hiking, where you may find the challenge of a steep mountain climb a healthy substitute for the thrill of betting.

Many people who quit the gambling habit experience withdrawal symptoms, including irritability, stomach distress, insomnia, and high blood pressure. Walking can help alleviate these physical discomforts by relaxing the body and enhancing peace of mind.

Workaholism

As you'll learn in the next chapter, workaholism is often associated with a "Type A" personality. It, like gambling, is an addiction, and it drives individuals to ignore every aspect of their lives save their careers.

With the growth of the Yuppie work ethic, workaholism has been given a good name. Slaving away 10 or more hours a day is considered part and parcel of being successful. However, as you learned in Chapter 2, stress *will* take its toll.

Take an hour out of your work schedule to walk each day. Use the time to visit with friends or family. You'll relieve the tension that's built up during the day, and you'll gain some perspective about where your career fits in with the rest of your life. There are, after all, other things in life besides work. For more information on changing your workaholic ways and "Type A" behavior, see Chapter 5.

Overexercising and Eating Disorders

Julie Morrison, now age 35, had the eating disorder bulimia (binge eating) since 1967, when she was 13 years old. Julie's binges were followed by crash dieting, and she was so obsessed with her weight that she weighed herself several times a day. As an adult, Julie sought psychological counseling (group therapy) at an outpatient treatment center for about 6 months. Although she learned a lot about herself and thought she had overcome her problem, she had not.

Julie was not actively bulimic for 20 years, but she was always obsessive, and this showed up in a running addiction. Running was the "in" thing to do. Julie also ran as part of her work—she had started a running magazine, *Running Journal*, with her husband. Running was a good workout, but not right for her particular body or personality. "I just did not enjoy running," said Julie. However, she pushed herself to be a better runner and was logging 20 to 40 miles per week and competing unsuccessfully in races.

One day, when Julie was getting over a bout of anemia, she decided to go out for a walk because she felt too weak to jog. She started out slowly but increased her pace because she was in a hurry. Suddenly, she was walking as fast as she could. "After about a mile, I realized I was breathing heavily, I was sweating—I was getting a workout. That's what made me stop running and take up racewalking," she said. To her surprise, Julie actually enjoyed walking. "Running sort of shocked my body, no matter if I started slow, I would always feel highly nauseous. But with walking, I never felt nauseous."

At first, however, walking, too, became an obsession. "I didn't just want to get a good workout, I wanted to be . . . a competitive racewalker, I wanted to be national class" Julie said. And she *was* a fairly competitive walker, winning many local races and even entering a marathon.

One day in late 1987 something clicked inside Julie. "I was trying to remember what kind of diet I was supposed to be on that day, and suddenly it sort of all crumbled. I said, 'I'm not going on a diet, I'm not ever going to diet again, I'm not going to compete or drive myself again. I want to enjoy life. . . . The emotional baggage, I don't want to carry it around with me anymore.' I stopped competing in races. I went back to taking a nice walk and enjoying it."

After her psychological breakthrough, Julie gained 20 pounds. But it did not faze her, because she now understood mental health is more important than physical perfection. (She has lost about 10 of those pounds, and she says she is still somewhat overweight by her own standards.) Walking does help her control her weight, but more important, walking serves as a reminder that Julie is finally in control—or rather, able to take a less compulsive, less control-oriented approach to exercise.

Because she wants to steer clear of rigidity, Julie maintains no real walking schedule. "I don't do it three times a week or watch my pulse or do any of the things you're 'supposed' to do in that way," she says. But she does walk nearly every evening, usually about 1 to 3 miles, although not always at an aerobic pace. "If I had realized what walking could do, I wouldn't have had the problems for 20 years!" she says.

As Julie Morrison's story demonstrates, you can do too much of a good thing. Overexercising is another example of compulsive behavior, and although in moderate amounts exercise is healthy, too much can cause injury or sickness through fatigue and can disrupt your life. One psychiatrist told us about a patient who missed his own wedding because it would have meant foregoing a workout. Walking has been used at the Benjamin Rush Center in Syracuse, New York, to treat patients with anorexia, who are usually compulsive about exercise as a way to keep down their weight. Health professionals there have found that introducing patients with anorexia to walking during their stay at the center has helped them adopt a moderate approach to exercise when they leave the center. Walking works better than other exercises because it is relaxing and can help lift the depression and anxiety that often lead to compulsive behavior.

If you are an exercise addict, you must undo some of the self-destructive ideas that you have about exercise. Don't feel guilty about missing a workout, and don't feel that you *must* exercise for a specified number of minutes each day. Rather, walk when you feel like it, and listen to your body. If you are tired, stop. Remember, walking is supposed to be enjoyable. Do not think of exercise as a solitary activity that dissociates you from others. Join a walking club or walk with family and friends.

It is best not to follow a formal walking program if you are compulsive about exercise. If you do find, over time, that you can handle a regimen, do not tax yourself. Start the walking maintenance program in Chapter 6 at Level I or II. You can increase the time you walk each day, but you should not progress higher than Level III.

Walking Intervention Program

Your first step is to be ready to quit or cut down your addiction or habit. Once you have made this decision, begin a Level I or II maintenance walking program (see Chapter 6) for at least 2 weeks prior to quitting so you'll be walking at a good pace by the time you're ready to begin lowering or ceasing your consumption. A brisk walk will deliver benefits much faster and stronger than a slow stroll.

Once you actually begin to quit, you will trade your one daily walk for a series of shorter walks, as outlined in the chart on page 321, to be taken at the times you have the urge for a sugar snack, cigarette, drink, or cup of coffee. Once you are in control of your habit (when you have been able to reduce your consumption to the desired level), then you can return to the maintenance program, where you will trade the intermittent walks for one long walk, which will help you maintain your fitness and keep you "clean." Of course, you can supplement the maintenance program with miniwalks whenever you feel the urge to indulge, but this should be increasingly unnecessary as time goes on.

Analyze how much and when you indulge in your habit of choice. Do you drink when you are tense and nervous? Do you crave sugar after your boss chews you out for a mistake? Do you smoke when you are bored? Choose a typical week and keep a log, like the one at the end of this chapter, of the times when and circumstances under which you indulge in your habit or habits. Then calculate your average daily consumption. (Note especially if you tend to consume more on certain days.) Once you know what drives you to your habit, you can begin to put the walking substitution in place when it's needed most. Take a brisk walk for the prescribed time period for your level every time you feel the urge to take a bite of that candy bar or smoke that cigarette or indulge in one of the other habits discussed here. Walk briskly, but make sure that you can talk as you walk. If you find you only turn to your habit at one time during the day, begin with the maintenance program, walking during the same time you would drink, smoke, or take drugs. Deep breathing is important. Make sure you are using your diaphragm when you breathe and are not just expanding your upper chest. If you are at Level V but only have 5 minutes, take the walk anyway. If you are on the high end of the scale, you may be walking an hour or more a day in 10- to 15-minute segments.

You don't always have to go outside to walk. Take a spur of the moment walk break by walking in place by your desk or in front of the television set. Both will provide the same benefits as going outside. Even moving your legs in a walking motion while sitting down (good for trains, cars, and airplanes) will give you extra energy or reduce tension. (See Book 4: Walkshaping for a variety of in-place walking techniques.)

If You Are Reducing Consumption over Time

The usual length of this intervention walking therapy is 6 to 8 weeks. Pick a level you want to eventually reach and make intermittent reductions, cutting your consumption by 20 percent each week. For example, if you smoke two packs of cigarettes a day, the first week you will cut out eight cigarettes (each day for a week you will smoke thirty-two cigarettes instead of your usual forty). The second week you would cut another 20 percent off your daily dose (in this case, about seven cigarettes, or a total of twenty-five per day for a week), and so on until you hit your desired level. On the chart below you can see that a two-pack-a-day smoker will be walking four to six times a day for 10 minutes each time. What times of the day you walk will depend on when you have an urge for a cigarette. By the third week, you will have dropped from Level IV to Level III, and you will probably be walking only three to four times a day.

If you are already very close to your goal, you may need only 1 or 2 weeks to reach your level. Start the maintenance program when you are at your desired level of consumption or when you reach Level III, whichever is highest.

If You Opt to Quit All at Once

Look at the following chart and find your consumption level, the prescribed number of walks per day, and their duration. Start on the maintenance program but feel free to take miniwalks whenever you have the urge to smoke, eat sweets, or drink coffee or alcohol. As time goes on, you will need less and less of these stop-gap walks and can begin replacing them with one 20- to 60-minute walk per day.

Diet

Proper diet is important when overcoming an addiction. Adopt a balanced diet like the one in Book 4: Walkshaping and Weight Control.

On pages 321–322, you'll find a chart of withdrawal symptoms for each of the addictions. Walking, as explained in this and earlier chapters, reduces all of the withdrawal symptoms associated with breaking addictions. Keep this handy to remind yourself that these feeling are normal.

Avoiding the Relapse

Once you quit, you may be faced with situations where the urge to smoke or drink will be overwhelming. Maybe it's in a crowded bar, maybe it's

Walking Prescription Keyed to Consumption of Sugar, Caffeine, Cigarettes, and Alcohol

WALKING LEVEL	I	II	III	IV	V
Amount of sugar per day (in teaspoons)*	0–10	11–20	21–25	26–35	35+
Milligrams of caffeine per day†	0–300	300–600	600–750	750–1500	1500+
Cups of coffee per day	0–2	3–4	5–6	7–10	10+
Cigarettes per day	0–5	6–10	11–20	21–40	40+
Alcoholic drinks per day‡	0–1	1–2	2–3	3–5	5+
Alcoholic drinks per week‡	0–5	5–9	10–14	15–21	21+
Length of walks (in minutes)	5	10	10	10	15
Approximate number of walks per day	1–2	2–4	3–4	4–6	4–6
Walking speed (mph)	3–5.5	3–5.5	3–5.5	3–5.5	3–5.5
MET level of exercise:	4–15	4–15	4–15	4–15	4–15
Level at which to begin maintenance program	I	II	III	IV	V

*See chart on page 309 for sugar content of selected foods.

†See chart on page 311 for caffeine content of selected foods.

‡One drink equals 2 ounces of hard liquor, 4 ounces of wine, or 8 ounces of beer.

Withdrawal Symptoms Associated with Selected Substances

SUBSTANCE	WITHDRAWAL SYMPTOMS	LENGTH OF WITHDRAWAL
Sugar	Headache, stomach ache, back ache, indigestion, depression	1–2 days
Caffeine	Nervousness, irritability, headaches, listlessness	1–2 days
Cigarettes	Edginess, irritability, insomnia, gloominess	Varies wildly, from a week to several months (depending on length of time and quantity you smoked)
Alcohol	Nervousness, irritability, depression, fear	3–4 days to several weeks

Withdrawal Symptoms Associated with Selected Substances (cont.)

SUBSTANCE	WITHDRAWAL SYMPTOMS	LENGTH OF WITHDRAWAL
Marijuana	Anxiety, depression, feeling "out of touch"	1–2 weeks
Tranquilizers* and sleeping pills	Agitation, anxiety, fear, insomnia; in severe cases, seizures or hallucinations	Total time 1–2 months; less severe cases, 2–5 days
Speed and cocaine	Severe depression, sluggishness, fatigue, confusion, disorientation, paranoia	Total time 1–2 months

*Tranquilizers' withdrawal symptoms may not start for 1 to 3 weeks, since the active ingredients are still found in the body's tissues and are still being released into the bloodstream.

because your boss has just let you go, or maybe it's because you've just had a fight with your spouse. These are all times when you may want to throw your hard work away and have a cigarette or a drink. Walking can help by giving you an out. Leave the smoky bar for a breath of fresh air, leave your office for 5 or 10 minutes, or take your spouse for a walk to continue your discussion.

If you do "fall off the wagon," begin from your present level of consumption and follow the preceding plan from the beginning. Don't be too hard on yourself if you do relapse. Relapses are part of the quitting process, and many people go through one or more before they are finally free of their habit or addiction. Don't use them as an excuse to give up the program.

Remember that if you fight your addiction, whatever it is, one walking day at a time, you can break your unhealthy habits.

The Habit Diary

For 1 week, record the time of day and the situation in which you were most apt to indulge in your habit. Make a copy of this form for each day.

Date: _____

TIME	SITUATION
_____	_____
_____	_____
_____	_____
_____	_____
_____	_____
_____	_____
_____	_____
_____	_____
_____	_____
_____	_____
_____	_____
_____	_____
_____	_____
_____	_____
_____	_____
_____	_____
_____	_____
_____	_____
_____	_____
_____	_____

Total: _____

4. Walking for Life's Major Traumas

Throughout our lives we all experience major traumas—the death of close relatives or friends, a divorce, the loss of a job, or a major, perhaps fatal, illness like cancer. For the most part, these are events over which we have no control, which is part of the reason these experiences can be so devastating.

In this chapter you'll learn how walking can help you with the big problems. These are the sorts of major stresses found in Levels III, IV, and V on our stress scale from Chapter 1. Here you'll read stories of people who faced death, sickness in their family, and other major events in their lives (many of them happening simultaneously) but who were able to cope and remain strong and well with the help of a regular walking program.

If you've experienced any of the events or problems outlined in this chapter or in the top tier of the stress list in Chapter 1, you should follow our maintenance walking program (Chapter 6). Notice that the walking times for these stresses can be as much as 4 hours (for the entire day, not necessarily all at once). Some walkers we interviewed have found that filling their time with an activity like walking can be therapeutic. But this is by no means an obligation. Even if you walk for 15 or 20 minutes, you will feel better and will be able to cope better with whatever problem you are facing.

Take the example of Marvel Svoboda, who, after she retired from her job 5 years ago, joined a walking club because she missed being around people during the day. She and her husband, Leon, who then had congestive heart failure, diabetes, and hypertension, started walking with the club everyday, but they never realized how important this daily routine would become for them.

About a year after they began to walk, Leon discovered a sore on his tongue. A biopsy was taken, the growth proved to be malignant, and a date for surgery was set. "There was an awful lot of stress in this house," said Marvel about the time before Leon's surgery. "I envisioned everything." She and Leon continued to walk 3 to 4 miles every day before Leon's surgery, which she said helped to diffuse the anxiety and fears.

"In the beginning, being diagnosed with cancer throws you for a loop," Leon says matter-of-factly. Leon was worried about what would happen to his speech after the surgery, as well as the risks of surgery itself and the threat of the cancer spreading to other parts of his body. "Walking really helped to keep my mind off it and think about other things. It also helped me relax and be positive."

The doctors successfully removed the cancer, along with half of Leon's tongue, but the walking helped him to recover quickly from the operation. "Everyone was worried that I wouldn't be able to talk. When my wife and daughter first came to visit me after the surgery, they brought a pad and pencil with them so I could write. As my daughter greeted me and handed them over to me to respond, I looked at her and said, 'What the hell are you doing with that?' "

It's been 4 years since Leon's operation, and the couple continues to walk 3 miles every day, and both are in better physical condition than ever before.

By far the greatest reactions to major changes or events in our lives are depression and fear. These feelings can paralyze you, keeping you from doing the things you need to do to cope with the situation. But sitting around, wallowing in your gloom will only sink you farther into the mire. A long walk at a casual pace can be especially helpful when you are experiencing depression. Even if it's only ¼ mile around the block, it is a small signal to yourself that you can take control. Coming to grips with bigger problems begins with convincing yourself you can manage the smaller ones.

Depression affects your neurochemistry by producing less serotonin and norepinephrine, chemicals in the brain that are responsible for positive moods. Usually, severely depressed patients (either ones who have experienced a traumatic event or who have a chemical imbalance) are given antidepressant drugs that help boost the manufacture of these chemicals. Psychiatrists, however, have noticed that depressed patients who exercise seem to produce more of these chemicals without the aid of drugs.

Dr. Bill Jones, a psychiatrist in Delaware, encourages his clinically depressed patients to walk once they have begun to get better: regain their appetite, become more social, and shake suicidal or self-destructive thoughts. Dr. Jones has also found that some patients who become more depressed during the fall and winter (called *seasonal affective disorder*) when sunlight, a known mood elevator, is at a minimum have been helped by walking outdoors during the winter months. In general, psychologists and psychiatrists encourage their clients to walk outside rather than walking indoors on a treadmill (which, to some people, may be a metaphor for expending lots of energy but going nowhere).

The most important factor with a depressed patient is to start the exercise off at a moderate level that won't discourage the patient. If the patient does not stick with walking, then he or she will become even more depressed because he or she has failed. Therefore, *keep it easy and make sure the goals are attainable.* Dr. John Simpson, a psychologist, had one client begin by taking a few extra steps every time she took the garbage out. Soon she was walking around the block.

Walking will also help you remember better times. The ability to access memories is influenced by mood. When you are in a bad mood, you remember unhappy memories; when you're in a good mood, you remember happy times. Walking is a known mood elevator, so an invigorating walk will help you to recall when you felt better or times that you came through difficult circumstances. Walking will help relax you to face challenges and will provide a time for you to escape. It will also keep you healthy, as studies have shown that major stress weakens the immune system and can make you susceptible to illness. Walking with a friend or family member can be extremely therapeutic, as during trying times walking and talking with those who are closest to us can be comforting. Other people prefer to walk alone, because the presence of others disrupts their thoughts as they try to work out a problem.

Another option is to join a walking club. People who have faced major life events have found that walking in a group provides a feeling of community and helps take their minds off their troubles. Floyd Davis, who joined the walking club at the Westdale Mall in Cedar Rapids, Iowa, after he was diagnosed with prostate cancer, said that walking has helped him both physically and psychologically. "You don't sit around thinking about your problems," he says. Floyd, who later had heart bypass surgery, has logged between 3000 and 4000 miles, averaging about 4 miles per day every morning. His cancer is now in remission.

Floyd finds the camaraderie of the walking club motivating. "Everyone hollers 'hi' as you go by, and if you stop to check your pulse, not more than three people will go by before someone asks if you're all right." He's also found the other walkers a source of motivation because many have similar or worse medical problems that they have overcome with walking.

Death of a Loved One

The death of one's spouse or loved one is considered the most stressful incident of a person's life. Dot Becker, age 62, has been walking since

February of 1989, soon after the death of her husband of 33 years. After his death, says Dot, "I felt at loose ends, apathetic, depressed. I realized I had to get out of the house and get my life back together again." So she started walking. She feels that walking was responsible for helping her to adjust to life without her husband. After 6 months of walking 2 miles 7 days a week, Dot feels active and interested in life again.

The best approach to the death is let yourself grieve. Don't make yourself "get over it" by a certain date. You can and should allow yourself time to be sad. Some psychiatrists report that is it not unusual for people to grieve for up to 2 years and intermittently after that for many more. It is healthier to grieve than to keep a stiff upper lip according to many psychiatrists. A walking program over those 2 years may help you because it is physical, goal-oriented, and elevates moods. It also will keep your body strong to fight illnesses that often strike those under extreme stress. Joining a walking group will also help you conquer loneliness.

Patty Adams, age 42, started experiencing panic attacks after the death of her 18-year-old daughter in a drowning accident. "Walking has carried me through the grief process of losing my only child. I tried support groups and counseling, but walking was the answer for me," said Patty, who walks 6 days a week, averaging 25 to 28 miles. Patty, who walks a 15-minute mile, feels walking is effective because it is a calming activity. "I will never be the same," she said, "but walking has provided the means of surviving this trauma."

Illness

Henry Heaton had a heart attack at age 66. He was told by his doctors that he was not strong enough to have bypass surgery and that he had only 3 months to live. It is now 3 years later, and Henry not only survived triple bypass surgery, but was the family's pillar of strength during the past 2 years, when his daughter-in-law had a kidney transplant and his wife was hospitalized for cancer tests. He feels his amazing comeback and optimism were due to a daily walking program at his local mall that his doctors initially warned him he was too weak to do. He's logged over 7000 miles since his original diagnosis and is still going strong, continuing his business, traveling frequently, and still walking 3 miles a day.

Research being done with AIDS and cancer patients shows that exercise, including walking, can provide a sense of accomplishment and hopefulness that helps deal with terminal illness. Giving terminal patients goals to attain, whether it is the number of steps they take or the number of miles they walk, fosters a feeling of control and self-worth.

Joan Simon, age 57, was diagnosed with breast cancer 10 years ago and has had several relapses since that first diagnosis. She believes that illness is aggravated by emotional problems and their repression, but that "walking is life motivating and life affirming." Joan chose walking because it was something she could do even when she didn't have a lot of energy. And most important, it made her feel a part of the world.

Joan is now in complete remission and reports that she feels great. She walks 3 miles four to five times a week, eats a healthy diet, and believes her positive attitude and lifestyle are responsible for her recovery.

Divorce or Separation

Divorce is considered the second highest cause of stress according to the Holmes and Rahe scale, but in some instances divorce can be even more painful than having a mate die. As with the death of a spouse, you will undoubtedly feel anger, guilt, and abandonment or some combination of these emotions.

Walking every day can be a good means of building confidence, fighting depression, and relieving anger. Joining a walking group can be a good antidote to loneliness.

If you are going through a separation or divorce, keep the following in mind:

1. Bereavement over divorce is similar to that over a death. As with a death, it is important not to deny the pain or cut short the period of grieving.

2. Don't deny the existence of your marriage or your ex-spouse. It is not realistic to pretend those 10 or 20 years never happened.

3. Don't run away. This is true in both the physical and the psychological realm. Don't jump into a new relationship too soon as a means of escape. Nor should you leave town, on the theory that a new environment will change everything. It won't, and it might make you more unhappy because you've left friends who will be particularly important to you during this time.

Retirement

Stress is often associated with having too much to do and too many responsibilities to meet. Stress can also be caused by boredom or by suddenly having nothing to do. This kind of stress is associated with retirement, both chosen and forced early retirement. One day you are a "productive" member of society—you have a job to go to 5 days a week and that job defines who you are. Along with your work comes a whole group of built-in friends. But literally the next day you no longer have a role. You may feel worthless because you lack a purpose. Added to this are the additional fears of financial hardship, ill heath, and death.

Walking can play an important role in adjusting to retirement. Following a walking program provides goals, which people are used to from work and are lost without when they retire. Walking every day will also give you energy, elevate your mood, and give you a reason to get out of the house and see the world. Joining a walking club can help you meet new friends. If there isn't one nearby, create one of your own. If you like to travel, take a walking vacation. There are many parts of the world that are great places to visit and walk, whether it's the beaches of California or the Great Wall of China.

Even if you have another job or time-consuming activities already lined up for your retirement years, walking once a day at lunch time or in the mornings or evenings will keep you feeling healthy and energetic.

Unemployment

Losing your job can be devastating. As with retirement, you no longer have a clear identity or role in the world, but even worse, you didn't choose unemployment, it chose you. You will undoubtedly feel out of control of your life, and walking can help you—by raising your morale, helping you look and feel better, and keeping you active. Studies show that stress, such as losing your job, depresses your immune system, and walking can help strengthen it. While the first few weeks after you lose your job are like a holiday, after that, your self-esteem may take a dive, and the longer it takes you to find a job, the worse you feel. Make looking for a job your full-time work. The more energy you spend looking, the faster you'll get one. Making yourself a schedule will help you get more done, and make a walking regimen part of that schedule. Walking will help reduce the stress of looking for a job. You may also lose some weight, and being slimmer will make you more confident during job interviews.

Although walking can't undo any of the traumatic experiences we all must face in our lives, many people have successfully used walking as a tool in helping them cope with the resulting stress, anger, and depression. Joan Simon, the walker with cancer you read about earlier, said, "If I can maintain a decent walking speed, it says I'm OK, and feeling better makes you better."

5. Walking for Personality Changes

Can walking really help change your personality? The answer is a resounding *yes*—although such changes won't occur overnight.

Walking is a natural motion, something our bodies are designed to do. Because we do it unconsciously, the way we walk reflects our personalities and moods. If this sounds farfetched, think about people you see on the street. If someone is shuffling along, his head down and eyes glued to the ground, you instinctively know he is sad or upset about something. You also know that someone taking staccato steps, with his shoulders hunched, is both hurried and worried.

By standing and walking properly, shoulders back, back straight, eyes looking forward, you will feel more relaxed and confident—and you will project that image to others. In short, you can change the way you feel by the way you move, and vice versa.

Before you analyze how you walk, however, and what that means about you, let's start with a nonphysical personality analysis: Are you a workaholic who spends 12 hours in the office everyday? Or do you balance work with play? Do you find it difficult to motivate yourself to do things? This chapter will test you for your personality type and, along with an analysis of the way you walk, will help you learn something about yourself and perhaps make some changes.

The "Type A" personality profile was first developed by Drs. Roseman and Friedman, two cardiologists who, in the late sixties, found a correlation between a certain personality type and an increased chance of developing heart disease. Type A personality was characterized by extreme competitiveness, an insatiable desire for achievement, aggressive behavior, impatience, restlessness, a feeling of being constantly under a great time pressure, and the feeling of overwhelming responsibility. Type A's are not very good at coping with stress, probably because they have an oversensitive sympathetic nervous system that sends out signals to prepare the body for a fight at the slightest provocation.

The opposing personality profile is what we'll call "Type C." Type C persons are phlegmatic. They feel no time constraints and no responsibility. Type C's may feel they have no real control over what happens to them and will postpone doing today what they can do tomorrow or next week. Type C's also tend to be submissive and passive, letting others take the lead.

The "Type B" personality is the balance between these two extremes. Such persons are assertive without being aggressive, and while motivated, they allow themselves to take time out to do things they enjoy. They do have a sense of responsibility for their actions, but they know when situations are beyond their control.

We are certainly not recommending that any type should dominate, nor that the extremes, Types A and C, be wiped out as if they were smallpox or the black plague. There is a place for a competitive nature, as there is for a passive one. But if you feel your Type A or C personality is chronic, that you constantly feel under pressure and hostile or that, on the other hand, you feel totally out of control of your life, then you may decide that it is time for a change. Walking can help you find a balance.

Dr. William Farrell, a dentist in Atlanta, Georgia, learned the value of moderation after he developed chronic fatigue syndrome (formerly Epstein-Barr syndrome), a condition nicknamed the "Yuppie disease" because it is brought on by chronic stress and has hit many overambitious, upwardly mobile professionals.

Dr. Farrell, an ultramarathoner (walking and running in multiday races), always led a very active life. In addition to running his own dental practice, he would exercise 6 to 8 hours a day: running, weight training, bicycling, and walking to prepare for his competitions.

About 2 years ago, his wife broke her leg, and Dr. Farrell spent four nights without sleep caring for her. He had just completed a 170-mile walk across Georgia and was recovering from a painful foot injury. In short, his life was packed full of both physical and emotional stress.

Shortly after his wife's injury, Dr. Farrell began having flulike symptoms that lasted a few days. He started to train again, but he had no energy. His fatigue grew worse. He was forced to lie down on his couch between patients, and some days he would arrive at the office so exhausted that he'd have to turn around and go home.

Finally, Dr. Farrell developed walking pneumonia that he could not shake. No one knew what was wrong with him until he found a friend who had the same symptoms who had been diagnosed with chronic fatigue syndrome.

Dr. Farrell's ailment seems to be in remission now, but he is careful about overtaxing himself. He's now down to 1- to 2-hour workouts daily. "If I don't feel good, I don't work out," he says. Although he plans to continue ultramarathons, he preaches to the walkers in the walking club he started to stay well within their limits.

What Type Are You?

The following test will help you to ascertain where you fall within the Type A to C personality spectrum. Circle the number that you feel most closely represents your own behavior.

1. Never late	7	6	5	4	3	2	1	Frequently don't keep appointments
2. Avoids competition	1	2	3	4	5	6	7	Very competitive
3. Finishes other people's sentences (interrupts others, etc.)	7	6	5	4	3	2	1	Doesn't pay attention when others speak
4. Always rushed	7	6	5	4	3	2	1	Never rushed
5. Does not mind waiting	1	2	3	4	5	6	7	Impatient
6. Always feel can give more	7	6	5	4	3	2	1	Everything is too much effort
7. Takes things one at a time	1	2	3	4	5	6	7	Tries to do many things at once
8. Emphatic and loud in speech	7	6	5	4	3	2	1	Speaks slowly and quietly
9. Needs work recognized by others	7	6	5	4	3	2	1	Gets no satisfaction from work
10. Fast (eating, walking)	7	6	5	4	3	2	1	Slow doing things
11. No motivation	1	2	3	4	5	6	7	Hard driving
12. Hides feelings	7	6	5	4	3	2	1	Dwells on feelings
13. Follower	1	2	3	4	5	6	7	Leader

14. Disappears in the   1 2 3 4 5 6 7   Dominates social
    crowd in social   situations
    situations

15. Inflexible to changes   7 6 5 4 3 2 1   Submissive
    and suggestions

Now add up your points. Scores range from 15 to 105. The higher the
score, the more Type A characteristics you have, and the closer the score
is to 15, the more you are a Type C personality. A score of 60 would make
you the quintessential Type B. Undoubtedly if you are a Type B, in some
instances you will fall closer to Type A and in others closer to Type C. A
high score (over 90) indicates that you may be at risk for stress-related
illnesses, including heart disease, and should use 10-minute walks throughout the day to diffuse stress. If you scored below 90, you are not in any
"danger," but walking can certainly help you recover from stressful times
in your life. If your score was below 50, you may not have enough stress
in your life. Remember, change is essential.

If you are a Type A, forget about any mileage or speed goals on longer
walks. Use your walking time to unwind. If you are a Type C, you might
benefit from entering short walking races (1 to 3 miles), which will increase
your feelings of accomplishment and belonging.

Now that you know where you stand, let's see if you manifest these
traits in the way you walk. Get a friend or family member to observe you
walking. They can compare what they see with the following chart. Of
course, there are undoubtedly Type A's who walk like Type C's, and vice
versa, but use this chart as a guideline to typical walking styles.

Watch your shoulders, which are one of the more expressive areas of
your body. If they are hunched up around your ears, then any tension
that has accumulated in your muscles is not being released. This may also
mean that you are depressed or anxious about something. And the tenser
your body, the more tense it will become. Relax your shoulders, pushing
them down and back. Imagining you are holding small weights in your
hands will help you position them correctly as you walk. Tenseness might
also be manifested in a robotic walk, where the arms, legs, and hips are
rigid.

It's also important to hold your head in a neutral position. Looking
down will cramp your breathing, making it shallower, and increase tension
in your neck. Fix your sight on a point at least 15 feet in front of you.

Also be aware of your breathing as you walk. A shallow breath might
indicate that you are tense as well. Breathe deeply using your diaphragm
so your stomach and chest expand with each breath. A deep breath will
give you energy if you are feeling lethargic and relax you if you are feeling
tense.

Walking Styles of Types A, B, and C

	TYPE A	TYPE B	TYPE C
Heel strike:	Very defined	Natural	Not defined
Stride length:	Very long and powerful	Moderate length	Slow and short
Arm pumping:	Arms almost jerk out of sockets	Strong but not exaggerated	Little to no arm movement
Breathing:	Shallow and quick	Deep and relaxed	Shallow
Posture:	Head down or neutral, shoulders hunched, leans forward at the waist	Head neutral, eyes ahead, shoulders down and relaxed	Head down, shoulders hunched

Your walking gait may not only represent your personality, but it may also be damaging your body. David and Deena Balboa, sports psychotherapists and directors of The Walking Center in New York City, tell the story of John W., a 41-year-old, upper-level manager in a large corporation. John, a racewalker, came to the Balboas because of a pain in his heel. John had a typical Type A personality, aggravated by a good deal of work-related stress, and this aggression manifested itself in the way he walked. John leaned forward at the waist, jamming his heels into the ground with each step and thrashing his arms back and forth in an attempt to increase his walking speed. The Balboa's videotaped John walking to help him see and correct his aggressive and inefficient walk. The Balboas taught John to keep his back straight and his pelvis tucked under, along with other techniques that helped him to smooth out his gait. Within three sessions, John had a much more relaxed, natural walking style, what David called "assertive" rather than "aggressive."

Your walking style can also say things about how you want others to perceive you. When one of our researchers went to interview the Balboas, they put her on the treadmill so she could experience first hand how they work. She is rather small, and as David pointed out, she walks with a very heavy step, as if to compensate for her size by saying, "I'm here, I'm bigger than you think I am. Pay attention to me." David and Deena explained that while this heavy step, which may have been useful for a child, remained a habit into adulthood, a light, elegant walk would serve her better, be more natural, and give her a more positive image to project to the world.

Is Walking Your Sport?

We mentioned earlier that how you move reflects your personality—either attributes you already possess or ones you'd like to have. Logically, then, the sport you choose says something about who you are. If you have a good deal of self-discipline, you may become a dancer. If you are aggressive and competitive, you may choose tennis or jogging. If you are a loner, you may take up bicycling or hiking. These sports all magnify specific qualities in a person. The sport you choose may also reflect the kind of personality you would like to have. If you are meek, you may take up judo to build assertiveness; if you are tense, you may take up yoga.

All the sports we've mentioned have a certain profile of characteristics associated with them, and walking is no different. Walking represents a balanced lifestyle. Walking is noncompetitive (unless you racewalk), it lends itself to social interaction (walking clubs, and walking with family and friends) and spontaneity. You don't have to be severely disciplined to walk (other than possessing the motivation to leave the house), nor do you have to be athletic. People who walk for exercise are usually less obsessive and less rigid than runners, for example, and less time-pressured.

Even if you like the sport you're currently involved in and feel it's a good reflection of your personality, walking as a secondary activity can give you additional physical and psychological benefits, as you can see from the following list.

Body Builder: The body builder who takes up walking can benefit from getting aerobic exercise and valuable calorie burn and give his or her joints a rest from the strain of lifting heavy weights. Walking will make you more flexible, more outgoing, and more multidimensional. It will take your attention away from yourself and your body and get you away from the confines of the gym to walk and see what's going on in the world. Body builders can follow the powerstepping and stroking program (See Book 4, pages 224–248), which includes walking with hand and ankle weights and weight-loaded backpacks, which will help to fine-tone the body.

Dancer: Walking can help relieve the stiffness of your leg joints and maintain flexibility after a workout. Walking will help you become more relaxed, taking you away from the studio and giving you a chance to meet nondancers. Former dancers, such as Shirley MacLaine and Cyd Charisse, often take up walking because the years of dancing have weakened their joints, so it's the only exercise they can do comfortably.

Runners: You probably can't imagine that walking could give you a fulfilling workout, but in fact, walking fast is even more physically demanding than running. Learning and mastering racewalking techniques (which can take 6 months to a year) also will provide a new challenge to your workouts. Walking is also a good way to stay in shape if running injuries are keeping you off the track. Finally, walking can help you to become less "Type A" about exercise.

Swimmers: You will burn more body fat walking than swimming. In fact, studies show that swimmers do not lose weight swimming. If you swim regularly, you lose your spatial coordination from being "suspended" in water, which can be regained by supplementing your swimming workout with walking. Getting out of the pool and into the fresh air can be a refreshing change and will give your hair, eyes, ears, and skin a rest from the chlorinated water. Walking will also give you a chance to socialize while you work out.

Racquetball and Tennis Players: Do you find that even if you're playing with your spouse, mate, or best friend, a feeling of aggression and anger comes over you if they get ahead by one or two points? Do you ever throw your racquet or yell at your partner when he or she misses a shot? Walking will teach you to be less competitive. While we don't denounce competition, there is a point at which it becomes destructive.

6. Walktherapy
Maintenance Program

Throughout this book, our general rule has been that your walking level should be tailored to your particular stress level. The more stressful your life, the more often you need to walk. Included in this chapter is the overall maintenance program as well as summaries detailing the programs for stress management, breaking bad habits and addictions, coping with traumatic events, and personality changes.

You may want to turn back now to the stress scale outlined in Chapter 1 and the results of your test. Use the results (along with the schedules outlined in Chapters 2 and 3 if you are following those programs) to choose your maintenance walking level.

Before You Start

As with the other walking programs in this book, a warm-up is important. Take 5 minutes and walk slowly to get your blood circulating. You should also do stretching exercises for your calves, thighs, and back and shoulders several times a week (see Book 2, pages 102–103, for stretching exercises).

Physical environment has a lot to do with the perception of stress. Some people like the controlled climate and environment of a gym (or any other place, like a mall, which offers consistency of temperature, plus visual and aural stimulation) because the exercise experience is always the same and the effect of the exercise on their well-being is identical. The regularity of the environment also reinforces motivation, because the effect of the walk is known with certainty ahead of time.

Others, however (especially if walking is an antidote for boredom), may benefit from varying the environment in which they walk. If this is your case, plan several routes of differing scenery and walking gradation (flat, hilly, etc.). You may intersperse these walks with treadmill walking or stair walking indoors or with the powerstepping programs outlined in Book 4 (pages 224–248).

In walktherapy, we measure walks in minutes. The intensity of the walks varies, as is explained in earlier chapters. For example, if you are walking to relieve stress and muscle tension, a brisk walk is prescribed, but if you are walking to combat depression, a slower pace is more beneficial.

The minutes listed in the following chart are totals for the whole day. Don't be alarmed by the high number of minutes in Levels IV and V. The high end of the range is included because in speaking with walkers who have faced major life changes we found that many chose to walk up to 4 hours a day. You may need less. Remember, walking should not become another obligation that will add even more stress to your life. Any amount of walking will help, and these numbers are included only as guidelines.

In earlier chapters we outlined the walking intervention techniques. Notice that the minutes in this chart are 10 to 20 minutes higher than those in the charts in chapters 2 and 3. The overall program time represents your total daily walking time. For example, if you are following a Level II in the intervention plan, then you are already walking 10 to 20 minutes a day total. The range in this chart is 20 to 40 minutes. So for you to integrate a regular maintenance program into your life, pick a time during the day and walk the difference between your intermittent walking and your total walking prescription, in this example, 10 to 20 minutes. As you use the intermittent program less, add more time to your maintenance

Overall Walking Program

	LEVEL I	LEVEL II	LEVEL III	LEVEL IV	LEVEL V
Your stress score:	100	100–175	176–250	251–300	300+
Total length of walks (in minutes)	20–30	20–40	40–60	60–80	80–240
Number of walks taken per day	1–2	1–5	1–5	1–8	1–10
Walking speed (mph)	2.5–5.0	2.5–5.0	2.5–5.0	2.5–5.0	2.5–5.0
MET level of exercise:	3.5–12	3.5–12	3.5–12	3.5–12	3.5–12

program, so that eventually you are walking 20 to 40 minutes a day in one session. Your stress hardiness will increase, and eventually you may be able to reduce your walking level or reduce the number of days you walk each week. (This should not fall below a weekly average of 90 minutes of walking.)

If you have just experienced a traumatic event like the ones described in Chapter 4, you may feel the need to increase your walking to Level IV or V until you feel the stress from that event diffusing (which could take 6 months or longer). Refer back to the stress test in Chapter 1 to monitor your stress and to make sure that you have picked a walking level suitable for your needs. You can learn to pace yourself, maybe increasing your stress-reduction walking program before holidays or vacations and returning to your normal schedule afterwards.

Of course, if the reason for your stress is a medical problem, like heart disease, arthritis, or back pain, follow the specialized walking programs for those ailments. The walking done in those programs will help you become both physically and emotionally stronger.

In the beginning, do not worry about your speed (2.5 to 3.5 miles an hour is an average walking speed), as long as you are walking at a somewhat hard level (see the RPE scale on page 159) or about 60 to 70 percent of your maximum heart rate. Eventually you may want to increase your speed. If, for instance, you currently walk at 3 miles an hour and want to get to 4 miles an hour, decrease your walking time per mile by 15 seconds every week until you reach your goal.

Below are summaries of our four walking maintenance programs for stress management, breaking habits and addictions, coping with traumatic events and major changes, and personality changes.

Stress Management

Walking for Cognitive and Emotional Stress

This program is to manage stress that does not cause muscle tension or other psychosomatic problems. It combats light depression and boredom and improves creativity and problem-solving capabilities.

Level: I to III

Speed and intensity: Slow to moderate (2.5 to 4.5 miles an hour or up to 8 METs)

Frequency and duration: Intermittent walks taken to meet low-level stresses combined with at least a 3-day-a-week walking program (90 minutes weekly)

Walking for Psychosomatic Problems

If you experience muscle tension or other physical symptoms, like headaches, back aches, insomnia, ulcers, or beginning signs of heart disease, you know stress is negatively affecting your body. Increase your walking intensity to squeeze the stress from your muscles and increase circulation.

Level: II to IV

Speed and intensity: Brisk (up to 6 miles an hour or up to 15 METs)

Frequency and duration: Brisk intermittent walks to combat stress, coupled with 3.5- to 5.5-mile-per-hour walks lasting 20 to 60 minutes or 1.5- to 3.0-mile-per-hour walks lasting 80 to 180 minutes. The latter should be done at least 5 days per week.

Breaking Bad Habits and Addictions

This program involves a more committed approach to walking, but it can be phased in with intermittent walks. Over several weeks, as you lower your consumption level of the substance you are trying to quit, you can increase the length of your walking sessions.

Level: II to IV

Speed and intensity: Brisk walks (up to 6 miles an hour or 15 METs). If withdrawal causes severe depression, moderate speeds (2 to 4.5 miles an hour or up to 8 METs) are recommended.

Frequency and duration: Walks should be taken intermittently (to replace the stimulant or relaxant effects of the substance you are trying to quit). These intermittent walks supplement a maintenance walking program, done at a moderate speed, which should be followed daily to help you remain free of your habit or addiction.

Walking for Trauma and Major Life Changes

This program involves longer, slower walks, although intermittent walks can be used to combat bouts of depression, anxiety, or tension. Walk 2 or more hours a day if you are facing major changes—this extended walking schedule can last anywhere from 6 months to 2 years.

Level: III to IV

Speed and intensity: Less than 4.5 miles an hour (or less than 8 METs)

Frequency and duration: Daily, with intermittent walks as needed. Walks can last anywhere from 20 minutes to several hours.

Personality Change

This involves a long-term walking program and varies depending on the type of changes you want to make.

Intensity, speed, and duration: If you are a Type A personality, be careful not to become too compulsive about your exercise. Don't spend more than an hour 3 to 5 days a week walking (or following exercisewalking programs of more than 12 METs). A Type C, on the other hand, might walk every day for 20 to 40 minutes at a moderate to brisk pace (3.5 to 6 miles an hour or 4 to 15 METs).

Techniques for All Programs

Keep your head neutral and eyes looking ahead about 15 feet.

Keep your shoulders down and slightly back.

Don't walk like a soldier, relax your hips.

Keep your back straight and your pelvis tucked in—"Walk tall."

The lesson of this book is that walking is a great exercise not only for your body, but also for your mind. People who follow a regular exercisewalking program are more positive about their lives (even in the face of grave sickness or stress), are more energetic, and feel more in touch with the world. In fact, walking makes such a difference in their lives that they can no longer imagine what it was like not to walk. Dorothy Chester (a walker you met in Chapter 3) sums it up best: "Walking is a big part of my life, and if for some reason I wasn't able to continue to walk, I am not sure my life would be the same."

THE WALKING SHOE AND FOOT BOOK

Creating a Firm and Comfortable Foundation

CONTRIBUTORS

Myron Boxer, D.P.M.

Dr. Boxer is chief of the Department of Podiatry at Gouverneur Hospital in New York City and coordinator of podiatric medical education at Peninsula Hospital Center in Far Rockaway, New York. Dr. Boxer's teaching appointments include adjunct clinical professor at New York College of Podiatric Medicine in New York City, adjunct clinical faculty at Pennsylvania College of Podiatric Medicine in Philadelphia, and clinical professor at California College of Podiatric Medicine in San Francisco. In 1961, Dr. Boxer received the Doctor of Podiatric Medicine degree from New York College of Podiatric Medicine. Walking is his primary method of exercise, and he walks 4 days and 6 miles a week. He lives in Woodmere, New York.

Richard T. Braver, D.P.M.

Dr. Braver, who specializes in sports medicine, is a fellow of the American Academy of Podriatic Medicine and has an appointment as clinical assistant professor at the New York College of Podiatric Medicine, Department of Orthopedics, in New York City. He is team podiatrist for all the athletic teams of Fairleigh Dickinson University in Teaneck, New Jersey, and of Montclair State College in Upper Montclair, New Jersey. Dr. Braver also conducts walking clinics in northern New Jersey. Dr. Braver received the Doctor of Podiatric Medicine degree from Dr. William M. Scholl College of Podiatric Medicine in Chicago, Illinois. He lives in Rivervale, New Jersey.

Harry F. Hlavac, D.P.M., M.Ed.

Dr. Hlavac is a podiatrist at the Marin Foot Health Center in Mill Valley, California, and president of Biosports Lab, also in Mill Valley. Dr. Hlavac is past president of the American Academy of Podiatric Sports Medicine and is the author of *Foot Book: Advice for Athletes*. A graduate of California College of Podiatric Medicine in San Francisco, where he is also a clinical professor, he received the M.Ed. degree in educational psychology from Temple University, Philadephia. Dr. Hlavac walks 4 to 5 miles a week 3 to 4 days a week and lives in Mill Valley, California.

Mark La Porta, M.D.

Dr. La Porta is an internist who practices preventive medicine, focusing on geriatrics, with a private practice in Miami, Florida. He has taught podiatric medicine and physical diagnosis at the Dr. William M. Scholl College of Podiatric Medicine in Chicago and has been a medical instructor at Rush Medical College in Chicago. Dr. La Porta received the M.D. degree from Northwestern University Medical School in Chicago in 1978. He walks 4 days a week and lives in Miami Beach, Florida.

Neil Sheffler, D.P.M.

Dr. Sheffler practices podiatry in Baltimore and is a member of both the American College of Sports Medicine and the board of advisors of the American Running and Fitness Association, a national organization. Dr. Sheffler graduated cum laude from New York College of Podiatric Medicine in 1971. Dr. Sheffler used to be a runner but switched to walking because of back and knee pain. He walks 15 miles a week and lives in Baltimore.

Terry Spilken, D.P.M.

Dr. Spilken is on the adjunct faculty of the New York College of Podiatric Medicine. He is the author of *Paddings and Strappings of the Foot* and *The Dancer's Foot Book*. He is also the podiatrist consultant to the Alvin Ailey American Dance Theater and Light Opera Company of Manhattan. Dr. Spilken prescribes walking exercises to dancers and other athletes to rehabilitate foot problems. Dr. Spilken received the Doctor of Podiatric Medicine degree from New York College of Podiatric Medicine. A 15-mile-a-week exercisewalker, he lives in New York City.

1. Feet First

CHOOSING A "WALKABLE" SHOE

The feet are the walker's Achilles heels. Eighty percent of Americans suffer from foot problems at some point in their lives, and many of those problems are preventable.

If so many foot problems are avoidable, why do so many people continue to suffer? The answer is that people neglect their feet. When you think about preparing to walk, you consider warming up, stretching your muscles, and learning techniques, but do you give a moment's thought to your feet?

And yet the feet are of paramount importance to walking, because if you have foot problems or even aching feet, you aren't going to be motivated to get out and take a walk. You need to learn how to pamper your feet if you want to be free of pain.

And then there's the shoe. Throughout *Walking Medicine* you've read repeatedly that one of the reasons walking is such a great exercise is because it is inexpensive and you don't need special equipment. Well you do need one thing—a pair of shoes that are comfortable to walk in, what we'll call "walkable" shoes. Improperly fitted and poorly constructed shoes are major reasons foot pain is such a common occurrence. Even if you have foot problems that predispose you to painful feet, the shoes that you wear can make the difference between a pleasurable and a miserable walk.

You aren't the only one who might have been ignoring your feet. To a large extent, shoe manufacturers did not hit the mark with their initial efforts in the walking shoe field. Although some companies have realized the need for really "walkable" shoes and have researched and designed to that end, others seem to have done little more than slap the label "walking shoe" onto their products, modeling them after running shoes and not making the effort to understand what kind of shoe the walker really *needs*. Still other companies, somehow not savvy to the growing number of walkers (65 million at last count), do produce good walking shoes but don't know it. They don't market them as such, but call them "comfort" or "cross training" shoes instead. Finally, a few athletic shoe companies are still holding out until the market gets bigger.

Despite the false starts and general slow going, the walking shoe industry still has great potential. The main problem has been that unlike the successful running shoe companies, there are few walking shoe companies, or walking shoe departments staffed or headed by walkers, so few people at the top know what a walker wants in a shoe. This minibook will educate you (and coincidentally the shoe manufacturers) in the most important design features of a walking shoe. Our hope is that the next generation of shoes will be improved because of this book.

Here you will also learn important facts about walking shoes that have until now been unavailable. Although various publications and associations have evaluated walking shoes, many of these analyses have been lacking, either because of inadequate testing or, in the case of health and fitness publications, because of a fear of insulting shoe companies who advertise in their pages. As a result, the reviews in many magazines tend to be neutral, not reflecting badly on any manufacturer, even if the shoes are inferior. Some editors of magazines that have reviewed walking shoes have had painful walks in poorly designed shoes but have still not negatively reviewed these shoes in their publications.

With proper shoes and proper foot care, as well as basic walking techniques (reviewed in Book 2: Walking for Arthritis, Back and Joints), you can be free of foot pain. Most of the ailments discussed in *Walking Medicine* can only be controlled, but the majority of foot problems can be cured. As in almost every area of life, sometimes the things that are easiest to help get ignored the most.

How to Use This Book

The two questions walkers most often ask Gary Yanker are "What kinds of shoes are best for walking?" and "Do I really need a special shoe to walk in?" Chapter 1, Feet First, answers these questions and teaches you which shoes in your closet are "walkable."

If you are a more advanced walker (level III or greater) or don't own any walkable shoes, Chapter 2, Choosing Your First Walking Shoe, will take you through the process of buying your first specialized walking shoe, including an 11-point system that ensures you'll find a shoe with the best walking features for you. Here you'll also find reference charts listing facts and features of over fifty walking shoes.

While you should look for the basic features stated in Chapter 2 in any shoe you buy, dress shoes, women's shoes, and children's shoes require special attention. Chapter 3, Special Fittings, outlines specific guidelines to finding a comfortable and fashionable dress shoe for both men and women and provides information on the development of children's feet, as well tips on buying and fitting shoes for children.

In Chapter 4, Aching Feet, you'll learn about walkers' top ten foot problems. Walking itself does not cause foot problems, but ill-fitting shoes, overtraining, or inherited ailments can take their toll on your feet. Here you'll find guidelines on foot care, including foot and leg exercises, to cure or prevent foot pain.

Chapter 5, Shoe Care, Repair, and Modification, will teach you how to stretch out the life of your walking shoe by protecting the uppers and lowers from moisture, scratches, and stains and knowing how and what you can repair.

Why You Need a Walking Shoe

Walking is a distinct pattern of movement that is different from running or, for example, playing tennis. The foot and leg actions involved in propelling the body forward are unique to walking and thus necessitate a shoe designed to assist the lower body through these movements. Does this mean you have to go out and buy a "walking shoe"? Not necessarily, at least if you're a beginning walker (Levels I and II). Shoes you might already own, whether made for running, tennis, basketball, or leisure, probably have some of the essential characteristics of a good walking shoe. Once your walking mileage increases, you may find that you want to invest in a specialized walking shoe that provides enhanced padding and support.

What makes a shoe "walkable"? The main features to look for are a cushioned, flexible sole and a top (called the *upper*) that lets air circulate around your feet and lets moisture escape. You also want a shoe that fits right—one that doesn't cramp your toes and that supports your foot at the heel and arch.

The shoe's main role is to protect the feet. When you walk, you take anywhere from 1500 to 2500 steps per mile, and your foot is on the ground 60 percent of the time. Your feet will become hot and sweaty from all those steps, so you want a shoe with an upper of leather, canvas, or nylon mesh that allows your feet to breathe. Stay away from plastic and rubber uppers, which do not allow air to circulate.

You also want a shoe with a durable, yet soft sole that will cushion your foot against the surface on which you're walking, especially at the heel, which bears about 25 percent of the body's weight with each step, and the ball of the foot and the toes (known scientifically as the *metatarsal head* and the *phalanges*), which also support much of the body's weight. Shoes can absorb up to a third of the shock of impact, which is why good walking shoes are especially important for arthritics and people with sports injuries of the feet, legs, or back.

Because the ball of the foot and toes support our full body weight as we walk, the toes tend to spread out when we push off for a step (known as the *toe-off*). For this reason, you want a shoe that does not crowd your toes. There should be at least one thumb's width room between your toes and the end of the shoe, and your toes should not be squashed against the top or sides of the shoe.

The shoes also need to support the heel and the arch. As you take a step, the foot first hits at the heel (the heel strike) and then rocks forward along the outer edge of the foot to the toe-off position. Support at the heel ensures that the foot will not roll inward too much (a little is normal). Find a shoe that is flexible at the toe to help with the toe-off, but stiffer toward the back of the shoe. Arch support is important for comfort. If the arch in your shoe is not high enough, buy an arch support insert at a sports store or pharmacy.

Now go to your closet and see what you find. A pair of running or cross-training shoes will probably be adequate, or maybe a casual canvas or leather shoe with a crepe or rubber sole. A sandal with straps at the heel and over the ball of the foot and a rubber bottom contoured to the shape of your foot would fit the bill for a summer day's walk.

Take the hands-on test to decide which shoe is best. Grab the shoe by the heel and push against the toe with your other hand. If the shoe flexes easily at the forefoot (where the ball of your foot would be), then it is flexible enough to walk in. Next, feel the inside of the shoe. There should be no protruding seams that could rub against your foot and cause blisters. Feel the bottom inside of the shoe. Is it padded and contoured like the bottom of your foot? Then it should be comfortable for a stroll. The sole itself should not be worn down and should provide some traction.

Finally, try the foot-in test:

Is your heel held in place, not slipping, when you walk?

Does the shoe fits snugly around the widest part of the foot?

Can you move your toes freely?

Is the shoe at least ½ inch longer than your longest toe?

If you've answered yes to all these questions, then you've found a "walkable" shoe.

Continue to evaluate your shoes after you begin walking in them. Are you developing blisters or sore areas on your foot? Do your arches and calves ache? If so, discard the shoe for serious walking.

In the next chapter you'll learn how to choose a specialized walking shoe, as well as additional features to look for to match a shoe with your foot type, special medical needs, and walking style.

2. Choosing Your First Exercisewalking Shoe

The earliest shoe dates back to the end of the last ice age, about 10,000 years ago. It was a sandal made of sagebrush bark, complete with a ridged bottom for added traction, straps around the back of the heel, and a large strap over the top of the foot. In Roman times, the sandal, with its open ventilation, allowed soldiers to average 21 miles a day over many months (and, in fact, the word "mile" comes from the latin for 1000 paces).

Over the years, the sandal, although still a good walking shoe, has been pushed aside to make way for more advanced designs to fit all occasions and situations. There are now walking shoes for indoor walking, race-walking, hiking, and even walking to work.

If you've found that the shoes you already own don't fit your walking needs, you'll need even more information on how to pick a specialized walking shoe, especially because you'll be making an investment of any-where from $40 to $180. You may be interested in buying a walkable dress shoe for work or a sandal, but more likely you'll be looking for a more athletic-style walking shoe.

As mentioned in Chapter 1, a cushioned sole and breathable, flexible upper are the minimum requirements, but now that you're probably walk-ing several miles a day, there are other aspects you'll need to consider.

Before you read about good walking shoe characteristics, however, you'll need to understand the basics of walking shoe construction. See the glossary on the next page and the figure on page 354 for shoe terms and shoe anatomy. You may wonder why you need to learn these technical terms, but the more you know, the easier it will be to navigate through all the information shoe salespeople will throw your way and find the shoe that's right for you.

The following is a glossary of shoe parts and what they do.

Arch bandage: Pieces of fabric sewn on the inside of the upper from the sole to the instep that provide stability and reinforcement.

Arch pad: Additional cushion for support.

Collar: The padded portion surrounding the ankle.

Combination last: A type of form used in shoe construction that determines the shape of the shoe. A shoe made from a combination last is narrow at the heel and wide at the instep. (See *Last* below.)

Curved last: A type of mold used in shoe construction that determines the shape of the shoe. A shoe made from a curved last bends inward slightly. (See *Last* below.)

Heel counter: A firm cup that surrounds the heel. It's main purpose is to stabilize the heel and reduce pronation (amount that the foot rolls inward after the heel strike).

Heel cup: That part of some sock liners that is contoured for the heel to provide extra support.

Insole: The part of the shoe your foot rests on.

Lacing system: The laces and eyes. Some shoes come with *variable lacing*, which gives the wearer two sets of eyelets to choose from so the width of the instep can be adjusted.

Last: The three-dimensional form over which the upper is stretched to shape the shoe.

Midsole: The part of the sole that is attached to the upper; its key role is shock absorption.

Metatarsal raise: A raised area in the sock liner right behind the heads of the metatarsal bones.

Outsole: Bottom of the shoe that comes in contact with the ground. This gives traction and contributes to shock absorption.

Shank: The part of the sole between the heel and the ball of the foot.

Sock liner: An insert (either removable or not) that runs the full length of the shoe, covering the insole. Some sock liners are molded to the shape of the sole, providing arch support and shock absorption, and holding the foot in place.

Straight last: Kind of form used in construction of a shoe. The toe of a shoe made from a straight last is lined up with the heel.

Toebox: The bottom, sides, and top of the upper covering the toes.

Upper: The top of the shoe. The *vamp* refers to the part of the upper that covers the forefoot. The vamp should have a minimum of stitching, since stitching can irritate the foot and cause blisters.

Wedge: This is between the midsole and the outsole and provides both shock absorption and heel lift.

Features and Functions

We've interviewed a wide variety of walkers, podiatrists who walk, shoe designers, and biomechanists to determine the characteristics essential to a good walking shoe. These features are listed below in their order of importance for the average walker.

Cushioning

You will be spending more time in your walking shoes than you would in a pair of running or tennis sneakers, which are usually worn only for an hour or two at the most. Walkers sometimes wear their shoes all day. Since walkers' feet are on the ground much more than those of runners or other athletes, cushioning becomes very important. *Cushioning* and *shock absorption* (see below) are often used synonymously. Although some parts of the shoe provide both cushioning and shock absorption, the distinction between the two concepts is important.

The purpose of cushioning is to protect your feet from pressure and friction created from walking on hard surfaces or to protect the foot from the shoe's upper. After all, even if you are sitting with your feet flat on the ground or standing still, your feet are constantly feeling the pressure of the shoes and the ground.

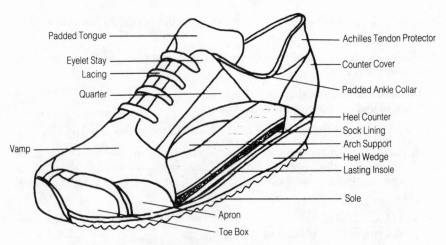

Construction of a Walking Shoe

If the bottom of your feet burn after walking as little as 2 miles or you develop blisters, painful calluses, or red, sore spots on your feet, then you may need a shoe with more cushioning. Too much cushioning, either in the midsole or in the inside of the shoe, can be counterproductive, since it allows the foot to sink too much into the shoe. The softest surfaces should be closest to your feet, and the materials should become harder and more durable the farther they are from your skin. If the cushioning is too soft, however, the foot and lower leg muscles will be forced to work too hard to take each step.

Where to look for cushioning:

- At the tongue to cushion the instep.

- Around the collar of the shoe.

- At the heel (both underneath and surrounding it), which will cut down on blisters and pain from the repeated heel strike. If you walk fast, you also should look for cushioning at the ball of the foot (the faster you walk, the closer you'll strike the ground to the ball of the foot). A variable-density sock liner may offer more cushioning at the heel or forefoot than a normal sock liner.

- A soft yet resilient midsole adds cushioning to the shoe (see further discussion under shock absorption).

Appropriate Last

The construction of a shoe begins with the last. Lasts vary from manufacturer to manufacturer, which is why in some makes you might wear a size 7 and in others a size 8.

Most people's feet curve slightly inward, so many companies make slightly curved lasts (the curve is approximately 7 degrees). However, straight-lasted shoes provide better support and are especially good for people with flat feet (see pages 360–363).

The last ultimately determines how well the shoe fits. The shoe should be wide enough at the ball of the foot, but narrow enough at the heel to hold it in place. A combination last allows for a wide discrepancy between the width of the heel and the toe. Women, who tend to have narrow heels and wider toes, will probably be more comfortable in a shoe with a combination last. You might also look for a company that makes shoes in a variety of widths.

Lasts also determine toe spring, the amount the shoe turns up in the front, a feature that helps rock the walker's body forward. In walking shoes, this should be 15 to 20 degrees.

Stability

Stability refers to all the properties of the shoe that keep the foot, and therefore the whole body, in proper alignment. Rear foot stability is par-

ticularly important because walkers land on their heels as they take a step,
rolling from this position to the outer edge of their foot. The shoe can
help keep the foot from rolling too far inward or outward.

Features that aid rear foot stability include.

- A stiff heel counter made of hard plastic or thermoplastic. Walking shoes
  usually have longer heel counters than running shoes, and the counter should
  extend almost to the middle of the shoe on the medial side (the inside of the
  foot). To test that the heel counter is firm, hold the shoe so you are grasping
  it around the heel counter. You should not be able to crush the shoe flat. If
  you tend to "roll over" the heel counter while walking, a firm heel counter
  is particularly important for you.

- A broad-soled shoe. Often manufacturers make the sole at the arch too narrow.
  If your foot is wider than the sole at the arch, you will not get the proper
  support.

- A heel that flares out (so that the part that touches the ground is wider than
  the part attached to the upper) provides greater stability.

- Firm midsole (use test described under shock absorption).

- A removable sock liner with a molded arch and heel cup.

- A longer lacing system or a variable lacing system. The more the last is
  different from the shape of your foot, the longer the lace portion of the shoe
  should be. A variable lacing system will also help you fit the shoe to your
  foot as it swells or contracts from weather or wear.

- A straight-lasted shoe (especially for flat-footed people).

- An upper that is stitched to the sole (this is unfortunately quite rare) is more
  stable than a shoe whose upper is glued to the sole.

Many people believe that a high-top shoe provides extra stability, but
this is not true (unless it is a hiking shoe with a stiff leather upper). If the
shoe does come up high on the ankle, make sure there is a cutout at the
back (called an *Achilles notch*). Otherwise the shoe might chafe the Achilles
tendon.

Flexibility

The shoe should be flexible at the ball of the foot, as walkers need a
forefoot that flexes about 45 to 55 degrees (runners need only about 30
degrees). Some shoes have grooves in the sole that make the shoe more
flexible for the toe-off.

Flexibility is determined in large part by lasting, the process of pulling
the upper over the last. The lasting includes the insertion of the heel
counter, the toe box, and the shank, which is the stiff part of the shoe
between the heel and the arch. After the shoe has been lasted, the insole,

midsole, and outsole are added. The kind of lasting affects how the shoe will fit your foot. A slip-lasted shoe is usually more flexible, while a board-lasted shoe offers more stability (prevents the foot from twisting from side to side), as does a combination lasting, which may combine a more flexible front portion with a more stable rear section. Flexibility is especially important for racewalkers. If you are a racewalker, consider a slip-lasted shoe.

A lower-cut shoe is also more flexible because it does not impede ankle flexion. The upper should also be made of flexible material, such as leather, although some walkers complain that the ultrasoft garment leather stretches and wears too quickly.

High and Wide Toe Box

The toe box (the toe of the shoe) should be high enough that the toes do not touch the top, even when they splay out for the push off. If you walk hills, you will need even more room in the toe box to accommodate the foot as it slides forward on the downhill inclines. If the toe of the shoe is too tight, you will end up with corns, joint pain, calluses, and black toe nails (for more information on these, see chapter 6).

Breathability

The shoe should be made of breathable fabrics that provide ventilation to the feet. This is especially important in walking shoes because the extra internal padding can make them hot. Both nylon mesh and leather breathe; nylon mesh, because it is lighter, is preferable for hot climates, and leather is better for colder temperatures. Some companies claim that their shoes have high-tech ventilation systems, but hard-core walkers report that these systems don't make a noticeable difference. Make sure the shoe is roomy enough that air can circulate inside the shoe. Air should escape by means of the collar with each step.

If you often walk in wet weather, you'll want a leather shoe that can be waterproofed, or even one that's made of a water-repellent substance (which should also be breathable). Keep in mind that you will be trading dry feet for decreased ventilation. To help the inside of the shoe stay dry, look for a shoe that is lined with a substance that wicks away moisture from your foot to the outside of the shoe.

Traction

Walkers also need a sole with a good traction because they walk on a variety of surfaces: sleek floors of an indoor track or mall, the gratings found in a city street, or even dirt paths. A waffle bottom provides a good no-slip surface. Watch out for shoes whose soles are too slick; this can lead to falls and possible broken bones.

Durability

Shoes should be made with more durable uppers to stand up to the thousands of steps a walker takes each mile. Both nylon and leather make good uppers, and some companies are coming out with synthetic materials that are also durable. The soles of the walking shoe should be tough as well, especially at the heel, where the foot strikes the ground. Carbon rubber is considered one of the sturdiest outsole materials. If you walk quickly, you may be wearing out the front of the toe with a vigorous toe-off. Look for a shoe with a toe guard.

Proper Heel Height

The heel should be ⅝ to ¾ inch high (not including the height of the sole), and the sole at the heel should be thicker than at the ball of the foot. Some walking shoes have a distinct heel, which was a cosmetic addition meant to make the shoe look less athletic. However, a wedge heel (like those found on running shoes) is preferred because it helps the foot rock from heel to toe.

Performance

Match a shoe's performance attributes with your walking style. If you walk at less than 5 miles an hour, you need not worry about special performance features. However, if you walk faster than 5 miles an hour, look for the following features:

Lightweight materials

More flexibility at the ball of the foot

A shoe that does not come up high on the ankle

Greater shock absorbency or cushioning at the ball of the foot

A snugger fit at the heel

A midsole that is firm for energy return

A heel that flares out for stability

Shock Absorption

The purpose of shock absorption, usually found at the heel and sometimes the ball of the foot, is to dissipate some of the forces that move through the entire body, from the toes to the head, each time we take a step. Some shock through the legs is good and actually promotes bone growth (helping to prevent osteoporosis). The need for shock absorption is generally overpromoted by walking shoe manufacturers, an advertising reflex from the running craze days. Walking causes forces of only 1 to 1½ times body weight on the joints, about 50 to 75 percent less than for high-impact sports like running and aerobics.

Nonetheless, shock waves still need to be absorbed to some degree because there is a cumulative effect of shock on the joints, especially for walkers who walk for long periods of time each day or have joint or back weaknesses. Walking in shoes with absolutely no shock absorption can cause muscle fatigue and pain in the feet and legs.

The midsole, the portion of the sole between the upper and the outsole, is responsible for shock absorption and cushioning, and it needs to be soft yet resilient so that it cushions the foot while remaining somewhat firm. If the midsole is too soft, you will sink into the material and fail to rebound, which will tire the muscles of the feet and legs sooner than if you were walking on a stiffer shoe. This is analogous to walking in mud, where you don't feel any shock but you tire very quickly. Too much shock absorption will also allow the foot to move too much inside the shoe, throwing off the alignment of your body as you walk. This is why walkers should generally take less shock absorption in return for more stability.

When shopping for shoes, take the midsole test: Grab the shoe at the heel, placing your thumb on the outsole of the shoe and your forefinger on the top of the midsole (right under the upper). Try to pinch the midsole together. If it collapses more than halfway, then the midsole is too soft. If it does not collapse at all, then it is too dense. Good midsole materials include EVA (ethylene vinyl acetate), and even more durable, compression molded EVA. These are two of the most popular materials for midsoles, but polyurethane and blown rubber are also good choices. (If you shop at a specialized athletic shoe store, the salespeople will be able to give you details on the shoes. Also see pagse 368–379 for a list of walking shoes and what they are made of.)

What About Walking Socks?

Socks protect your feet from your shoes and are to a large extent responsible for the environment your foot "lives in" inside the shoe. There are three basic types of socks, and the features they emphasize depend on what the manufacturers believe is important in a sock. Some make padded socks to provide extra cushioning to the feet at strategic points like the heel, the upper, and the toe. This padding decreases friction inside the shoe.

Padded socks may add to comfort if your shoes are roomy, but if your shoes are snug, padded socks may make them too tight. They may also make your feet sweat if there is not enough room for air to circulate around the foot.

Other manufacturers believe that socks should control temperature and humidity inside the shoe. Some companies now make socks of fibers for warm and cold weather that wick away moisture from the foot twice as fast as polypropelene and fourteen times as fast as cotton. These socks offer no extra padding.

A third type of sock is a traditional cotton or wool model. Some sock manufacturers contend that cotton is a bad material to put next to your feet during exercise because it traps moisture next to your skin, causing blisters and promoting bacterial problems like athlete's foot. However, some serious walkers, like Steven Newman, who walked around the world over a 4-year period, wore only cotton socks and had no complaints. Silk (for liners) and wool are considered good materials for socks. Although wool absorbs up to 70 percent of its weight in water, it does not mat with moisture absorption, so the water stays on the outside of the sock, away from the skin. Wool, however, can cause the skin to itch. If your main problem is blisters or sweaty feet, try a sock made from synthetic material or wool.

Now that you know the basic characteristics of a good walking shoe and sock, look at your feet to decide which characteristics are most important for you. Because everyone's feet are different, there is no one shoe that will fit everyone's needs. What works for you depends on what kind of arch you have, how wide or narrow your feet are, as well as any particular foot or leg injuries or structural irregularities you may have. Ultimately, this means that you (and perhaps your podiatrist) will be the best judge of what shoe is right for you. The brand your best friend swears by may make you miserable.

Your Foot Profile

The most important thing to consider when choosing a shoe is your arch type. The arch of your foot is made up of five of the twenty-six bones in the foot and serves as the body's natural shock absorption, alignment mechanism, and body support. The plantar fascia, the ligament that connects the heel bone to the big toe, is also part of the body's shock absorption equipment.

Arches can be normal, high, or low. To find out which you have, wet the bottom of your foot and make a footprint on the floor. If you can see the outline of your toes, heel, and the crescent shape of your arch, you have a normal arch. If the entire bottom of your foot appears, then you suffer from flat feet (or fallen arches). If only your toes and heel appear, you have a high arch. Another simple test for fallen arches is to balance on one foot. If you fall over easily, then you have unstable, usually flat, feet. A high or low arch can cause foot and leg pain (although not in all instances).

Most people think of only flat feet as being problematical, but high arches can be painful, especially if the joints of your foot are very rigid.

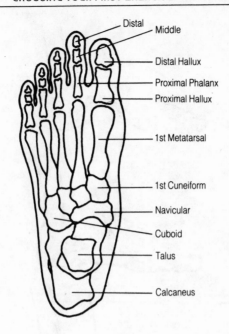

Distal
Middle
Distal Hallux
Proximal Phalanx
Proximal Hallux
1st Metatarsal
1st Cuneiform
Navicular
Cuboid
Talus
Calcaneus

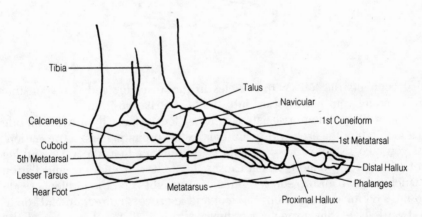

Tibia
Talus
Navicular
1st Cuneiform
Calcaneus
1st Metatarsal
Cuboid
5th Metatarsal
Distal Hallux
Lesser Tarsus
Phalanges
Rear Foot
Metatarsus
Proximal Hallux

The Foot

This condition is known as the *rigid cavus foot,* and this means that the foot cannot absorb shock effectively. These rigid high arches can often cause localized or radiating pain (pain that moves up the leg and sometimes to the back) because nerves in the foot are pinched and squeezed. A rigid arch is also often associated with an inflexible Achilles tendon, the cord

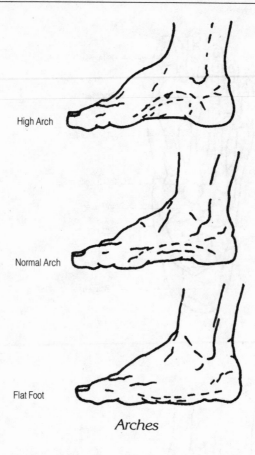

High Arch

Normal Arch

Flat Foot

Arches

that connects the heel with muscles in the lower leg and is responsible for bending your foot upward into the heel-strike position.

The main problem associated with flat feet (especially a hypermobile flat foot, when the arch is very loose) is excess pronation or overpronation. As you take a step, supporting your weight on one foot, the ankle and leg rotate inward (pronate), which causes the arch to stretch out and flatten (which helps to absorb shock). Once your weight is on the forefoot, ready to push off for the next step, the foot and leg reverse direction and rotate outward. Everyone pronates as they walk, but 20 to 40 percent of the population overpronate, the ankle and leg rotate too far inward, thus throwing off the alignment of the legs and hip. If your shoes wear first on the inside (medial side) of the sole or you notice that the uppers lean inward, then you pronate excessively. If you overpronate, the forces created when the foot hits the ground do not travel linearly up the leg, which places undue stress on the leg and back joints and can cause injuries.

A less common problem is oversupination, which is the opposite of pronation and affects about 5 percent of the population. You supinate when you roll on the outside of your foot after the heel strike, and if you oversupinate, then your weight stays on the outside of your foot, never moving medially. If your shoes wear on the outside of the sole first, then you probably supinate excessively, which also throws off your body's alignment, eventually causing injury to the legs and back. Oversupination is associated with high arches.

The kind of shoe you buy will depend on whether you have normal, high, or low arches, as well as the length and width of your feet. Depending on your foot type, your history of foot or leg injuries, your predisposition to foot problems, and various medical conditions, you might reorder the sequence of the eleven shoe features described in this chapter. For example, there is a tradeoff between stability and cushioning or shock absorption, since extra cushioning and shock absorption in the midsole make for a softer shoe that dissipates energy but does not hold the foot in place as well. Generally, walkers should opt for a firmer midsole with cushioning inside the shoe. However, if you have high arches, shock absorption becomes more important because the arch does not supply it naturally.

In the following shoe quiz, write down the recommendations that apply to you. Then take this list and compare it with the charts at the end of this chapter (pages 368–383). Use these to narrow down a list of walking shoes appropriate for you and your feet. Once you narrowed the list down, go to a good shoe store specializing in sports shoes and try on lots of shoes, using the criteria in the Chapter 1, as well as those on page 366 to help you buy the right shoe.

A Foot and Shoe Quiz

How Your Shoes Wear

Looking at the way you wear your shoes (even nonathletic shoes) will tell you about the way you walk and what you should look for in a walking shoe.

1. Where are your soles worn out? On the inside of the heel or toe, the outside of the heel or toe, or at the back? Look at your shoes from the back. Do they lean outward or inward? If your heels are worn out on the *inside*, you need a stiff heel counter plus an outflared heel and a sock liner that holds your heel in place. The shoe should also be constructed with a board last. If your shoes are worn on the *outside* or they lean outward, a stiff heel counter is necessary. If your heels wear out in the back first, then you are probably a heavy heel striker and land on your heel with much force. Look for a higher heel and an outsole made of carbon rubber. If the uppers of your shoes wear out at the front of the toe, look for a shoe with a toe guard.

2. Are your shoe uppers stretched, especially around the toes or midfoot? Do your feet get numb from long walks? If so, you need a wider shoe.

3. Do you get holes or toe marks where your big toe pushes against the upper? Do you develop bruises under your toe nails? If yes, you need a higher toe box or a longer shoe.

4. Do you have any lumps or other projections on your feet? If so, leather uppers will mold to these irregularities. Nylon will not.

Foot Characteristics

5. Do your feet perspire greatly? If yes, look for a sock liner made of terry cloth or, better, some synthetic material that wicks away moisture. You'll also want a removable sock liner.

6. Do you have a high arch? If so, you need a shoe with good shock absorption in the midsole, as well as a good arch support, such as an "arch cookie" (a special supportive insert).

7. If you have flat feet, you need a shoe that offers much stability, including a long, stiff heel counter and a heel cup to aid against pronation.

8. If you have weak ankles or often sprain them, you need a shoe that offers rear foot stability.

9. Is your second toe longer than your big toe? This is called a *Morton's foot* (or Morton's toe). Look for a shoe with a soft insole under the second metatarsal head.

Injuries and Conditions

10. If you have a knee injury on the medial side of your knee, look for a stable shoe with an outflared heel, stiff heel counter, and a good lacing system. If you have a knee injury on the outside of your knee, look for greater shock absorption.

11. Have you ever had plantar fasciitis (inflammation of the tendon that runs along the bottom of your foot), heel spurs, or heel pain? If so, look for a shoe with a wide sole at the arch, a supportive sock liner (removable in case you want to use an orthotic in the shoe), padding at the heel, and proper shank support. (This is tested by pushing down on the shank—the portion between the heel and the ball of the foot—from the inside of the shoe. There should not be any give.)

12. Have you ever had Achilles tendonitis? Look for a shoe that, if it comes up high on the ankle, has an Achilles notch. Also make sure the heel of the shoe is the on the high end of the acceptable range.

13. Do you often get shin splints? If so, your shoes may be too flexible at the ball of the foot.

14. If you are pregnant, your ligaments (the cords connecting bone to bone) become looser and your feet will spread out. Look for a shoe with a higher heel, a long lacing system (variable lacing would be especially helpful), and arch bandages (a piece of material, usually about 2 inches wide, that's found in the inside of the shoe and secures the sole to the instep).

15. If you are over 60, cushioning in the forefoot and a heel cup are important because as you grow older, you lose the fat padding on the bottom of your feet.

16. Are you overweight (above the high end of the range for your height and age)? Look for shoes with lots of cushioning in the heel and arch.

17. Is your foot very narrow or very wide? Look for a shoe that comes in many widths. If you have a wide forefoot and narrow heel, look for a shoe made with a combination last. Variable lacing also will help you to customize the fit to your foot (see page 402 for tips on lacing shoes).

Walking Style and Environment

18. On what kind of surface do you walk? On rugged terrain, on a granular surface, on a smooth, slick surface (such as the floor of a shopping mall), or on a sidewalk? Pick a shoe with an outsole to match the terrain you walk on.

19. If the weather where you walk is hot and humid, look for a mesh upper. If the weather is cold and damp, look for a waterproof upper (or at least a leather upper that can be treated to repel water).

20. If you racewalk, look for a flexible shoe that is slip-lasted and has cushioning in the forefoot. Are you willing to sacrifice support for speed?

If the Shoe Fits . . .

When you go to a store to try on shoes, try several different kinds, and take the hands-on test with all of them (see page 350). You should be able to tell immediately if a shoe is comfortable. It should feel good right away and should need little or no breaking in period. (Stiff leather shoes may require a few days.) It is also important to find a store with knowledgeable salespeople who can help you. Luckily, specialty athletic shoe stores are becoming more common. Shop around. Getting second and third opinions will help you make a more knowledgeable choice.

Here are some basic rules for shoe shopping:

1. Your feet are probably not both the same size. Buy for the larger foot. You can always place an innersole or heel pad in the smaller foot's shoe or lace the shoe in ways to make it fit better (see page 402). Don't assume that your foot size remains the same year after year. Often beginning walkers find that after eight months or so of walking, they need a larger shoe.

2. Go shoe shopping at the end of the day. Your feet swell during the day, so they will be largest during the late afternoon.

3. When trying on shoes, find an uncarpeted area to walk on. This will give you a better idea of how comfortable the shoes will be when you're walking on the hard sidewalk. If there is no hard surface to walk on inside, try to persuade the shoe salesperson to let you go outside.

4. Stand on one foot to see how tight the shoes are at the ball of the foot when it is supporting all your weight. Practice the heel strike and the heel-toe roll (see page 98) in place and while walking to check out the shoe flexibility and cushioning.

5. If you wear shoe inserts (like an orthotic device, a custom-made support made by a podiatrist), be sure to take them with you when you shop.

6. Be certain that the ball of your foot is located in the widest part of the shoe.

7. Your heel should not move around or come out of the shoe.

8. Make sure there is plenty of room for your toes, in terms of length, width, and height. There should be ½ inch between your longest toe and the tip of your shoe.

9. Have your foot measured each time you buy shoes. The fitter should measure your foot from the heel to the ball of the foot to better determine your size. For the most accurate results, stand up when your foot is being measured.

Rating the Walking Shoes

As the market for specialized walking shoes has grown, so has the need for a shoe survey to educate the consumer. Back in 1971, when running became the fitness craze, *Runner's World* magazine began publishing a shoe survey to highlight the positive and negative features of the running shoes on the market. This survey was based on laboratory testing of shoes for various features like shock absorbency and stability. This survey naturally angered those companies who received low ratings, but it also motivated them to improve their shoes, since they found that the rating greatly influenced the sales of their products.

Unfortunately, no publication or organization has, as of yet, provided the same service to walkers. Yes, many magazines have provided information about how to pick a walking shoe, but no formal, objective listing comparing the features of each brand exists. Therefore, we offer the results of our walking shoe survey, which was sent to over fifty walking shoe companies, both those established in the walking field and newcomers who have produced promising shoes. We asked detailed questions about how the shoes were made, their performance, and their special features. We feel that this survey provides the most complete information available so far.

Walking Shoe Survey

	Price	Type of Shoe	Speed (m.p.h.)	Year Introduced	Upper Material	Midsole Material	Outsole	Lining	Shape of Last	Method of Lasting	Distinct Heel	Wedge Heel
Adidas Racewalk (Men's)	$$$$$	Race-walking	N/A	N/A	N/A	EVA	Rubber, at toe	N/A	N/A	N/A	~	N/A
*Asahi Mens GTW-1	$$$	Casual	3–4	1987	Leather	Rubber sponge	Com-pressed rubber sponge	Cambrelle	Semi-curved	Board	X	~
*Asics Tiger Gel Urban Walker	$$$	Multi-terrain	3–4	1989	Nappa Leather Split Suede	EVA	Molded rubber	Cambrelle	Semi-curved	Board	~	X
Gel- and Lady Gel-Strider	$$	Casual, Power walking	4–5	1987	Nappa Leather	EVA	Blown rubber	Foam and tricot	Semi-curved	Board	+	+
Gel-Walker	$$$	Casual, Power walking	4–5	1987	Nappa Leather	Compres-sion molded EVA	Blown rubber w/ carbon rubber heel	Cambrelle	Semi-curved	Board	X	~
*Autry Women's Cus-tom Walker Men's Deluxe Walker	$$	Athletic	4	1989	Leather	EVA	Rubber	Spenco	Straight	N/A	~	X
Avia 350 Arc, Men's and Women's	$$$	Athletic	N/A	N/A	Mesh	Polyure-thane and ARC®	Rubber	N/A	N/A	N/A	~	X
Bass Missv	$$	Casual	N/A	N/A	N/A	Polyure-thane	Polyure-thane	Cambrelle	N/A	N/A	~	X

Key:
N/A = Not available
X = yes
~ = no
+ = cross between a distinct heel and a wedge heel
* = companies who responded to our questionnaire

Price List
(in U.S. dollars)

$ = 46–65

$$ = 66–79

$$$ = 80–110

$$$$ = 111–180

$$$$$ = Over 180

External Heel Stabilizer	Removable Sock Liner	Ventilation	Padded Tongue	Achilles Tendon Notch	Hi Top Models	Oxford Style	Men's Sizes	Women's Sizes	Kids' Sizes	Flared Heel	Arch Cookie	Various Widths	Variable Lacing System	Toe Guard	Heel Counter on Medial Side	Notch Sole at Ball of Foot	Variable Density Midsole	Fits an Orthotic	Cushion at Heel	Cushion at Ball of Foot
N/A	N/A	N/A	N/A	N/A	~	X	X	~	~	N/A	N/A	~	N/A	N/A	N/A	N/A	N/A	N/A	N/A	N/A
~	X	X	X	X	~	X	X	~	~	~	~	~	~	X	~	X	X	N/A	X	N/A
X	X	X	X	X	X	X	X	X	~	X	~	~	~	X	~	X	~	X	X	~
~	X	X	X	X	~	X	X	X	~	~	~	~	~	~	~	X	~	X	X	~
X	X	X	X	X	~	X	X	~	~	~	~	~	~	~	~	X	X	X	X	~
~	X	X	~	X	~	X	X	X	~	~	~	~	~	X	~	X	~	~	N/A	N/A
~	X	X	X	X	~	X	X	X	~	X	~	~	X	X	X	X	~	X	~	~
N/A	N/A	N/A	N/A	N/A	~	X	~	X	~	N/A	X	N/A	N/A	N/A	N/A	N/A	N/A	N/A	N/A	N/A

Walking Shoe Survey (continued)

	Price	Type of Shoe	Speed (m.p.h.)	Year Introduced	Upper Material	Midsole Material	Outsole	Lining	Shape of Last	Method of Lasting	Distinct Heel	Wedge Heel
*Brooks Strideflow	$$$	Athletic	2–5	1989	Leather	EVA and hydroflow	Solid rubber	Brushed tricot	Semi-curved	Board	~	X
Stridewalker	$$	Athletic	3–4	1988	Full grain leather	EVA	Solid rubber	Foam tricot and brushed tricot	Semi-curved	Board	+	+
Stroll	$	Athletic	1–4	1989	Leather	EVA	Solid rubber	Brushed tricot	Semi-curved	Board	+	+
Horizon	$$	Athletic	2–5	1989	Full grain leather	EVA	Solid rubber	Brushed tricot	Semi-curved	Board	~	X
Destination	$$$	Athletic	2–5	1989	Full grain leather	EVA, PU, and hydroflow	Solid rubber	Brushed tricot	Semi-curved	Board	~	X
Cherokee Camprocker	$$$	Athletic	N/A	N/A	N/A	N/A	N/A	Terry	N/A	N/A	N/A	N/A
Clarks of England Air Traveler	$$$$$	Casual/Dress	N/A	N/A	Leather	N/A	Polyurethane	N/A	N/A	N/A	~	X
Coleman-Wolverine Gore-Tex Hiker	$$$$	Off-road/Rugged	N/A	N/A	Gore-Tex	N/A	Rubber	N/A	N/A	N/A	~	X
*Converse Wave Walker	$$	Athletic	2–3	1989	Leather	EVA	Rubber	N/A	Semi-curved	Board	+	+
*Danner Mid-High Cross-Hikers	$$$	Hiking	2–3	1989	Leather and Fabric	EVA	High abrasion resistant rubber	Polyester abrasion resistant lining	Semi-curved	Combination	~	X
*Dexter Weatherwalker A274 Series (Mens) L62 Series (Women)	$$$	Casual	3–4	1988	N/A	6 Iron	N/A	N/A	Semi-curved	Board	~	X

External Heel Stabilizer	Removable Sock Liner	Ventilation	Padded Tongue	Achilles Tendon Notch	Hi Top Models	Oxford Style	Men's Sizes	Women's Sizes	Kids' Sizes	Flared Heel	Arch Cookie	Various Widths	Variable Lacing System	Toe Guard	Heel Counter on Medial Side	Notch Sole at Ball of Foot	Variable Density Midsole	Fits an Orthotic	Cushion at Heel	Cushion at Ball of Foot
X	X	X	X	X	~	X	X	~	~	X	~	~	X	X	X	X	X	X	X	~
X	X	X	X	X	~	X	X	~	~	X	~	~	X	X	X	X	X	X	X	~
X	X	~	X	X	~	X	X	X	~	X	~	~	X	X	X	X	~	X	X	~
X	X	X	X	X	~	X	X	X	~	X	~	~	X	X	X	X	X	X	X	~
X	X	X	X	X	~	X	~	X	~	X	~	~	X	X	X	X	X	X	X	~
N/A	N/A	X	N/A	N/A	N/A	N/A	X	~	~	N/A	N/A	N/A	N/A	N/A	N/A	N/A	N/A	N/A	N/A	N/A
N/A	N/A	N/A	N/A	N/A	~	X	X	X	~	N/A	N/A	N/A	N/A	N/A	N/A	N/A	N/A	N/A	N/A	N/A
N/A	N/A	N/A	N/A	N/A	X	~	X	~	~	N/A	N/A	N/A	N/A	N/A	N/A	N/A	N/A	N/A	N/A	N/A
~	X	~	~	X	~	X	X	X	~	~	~	~	~	~	~	~	~	~	X	~
~	X	X	X	X	~	~	X	X	~	~	~	~	X	~	~	~	~	X	~	~
~	X	~	X	~	~	X	X	X	~	~	~	X	~	X	~	~	~	~	~	~

Walking Shoe Survey (continued)

	Price	Type of Shoe	Speed (m.p.h.)	Year Introduced	Upper Material	Midsole Material	Outsole	Lining	Shape of Last	Method of Lasting	Distinct Heel	Wedge Heel
*Dingo Territory (Acme Boot Company)	$$$	Casual	N/A	N/A	A variety of leathers	Dual density rubber	Vibram rubber	Cambrelle covered poron cushion	N/A	N/A	N/A	N/A
*Easy Spirit Mach I (U.S. Shoe)	$$$	N/A	4–5	1987	Leather	Flexible combination board	Blown PVC	Foam and Coolmax™	Curved/contoured	Board, slip	N/A	N/A
*Etonic Pace Walker	$$	Casual/Athletic	4–5	1989	Full grain garment leather	EVA	Solid rubber	Brushed nylon	Semi-curved	Board	X	X
Stable Stride	$$$	Casual/Athletic	3–5	1989	Full grain garment leather	EVA	Blown rubber w/ carbon rubber plugs	Brushed nylon	Semi-curved	Board	X	X
Trans Am Walker	$$	Casual	1–4	N/A	Full grain	EVA	Expanded rubber w/ solid rubber heel plug	Brushed nylon	Semi-curved	Board	X	X
Footjoy Promenade	$$	Athletic	N/A	N/A	N/A	EVA	N/A	N/A	N/A	N/A	N/A	N/A
Hersey Custom Shoe	$$$$$	Shoes custom built for individuals' needs						Build according to need				
Hi-Tec Walk Lite (Women's)	$$	Athletic	N/A	N/A	Leather	EVA	N/A	N/A	N/A	N/A	N/A	N/A
Hush Puppies Ventura (Women's)	$$	Casual/Sandal	N/A	N/A	N/A	N/A	N/A	N/A	N/A	N/A	N/A	X

External Heel Stabilizer	Removable Sock Liner	Ventilation	Padded Tongue	Achilles Tendon Notch	Hi Top Models	Oxford Style	Men's Sizes	Women's Sizes	Kids' Sizes	Flared Heel	Arch Cookie	Various Widths	Variable Lacing System	Toe Guard	Heel Counter on Medial Side	Notch Sole at Ball of Foot	Variable Density Midsole	Fits an Orthotic	Cushion at Heel	Cushion at Ball of Foot
N/A	N/A	N/A	N/A	N/A	X	N/A	X	~	~	N/A	N/A	N/A	N/A	N/A	N/A	N/A	N/A	N/A	N/A	N/A
X	~	~	X	X	X	X	~	X	~	~	X	X	X	X	~	X	X	~	N/A	N/A
X	X	X	X	X	N/A	N/A	X	X	~	~	~	~	~	X	~	X	~	N/A	~	~
X	X	X	X	X	N/A	N/A	X	~	~	~	~	~	~	X	~	X	X	N/A	X	~
X	~	X	X	~	N/A	N/A	X	X	~	~	~	X	X	X	~	~	~	N/A	~	~
N/A	N/A	N/A	N/A	N/A	N/A	N/A	~	X	~	N/A	N/A	N/A	N/A	N/A	N/A	N/A	N/A	N/A	X	N/A
specs meet individuals' needs													specs meet individuals' needs							
N/A	N/A	N/A	N/A	N/A	N/A	N/A	X	X	~	N/A	N/A	N/A	N/A	N/A	N/A	N/A	N/A	N/A	N/A	N/A
N/A	N/A	N/A	~	N/A	~	~	~	X	~	N/A	N/A	N/A	N/A	N/A	N/A	N/A	N/A	N/A	N/A	N/A

Walking Shoe Survey (continued)

	Price	Type of Shoe	Speed (m.p.h.)	Year Introduced	Upper Material	Midsole Material	Outsole	Lining	Shape of Last	Method of Lasting	Distinct Heel	Wedge Heel
*Kappa 8100 Tour Walker (Women's) 8010 Miler (Men's)	$$	Casual	3–4	1989	Leather	EVA	Endura Rubber®	Spenco K-Tex®	N/A	N/A	X	X
Kangaroos Dynacoil Pacer	$$$	Athletic	N/A	N/A	Leather	EVA	Rubber	N/A	N/A	N/A	N/A	N/A
*Ked's Light Walker	$$	Athletic	N/A	1989	Leather	EVA	Rubber	Taiwanese Cambrelle	N/A	N/A	~	X
Kinney-Stadia Easy Walkers (Women's)	$	Athletic	N/A	N/A	N/A	N/A	N/A	N/A	N/A	N/A	N/A	N/A
*Masterpeace Beach Cruisers	$	Sandal	N/A	1989	Nylon straps		EVA	None	N/A	N/A	N/A	N/A
Hey! Sailor	$	Sandal	N/A	early '80's	Poly-propyl-ene		EVA	None	N/A	N/A	N/A	N/A
Vagabond II & III	$$– $$$	Sandal	N/A	1989	Leather Molded		Rubber 15 iron	N/A	N/A	N/A	N/A	N/A
Mason Slip-less Walker (Women's)	$$	Casual/ Dress	N/A	N/A	Leather	N/A	Non-slip rubber	N/A	N/A	N/A	N/A	N/A
Walkabout Sport Shoe (Men's)	$$$	Casual/ Dress	N/A	N/A	Leather	EVA	Vibram rubber	N/A	N/A	N/A	N/A	N/A
Mephisto Castallet (Women's) Dragster (Men's)	$$$$$	Athletic	N/A	N/A	Leather	Latex	Rubber	N/A	N/A	N/A	~	X
Merrell Trail	$$	Off-road/ Rugged	N/A	N/A	Mesh/ Suede	EVA	Deep lug tread	N/A	N/A	N/A	N/A	N/A

External Heel Stabilizer	Removable Sock Liner	Ventilation	Padded Tongue	Achilles Tendon Notch	Hi Top Models	Oxford Style	Men's Sizes	Women's Sizes	Kids' Sizes	Flared Heel	Arch Cookie	Various Widths	Variable Lacing System	Toe Guard	Heel Counter on Medial Side	Notch Sole at Ball of Foot	Variable Density Midsole	Fits an Orthotic	Cushion at Heel	Cushion at Ball of Foot
X	X	X	X	X	~	~	X	X	~	~	X	X	X	X	~	X	~	X	~	~
N/A	N/A	N/A	N/A	N/A	N/A	N/A	X	X	~	N/A	N/A	N/A	N/A	N/A	N/A	N/A	N/A	N/A	N/A	N/A
~	X	~	~	X	~	X	~	X	~	~	X	X	~	~	~	~	~	~	X	~
N/A	N/A	N/A	N/A	N/A	N/A	N/A	~	X	~	N/A	N/A	N/A	N/A	N/A	N/A	N/A	N/A	N/A	N/A	N/A
~	~	X	~	~	~	~	X	X	~	N/A	N/A	N/A	~	~	~	N/A	N/A	~	N/A	N/A
~	~	X	~	~	~	~	X	X	~	N/A	N/A	N/A	~	~	~	N/A	N/A	~	N/A	N/A
~	~	X	~	~	~	~	X	X	~	N/A	N/A	N/A	~	~	~	N/A	N/A	~	N/A	N/A
N/A	N/A	N/A	N/A	N/A	N/A	N/A	~	X	~	N/A	N/A	N/A	X	N/A	N/A	N/A	N/A	N/A	N/A	N/A
N/A	N/A	N/A	N/A	N/A	N/A	N/A	X	~	~	N/A	N/A	N/A	X	N/A	N/A	N/A	N/A	N/A	N/A	N/A
N/A	N/A	N/A	N/A	N/A	N/A	N/A	X	X	~	N/A	N/A	N/A	X	N/A	N/A	N/A	N/A	N/A	N/A	N/A
N/A	N/A	N/A	N/A	N/A	N/A	N/A	X	X	~	N/A	N/A	N/A	N/A	X	N/A	N/A	N/A	N/A	N/A	N/A

Walking Shoe Survey (continued)

	Price	Type of Shoe	Speed (m.p.h.)	Year Introduced	Upper Material	Midsole Material	Outsole	Lining	Shape of Last	Method of Lasting	Distinct Heel	Wedge Heel
Mile Sport Shoes Doctor (Women's) Officer (Men's)	$$	Athletic	N/A	N/A	Leather	EVA	Ridged, cleated	N/A	N/A	N/A	N/A	N/A
Musebeck Suburban	$$$$– $$$$$	Athletic	N/A	N/A	Leather	EVA	Vibram rubber	N/A	N/A	N/A	~	X
New Balance Model 405	$$	Athletic	N/A	N/A	Leather	EVA	Rubber and EVA	N/A	N/A	N/A	N/A	N/A
*Nike Health-walker Max	$$$$	Athletic	N/A	N/A	Dura-beck (Syn-thetic leather)	EVA	Rubber	N/A	N/A	N/A	~	X
*Propet Chelsea (Women's) Tanner (Men's)	$–$$	Athletic	2–3	1987	Full grain leather	EVA, PU with fiber sole-bed	Rubber	Brushed nylon and cambrelle	Semi-curved	Com-bina-tion board, slip	X	X
Reebok ERS Techwalker	$$$$	Athletic	N/A	N/A	N/A	Polyure-thane	Rein-forced arch and non-slip rubber	N/A	N/A	N/A	N/A	N/A
*Revelations Racer	$$	Athletic	2–3	1989	Cow-hide Full grain	Fiber with Texon	Polyure-thane	Tricotknit	Semi-curved	Board (ce-ment-ed)	~	X
*Rockport Prowalker® 7100	N/A	Casual	4–5	1988	Leather	Highflex® EVA	High Abrasion Rubber	Polyester blend	Semi-curved	Com-bina-tion	X	~
Prowalker® 7300	N/A	Athletic	2–3	1989	Leather	N/A	Polyure-thane	Polyester blend	semi-curved	Board	X	~

External Heel Stabilizer	Removable Sock Liner	Ventilation	Padded Tongue	Achilles Tendon Notch	Hi Top Models	Oxford Style	Men's Sizes	Women's Sizes	Kids' Sizes	Flared Heel	Arch Cookie	Various Widths	Variable Lacing System	Toe Guard	Heel Counter on Medial Side	Notch Sole at Ball of Foot	Variable Density Midsole	Fits an Orthotic	Cushion at Heel	Cushion at Ball of Foot
N/A	N/A	N/A	N/A	N/A	N/A	N/A	X	X	~	N/A	N/A	N/A	N/A	N/A	N/A	N/A	N/A	N/A	N/A	N/A
N/A	N/A	N/A	N/A	N/A	~	X	X	X	~	N/A	N/A	X	N/A	N/A	N/A	N/A	N/A	N/A	N/A	N/A
N/A	N/A	N/A	N/A	N/A	N/A	N/A	X	X	~	N/A	N/A	N/A	N/A	N/A	N/A	N/A	N/A	N/A	N/A	N/A
X	N/A	N/A	X	X	~	X	X	X	~	N/A	N/A	N/A	N/A	X	N/A	X	N/A	N/A	N/A	N/A
X	X	X	X	X	~	X	X	X	X	X	X	X	X	X	~	X	X	X	X	X
N/A	N/A	N/A	N/A	N/A	N/A	N/A	X	X	~	N/A	N/A	N/A	N/A	N/A	N/A	N/A	N/A	N/A	N/A	N/A
~	X	X	X	X	~	X	X	X	~	X	X	X	X	~	~	X	~	~	~	~
X	~	X	X	~	~	X	X	X	~	~	X	X	~	X	~	~	~	X	N/A	N/A
~	~	X	X	X	~	X	~	X	~	~	X	X	X	~	X	~	~	X	N/A	N/A

Walking Shoe Survey (continued)

	Price	Type of Shoe	Speed (m.p.h.)	Year Introduced	Upper Material	Midsole Material	Outsole	Lining	Shape of Last	Method of Lasting	Distinct Heel	Wedge Heel
*Rockport Prowalker® 9000	N/A	Casual	3–4	1985	Leather	Vibram More-flex® EVA	Vibram Super More-flex®	Leather	Semi-curved	Board	+	+
*Ryka 560	$$$	Athletic	3–4	1990	Full grain leather	PU w/ Nitrogen energy spheres	Abrasion rubber, 5-color	Cambrelle, brushed nylon	Semi-curved	Board	X	~
*Saucony Instep Power (Women's) Instep (Men's)	$$	Casual	N/A	1987	Full grain leather	EVA	Rubber	Non-woven nylon	Straight	Combination	X	~
Soft Spots Bonus (Women's)	$$	Athletic	N/A	N/A	Leather	N/A	N/A	N/A	N/A	N/A	N/A	X
Street Cars GW-700 (Men's)	$$$	Athletic	N/A	N/A	N/A	EVA	N/A	N/A	N/A	N/A	N/A	X
Tecnica Pioneer	$$$	Off-road/ Rugged	N/A	N/A	Water-resistant leather and codura	Bi-density leather	Triangular rubber cleats	Nylon and cambrelle	N/A	N/A	N/A	N/A
Timberland Model 91352 (Women's)	$$$$$	Casual/ dress	N/A	N/A	oiled leather	N/A	Polyurethane lug	N/A	N/A	N/A	N/A	N/A
Model 57033 (Men's)	$$$$$	Casual/ Dress	N/A	N/A	Leather	N/A	Vibram rubber	Waterproof Gore-Tex	N/A	N/A	N/A	N/A
*Vasque Windwalker	$$$$	Casual/ Athletic	4–5	1988	Nappa leather	EVA	Rubber	Leather	Curved	Combination	X	X

External Heel Stabilizer	Removable Sock Liner	Ventilation	Padded Tongue	Achilles Tendon Notch	Hi Top Models	Oxford Style	Men's Sizes	Women's Sizes	Kids' Sizes	Flared Heel	Arch Cookie	Various Widths	Variable Lacing System	Toe Guard	Heel Counter on Medial Side	Notch Sole at Ball of Foot	Variable Density Midsole	Fits an Orthotic	Cushion at Heel	Cushion at Ball of Foot
X	X	X	X	X	~	X	X	X	~	~	X	X	~	~	~	~	~	X	X	X
~	X	~	X	X	~	~	~	X	~	X	~	~	X	~	X	X	~	~	~	~
X	X	~	X	X	~	X	X	X	~	X	~	~	~	X	~	X	~	~	~	X
N/A	N/A	N/A	N/A	N/A	N/A	N/A	~	X	~	N/A	N/A	X	N/A	N/A	N/A	N/A	N/A	N/A	N/A	N/A
N/A	N/A	N/A	N/A	N/A	N/A	N/A	X	~	~	N/A	N/A	N/A	N/A	N/A	N/A	N/A	N/A	N/A	X	N/A
N/A	X	N/A	N/A	N/A	N/A	N/A	X	X	~	N/A	N/A	N/A	N/A	N/A	N/A	N/A	N/A	N/A	N/A	N/A
N/A	N/A	N/A	N/A	N/A	X	N/A	~	X	~	N/A	N/A	N/A	N/A	N/A	N/A	N/A	N/A	N/A	N/A	N/A
N/A	N/A	N/A	N/A	N/A	N/A	N/A	X	~	~	N/A	N/A	N/A	N/A	N/A	N/A	N/A	N/A	N/A	X	N/A
X	X	~	X	~	~	X	X	X	~	X	X	X	X	X	X	X	X	N/A	X	~

Shoe Survey: Additional Comments on Selected Brands

Asahi: A series of holes on the insole called the "Air Ventilation System" enhances breathability.

Asics: In all Asics shoes, shock absorption and stability are provided by Asics' Gel technology, a semi-fluid, silicone-based substance encapsulated in pads set under the removable sockliner.

Autry: A "Shox" insole system customizes the shoe to the gait and weight of the walker.

Avia: All Avia walker exercise and power walker shoes have an Arch Rocker® midfoot design—extra material that protrudes under the arch to give the arch greater support when pressure is exerted on the midfoot. The Cantilever® outsole design, a layer of dense rubber shaped concavely at the heel, provides shock absorption.

A light shoe (women's size 6 weighs 5.5 ounces), it also has invisibly stitched uppers for smooth styling.

Brooks: The HydroFlow™ custom cushioning system, a regulated flow of silicone fluid from one chamber set in the back part of the heel to another set in the front of the heel, absorbs shock and stabilizes the shoe. The transfer of fluid differs according to the gait and weight of the walker; quicker gaits or heavier walkers will find themselves walking in a stiffer shoe than a lighter or slower walker.

Converse: A perforated toe box enhances ventilation, while the Energy Wave midsole material in the heel adds cushioning and stability to the shoe.

Danner: A special arch support system called the Danner Airthotic makes this shoe more suitable to someone with a higher arch.

Easy Spirit: The shoe has two layers of shock foam extending from heel to toe and an injection-molded concave sole. It also comes in 45 sizes.

Etonic: Etonic shoes provide a good variety of widths and sizes in both men's and women's shoes.

Hersey: Hersey is the only custom-made shoe. Not available in stores.

Kappa: Has a patented Lace Lock lacing system that allows for two separate lace tensions according to the individual shape and build of the wearer's foot.

Kangaroos: For cushioning it has a Dynacoil™ system, a NASA development: tubular mesh of polypropylene, nylon and saran, that forms an interlocking coil structure resting in polyurethane foam.

Kinney: Good for pronaters because it has a tendency to rock from the inside heel to the outside toe.

Masterpeace: Comfortable sandals with a molded toe arch; not lasted.

Mason: Practical, durable shoes.

Mephisto: Mephisto shoes are made entirely from natural materials. They provide lots of room in the toe box, and are designed to put no pressure on any part of the foot.

Merrell: A hiking shoe with unique fit characteristics: it's wider at the ball of the foot and narrower at the heel than most shoes, creating a snug fit at the instep.

Musebeck: The shoe comes in a large range of sizes (7AAA to 17EEEEE for men and 5AAAAA to 11EEE for women).

Nike: The insole is connected to the tongue by a Dynamic-Fit Sleeve, an elastic mesh band, creating a snug compartment for the foot.

Propet: There's a heel stabilizer and an extra wide heel for added stability. It's one of the few shoes available in children's sizes.

Reebok: The ERS is an "Energy Return System," Reebok's patented cushioning design, in which tubes of a springy plastic called Hytrel pass through the midsole.

Revelations: The shoe is highly flexible and breatheable, with a very heavy tread. It is available in all widths.

Rockport: Rockport has a broad line of shoes, with products for all levels of walkers. All shoes feature high and wide toe boxes.

Ryka: The Nitrogen Energy System™, shock absorbers placed along the entire foot strike pattern, provides a good deal of cushioning and also enhances the shoe's durability. The last design runs narrow at the forefoot so the shoe fits narrower feet better than wide feet.

Soft Spots: There are a good variety of width selections (sizes 5–12, N–WW).

Street Cars: The shoe has a "Cordian Flex" design in the midsole, an accordion-like set of rubber grooves that run across the forefoot and stretch as your foot flexes, allowing a wide range of motion.

Tecnica: The sockliner is bacteria-resistant and the collar is quite low cut to give the ankle bone some room. These are sturdy shoes, good for heavier or more forceful walkers.

Timberland: Heavily stitched for toughness and durability.

Vasque: Stable, although heavy (men's size 9 weighs 13.5 ounces, and women's size 7 weighs 10.5 ounces).

Shoe Statistics (in centimeters)

BRAND NAMES	THICKNESS OF SOLE	WIDTH OF TOE BOX	HEIGHT OF TOE BOX	HEIGHT OF HEEL	WIDTH AT BALL OF FOOT	HOW MANY MILES CAN IT BE WORN BEFORE NEEDING REPLACEMENT
Asahi (M9)	0.3	8.2	2.2	n/a	9.2	not avail.
Brooks						
Strideflow (M9)	1.6 (forefoot)	8.4	4.2	1.2	9.5	500 miles +
Stridewalker (M9)	1.2 (forefoot)	8.4	4.2	1.2	9.5	500 miles +
Stroll (M9)	1.2 (forefoot)	8.4	4.2	1.2	9.5	500 miles +
Horizon (M9)	1.6 (forefoot)	8.4	4.2	1.2	9.5	500 miles +
Destination (W7)	1.5	7.5	3.1	1.0	9.0	500 miles +
Converse (M9)	0.6	7.2	2.3	1.9–2	8.9	Depends on gait and weight
Danner (M9)	0.6	8.9	3.2	11.2	10.0	605 miles
Dexter						
(W7)	1.1	6.2	2.2	1.1	8.8	Depends on wearer
(M9)	1.1	7.2	2.5	1.1	10.0	

Easy Spirit (W7)	0.7	not avail.	4.1	6.3	not avail.	Varies, ~100 miles
Etonic Pace Walker (M9)	2.5	9.5	3.5	6 (medial) 5.5 (lateral)	10.3	600–900 miles
Stable Stride (M9)	not avail.	9.5	4.0	3.5	10.5	500–700 miles
Trans Am (M9)	3.0	9.5	3.5	5.0	9.5	500–700 miles
Kappa (W7)	1.8	8.3	5.0	7.0	8.2	350 miles
Keds	0.4 rubber 0.4 EVA	not avail.	not avail.	not avail.	not avail.	not avail.
Propet	3.7	6.3	2.5	8.8	7.5	500 miles
Revelations (W7)	1.1	5.5	2.3	1.9	8.4	1 year
Rockport Prowalker 7100 (W7)	.8 EVA .5 Rubber	not avail.	not avail.	1.0	not avail.	not avail.
7300 (W7)	1.3	7.0	2.6	1.0	8.2	not avail.
9000 (M9)	1.8	7.8	3.2	1.0	not avail.	not avail.
Saucony (W6)	0.4	6.2	2.6	1.6	8.1	varies

3. Special Fittings

While many of the features that make a shoe "walkable" are the same for men's and women's dress shoes and children's footwear, there are other aspects to choosing these special shoes that have not been discussed in the first two chapters. You should know about these before you go shoe shopping.

Men's Dress Shoes

Although men's dress shoes don't have the same cushioning found in athletic shoes, many have "walkable" qualities. For example, the classic wing tip, the "uniform" of the corporate lawyer and Wall Street broker, is a comfortable walking shoe because it is wide and the leather upper and sole are flexible. The only feature the shoe lacks is arch support. Adding a commercial arch support insert will alleviate any arch pain and increase cushioning. Bring arch pads with you when shopping for shoes to ensure that they will fit in the shoes. If you plan on wearing padded walking socks with your dress shoes, wear them when trying on shoes.

Some companies make dress walking shoes for men. Because they have more cushioning and support than a normal dress shoe, they tend to be clunky. Some men, therefore, wear these to walk to work and change into more traditional dress shoes upon arrival.

Women's Dress Shoes

Women have a love-hate relationship with dress shoes—fashion often takes precedence over comfort. As a result, women are forced to visit podiatrists twice as frequently as men.

The American Podiatric Medical Association conducted a study on American women who wear high heels (higher than 3 inches). Fifty-nine percent of those interviewed wore high heels for up to 8 hours a day. Of those 59 percent, 37 percent wore high heels "in spite of the pain." The study also found that 66 percent of those women who didn't wear high heels cited discomfort as their chief reason for not doing so. But this battle between foot health and fashion does not have to be. In this chapter you'll learn to choose the shoes that are right for your feet without sacrificing fashion.

Women who wear high heels spend the better part of their lives walking on an inclined plane, taking all their body weight on the balls of their feet. This is quite unnatural because, as you learned earlier, the body is normally supported by the heel, the big toe, and the ball of the foot. To then place all the body's weight on two points (the ball of the foot and the big toe) instead is equivalent to sitting on a two-legged stool. It results in a strenuous balancing act. This unnatural position causes pain not only at the ball of the foot, but also in the arches and lower leg. The lower back is often affected as well, since the high-heel shoe wearer tends to lean back to keep from falling forward.

One of the main problems with high heels is that over time, the tendons and muscles in the calfs shorten. Wearing flat shoes is then uncomfortable because the calf muscles have to stretch so that the heel can rest on the ground. If you are used to wearing very high heels, try wearing shoes with increasingly lower heels; once your leg muscles are stretched, you can vary the height of your heels. Doing calf-stretching exercises will also help (see page 399).

Women should change their shoes often. Try to wear at least three different styles of shoes daily. This may sound unusual, but you probably already change your shoes that often throughout the day. For example, when you walk to and from work, wear sneakers or casual walking shoes. At work, wear your dress or "office" shoes. If you plan on walking during lunch, put your casual shoes or sneakers back on. This strategy is not only good for your feet and legs, but will also prolong the life of your dress shoes, especially in the city where one grating or crack in the sidewalk can destroy a heel.

The right height for you is what is comfortable, although a good guideline for everyday wear is a heel that is ¾ to 1 inch high. If you are used to higher heels, don't buy very flat shoes, which may hurt your knees and calves. If you are a sneaker person, any heel over an inch will make you feel like you are falling forward. Some podiatrists recommend touching your toes to find out what heel height is right for you. If you can easily reach your feet or even the floor, flat shoes are probably more comfortable for you. If you are very inflexible, higher heels are better. However, you should try to stretch out those muscles and tendons at the backs of the legs, inflexibility can lead to lower back problems (see stretches in Chapter 4, page 399).

Certainly you can wear higher heels for special occasions. The idea here is merely that you not wear the same shoes (or same style) every day.

Fitting the Shoe

The parts of a woman's pump shoe are basically the same as the shoe parts outlined in the walking shoes section. These shoes also have heel counters, a sock liner (which keeps perspiration from staining the shoe and covers seams), as well as a toe box, vamp, and shank. The part of the shoe that touches your foot at the toe is called the *throat*.

The three biggest problems fitting women's dress shoes are in the heel, arch, and toes. If the shoes fit the heel, they are often too narrow at the toe. Often, the arch does not fall in the proper position. This general problem can be even more frustrating if you have particularly narrow heels or very wide feet at the toe.

If your toes overlap, the shoe toe is too narrow. Narrow-toed shoes are not only uncomfortable, but can cause calluses and bunions and aggravate hammertoes. If you have problems finding shoes that are wide enough in the toe area, buy shoes designed with a long vamp, which tend to be roomier (a long vamp will come father up on your foot). Also look for shoes

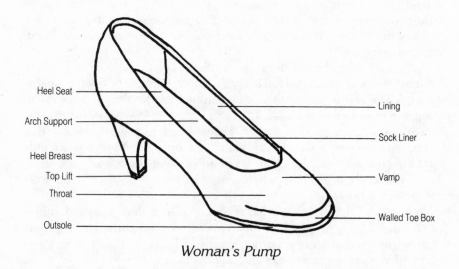

Heel Seat
Arch Support
Heel Breast
Top Lift
Throat
Outsole

Lining
Sock Liner
Vamp
Walled Toe Box

Woman's Pump

with a walled toe box (see figure on page 386), which creates height in the toe area and prevents crowding.

Also make sure that the shoe's arch fits your arch. If your foot slides forward too much, then your arch will not be supported. To ensure correct fit, the ball of your foot should fall right at the end of the shoe's arch. If the arch is in the wrong place, then your toes will be scrunched up at the front of the shoe. If your shoes begin to wrinkle at the instep, the ball of your foot is too far forward. Shoes with open sides, as well as unlined and suede shoes (which tend to stretch at the ball of the foot), also promote this forward slippage.

Heel fit is perhaps the biggest problem. Realistically, you will usually have to trade off between a snug heel and a wide enough toe. Try buying sandals, which hold your foot at the instep with straps; slingbacks, which can be adjusted in the back to fit your heel; oxfords, which can be laced at the appropriate tightness to hold your foot; or boots, which support all your foot.

Once you buy a shoe, flex the soles a few times with the heel of your hand. Adding flexibility to the sole at the ball of the foot (where the shoe needs to bend) will help keep the heel in place. Various companies make pads that stick to the heel counter to make the shoe fit more closely at the heel.

When you try on shoes, make sure the fit is snug but not tight. Unlike athletic-style walking shoes, leather dress shoes will take some breaking in. Leather, canvas, and suede will eventually mold to your foot, but synthetic uppers will not. However, don't expect a too-tight pair to *ever* fit properly.

If you buy your shoes too small, they might stretch too much and you'll be fighting to keep them on within a few months. Shoes may stretch at the ball of the foot, but never at the toes, so if the toe box doesn't fit at the time of purchase, it never will.

Children's Feet and Children's Shoes

Most foot problems are avoidable if they are caught at a young age. The foot is not totally formed until age 20 (before that there is cartilage at the ends of the bone), so children's feet are fairly malleable. This is why teaching your children to walk correctly, caring for their feet, and putting them in shoes that fit will avoid foot problems later on.

Parents are often worried because their toddlers develop what may seem to be bad walking habits. But many of these are perfectly normal. For example, children are naturally bowlegged until they are 2, become knock-kneed from 2 to 4, and then bowlegged again until about age 6 for boys and age 8 for girls. Until age 8, children also often walk pigeon-toed or duck-footed to aid stability. Children's feet also appear to be flat until they are about 4, when the fat pad over their arch disappears.

Most foot or leg conditions that show up in infancy are easily fixed. Some infants severely turn their feet in or out; this is caused by muscle contraction in the legs. In such cases, doctors will probably prescribe a night splint (a bar placed between the baby's feet to hold them in a neutral position) to correct the problem. Children should be discouraged from sitting on their feet, because doing so pushes their feet outward or inward (depending on how they sit) even more.

Probably the most serious problem parents overlook is so-called growing pains. These have nothing to do with the growth of muscles or bones but are caused by some structural misalignment or biomechanical problem that is placing strain on the joints, muscles, ligaments, and tendons of the child's legs. If your child often complains of leg pains, take him or her to an orthopedist or podiatrist.

Until a baby is ready to stand, many doctors believe he or she does not need shoes. Cotton socks with plenty of room in the toes should be worn for warmth until then. It is important not to crowd the foot at any time, and parents should make sure not to tuck the child's blanket too tightly around the feet when he or she is sleeping.

Either low or high shoes are fine for babies. The conventional wisdom used to be that babies needed the ankle support of an ankle-high boot, but the belief now is that the child should develop ankle strength on his or her own.

Babies' feet grow at different rates, but generally, between the ages of 2 and 6 a child may need new shoes as often as every 1 to 2 months. This growth spurt subsides as the child gets older. From ages 6 to 10, new shoes may be needed every 2 to 3 months; from ages 10 to 12, every 3 to 4 months; from ages 12 to 15, every 4 or 5 months; and from ages 15 to 20, every 6 months. Parents should be sure that their children's shoes are roomy, with at *least* ½ inch between the end of the shoe and the longest toe. This will not only make the shoe more comfortable for the child, but also will save parents from replacing shoes as often.

If your child is constantly taking off his or her shoes, he or she may be trying to tell you that the shoes are too tight. Look for red marks on the child's feet. Finally, if your child's feet sweat heavily, this may be a sign that his or her muscles are working too hard to walk within a poorly fitting shoe.

4. Aching Feet

Walkers beware. You may have seen articles that say, "Walkers now suffering injuries" or "Walking may not be good for you," as an explanation for foot problems. The fact is that walking is one of the safest exercises for your lower extremities. Then why all the negative press? What most people don't realize is that the foot problems that walkers experience are *not* inherent to walking, but rather are caused by poorly fitting footwear, inadequate warm-up, overtraining, surface factors (holes in road, cant of the road, etc.), poor walking technique, preexisting injuries or structural weaknesses, or some combination of these factors. *Walking, by itself, does not cause injuries or foot problems.*

That said, a survey of sports podiatrists and walkers produced this top-ten list of common foot problems that walkers experience: blisters, calluses, corns, black and ingrown toenails, sweaty (and smelly) feet, shin pain, strained arches, plantar fasciitis, heel spurs, and tight Achilles tendons.

You may find these topics distasteful. After all, who wants to read about blisters and smelly feet? However, they are a fact of walking life, and if you suffer from any of the top-ten problems, knowing how to prevent and cure them will go a long way toward making walking an enjoyable sport for you.

Top-Ten Problems

Blisters

If anyone knows what foot problems are most common to walkers, it's Rob Sweetgall. He walked 11,208 miles through all fifty states in 364 consecutive days in weather from −30°F (wind chill) to 100°F. Rob averaged 50,000 footsteps per day that year, for which he claimed "hot, sensitive feet" as his biggest foot concern.

Hot feet lead to *blisters*, which occur when two upper layers of skin rub against one another and separate, causing fluid to collect between the two layers. Blisters can usually be avoided by keeping your feet dry and free of irritation, which is why proper shoes and socks are so important. Shoes that are too small will cause your feet to perspire, which produces friction between the shoe and the foot. If the socks trap moisture next to the skin and if the shoes are not properly padded, or if your foot is not held in the shoe securely and thus moves around, then you will certainly get a blister. Blisters are not only painful, but can lead to more serious aches and pains if you are forced to favor one foot as you walk.

If you plan on walking long distances over several hours, take off your shoes and socks whenever possible to air your feet. On Rob Sweetgall's cross-country walk, he removed his shoes and socks every hour. If your socks feel damp, change them. Massaging your feet also will reduce any burning sensations you might feel. Rob also powders his feet with cornstarch to help prevent blisters. He claims that cornstarch worked better than any other commercial foot powder. (Cornstarch absorbs sweat and lubricates the foot inside the shoe.) To apply, take off your shoes and socks and wipe your foot with a wet washcloth. Allow your feet to air dry, since the evaporating water will draw heat out of your feet. When you first take your shoes off, your feet will look slightly pinkish. Once they return to their normal color, apply the cornstarch. In what Rob calls the "shake and bake" method, place your foot into a plastic bag that contains a handful of cornstarch. Once all the surfaces of your foot have been covered with the powder, remove your foot and put on a clean, dry pair of socks. (You can follow this method before you begin walking, too.) When the temperature drops below freezing, Rob rubs his feet with Bag Balm (a veterinary product used on cow teats) to help lubricate his feet.

If you develop a red spot on your foot, this is the beginning of a blister. Place a bandage over the spot to help avoid further friction. If there is pain, the blister should be popped using a sterile needle, but make sure to leave on the top layer of skin, which will act as a natural dressing and protect against infection. An antibiotic cream also should be applied to the wound. If you experience increased pain or notice redness or pus, see a podiatrist.

Calluses

A *callus* is any buildup of tough skin that grows in response to friction or pressure. People develop calluses most often on the heels or balls of their feet, since these are the areas that bear the most pressure. Calluses can act as a cushion to protect the bone underneath the skin, and a small amount of callus is usually not bothersome or uncomfortable.

Calluses can, however, be quite painful if they become too thick and begin to irritate the soft skin underneath. Callus buildup will tend to arise because of improper bone alignment (which often happens at the ball of the foot—called the *metatarsal heads*). In fact, people with Morton's toe (when the second toe is longer than the first) frequently develop calluses at the base of the second metatarsal head. Place a metatarsal pad, a small, self-adhesive cushion, behind the callus to raise the area and protect it from pressure. An orthotic device with a Morton's extension can also help to relieve pressure from that area. If you have an irregular gait, which places stress on a part of the foot that is usually pressure-free (such as the medial side of the big toe), you may develop a callus. Shoes that are too narrow or tight can also cause callus buildup.

Layers of callus should be periodically removed to keep them from getting too thick. One way to "dissolve" a callus is to rub nonallergenic lanolin lotion into any place where hardened skin has developed. You can also use a pumice stone, a rough, porous material available in most pharmacies. Soak your feet in warm water and rub the stone over the callus. This will not hurt, since the callus is dead skin with no nerve endings. If the area still hurts when you walk, place a pad or piece of soft material such as moleskin over the calloused area for extra padding.

Corns

Corns, the toes' equivalent of calluses, are hardened, cone-shaped growths of deadened skin that usually develop on top of or between toes as a result of friction or pressure. Corns (so named because the surface looks like a kernel of corn) are painful because they irritate the nerves and fluid that surround the joints under the skin. Corns are frequently caused by shoes that cramp the toes. As with calluses, reducing the friction or pressure will stop the corns from hurting. Corns can also be caused by toe deformities, such as hammertoes (see page 397 "joint problems"), which a podiatrist can treat. Corns are best removed by a professional, too. Over-the-counter corn medication is not effective and may be dangerous.

If you don't want corns to interrupt your walking routine, try corn pads (a round spongy pad with a cutout that fits over the corn) to relieve pressure until the corn can be removed. Soaking your feet in warm water and epsom salts after a walk may relieve the pain. A pumice stone can be used on the corn to remove some of the deadened skin on top, which will reduce the surface that rubs against your shoe and reduce discomfort.

Sweaty Feet

Some people's feet sweat more than others. Almost everyone knows someone whose feet sweat so profusely and thus smell so strongly that he or she is not allowed to remove his or her shoes in polite company. One walker told us that his wife can't fall asleep if his shoes are in the bedroom because the odor is so strong.

Each foot has 125,000 sweat glands, so the potential to have feet that perspire heavily (known as *bromhidrosis* from the latin *bromis* for "bad smell" and *hidrosis* for "sweat") is great. Normally, we excrete ½ cup of sweat per foot per day. You sweat more when you exercise, and naturally, because the foot is closed up inside the shoe, it sweats more than other parts of your body.

Look for shoes and socks that wick sweat away from your feet, and don't wear shoes or socks that are too tight, which will aggravate the problem by reducing air circulation around the feet. Try following the cornstarch "shake and bake" method (see page 390) at the beginning of the day and before you walk. Some podiatrists recommend using an antiperspirant deodorant on your foot to fight both odor and perspiration.

Black and Ingrown Toenails

A low, sleek toe box is the main cause of a black toenail, which is a bruise underneath the nail. The nail appears black because the constant pressure of the upper against the shoe causes blood vessels to break, and blood then gets trapped under the nail. This causes even more pressure under the nail and can make it sensitive to the touch. Racewalkers frequently complain of black toenails because the speed and style of their walk can jam the toes against the front of the shoe, and many racers actually lose their toenails to this constant pressure. Walking downhill can also cause black toenails.

Some racewalkers relieve this problem by cutting a slit in the toe of the shoe with a razor blade, which gives the toe room to move. If you have a black toenail that hurts, you can have a podiatrist drill a small hole in the nail, which will relieve some of the pain.

Ingrown toenails are usually thought to occur from improper cutting. This is one cause, but an inherited tendency for part of the nail to curve inward as it grows is a far more common one. This curve digs into the skin surrounding the nail, causing pain and tenderness to the area, which often becomes infected. If you develop an ingrown toenail, wear opened-toed shoes or cut a hole in an old pair so that no pressure is put on the irritated toe.

If you have chronic ingrown toenails, a podiatrist, in a simple surgical procedure, can permanently solve the problem by removing the offending portion of the toenail root. This procedure is done in the doctor's office, and the patient will experience little discomfort afterward.

Shin Pain

A big complaint of beginner and advanced walkers alike, shin pain is usually the result of insufficient warm-up or stretching, overtraining, or lack of flexibility. Shin splints are the most common shin pain, and these occur when the muscles on side of the shin bone (the tibia), which are responsible for raising the foot into the heel-strike position, pull away from the bone because they fatigue and begin to tighten. As the muscles pull away, the tissue covering the bone (called the *periosteum*) becomes inflamed and any force placed on the bone (as when you walk) hurts.

If you are a beginning walker, you may suffer shin splints because of weak muscles in the fronts of the legs. Even if you've been involved in other sports, like running, you will not have practiced the continuous flexion of the foot necessary for walking. If you are just starting out, don't do too much hill walking, as this requires even stronger muscles than walking on flat ground. Advanced walkers are also prone to shin splints, especially if they skip the 10- to 15-minute slow-walk warm-up, do not stretch their shin muscles adequately, or try to increase their pace before their muscles are strong enough.

Other causes of shin splints include overpronation and improper posture, as people who lean forward too much when they walk often develop shin pain. Finally, shoes that flex too much at the ball of the foot can contribute to shin splints. If you have recurring problems with shin pain, try a stiffer shoe that allows the foot to rock easily from heel to toe.

Your shin muscles will develop properly with time. The best cure is to continue walking at a comfortable pace. In the meantime, if your shins hurt, apply ice for 15 to 20 minutes after you walk (this can be done with a commercial ice pack, a plastic bag of ice, or a bag of frozen vegetables. Be sure to place a towel over your skin before applying ice). Also, wrap an Ace bandage around your shin before going for a walk. Practicing the exercises and techniques on page 399 will strengthen the muscles in the fronts of your legs.

Highly competitive racewalkers sometimes suffer from a much rarer condition called *compartment syndrome*. This is a burning pain in the shin caused by overdevelopment of the muscles that surround the tibia. These muscles get so big that they expand beyond the sheath (fascia) that holds them together. The treatment is surgery to slit the fascia and let the muscles expand and the fascia to regenerate around the area.

Arch Pain and Strain

Arch pain is usually caused by overexertion, ill-fitting shoes, or biomechanical problems. The most common (and least severe) discomfort is arch strain caused by sore muscles. This can happen either because you have walked for a longer-than-usual distance or because you have stood for a long time.

Another cause of arch pain is tendonitis (inflammation of the tendons). This is usually the result of overpronation, since the tendons must fight to keep the foot from rolling inward. You are especially susceptible to tendonitis if your shoe does not provide proper arch support or does not fit your arch properly.

If you develop arch strain, try the exercises on page 399 to strengthen the muscles surrounding the arch. Icing the arch for 15 minutes after walking will also help relieve pain. Placing arch supports in your shoes (these are made by a number of companies) can help avoid discomfort. If you have chronic arch pain, being fitted with an orthotic, a custom-made device that improves foot function, can also reduce pain.

Plantar Fasciitis

Another kind of arch pain is the inflammation of the plantar fascia, the main ligament that runs along the bottom of your foot and connects your heel bone to your toe bone. People with high arches are especially prone to it. Plantar fasciitis occurs when the foot twists unnaturally after the heel strike. Over a period of time, the ligament pulls away from the heel bone and becomes inflamed.

If you develop plantar fascitiis, the initial treatment is to rest the foot and ice it for 10 to 15 minutes once or twice a day until the pain has receded (probably about a week). After that, you can begin walking again. If the pain does not go away, visit a podiatrist or orthopedist, who will probably give you an orthotic.

Heel Spurs

Heel spurs are another condition related to the plantar fascia and are normally an overuse injury, although some types of arthritis can also cause heel spurs. If you continually overstretch the plantar fascia by walking more than you are used to or strain it through poorly fitting shoes, the plantar fascia begins to tear away from the heel. This causes bleeding, and the blood in the area calcifies, creating tiny growths or spurs on your heel bone. These spurs poke into the ligament and produce a pain that feels like a bruise on the heel.

The pain will actually be worse after a night's sleep because your plantar fascia has not been moved or stretched for several hours. Walking for a few moments will improve the situation, although you should not use the foot extensively until the pain has subsided. The heel should be iced for 10 or 15 minutes once or twice a day. You may be able to walk again after a week, although you should take the precaution of placing foam padding in the heels of your shoes to cushion the sensitive area. Often a visit to a podiatrist will be necessary. An orthotic to cup the heel, medications, and physical therapy may be prescribed. Rarely, and only as a last resort, surgery is performed.

Tight Achilles Tendons

Walkers often suffer from a tight Achilles tendon, the cord that stretches up the back of the leg from the heel, because walking exercises (and thus tightens) the muscles in the backs of the legs. Women especially can have considerable Achilles tendon pain if they are used to wearing high-heel shoes. Switching from a high heel to a relatively flat athletic shoe will surely cause pain along the backs of the calves. Overpronation can also irritate the Achilles tendon. The only remedy is to apply ice to the area (for 10 to 15 minutes once or twice a day) if it is sore and to stretch the back of the leg (see page 399) to help even out muscle development.

Everyday Problems

Unlike the problems just discussed, which can happen as a result of your walking routine, the following are foot disorders that anyone can get. Knowing how to treat them will help you avoid discomfort while you walk.

Athlete's Foot

Athlete's foot, the most common skin problem in America, is caused by a fungus that usually grows between the toes or on the bottoms of the feet. It normally causes itching or burning that will be aggravated by heat buildup inside the shoes. Sometimes the toenails will become infected by the fungus, becoming brittle, discolored, thickened, and perhaps painful.

The best treatment is prevention. Change your socks and shoes often, especially after a walking workout. A warm environment, which is what the insides of your shoes are like after a few miles, will just promote more fungal growth. The fungus can get into cracks in your feet and be very painful. Over-the-counter medication often relieves the problem in a few days. If your toenails become infected, see a podiatrist. Clearing up the nail fungus is much more difficult than clearing up the skin fungus (it can take up to twelve weeks). If it is not treated, it is likely that the fungus will spread back to the skin. To help avoid athlete's foot, stay away from socks made from synthetic materials that trap moisture next to the foot.

Allergies

Contact dermatitis is a painful, red, bumpy rash caused by an allergy to materials in shoes or socks, including synthetic fibers or chromates (made from nickel), used in leather dye or curing, or rubber cement, used to glue parts of shoes together. You might also be allergic to the ingredients in skin creme (like perfumes or lanolin) that you have rubbed into your feet. These irritations are aggravated by heat, friction, and foot perspiration.

As with athlete's foot, if you have allergies, be sure to change your shoes and socks often to avoid further irritation. You can also apply cornstarch to your feet to reduce friction and heat inside your shoes. After you walk, try soaking your feet in warm tea for 20 minutes. The tannic acid soothes them and reduces the allergic response. (A tea bath is also a good cure for sunburned feet.) Your doctor may prescribe cortisone cream for severe rashes.

Plantar Warts

A wart on the sole of your foot is called a *plantar wart* (*plantar* refers to the sole of the foot). Although these warts may cause you no pain and in most cases will not curtail normal activity, you will probably be bothered by them if they are located on the ball of your foot, either as an annoying itchy spot or as a tender area.

A wart will usually go away on its own accord after a few years, but a new wart may spring up in its place. Leaving them alone presents risks of spreading. If left untreated, these warts, caused by a virus, can multiply, so it is best to get rid of them as soon as they appear.

Warts can be removed with over-the-counter medication or by a physician. Drug-store remedies include salicylic acid pads or other commercial salicylic acid preparations. Doctors' methods vary and include cutting the wart out of the skin, applying acid, or using lasers or ultrasound to "zap" the wart. If you want to continue walking before the wart has been removed, place a pad around the wart to relieve the pressure.

Circulation Problems

Diabetes

Diabetes causes decreased circulation, especially in the eyes, hands, and feet, but walking can alleviate the problem and may even save your feet and legs from serious infection.

Take Walter Stein, for example, the 49-year-old racewalker with diabetes who you met in Book 4. Before Walter began walking, he complained of burning, numb feet (called *neuropathy*). He also had sores all over his feet and legs, a common problem among diabetics, since their inadequate circulation decreases the number of white blood cells that reach and heal small cuts or scratches on the feet and legs. If a sore becomes infected, gangrene can set in and amputation may be required.

After only a few weeks of walking a mile a day, Walter's sores had cleared up and the tingling in his feet subsided. Walking had promoted the growth of new blood vessels (called *collateral circulation*) around the blocked arteries in his feet and legs. Diabetics should get clearance from their doctors before they start a walking program, however.

Cold Feet

"Cold feet, warm heart," is what my mother always told me, but chronically cold feet can make you miserable and curtail all outdoor walking once the weather turns chilly. Chronic cold feet may indicate a circulatory problem. It can mean that your arterioles (small arteries) may be constricting and not letting blood flow to your feet. This constriction can be caused by nicotine and caffeine, amphetamines, and some nasal congestion medication. In fact, smoking one cigarette can reduce the blood flow to your feet by up to 50 percent. Stress also can cause constriction of your arterioles, and this is likely the genesis of the expression "having cold feet."

Walking is the best answer for cold feet, whether or not you have a circulation problem. It increases blood flow to the extremities and thus warms them up. Wearing warm socks, either a double layer of silk covered with wool or a single sock of polypropylene or other synthetic material, should keep your feet toasty. You might also try placing a lining of sheepskin (either real or synthetic) in your shoes during the winter months. Leg warmers will also help to keep your legs and feet comfortable.

Joint Problems

One of the more common joint problems of the feet is hammertoes. This is when a toe, usually the second toe, buckles under to resemble a small hammer. Some people are born with hammertoes, although you can get them from a toe injury or from wearing narrow-toed shoes (especially if you have a Morton's toe). People who pronate are susceptible to hammertoes.

A hammertoe itself may not be painful, but if you wear shoes that crowd the deformed toe, it can be extraordinarily so. If you have a hammertoe, look for shoes with a high, wide toebox or wear opened-toed shoes in warm weather. If the hammertoe causes you a great deal of pain, a podiatrist can perform minor surgery to straighten the toe out by lengthening tendons attached to the toe bones. This surgery requires only a few weeks recuperation at most, the incisions are very small. If the toe is more severely bent, the bone might be shortened, which is also minor surgery. This operation will take a few more weeks to heal.

Pain in the Ball of the Foot and Bunions

Pain in the ball of the foot, also known as *metatarsalgia*, is usually associated with high rigid arches, although people with low arches who pronate excessively can also develop it. Misalignment of the first metatarsal can also cause metatarsalgia. You will usually feel a burning or aching in the ball of the foot, with numbness and pain in the third and fourth toes. Walking more than a few blocks will be difficult. This pain is caused by nerves being squeezed by the two metatarsal bones, resulting in nerve irritation (called *neuritis*) and often nerve enlargement (called *neuroma*). Massaging the foot will help temporarily, but walking any great distance will be difficult. Shoes that are tight at the ball of the foot will cause further discomfort and will enlarge the area of pain. Possible treatments include placing a special foot pad over the sensitive area, being fitted with an orthotic, receiving cortisone injections, undergoing physical therapy, or as a last resort, having surgery to remove the neuroma or shorten the bone that is rubbing against the nerve.

Bunions, an overgrowth of bone at the base of the big toe, often results from a misalignment of the metatarsal bone, known as *hallux valgus*. This misalignment causes the big toe to bend in the direction of the little toe and the big toe bone to enlarge and protrude out the side of the foot. Although bunions are often inherited or caused by arthritis, wearing shoes with too narrow toes or too high heels can both also bring on bunions. Bunions do not develop all at once but will grow over time, especially if they are irritated by shoes too small at the toe box. An orthotic device can help delay the formation or progression of bunions.

There is no permanent cure for bunions other than a bunionectomy, in which part of the first metatarsal bone is removed. This operation can now be done with a minimal incision, and most patients can be walking around the same day and wearing shoes within a week. Patients have been known to compete in a race within 2 weeks of surgery (although doctors don't recommend this). If surgery involves straightening a misalignment, recovery will take approximately 4 weeks.

If a bunion develops, buy shoes with a wide toe box and consult a podiatrist for further treatment. Ignoring bunions can lead to pain and arthritis in the joint.

Alignment Problems

Some alignment problems are caused by an abnormal shift in your center of gravity due to poor posture, pregnancy, or carrying a backpack. When your center of gravity is out of line, it causes imbalances in your muscles, ligaments, tendons, and joints and may even result in nerve damage. Such imbalances often manifest themselves in foot problems. For example, if the body is shifted too far forward, calluses will build up on the balls of the feet. If the foot itself is out of alignment, then conversely, the imbalances will exhibit themselves as knee, ankle, and even lower back pain.

Bowlegs and knock-knees are congenital structural misalignments, and a person with them puts unnatural stresses on his or her feet and legs when he or she walks. They can cause shin splints and pain in the heel, arch, leg, and big toe. These conditions can be helped with an orthotic, which will help to realign the foot and leg.

Foot and Leg Exercises and Exercisewalking Techniques

Exercises for Shin Splints and Tight Achilles Tendons

1. Sit in a chair and stretch out one leg. Tie your walking shoes together by the laces, and hang the shoes over your foot. Flex your foot up and back. Repeat ten to thirty times.

2. To build up the muscles at the front of your legs, walk backwards for 3 to 5 minutes at both the beginning and end of your workout.

3. Pretend you are holding a pen with your toes and try to "draw" figure eights. Make ten figures with each foot.

4. Stand 1 or 2 feet from a wall. Lean into the wall, supporting yourself with your arms, and feel the stretch in the backs of your calves. The more you bend your arms, the more you'll feel the stretch. Hold position for at least 15 seconds (30 to 60 seconds is more effective). Repeat ten times, three times a day. This is also an excellent exercise to prevent nocturnal calf cramps.

5. Stand on a step with both legs together and your heels hanging off the edge. Lower your heels so that you feel a stretch in the backs of your calves. Hold this position for at least 15 seconds (30 to 60 seconds is more effective).

6. Sit on the floor with your legs together straight in front of you. If you can reach your toes with your hands, pull them toward you. If not, just lean forward as far as you can with your arms stretched toward your toes. Hold this position for at least 15 seconds (30 to 60 seconds is more effective).

Arch Pain

Roll a golf ball under your arch for 10 to 15 minutes before you go out walking. This will massage all the muscles on the bottom of your foot.

Exercisewalking Technique

While you walk, practice the follow techniques you learned in Book 2:

The *heel-toe roll* (see page 98). This will strengthen the muscles at the fronts and backs of the calves.

The *heel strike* (page 98). This is especially helpful to practice if you overpronate or supinate.

The moral of this chapter is that you can't afford to ignore your feet if you want walking to be a pleasurable activity.

5. Shoe Care, Repair, and Modification

Once you've found a walking shoe you like, you'll want to keep it as long as possible. Anyone who has ever had a favorite pair of shoes knows it is a sad day when it's time to throw them out. With walking shoes becoming increasingly expensive, there is even greater incentive to keep them in good shape. In this chapter you'll learn how to preserve the life of your shoes, both dress and athletic.

Athletic Shoes

Upper and Interior

Wear on the upper of a shoe is caused by perspiration, humidity, bacterial growth, and the heat produced by your foot. The first rule in fighting shoe wear is to switch off among several pairs of shoes. If you wear one pair all day, you should not wear it the next. If you allow your shoes to air out for 24 hours, perspiration and moisture will not build up inside the shoe and you'll prevent fungal growth and a smelly interior. The best way to prolong the life of your walking shoes is to wear them only for your walking workout.

If your shoes get wet, don't place them on or near a heater. Instead, fill them with loosely packed newspaper and allow them to dry naturally. Excessive heat will cause uppers to become inflexible, and the leather may crack.

Keep the uppers clean. If they are hard leather, treat them with a water repellant and polish them often. Soft leather can be cleaned with a damp cloth. Suede uppers can be brushed clean. Nylon uppers should be cleaned with a damp cloth or soft brush. For extra protection, you can spray them with Scotch-Guard. This will make spot removal easy, although it may impede ventilation slightly.

Canvas uppers can be washed by hand or in the washing machine. Hand washing is preferred because other fabrics in the shoe do not stand up well to the abuse of a washing machine. Spray the canvas uppers of new shoes with starch to keep dirt from getting deep into the fibers of the material.

If a hole develops in the upper of a nylon walking shoe, try placing a little duct tape over the hole. Although this might not be the height of fashion, it will prevent the upper from tearing further.

If your shoe has a removable sock liner, you can wash it separately (by hand with mild detergent).

The Sole

It is now possible to give new life to the soles of your fitness exercisewalking shoes. If you like at-home methods, try a product such as Shoe Goo, a rubbery adhesive substance used to stop up holes in the soles or heels. Or you may be able to find a cobbler who specializes in athletic shoe repair. Ask your shoe dealer for cobblers in your area. This resoling usually costs about a third to half the price of a new pair of shoes. Even new midsoles, which usually collapse after several hundred miles, can be added. Sock liners, innersoles, and laces can also be replaced to give your walking shoes a second life. Beware that if your shoes undergo major repair, they probably won't give you the same performance as when they were new. Therefore, it might be healthiest in the long run to buy a new pair when the old ones wear out.

If you can't find a cobbler who can replace the midsole or sole, don't continue to wear your shoes. Once the midsole has collapsed (check it from time to time; if you can push it together more than halfway, it is no longer wearable) or your heels have worn down, the shoe can no longer do its job and could cause leg and foot injuries.

Dress Shoes

Maintenance for leather dress shoes is much the same as that for athletic shoes. Treat shoes before you wear them with a leather lotion (which you can buy at a cobbler or shoe store) to protect against scuffs and dirt. The treatment will also keep the uppers supple and breathable. Follow this routine at least once a month. You should also cover your shoes with a water-repellant spray to avoid salt spots and damage from rain or snow. Polishing your shoes often and brushing off dirt after you wear them will also help protect the leather.

Repairing the soles and uppers of leather dress shoes or boots is a simple process, but many people let their shoes go until it is too late. As soon as you notice wear on the heel or the sole, bring the shoes into your cobbler for repair. Cobblers can repair a wide variety of problems, including gouges on the heels of high-heeled shoes and uppers that have become unstitched or unglued from the soles. They can also replace innersoles and remove wrinkles from the upper.

Shoe Modifications

Several modifications can be made to walking shoes to make them more comfortable. The easiest is to add cushioning or sock liners to shoes with little or insufficient cushioning. When Gary Yanker walked from New York to Florida, he placed several foam pads over the sock liners in his shoes to provide extra cushioning. Liners with an arch support and heel cup are made by several companies, some even make a plastic form that you place in hot water and then step on. This is a good solution for people who seek extra support or stability from their shoe. (Both items can be found at athletic shoe stores.)

Lacings can also be modified to alter the way the shoe fits. If your toes tend to swell as you walk, try lacing your shoes looser at the toes and tighter at the instep to allow extra room and reduce pressure. Lacing your shoes in the normal X lacing pattern provides the most even distribution of pressure over the eyelets. If you have two eyelets at the top of the shoe and want to make the shoe fit better at the heel, try the following lacing approach: Run the laces through the outer eyelets, then back through the

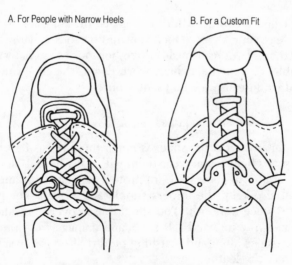

A. For People with Narrow Heels   B. For a Custom Fit

Lacing Systems

inner eyelets, across the tongue, and through the loops created on either side. If you have four holes at the top of the shoe, you can slip the lace into the second hole and out the fourth before tying them.

Finally, extreme modifications can be made in the uppers of the shoes to increase ventilation. When Rob Sweetgall walked across America, his feet got so hot from his daily 35- to 40-mile regimen that he slit the toes of his walking shoes to provide air-conditioning. This does not destroys the shoe's function, since little support is given by the upper at the toe. If you live in a hot climate and have a pair of leather walking shoes that you never wear because they are too hot, you might consider this solution. If not, try buying a pair of walking sandals for ventilation.

Now that you know how to choose the right walking shoe for you and how to take care of your shoes and feet, you are ready to walk a lifetime of comfortable miles.

WALKING DOCTOR AND HEALTH PROFESSIONAL DIRECTORY

A State-by-State Listing

Our Walking Doctor and Health Professional Directory creates for the first time a walking medicine establishment to counterbalance the sports medicine establishment. While sports medicine focuses primarily on treating already-injured athletes, walking medicine emphasizes *both* preventive and rehabilitative medicine.

Walking is the leading rehabilitative and preventive exercise for everything from heart disease and arthritis to weight control, diabetes, and hypertension, yet very few in the medical profession actually know enough about walking to prescribe specific exercisewalking techniques and programs to their patients.

This is why we have developed this network of doctors and health professionals who walk and prescribe walking to their patients.

Why should such a network be established? You, the walker, need a source of medical advice from health professionals who are sympathetic to your needs because they are walkers themselves. What's more, many of the doctors listed here have "healed themselves" with walking. For example, Dr. Scott Patterson, a psychiatrist practicing in Georgia, and Dr. Jack Stern, a cardiologist from Arizona, have both walked to rehabilitate from the physical and psychological effects of cancer. Both are now in remission and consider their walking programs as one of the reasons they are strong and healthy today. Dr. Darwin Strickland, a podiatrist from Colorado, has achieved a drastic weight loss and has lowered his cholesterol count through walking. Dr. Donnica Moore, a general practitioner from New Jersey, rehabilitated from spinal surgery through walking. Such walking doctors serve as both examples and motivation to their patients.

Doctors who practice what they preach, as do the doctors and health professionals in this directory, are "walker friendly." There is a "connectedness" between a health professional and his or her patient if they both participate in the same activity. Many runners found this to be true when they sought advice from running doctors. Now, with the help of our directory, walkers can seek advice from walking doctors.

The doctors in our directory can give you specific programs for your condition, whether it is heart disease, arthritis, or weight control, and help you apply the exercisewalking techniques and programs in *Walking Medicine* because they have practical experience in walking for exercise. For example, you'll find health professionals such as Nadine Baustein, a dietician in Massachusetts, who walks with her patients during nutritional counseling sessions; or Dr. Eric Shultz, a sports podiatrist practicing in Florida, who has set up a walking track in the parking lot of his clinic and teaches walking techniques at the local hospital.

How to Use Our Directory

Through the Walking Doctor and Health Professional Directory, you can locate doctors and other health professionals who walk and prescribe walking to their patients. Their specialties are coded beside their name and addresses. All the medical areas covered in *Walking Medicine* are represented in our directory, including pediatrics, geriatrics, heart and lung disorders, arthritis, orthopedics, foot problems, psychology and psychiatry, and nutrition and weight control. The listings also include information on the health professionals' personal walking regimens.

You can use this directory to find a general practitioner or internist who can give you the go ahead to start a walking program (this is especially important if you are over 35 and have been sedentary for more than one year), if you have an injury from another sport or an accident and want to use walking as a means of rehabilitation, or if you have one of the conditions discussed in *Walking Medicine* and want to use walking as part of your treatment.

Some of the health professionals listed here are university professors, researchers, or employees of large companies. Although they can't treat you, they are included here because they can be used as sources of referrals to doctors who can. If the doctors listed in your state are not specialists in the areas you need, use them to get referrals to other walking doctors who specialize in the area you need.

Future Listings

If you are a health professional who walks and prescribes walking to your patients and wish to be listed in our directory, fill out the questionnaire at the back of this book and send it to:

Walking Doctor Directory
c/o Walking World
PO Box K, Gracie Station
New York, NY 10028

If you are in search of a walking doctor in your area, you also can write us at the above address (please address the envelope to Ask Your Walking Doctor).

Key to Medical Specialties Code

AG = aging (geriatrics)
AR = arthritis
 B = back and joint problems
BM = biomechanics
 D = dermatology
EP = exercise physiologist
 F = foot problems
GP = general practitioner, family medicine
GS = general surgery
 H = heart and vascular disorders and related specialties
HE = health education
IM = internal medicine
 L = lung ailments
 N = neurology
 O = orthopedics
OB = obstetrics and gynecology
OC = occupational medicine
OP = ophthalmology, optometry
PA = pain management
PD = pediatrics
PE = physical education
PL = plastic surgery
PM = preventative medicine
PS = psychology, psychiatry
PT = physical therapy
RM = rehabilitative medicine, physiatrist

S = sports medicine
U = urology
V = veterinary medicine
W = weight control

Key to Professional and Scientific Degree Codes

A.B.   = Associate Degree
B.S.N.   = Bachelor of Science and Nursing
C.S.W.   = Certified Social Worker
D.C.   = Doctor of Chiropractic
D.O.   = Doctor of Osteopathic Medicine
D.P.M.   = Doctor of Podiatric Medicine
Dr.P.H.   = Doctor of Public Health
D.V.M.   = Doctor of Veterinarian Medicine
F.N.P.   = Family Nurse Practitioner
M.P.H.   = Master of Public Health
M.S.   = Master of Science
M.S.W.   = Master of Social Work
O.T.R.   = Occupational Therapist
P.A.   = Physician's Assistant
P.E.D.   = Physical Education Doctor
Psy.D.   = Doctor of Psychology
R.D.   = Registered Dietician
R.P.T.   = Registered Physical Therapist

Note: An (S) or (P) at the end of the listing indicates that the doctor or health professional specifically named walking as his or her primary (P) or secondary (S) exercise.

Directory

Alabama

Birmingham

William Koopman, M.D. (AR)
Director
Division of Clinical Immunology &
   Rheumatology
University of Alabama
UAB Station
Birmingham, AL 35294
(205) 934-5306

Dr. Koopman is head of the Multipurpose Arthritis Center at the University of Alabama and director of the Division of Clinical Rheumatology and Immunology. He is a Harvard Medical School graduate. Dr. Koopman walks about 10 miles a week.

Cullman

Lawrence J. Downs, D.P.M. (F,S)
412 First Avenue S.E.
Cullman, AL 35056
(205) 734-8782

Dr. Downs is an ardent walker, logging 2 to 3 miles every day.

Alaska

Eagle River

Kevin P. Maguire, D.O. (GP,PM)
Medical Data Systems
Box 77234
Eagle River, Alaska 99577
(907) 552-4957

Dr. Maguire walks 30 miles a week, 6 days a week, on rugged Alaskan terrain. He walks in all seasons, sometimes with his family. (P)

Arizona

Phoenix

Janice Bebe Dorn, M.D., Ph.D. (PS)
4227 North 32nd Street
Suite 108
Phoenix, AZ 85018
(602) 224-9277

Dr. Dorn walks 2 hours every day.

Scottsdale

James Asher, D.O. (PA)
The Headache & Stress Center
7330 East Earll Drive
Suite B
Scottsdale, AZ 85251
(602) 990-2382

Dr. Asher is a general practitioner who specializes in pain management. His practice includes acupuncture, massage, biofeedback, counseling, and other therapy. He walks 4 days a week, 2 to 3 miles a day.

Tempe

James S. Skinner, Ph.D. (EP)
Arizona State University
Department of Health and Physical
   Education
Tempe, AZ 85287-0404
(602) 965-4928

Dr. Skinner is director of the Exercise Research Institute in Arizona. He walks an hour a week over 2 days.

Christine L. Wells, Ph.D. (EP)
Arizona State University
Department of Health and Physical
  Education
CY1 1001/100261
Tempe, AZ 85287-0404
(602) 965-4928

As an exercise physiologist, Dr. Wells prescribes walking to previously sedentary people for weight control and to injured athletes.

Tucson

Todd J. Raemisch, D.C. (B)
Raemisch Chiropractic Center, Ltd.
2606 East Grant Road
Tucson, AZ 85716
(602) 325-0161

Jack I. Stern, M.D. (IM,H)
5400 North Via Velazquez
Tucson, AZ 85715
(602) 577-8429

Dr. Stern's specialty is internal medicine and cardiology. He loves aerobic dancing, but also gets a terrific workout by racewalking 11 minute-miles 7 to 8 miles a day 4 days a week.

Arkansas

Little Rock

Hampton Roy, M.D. (OP,AG)
Arkansas Cataract Center
1000 Medical Towers Building
9601 Lilie Drive
Little Rock, AK 72205
(501) 227-6980

Dr. Roy specializes in ophthalmology and is an associate professor at the University of Arkansas School of Medicine. He walks 7 miles a day 3 days a week for a total of 21 miles weekly.

California

Anaheim

John N. Strand, M.D. (GP)
Family Practice
1110 W. La Palma
Suite 4
Anaheim, CA 92801-2823
(714) 520-3000

Dr. Strand recommends walking to all his patients. He walks 20 miles a week, averaging 5 miles 4 days a week.

Anaheim Hills

Jeffrey H. Katz, D.P.M. (F,S)
Anaheim Hills Podiatry Group
6200 E. Canyon Rim Road
Suite 111E
Anaheim Hills, CA 92807
(714) 974-3338

Dr. Katz specializes in preventive and sports medicine. He walks 3 days a week for 2 hours at a time.

Beverly Hills

Howard Flaks, M.D. (W)
9400 Brighton Way
Suite 202
Beverly Hills, CA 90210
(213) 858-7641

Dr. Flaks is the public relations chairman of the American Society of Bariatric Physicians (specializing in the treatment of obesity). He enjoys walking on all sorts of terrain and does so daily, logging 20 miles a week. (P)

Mark Forrestal, M.D. (H)
Vein Clinics of America
8383 Wilshire Boulevard
Beverly Hills, CA 90210
(213) 852-0605

Dr. Forrestal recommends a brisk walk to all his patients with vascular disorders to improve circulation. He walks 3 miles a day 4 days a week.

Fontana

Ardis Beckner, R.D., M.S. (W)
9985 Sierra Avenue
Fontana, CA 92335
(714) 829-6054

Ms. Beckner is a registered dietician with an M.S. in nutrition. She is part of the Kaiser Permanente Group, with 12 years in their preventive medicine department. They see 34,000 patients a year, and nearly all are put on walking programs for weight and diabetes control. She walks every day for 2 to 3 miles and also climbs 12 flights of stairs daily to train for long hikes. (P)

Dave Roadruck, M.P.H. (W)
Kaiser Permanente
9985 Sierra Avenue
Fontana, CA 92335
(714) 824-7022

Dr. Roadruck, a Doctor of Health Science with a masters degree in public health, has 25 years of experience and hasn't met a successful weight-loss patient yet who did not incorporate exercise into his or her treatment. He walks 7 days a week, 2 miles a day. (S)

Greenbrae

Keith Denkler, M.D. (PL)
599 Sir Francis Drake Boulevard
Greenbrae, CA 94904
(415) 925-1012

Dr. Denkler is an instructor at the University of California, San Francisco. He walks an hour a day 5 days a week. (P)

Hayward

Steven O. Subotnick, D.P.M., M.S.
   (F,S)
Hesperian Medical Center
19682 Hesperian Boulevard
Hayward, CA 94541
(415) 783-3255

A leading podiatrist in the field of sports medicine, Dr. Subotnick is a clinical professor in the Departments of Biomechanics and Surgery at California College of Podiatric Medicine and an adjunct professor in the Department of Kinesiology at the California State University in Hayward. Dr. Subotnick is also on the staff of Turntec, an athletic shoe company and is the creator of the Varus wedge, a support system found in many athletic shoes. He walks twice a week, 5 miles a day.

Livermore

Harold M. Kuritz, D.P.M. (S,F)
Sunset Office Plaza
1364 Concannon Boulevard
Livermore, CA 94550
(415) 449-8333

Dr. Kuritz specializes in sports medicine and podiatric surgery and walks 5 days a week for 3 miles. (P)

Long Beach

Pamela R. Kushner, M.D. (GP,PM)
2865 Atlantic Avenue
Suite 151
Long Beach, CA 90806
(213) 895-6770

Dr. Kushner has a family medicine practice with an emphasis on preventive medicine. She walks 3 days a week, 1 mile a day.

Robert Thayer, Ph.D. (PS)
Department of Psychology
California State University
Long Beach, CA 90840
(213) 985-5026

Dr. Thayer walks 5 to 10 miles per week,
5 to 7 days. (P)

Los Angeles

Leonard J. Faye, D.C. (B)
10780 Santa Monica Boulevard
Suite 400
Los Angeles, CA 90025
(213) 420-1225

Dr. Faye walks 21 miles per week.

Robert Girandola, Ph.D. (EP)
University of Southern California
Department of Physical Education and
   Exercise Sciences
Los Angeles, CA 90089-0652
(213) 743-7360

Dr. Girandola received the Ph.D. degree
in exercise physiology from the University
of California, Berkeley. He walks every
day, 10 to 12 miles a week at a fast pace.
(S)

Keith L. Gurnick, D.P.M. (F)
2080 Century Park East
Suite 204
Los Angeles, CA 90067-2091
(213) 553-7691

Dr. Gurnick walks 5 days a week, 3 miles
a day.

Martin Hauptschein, M.D. (IM)
1831 Barry Avenue, #14
Los Angeles, CA 90025
(213) 477-5070

Dr. Hauptschein walks 2 miles a day, 2
days a week. (S)

Ruth Lerner, Ph.D. (PS)
1314 Westwood Boulevard, #106
Los Angeles, CA 90024
(213) 470-4410

Dr. Lerner, a clinical psychologist concentrating in sports psychology and whol-
istic health, incorporates walking into her
therapy sessions with depressed patients
because she believes walking helps to create the feeling of "movement" and "control" in one's life. She prescribes walking
to many of her other patients as well. Dr.
Lerner walks 16 hours a week, 4 days a
week.

Kathryn Welds, Ph.D. (PS)
11625 Texas Avenue, #201
Los Angeles, CA 90025
(213) 479-5457

Dr. Welds earned a Ph.D. in personality/
developmental psychology from Harvard
University. She specializes in helping individuals and organizations realize their
potential production capacity by evalu-
ating and developing career goals, com-
munication skills, and management
techniques. Dr. Welds walks 7 days a week.

Clifford J. Wolf, D.P.M., F.A.C.F.O.
   (F)
Mid-Wilshire Foot Clinic
5901 West Olympic Boulevard
Suite 400
Los Angeles, CA 90036
(213) 933-5064

Dr. Wolf specializes in foot and ankle surgery. He walks a fast 2 miles a week on
rugged terrain.

Mill Valley

Harry F. Hlavac, D.P.M., M.Ed. (F,S)
Marin Foot Health Center
100 Shoreline Highway
Suite 150
Mill Valley, CA 94941
(415) 331-3332

Dr. Hlavac is a professor in the Biomechanics Department at the California College of Podiatric Medicine in San Francisco and a former consultant to Nike Shoes. He walks 3 to 4 days a week, 1 to 2 miles a day on rugged terrain.

Mission Viejo

Allison Purtell, M.D. (AR,IM)
27800 Medical Center Road
Suite 459
Mission Viejo, CA 92691-6424
(714) 364-1989

Dr. Purtell practices both internal medicine and rheumatology. She bikes, swims, and walks 2 miles a day, 7 days a week.

Napa

Sarah Miller, Ph.D. (PS,W)
1447 4th Street
Napa, CA 94559
(707) 224-7411

Dr. Miller, a clinical psychologist, works with very overweight individuals (40 pounds and more) and has helped them achieve their health goals with a walking program. Dr. Miller walks 3 miles a day, 5 to 7 days a week.

Newport Beach

Darlene Landis, D.C. (B)
4121 Westerly Place
Suite 116
Newport Beach, CA 92660
(714) 752-5753

Dr. Landis has been an educator, trainer, and coach at Costa Mesa High School for over a decade and was also a chiropractor in India for some time. She walks 10 miles or more a week.

Northridge

Thomas Neuman, D.P.M. (F,S)
9435 Reseda Boulevard
Suite 201
Northridge, CA 91324
(818) 885-8400

Dr. Neuman is chief of podiatry at Granada Hills Community Hospital and specializes in sports medicine and podiatric surgery. He walks 5 days a week, 5 miles a day.

Orange

Grant Gwinup, M.D. (W)
University of California, Irvine
California College of Medicine
Department of Medicine
101 City Drive South
Orange, CA 92668
(714) 634-5125

Dr. Gwinup, an endocrinologist and a metabolism and nutrition specialist, is the developer of the Gwinup exophthalometer, used throughout the world to measure exophthalmus, a protrusion of the eyeball caused by a swelling of the soft tissue in the eye socket. Currently a professor of medicine at Irvine's College of Medicine, Dr. Gwinup has published books and articles about weight control, among other subjects. (S)

Petaluma

David R. Amundsen, D.C. (B,PM)
1112 B Street
Petaluma, CA 94952
(707) 763-1156

Dr. Amundsen emphasizes preventive health care in his practice. He walks 3 days a week, 3 miles a day.

Playa Del Rey

Marcy Atwood, M.A., O.T.R. (AR,PT)
314 Pershing Drive
Playa Del Rey, CA 90293
(213) 823-4436

Ms. Atwood is an occupational therapist who specializes in pediatric rheumatology and musculoskeletal and adolescent disorders. She works closely with the Childrens Hospital of Los Angeles and has supervised a community-based program to develop vocational and independent living skills. She prescribes walking to her patients, and herself walks 5 to 6 days a week, 4 miles a day.

Sacramento

Randall Brown, D.C. (S)
2729 P. Street
Sacramento, CA 95816
(916) 457-8825

Dr. Brown is a sports chiropractor. He walks 4 to 6 days a week. (P)

Deepak D. Chabra, M.D. (U)
2025 Morse Avenue
Sacramento, CA 95825
(916) 973-6250

Dr. Chabra's patients facing major cancer surgery are put on a deep-breathing/walking program. He finds that the walking works wonders for successful postoperative recovery, inducing minimal complications and a shorter hospital stay. Dr. Chabra enjoys walking with his family and hikes 2 to 3 days a week, 1 to 2 miles a day.

San Diego

Peter R. Francis, Ph.D. (BM)
WG1 Biomechanics Laboratory
San Diego State University
San Diego, CA 92182
(619) 594-5625

Dr. Francis, whose Ph.D. degree is in biomechanics, is a researcher and professor at San Diego State University. He walks 10 to 15 miles a week.

Jeffrey D. Korn, D.P.M. (F)
2307 Meade Avenue
San Diego, CA 92116
(619) 298-6400

Dr. Korn finds walking more enjoyable and less stressful to the joints than jogging. He covers 10 miles every 3 to 4 days. (P)

San Francisco

Lisa C. Bardaro, M.D. (OB)
558 Clayton Street
San Francisco, CA 94117
(415) 431-1716

Dr. Bardaro, who runs a family practice and practices some obstetrics and gynecology, feels walking is the safest and healthiest form of exercise for all her patients. She is a retired dancer and now does weight training and walks with weights 7 days a week, 2 miles a day. (S)

Nancy J. Bohannon, M.D. (IM)
1580 Valencia Street, #504
San Francisco, CA 94110
(415) 648-7622

Dr. Bohannon practices fast walking. (S)

David L. Chittenden, M.D. (F,O,S)
450 Sutter Street, #905
San Francisco, CA 94108
(415) 433-5284

Dr. Chittenden walks 1 to 2 days a week, 2 to 3 miles a day.

Terri Merritt, M.S. (EP,H)
CCMP, Cardiac Rehabilitation
2360 Clay Street
San Francisco, CA 94115
(415) 923-3395

Ms. Merritt, who received a master's degree in physiology, is a co-chairperson of the San Francisco May Day Run. She walks 12 to 15 miles a week, 3 days a week, on stairs or rugged terrain.

Kathleen Bell Unger, M.D. (PS)
A Medical Corporation
200 Van Ness Avenue
San Francisco, CA 94109
(415) 776-0456

Dr. Unger is a psychiatrist specializing in chemical dependency. She walks 5 days a week and logs 20 miles.

San Leandro

Darrell Heppner (B)
367 Bancroft Avenue
San Leandro, CA 94577
(415) 632-2200

Mr. Heppner runs Darell Heppner Risk Management Services, Inc., an organization that provides information and equipment designed to prevent injury to the back. He walks 2 miles a day for relaxation.

Santa Barbara

Ronald Kapp, Ph.D., M.D. (GP)
PO Box 23133
Santa Barbara, CA 93121
(805) 763-4211

Dr. Kapp strides a speedy 5 to 6 miles per hour and covers 3 miles a day, 4 days a week.

Santa Rosa

Drs. Janet and Bill Albers, D.C.
  (B,S,PM)
108 Wikiup Drive
Santa Rosa, CA 95403
(707) 528-3255

Both doctors emphasize preventive medicine in their practices, which specialize in nutrition and sports medicine. Dr. Janet Albers sustained a knee injury while running in the Chicago Marathon and switched to walking. Her knee is now completely recovered. Now she and her husband both walk 7 days a week, 1 to 2 miles a day, and hike on weekends.

Sausalito

Dean Ornish, M.D. (H)
Preventive Medicine Research Center
7 Miller Avenue
Sausalito, CA 94965
(415) 332-2525

Dr. Ornish has led major research studies on how heart patients can reduce the blockage of their coronary arteries through exercise, proper diet, stress reduction, and quitting smoking. He walks 1 to 2 miles a day, 3 days a week, and enjoys tennis and basketball.

Sherman Oaks

Peg Jordan, Editor (H,W,S)
American Fitness Magazine
15250 Venture Boulevard
Suite 310
Sherman Oaks, CA 91403
(818) 905-0040

Ms. Jordan's *American Fitness* is the official magazine of the Aerobics and Fitness Association of America. She is also a cardiac rehabilitation consultant for the Daniel Freeman Hospital in Marina del Rey. She enjoys the fresh air and California sunshine by walking 4 days a week, 3 miles a day.

Allen Selner, D.P.M. (F,S)
MedStar Foot & Ankle Center
13320 Riverside Drive, #216
Sherman Oaks, CA 91423
(818) 784-6231

Dr. Selner specializes in sports medicine for women. He walks at least a mile every day of the week.

Sonora

Richard E. Behymer, M.D. (GP)
Greenley Family Practice Center
940 Sylva Lane
Suite D
Sonora, CA 95370
(209) 533-0433

Dr. Behymer hikes in the foothills of the Sierras 2 to 3 days a week.

Sunnyvale

S. Marvin Sussman, D.P.M. (F)
Mary-El Medical Center
972 West El Camino Real
Sunnyvale, CA 94087
(408) 739-2277

Dr. Sussman specializes in podiatric medicine and surgery. He walks every day of the week, averaging 7 miles a day, for a total weekly mileage of 49 miles. (P)

Upland

Robert C. Clark, D.O. (B)
99 North San Antonio, #200
Upland, CA 91786
(714) 982-9855

Dr. Clark likes to beat California traffic by walking to and from work. He walks 2 to 4 miles, 5 to 6 days a week. (P)

Van Nuys

Neil H. Hecht, D.P.M. (F)
6900 Van Nuys Boulevard
Suite 6
Van Nuys, CA 91405
(818) 782-2227

Dr. Hecht specializes in podiatric medicine and surgery. He actively encourages his patients to participate in walking programs and monitors their activity. Dr. Hecht walks an average of 3 miles a day, 2 to 3 days a week.

Westminster

Amy L. Abt, M.D. (OB)
7631 Wyoming Street
Suite 204
Westminster, CA 92683
(714) 891-8872

Dr. Abt specializes in obstetrics, gynecology, and infertility. She recommends walking to all her patients for overall conditioning and stress reduction. Dr. Abt walks an hour a day, 4 days a week.

Whittier

Marica Ehinger, M.D. (GP,PD)
13203 Hadley Street
Suite 101-A
Whittier, CA 90601
(213) 945-1637

Dr. Ehinger practices general medicine with an emphasis on health care for women and children. She walks or hikes 5 days a week, 2 miles a day. (S)

Colorado

Boulder

Michael A. Goldman, D.P.M. (F,S)
Alpine Foot and Ankle Clinic
1120-B Alpine Avenue
Boulder, CO 80302
(303) 442-3500

Dr. Goldman is a podiatrist specializing in sports medicine with a background in biomechanics. He treats all levels of athletes from weekend tennis players to Olympic contenders. He walks approximately 10 miles a week with his family and enjoys backpacking on weekends.

Colorado Springs

Edmund R. Burke, Ph.D. (EP)
The Edmund R. Burke Company
Suite B
3508 Queen Anne Way
Colorado Springs, CO 80917
(719) 380-1473

Dr. Burke, a writer and consultant to the fitness industry, currently conducts research on the subjects of exercise physiology, cycling safety, and cycling biomechanics. He walks 30 miles a week, 6 days a week, on rugged terrain.

Stanton C. Southward, D.P.M. (F)
1900 East Pikes Peak
Colorado Springs, CO 80909
(719) 473-1828

Dr. Southward is president of the International Academy of Ambulatory Foot Surgery and promotes the benefits of minimal incision surgery, a treatment especially helpful to patients with bunions, hammertoes, ingrown toe nails, corns, and heel spurs. Dr. Southward walks 2 miles every day.

Denver

Othneil Seiden, M.D. (GP)
3654 South Oneida Way
Denver, CO 80237
(303) 758-5405

Dr. Seiden is a member of Doctors to the World, a group that provides medical aid to disaster-stricken areas all over the world. He walks 5 to 6 days per week, 4 to 6 miles a day.

Darwin J. Strickland, D.O. (F,S)
9669 North Huron Street
Denver, CO 80221
(303) 428-7509

Dr. Strickland has a private podiatric clinic specializing in family and sports medicine. He votes walking the number one exercise and has himself experienced a substantial weight loss and lowering of his cholesterol level since he began a walking program 9 years ago. He walks a brisk 3 miles a day.

Englewood

Connecticut

William Evans, M.D. (B)
125 East Hampden Avenue
PO Box 2901, Dept. 1099
Englewood, CO 80150-0101
(303) 788-6356

Dr. Evans specializes in spine rehabilitation and is currently researching the aging of lumbar disks in walkers. He walks 5 days a week, 5 miles a day.

Meredith H. Miller, M.D. (N)
South Denver Neurosurgical Associates
601 East Hampden
Suite 340
Englewood, CO 80110
(303) 788-4000

Dr. Miller specializes in neurosurgery and uses walking for his patients' postoperative rehabilitation programs. He hikes 12 miles a week at 3½ miles an hour on rugged terrain. (P)

Fort Collins

Alma R. Morgan, M.D. (GP)
1136 East Stuart, #3200
Fort Collins, CO 80525
(303) 221-4131

Dr. Morgan walks 12 to 20 miles every week. (P)

William A. Jones, M.D. (PS)
1025 South Lemay Avenue
2nd Floor-East Suite
Fort Collins, CO 80524
(719) 493-3040

Dr. Jones counsels families, couples, and individuals. He walks with weights 2 days a week at 4 miles an hour for a total of 8 miles. (P)

Bridgeport

Robert Lang, M.D. (AR,IM)
4699 Main Street
Bridgeport, CT 06606
(203) 372-7715

Dr. Lang is medical director of The Osteoporosis Diagnostic and Treatment Centers in New Haven and Bridgeport and the executive vice president and medical director of Working Well International, Guilford. He is certified in internal medicine, endocrinology, and metabolism. He walks 3 to 5 days a week, 3 miles a day.

Darien

Robert F. Weiss, D.P.M. (F,S)
800 Post Road
Darien, CT 06820
(203) 656-1696

Dr. Weiss is very involved in podiatric sports medicine and served on the Medical Advisory Committee for the 1984 and 1988 U.S. Olympic Men's Marathon Trials. He walks 5 days a week, 2 miles a day.

Farmington

Gail P. Dalsky, Ph.D.
University of Connecticut Osteoporosis
   Center
Farm Hollow
Suite C208
Farmington, CT 06032
(203) 679-3855

Dr. Dalsky conducts research at the University of Connecticut on the effects of exercise on the aging process, particularly on how exercise prevents osteoporosis. She walks 12 miles a week, 2 days a week.(S)

Norwalk

Myra L. Skluth, M.D. (IM,PM)
87 East Avenue
Norwalk, CT 06851
(203) 866-4455

Dr. Skluth emphasizes preventive medicine in her practice and urges many of her patients to walk. She averages 4 miles a day, 4 days a week, for a total of 16 miles.

Torrington

Richard T. Kramer, M.D. (PS)
199 Migeon Avenue
Torrington, CT 06790
(203) 489-8117

Dr. Kramer is a psychiatrist who walks 1 to 3 days a week. (S)

Delaware

Newark

Robert Neeves, Ph.D. (EP)
Sports Science Laboratory
University of Delaware
Newark, DE 19716
(302) 451-6816

Dr. Reeves is an associate professor of exercise physiology and codirector of the Human Performance Laboratory at the University of Delaware. He walks 15 miles a week.

Robert Sweetgall
Creative Walking, Inc.
P.O. Box 699
Newark, DE 19715
(302) 368-2222

Mr. Sweetgall is president of Creative Walking, Inc., an organization that helps hospitals, doctors, schools, and individuals create walking programs. He has walked 22,000 miles across the United States on two major foot tours of more than 10,000 miles each, and has found walking to be one of the most beneficial and least punishing exercises. He now walks a mile a day, seven days a week.

Florida

Coral Gables

Jack E. Young, M.D. (S,PM,RM)
Medical Director
Health and Fitness Institute
Doctor's Hospital
5000 University Drive
Coral Gables, FL 33146
(305) 666-2111, ext. 342

Dr. Young is the team physician for the Miami Hurricanes, football team of the University of Miami.

Coral Springs

Andrew S. Wasserman, D.C. (B,S)
9441 West Sample Road
Suite 206
Coral Springs, FL 33065
(305) 755-1980

Dr. Wasserman treats many amateur and professional athletes. He walks 18 miles a week, 6 miles a day, 3 days a week.

Delray Beach

Rodolfo C. Juantorena, M.D. (PS)
16155 South Military Trail
Delray Beach, FL 33484
(407) 495-0522

Dr. Juantorena provides outpatient services to psychiatric patients. He strongly recommends walking to his clients, friends, and family members. By following a regular walking program, Dr. Juantorena has been able to control his diabetes, and has all but eliminated severe pain in his Achilles tendon caused by bursitis.

Susan Puls, M.D. (O,B)
2150 Lake Ida Road
Suite 5
Delray Beach, FL 33445
(407) 276-3051
(407) 734-4508

Dr. Puls specializes in orthopedic surgery and prescribes walking to treat many of her patients with chronic lower back pain. She walks 5 days a week, 3 miles a day, and she also swims.

Fort Myers

Richard Vahl, D.C. (B,S)
Denise Vahl, D.C.
12995 South Cleveland Avenue
Pinebrook Park
Suite 132
Fort Myers, FL 33907
(813) 936-4357

Both Drs. Vahl prescribe walking to many of their patients. Richard Vahl walks 7 days a week, 5 miles a day, and Denise walks 5 days a week, 4 miles a day.

Gainesville

Michael L. Pollock, Ph.D. (EP)
Division of Cardiology
College of Medicine, Box J-277
University of Florida
Gainesville, FL 32610
(904) 392-9575

Dr. Pollock, an exercise physiologist, is director of the Center for Exercise Science at the University of Florida. He was one of the first to research walking's effect on the cardiovascular system. (S)

Indian Harbor Beach

William A. Harr, D.P.M. (F)
2040 Highway A-1A
Suite 211
Indian Harbor Beach, FL 32937
(407) 777-4774

Dr. Harr prescribes walking to many of his patients. He enjoys a 5-mile beach walk twice a week.

Jacksonville

Eric Shultz, D.P.M. (F,S)
2550 Park Street
Jacksonville, FL 32204
(904) 387-0433

As a specialist in sports podiatry, Dr. Schultz prescribes walking to all his patients. He has a walking track in his parking lot, and he teaches racewalking at St. Vincent's Hospital in Jacksonville. Dr. Shultz racewalks a blistering 9 minutes per mile for 6 miles, 5 days a week.

Jupiter

Dr. Ron Grassi, D.C., P.A. (B,SM)
6390 West Indiantown Road, #27
Chasewood Plaza
Jupiter, FL 33458-3958
(407) 746-3544

Dr. Grassi walks 15 miles in 3 hours, 5 days a week.

Margate

Jay A. Lieberman, D.P.M. (F,S)
Northwest Broward Podiatry Association
Palm Lakes Plaza
7336 West Atlantic Boulevard
Margate, FL 33063
(305) 975-2007

Dr. Lieberman specializes in sports and podiatric medicine and surgery of the foot. He walks 4 days a week, 3 to 4 miles a day.

Melbourne

Richard C. Wilson, D.P.M. (F,S)
Melbourne Podiatry Association
211 East New Haven Avenue
Melbourne, FL 32901
(407) 723-3500

Dr. Wilson, who specializes in podiatry and sports medicine, treats many geriatric walkers. He frequently prescribes walking to his patients to help control peripheral vascular disease and has also used walking regimens to successfully control diabetes. He walks 3 days a week, 3 to 4 miles a day, in addition to weight training.

Miami

Joseph W. Accurso, D.C. (B)
6030 Bird Road
Miami, FL 33155
(407) 667-1188

Dr. Accurso helps patients to help themselves with a regular walking program. He walks a fast 7 to 8 miles a day, 4 days a week.

Karen R. Kade, M.D. (D)
7000 South West 97 Avenue, #108
Miami, FL 33173
(305) 596-0020

Dr. Kade enjoys competitive racewalking 3 days and 9 miles per week.

Miami Beach

Mark A. La Porta, M.D. (PM)
Internal Medicine
1040 71st St.
Miami Beach, FL 33141
(305) 866-4220

Dr. La Porta, who walks a varied amount 4 days a week, prescribes walking to his patients.

Orlando

Hugh B. Morris, M.D. (AR)
2501 North Orange Avenue
Suite 137N
Orlando, FL 32804
(407) 844-3973

Dr. Morris specializes in sports medicine and joint replacement surgery and says that walking is the best exercise for his patients' recovery from surgery. Dr. Morris walks 2 miles a day, 5 days a week.

Robert W. Westergan, M.D. (S,W,O)
7300 Sandlake Commons Boulevard
Suite 127
Orlando, FL 32819
(407) 345-1646

Dr. Westergan practices preventive and sports medicine, with a specialty in knee and hip reconstructive surgery. He recently lost over 30 pounds by walking 3 days a week, 3 miles a day. (S)

Palm Beach Gardens

Jeffrey A. Gala, D.C. (B,S,N)
1951 Bomar
PGA Boulevard and U.S. 1
Palm Beach Gardens, FL 33408
(407) 848-2700

Dr. Gala is a neurologist with degrees in chiropractic and sports medicine. He is doctor to several nationally ranked athletes and studies ways to help them achieve peak conditioning for competition. Dr. Gala walks 2 miles a day, 5 days a week.

Rockledge

Patricia J. Bryan (EP,H)
Wuesthoff Hospital
Cardiac and Pulmonary Rehabilitation
P.O. Box 6, #14
Rockledge, FL 32955
(407) 452-2506

Ms. Bryon is an exercise physiologist who customizes walking and exercise programs for cardiac rehabilitation patients.

St. Petersburg

Charles L. Eichenberg, Ph.D. (W)
The New Start Health Center
.5768 5th Avenue North
St. Petersburg, FL 33710
(813) 347-5581

Approximately 70 percent of Dr. Eichenberg's practice deals with weight control, but he also treats smoking cessation, stress management, and cholesterol control. Walking is an integral part of all the programs offered at his center, The NewStart Health Center. One such program is the Lifestyles Club, a walking club open to the community. Dr. Eichenberg walks 6 days a week, 6 miles a day. (P)

Tallahassee

Emily Haymes, Ph.D. (EP)
205 Montgomery Gym
Florida State University
Tallahassee, FL 32306-2033

Dr. Haymes, a member of the American College of Sports Medicine, walks every day, 20 miles per week. (P)

Frederick S. Kaye, Ph.D. (W)
1108 East Park Avenue
Tallahassee, FL 32301
(904) 224-1108

Dr. Kaye holds a Ph.D. in nutrition, and he designs both diet and walking programs for his patients. Dr. Kaye enjoys all sports, including Nautilus training, and he walks six days a week, 2 miles a day. (S)

West Melbourne

Kory Ann Casey, D.C. (B,O,S)
1938 South Dairy Road, #5
West Melbourne, FL 32904
(407) 676-5600

Dr. Casey stresses holistic, preventive, and rehabilitative medicine in her practice. She is a past president of the Council on Orthopedics and was a sports physician at the 1984 Olympics in Los Angeles. She walks 3 days a week, 5 miles a day.

Winter Park

Richard Shure, M.D. (AR,O)
1285 Orange Avenue
Winter Park, FL 32789
(407) 647-2287

Dr. Shure specializes in surgery of the hand and shoulder and walks, swims, and lifts weights.

George M. White, M.D. (AR)
1285 Orange Avenue
Winter Park, FL 32789
(407) 647-2287

Dr. White prescribes walking to his patients as an excellent way to maintain general fitness while they recover from hand surgery, which is his specialty. He clocks a 12-minute-mile pace and walks 3 miles a day, 3 days a week.

Georgia

Atlanta

Susan Cartwright, R.N. (H)
Cardiac Health and Rehabilitation
5665 Peachtree Dunwoody Dr.
Suite 275
Atlanta, GA 30342
(404) 851-7633

Ms. Cartwright works with a mall walking club designed to help people achieve cardiovascular fitness. In 5 days, she covers 15 miles. (S)

Joseph Citron, M.D. (OP)
Citron Eye Clinic
705 Juniper Street N.E.
Suite 100
Atlanta, GA 30308
(404) 875-2020

Dr. Citron walks 1 hour a day, 3 to 6 days a week, and is a biking enthusiast as well.

Sheldon B. Cohen, M.D., P.A. (PS)
490 Peachtree Street, N.E.
Suite 251B
Atlanta, GA 30308
(404) 525-6158

Dr. Cohen prescribes walking to his patients to boost moods and morale. He enjoys a 3-mile walk 2 to 3 days a week. (S)

Scott Patterson, M.D. (PS)
3280 Howell Mill Road, N.W.
Atlanta, GA 30327
(404) 355-2234

Dr. Patterson offers treatment for stress management, behavior modification, and biofeedback. He walks 4 miles an hour and totals 15 miles a week. Walking was an important part of his personal recovery program from prostate cancer, and every workout continues to be cause for celebration. (P)

Paula Pullen, M.Ed. (AG,H)
5667 Peachtree Dunwoody Road
Suite 275
Atlanta, GA 30342
(404) 851-7001

Ms. Pullen specializes in adult fitness and cardiac rehabilitation at Saint Joseph's Hospital of Atlanta.

Augusta

Alfred L. Brannen, M.D. (H)
Augusta Diagnostic Associates
3623 J. Dewey Grey Circle
Suite 100
Augusta, GA 30910
(404) 868-0273

Dr. Brannen encourages all his patients with cardiopulmonary disorders to start walking programs. He walks 5 days a week, covering 25 to 30 miles. (P)

Decatur

Catherine L. Bray, M.D. (GP)
755 Commerce Drive
Suite 705
Decatur, GA 30030
(404) 377-3436

Dr. Bray, who walks 5 miles a week with arm weights, prescribes walking for a whole host of conditions, including high cholesterol, hypertension, diabetes, obesity, and PMS. She also prescribes walking as a preventive measure against osteoporosis, heart disease, and other degenerative conditions.

Robert Monett, M.D. (GP)
755 Commerce Drive
Decatur, GA 30030
(404) 377-3436

Dr. Monett walks 20 miles in a 3-day period.

Tunnel Hill

Richard Ruhling, M.D. (H,IM)
Route 1, Box 1129
Tunnel Hill, GA 30755
(404) 965-7555

Dr. Ruhling is a cardiologist and a board-certified internist and holds a masters degree in public health with emphasis in nutrition. He currently leads his "Total Health" seminars at various wellness centers around the country. Dr. Ruhling walks 2 to 3 days a week at a 15-minute-mile pace.

Warner Robins

G.V. Raghu, M.D. (OB)
PO Box 2105
Warner Robins, GA 31099
(912) 922-9944

Dr. Raghu specializes in obstetrics and gynecology and walks 5 days a week, 3 miles a day.

Hawaii

Pearl City

Gerald Seto, M.D. (B)
945 Kam Highway, #13
Pearl City, HI 96782
(808) 456-7077

Dr. Seto is head of Backworks Hawaii, a back rehabilitation clinic. He walks 6 days a week, 3 miles a day.

Idaho

Boise

Arlee Kawakami (PT)
Director of Physical Therapy
Idaho Elks Rehabilitation Hospital
204 Fort Place
Boise, ID 83702
(208) 343-6227, ext. 295

Ms. Kawakami enjoys extensive walks through the mountainous Idaho countryside. In a week she covers 20 miles, over 3 days.

Illinois

Bloomington

Barry Slotky, M.D. (OB)
107 North Regency Drive
Bloomington, IL 61701
(309) 663-6338

Dr. Slotky practices obstetrics and gynecology and is medical director of Planned Parenthood, McLean County. He walks 1 to 2 days a week, 3 to 4 miles a day.

Chicago

Harold J. Feder, D.P.M. (F,SM)
Mark Feder, D.P.M.
2348 Irving Park Road
Chicago, IL 60618
(312) 583-7700

Both doctors consider walking their primary method of exercise. They walk at a fast pace (12 to 13 minutes per mile). Harold walks 9 miles per week; Mark, who also walks stairs, logs 15 miles per week.

Noel D. Nequin, M.D. (H)
Cardiac Rehabilitation Center
Swedish Covenant Hospital
5145 North California Avenue
Chicago, IL 60625
(312) 878-8200

Dr. Nequin is medical director at the Cardiac Rehabilitation Center of the Swedish Covenant Hospital, the Human Performance Laboratory of Northeastern Illinois University, Multiplex Medical Institute in Dearfield, and the Exercise Physiology Laboratory at The Quaker Oats Company in Barrington. Dr. Nequin prescribes walking to his patients, and participates in such challenges as 50-mile ultramarathons and 100-mile mountain endurance runs.

Jadwiga Roguska-Kyts, M.D., S.C. (IM)
Suite 800
707 North Fairbanks Court
Chicago, IL 60611
(312) 944-0944

Dr. Roguska-Kyts recommends walking to her patients for a variety of conditions, including the prevention of osteoporosis, the treatment of PMS, and as a means to control weight and diabetes. She walks 1 mile a day, 4 days a week.

Leonard Winston, D.P.M. (F)
6426 North Western Avenue
Chicago, IL 60645
(312) 274-1878

Dr. Winston routinely prescribes walking as the best all-round exercise. He enjoys walking a bike path in the woods 4 days a week, 4 miles a day.

Lake Forest

Marie F. McHugh, Psy.D. (PS)
1401 N. Western Avenue
Lake Forest, IL 60045
(708) 234-6777

Dr. McHugh is a licensed clinical psychologist who specializes in behavioral medicine. She promotes walking for its physical benefits and also believes it works wonders for the human spirit. Personally dedicated to a walking program—it got her off insulin within 5 months and enabled her to lose 65 pounds—she strides an hour per day, 7 days a week.

Palos Heights

Phyllis Levine (PT)
C.O.R.S.
7600 West College Drive
Palos Heights, IL 60463
(708) 361-0608

Ms. Levine is a registered physical therapist who specializes in orthopedics and sports medicine. She conducts research on, among other subjects, physical therapy and arthritis. .

Scott Air Force Base

Frank C. Budd, Ph.D. (PS)
Mental Health Clinic
USAF Medical Center
Scott Air Force Base, IL 62225
(618) 256-7386

Dr. Budd has a Ph.D. in counseling psychology and specializes in behavior medicine and health promotion. He is involved in psychotherapy as well as group therapy and has designed programs for smoking cessation, relaxation, and pain and stress management. Dr. Budd walks 4 days a week, 3 miles a day.

Skokie

Dejan Markovich, M.D., S.C. (PS)
64 Old Orchard Road
Skokie, IL 60077
(312) 674-4000

Dr. Markovich specializes in psychiatry and has been a clinical assistant professor for the Abraham Lincoln School of Medicine, University of Illinois, since 1968. He is also the clinical director of the Mental Health Unit at the N.W. Community Hospital in Arlington Heights. He walks 3 to 4 days a week. (P)

Indiana

Fort Wayne

Frank D. Byrne, M.D., F.C.C.P. (L)
2828 Fairfield Avenue
Fort Wayne, IN 46807
(219) 744-8220

Dr. Byrne uses walking to help in pulmonary rehabilitation for his emphysema patients. He walks an hour a day, 3 days a week.

Karen Lou Kennedy, R.N. (FP,AG)
12101 Lima Road
Fort Wayne, IN 46818
(219) 637-3166

Ms. Kennedy has extensive experience in geriatric care, including expertise in pressure ulcers and Alzheimer's disease. She walks 5 days a week.

Indianapolis

Bud Getchell, Ph.D. (EP)
National Institute for Fitness and Sport
250 North University Boulevard
Indianapolis, IN 46202
(317) 274-3432

Dr. Getchell is currently executive director of the National Institute for Fitness and Sport, and is also a professor in the School of Health, Physical Education and Recreation at Indiana University, Bloomington, where he teaches the graduate program.

Arthur Lorber, M.D. (AR,O)
Indianapolis Bone and Joint Clinic, Inc.
3171 North Meridian
Suite 107
Indianapolis, IN 46208
(317) 923-3632

Dr. Lorber specializes in orthopedic surgery. He walks daily.

Shelbyville

Ms. Dottie Soller, R.N. (AG)
Major Hospital
150 West Washington Street
Shelbyville, IN 46176
(317) 392-3211

Ms. Soller recommends walking to promote good bone and muscle health in aging people. She walks at a fast pace at least 5 hours per week.

Iowa

Monroe

Eileen M. Robb, M.D. (IM,GP)
Monroe Medical Clinic
P.O. Box 707
Monroe, IA 50170
(515) 259-3434

Dr. Robb treats patients of all ages. She walks 2 to 3 miles a day, 4 days a week.

Kansas

Overland

Roger West Hood, M.D. (O)
8300 College Boulevard
Suite 105
Overland, KS 66210
(913) 451-9310

Dr. Hood specializes in total joint replacements, and all postoperative patients are instructed to walk 3 miles a day for the rest of their lives. He walks 7 days a week, 3 miles a day.

Overland Park

Mark E. Landry, D.P.M. (F,S)
10000 College Boulevard
Overland Park, KS 66210
(913) 661-9898

Dr. Landry is a board-certified podiatric surgeon and holds a master's degree in biomechanics. He walks a mile every day of the week and also enjoys running, biking, and swimming.

Wichita

Antonio L. Osio, M.D. (GP)
4127 East Kellogg
Wichita, KS 67218
(316) 689-8677

Dr. Osio lost nearly 50 pounds through dieting and walking. He walks a brisk 10-minute-mile pace for 30 minutes every day.

Louisiana

New Orleans

Albert Barrocas, M.D. (H)
Medical Center East of New Orleans
5640 Read Boulevard, #640
New Orleans, LA 70127
(504) 241-4547

Dr. Barrocas recommends progressive exercise walking to avoid or delay complex vascular surgery. He believes it acts as a substitute "medical bypass" through the stimulation of colateral circulation. He walks primarily during work, fast and up stairs, three to four days per week.

Maine

Scarborough

Linda M. Demers (PT)
Milliken Physical Therapy Center
605 U.S. Route 1
Scarborough, ME 04074
(207) 883-3406

Ms. Demers is co-owner of the Milliken Physical Therapy Center, where she specializes in industrial (occupational) rehabilitation. Part of her treatment of patients with acute and chronic pain is to start them on walking programs. Ms. Demers walks 15 miles in 5 days each week.

Maryland

Baltimore

Donna Bernhardt, R.N. (GP)
Good Samaritan Hospital
5601 Loch Raven Boulevard
Baltimore, MD 21239
(301) 323-2200

Ms. Bernhardt is a surgical nurse who walks
21 miles a week to relieve personal stress.
She also does daily aerobics and some
weight training. (P)

Neil Scheffler, D.P.M. (F,S)
5205 East Drive
Baltimore, MD 21227
(301) 247-5333

Dr. Scheffler, an injured runner who
turned to walking, counsels many of his
patients to do the same. As a medical consultant to the Maryland Marathon, he sees
a lot of runners with lower back and knee
problems, but sees very few walkers with
these ailments. Dr. Scheffler walks a brisk
11-minute-mile pace, 3 days a week, 5 to
7 miles a day.

Margaret Vaughan, M.D., M.P.H.
  (IM,PM)
Cross Keys
222C Quadrangle
Baltimore, MD 21210
(301) 433-9393

Dr. Vaughan, who walks 5 miles a week,
says walking is the only exercise program
that many middle-aged to older patients
have the confidence to start.

Ellicott City

Linda Ciotola, M.Ed (HE)
3986 View Top Road
Ellicott City, MD 21043
(301) 465-4026

Ms. Ciotola likes walking because it is a
safe and pleasant way to ease into physical
fitness, and she has found it to be excellent for stress management. She walks 4
to 5 miles a day, 3 to 4 days a week. (P)

Massachusetts

Chestnut Hill

Nadine Braunstein, M.S., R.D. (W)
25 Boylston Street
Suite 309
Chestnut Hill, MA 02167
(617) 232-3949

Ms. Braunstein is a registered dietician
with a master's degree in nutrition. She
not only recommends walking to her patients to help with weight management
and to reduce cholesterol, but also walks
with them as part of their nutritional
counseling sessions. She walks 3 to 4 days
a week, 4 to 5 miles a day. (P)

Medford

Martin L. Fenton, M.D. (AG,PS,IM)
92 High Street
Medford, MA 02155
(617) 396-4514

Dr. Fenton specializes in internal medicine and psychiatry. He walks 3 to 4 days
a week, covering 20 miles. He promotes
walking for its physical and emotional
benefits and prescribes it for people who
have overcome serious illnesses to restore
their self-confidence and well-being. (P)

Plainville

Martin C. Harris, D.P.M., P.C. (F)
7 Wilkins Drive
Plainville, MA 02762
(508) 695-1444

Dr. Harris walks 2 days a week, 2 miles a day.

Michigan

Birmingham

Barry Franklin, Ph.D. (H,EP)
Barnum Health Center
746 Purdy
Birmingham, MI
(313) 258-3705

Dr. Franklin holds a Ph.D. in physiology with a specialization in exercise. He is director of cardiac rehabilitation at the William Beaumont Hospital in Royal Oak, Michigan, and is an associate professor of physiology at the Wayne State University School of Medicine in Detroit. He walks 3 to 4 miles a day, 3 to 4 days a week.

Sharon

Susan Cable, R.P.T. (PT,PD)
43 Greenwood Road
Sharon, MA 02067
(617) 784-5258

Ms. Cable is a physical therapist who presently works with children but who has treated patients of all ages. She walks 3 to 5 days week, 3 miles a day.

Canton

Kathleen C. Israel, M.A. (AG)
39683 John Drive
Canton, MI 48187
(313) 455-4567

Ms. Israel is currently working on her graduate degree in gerontology. She uses walking in her health and exercise classes for seniors. Ms. Israel walks 2 miles a day, 4 days a week.

Somerville

Andy Ruina, Ph.D. (BM)
12 Carter Terrace
Somerville, MA 02143
(617) 253-8115

Dr. Ruina conducts research at M.I.T. in the fields of biomechanics and applied mechanics. He walks 1 to 2 hours a day, 7 days a week.

Jackson

Kenneth S. J. Murkowski, D.C. (B,S)
Northwest Chiropractic Life Center
645 St. Clair
Jackson, MI 49202
(517) 784-9123

Dr. Murkowski specializes in pediatrics and sports and industrial medicine. Because of past knee injuries, he took up walking and now logs 3 miles a day, 3 to 4 days a week. He also enjoys biking and swimming.

Wilmington

Kathy Petrillo, R.D. (W)
4 Ridge Road
Wilmington, MA 01887
(508) 657-4584

Ms. Petrillo is a registered dietician and counsels on nutrition. She walks 3 days a week, 4 miles a day. (S)

Mount Clemens

Thomas C. Hosey, D.P.M. (F)
253 South Gratiot
Mount Clemens, MI 48043
(313) 468-5445

Dr. Hosey is an adjunct professor at Pennsylvania College of Podiatric Medicine in Philadelphia. He is a foot and ankle specialist who walks 4 days a week, 5 miles a day.

Muskegon

Gerald J. Applegarth, D.P.M. (F)
Podiatry Association of Western
  Michigan
1576 Peck Street
Muskegon, MI 49441
(616) 726-6658

Dr. Applegarth is a podiatrist and foot surgeon. He enjoys a daily 2-mile walk along Lake Michigan.

Petoskey

Russell F. LaBeau, M.D. (PD,S)
Burns Clinic Medical Center
560 West Mitchell
Petoskey, MI 49770
(616) 347-7000

Dr. LaBeau specializes in pediatrics, sports medicine, and allergies. He walks 3 to 5 days a week for an hour.

Southfield

Earl J. Rudner, M.D. (D)
4400 Town Center, #105
Southfield, MI 48075
(313) 354-9595

Dr. Rudner specializes in disorders of the skin. Besides jogging and swimming, he also enjoys walking 1 mile a day, 2 to 3 days a week.

Minnesota

Eden Prairie

Jay P. Wilson, D.C. (B)
Wilson Chiropractic Center
6405 City West Parkway
Shady Oak Center
Eden Prairie, MN 55344
(612) 942-9700

Dr. Wilson considers walking the safest and best all-around exercise. He walks 5 days a week, 1 to 3 miles a day.

Minneapolis

Robert Benjamin, M.D. (GS)
5000 West 39th Street
Minneapolis, MN 55416
(612) 927-3180

Dr. Benjamin walks 12 to 25 miles every week, 4 to 7 days.

Arthur S. Leon, M.D. (H)
Division of Epidemiology
University of Minnesota
c/o Stadium Gate 27
Minneapolis, MN 55455
(612) 624-9965

Dr. Leon is a professor and director of applied physiology at the University of Minnesota. He walks every day for an hour, covering 3 miles.

William B. Lockner, D.P.M. (F)
517 Medical Arts Building
Minneapolis, MN 55402
(612) 332-7720

Dr. Lockner specializes in podiatry. He walks 20 miles, 5 days a week.

Alfred Pheley, M.D. (PM)
5000 West 39th Street
Minneapolis, MN 55416
(612) 927-3012

Dr. Pheley walks 5 days, 20 miles a week. (P)

Virginia

James J. Salonen, D.P.M. (F)
Washington Building
801 North Ninth Street
Virginia, MN 55792
(218) 741-8211

Missouri

Columbia

Rick Rother, P.T. (PT,O,S,H)
1701 East Broadway
Columbia, MO 65284
(314) 875-3870

Mr. Rother is a physical therapist with interests in orthopedics, sports, and cardiac rehabilitation. He is an accomplished triathlon athlete and finds time to swim, run, and bike, as well as walk 2 miles daily.

St. Charles

Robert J. Brown, M.D. (OB)
2730 Highway 94 South
St. Charles, MO 63303
(314) 441-6441

Dr. Brown recommends walking to his pregnant patients. He speed walks 5 to 6 days a week, at a pace of 5 miles an hour. (S)

St. Joseph

Helen Nguyen, M.D. (PD)
P.O. Box 8095
3817 Frederick Boulevard
St. Joseph, MO 64506
(816) 279-1113

Dr. Nguyen specializes in pediatrics and allergy immunology. She divides her exercise time between golf, swimming, weight training, and walking 2 miles a day, 3 to 4 days a week.

St. Louis

Jerome J. Gilden, M.D. (AR,O,S)
Jewish Hospital of St. Louis
216 South Kingshighway Boulevard
P.O. Box 14109
St. Louis, MO 63178
(314) 454-8700

Dr. Gilden is director of the Division of Orthopedic Surgery, Jewish Hospital, Washington University Medical Center in St. Louis. He prescribes walking to his postoperative joint replacement patients. He walks 3 days a week, 3 miles a day.

Ardy Janku (W)
530 Des Peres Drive
St. Louis, MO 63131
(314) 966-9525

Ms. Janku is an exercise therapist who specializes in weight control. She prescribes walking to many of her patients as a permanent solution to weight control and behavior modification. She walks daily for a total of up to 50 miles a week. (S)

Montana

Great Falls

James D. Watson, M.D. (H)
1400 29th Street South
Great Falls, MT 59403
(406) 454-2171

Dr. Watson is director of Cardiac Rehabilitation at the Montana Deaconess Medical Center in Great Falls. He also practices
clinical and invasive cardiology at the Great
Falls Clinic. He walks 5 to 7 days per
week, 10 hours per week.

Nebraska

Omaha

Nikola Boskovski, M.D., Ph.D. (AN)
University of Nebraska Medical Center
Department of Anesthesiology
42nd Street and Dewey Avenue
Omaha, NE 68105
(402) 559-4081

Born and educated in Yugoslavia (his M.D.
is from Skopje University and his Ph.D.
is from University of Belgrad), Dr. Boskovski is currently assistant professor of
anesthesiology at the University of Nebraska. He walks every day, for a total of
10 miles a week.

New Hampshire

Laconia

Suzanne C. Beyea, R.N. (GP)
Laconia Clinic
724 Main Street
Laconia, NH 03246
(603) 528-1841

Ms. Beyea is a nurse practitioner in adult
health. She chooses walking as her primary exercise because it is relaxing, reduces stress, and promotes heart health
and weight control. She walks with weights
a mile daily. (P)

Nashua

Michael Huffman, M.D. (RM,PA)
Medical Director
New England Rehabilitation Center of
    Southern New Hampshire
505 West Hollis Street
Suite 104
Nashua, NH 03062
(603) 886-2710

Dr. Huffman specializes in physical medicine and rehabilitation, prescribing a progressive walking program for pain
management and for increased strength
and endurance. He walks 4 days a week,
2 miles a day, at a 3 mile an hour pace.
He also swims and rides a stationary bike.
(P)

New Jersey

Cinnaminson

Ronald J. Pollock, A.B., D.C. (B)
1507 Highland Avenue
Cinnaminson, NJ 08077
(609) 829-6565

Dr. Pollock's patients have reduced their
blood pressure, controlled their weight,
and experienced emotional relief through
walking. He walks 5 days a week, 2 to 3
miles a day.

Elizabeth

Eugene P. Cinaciulli, D.C., M.S. (B)
422 Elmora Avenue
Elizabeth, NJ 07208
(201) 289-6515

Dr. Cinaciulli is a chiropractor who also holds a master's degree in biology and a certification in human nutrition. He walks 15 to 20 miles a week.

Englewood

Richard T. Braver, D.P.M. (F,S)
Foot-Wise Podiatry Center
140 Grand Avenue
Englewood, NJ 07631
(201) 569-7672

Dr. Braver is involved in sports medicine with emphasis on dance, running, and sports injuries. He is also a consultant to Brooks Shoes. He walks regularly and conducts walking clinics in New Jersey.

Fair Lawn

Albert P. Rosen, M.D. (PD)
28-02 Fair Lawn Avenue
Fair Lawn, NJ 07410
(201) 796-0401

Dr. Rosen specializes in pediatrics. He teaches a course in hiking for the Fair Lawn Community School and has hiked Mt. Kilimanjaro, the Grand Tetons, the Himalayas, the Tien Shew Mountains in the Soviet Union, and peaks in Greece, Yugoslavia, Bulgaria, Romania, Peru, and the Swiss Alps, among others.

Hillsdale

Howard S. Rosenbaum, D.P.M. (F,S)
Pascack Professional Center
Bergen Podiatry Group
185 Broadway
Hillsdale, NJ 07642
(201) 666-0700

Hoboken

John Skelly (PT)
613 Park Avenue, #8
Hoboken, NJ 07030
(201) 358-3242

Mr. Skelly works at the Department of Physical Medicine and Rehabilitation, Pascack Valley Hospital, in Westwood, New Jersey. He walks regularly.

Jersey City

Ms. Elizabeth Boyce, R.N. (OB)
13 Henry Street
Jersey City, New Jersey 07306
(201) 792-9427

Ms. Boyce, who's in training to become a midwife, walks 15 miles per week.

Livingston

Arthur Winter, M.D. (N)
22 Old Short Hills Road
Livingston, NJ 07039-5691
(201) 992-3300

Dr. Winter specializes in neurosurgery. He is director of the New Jersey Neurological Institute and has just developed a memory clinic, where he prescribes walking as a way to improve memory. He walks 2 days a week, 1 to 2 miles a day.

Mt. Holly

Donnica L. Moore, M.D. (GP)
160 Madison Avenue
Mt. Holly, NJ 08060
(609) 261-7035

Dr. Moore is a staunch walking advocate who has experienced its rehabilitative powers first hand. She began walking after spinal surgery last year and has built up her walking program to 2 to 3 miles a day, 5 days a week.

Princeton

Philip Erlich, M.D. (PS)
905 Herrontown Road
Princeton, NJ 08540
(609) 924-2685

Dr. Erlich improves his cardiovascular fitness by walking a brisk 3 miles a day, 6 days a week. (P)

Somerset

Trish Stypka, D.C. (B)
1075 Hamilton Street
Somerset, NJ 08873
(201) 828-7070

Dr. Stypka uses a holistic approach in her chiropractic practice. She recommends walking for osteoporosis prevention. Dr. Stypka walks 2 miles a day, 1 to 5 days a week.

South River

V. Gary Petrie, D.C. (B)
77A Water Street
South River, NJ 08882
(201) 257-5222

Dr. Petrie is an avid hiker. He walks 4 to 5 days a week, 4 miles a day.

Spring Lake

Walter F. Judge, M.D. (AG)
316 Brighton Avenue
Spring Lake, NJ 07762
(201) 449-5519

Dr. Judge specializes in endocrinology and is so inspired by his daily 2-mile walks that he even penned a poem about walking.

Springfield

David Plotkin, P.A. (F,S)
619 Morris Avenue
Springfield, NJ 07081
(201) 379-9333

Dr. Plotkin's practice covers podiatric medicine, sports medicine, and foot surgery. He is acting chief of podiatry, Department of Surgery, at Overlook Hospital in Su███ ██w Jersey. Many of his patien█ ███unning injuries and then tur██ ████ Dr. Plotkin walks a brisk 1 to ████ ██ay, 4 days a week.

Waldwick

Dale Fairchild, D.C. (B)
51 East Prospect Street
Waldwick, NJ 07463
(201) 445-3434

Dr. Fairchild offers care to the entire family. She gives health talks on spinal care, wellness, holistic health care, and stress management. She walks 12 to 15 miles a week.

Kenneth Harris, D.C. (B)
51 East Prospect Street
Waldwick, NJ 07463
(201) 445-3434

Dr. Harris offers in-office and community lectures and classes on spinal health care. He has been on the faculty of the New York Chiropractic College, where he taught anatomy and physiology. He walks 15 to 18 miles a week.

West Paterson

Marc S. Kitrosser, D.P.M., P.A.
(F,S,W)
Park West Meadows Medical Center
1031 McBride Avenue
West Paterson, NJ 07424
(201) 256-0002

Dr. Kitrosser practices podiatric and sports medicine and treats patients with weight-control problems. His patients find that a walking program not only makes them feel better and lowers their cholesterol, but also suppresses their appetite. He walks with weights 4 days a week, 5 miles a day.

New Mexico

Albuquerque

Dennis A. Cohen, M.D. (GP)
1812 Candelaria, N.W.
Albuquerque, NM 87107
(505) 768-5465

Dr. Cohen tells all patients in his family practice about the benefits of walking. He enjoys "walk talks" with his wife 7 days a week, 2 to 3 miles a day.

Donna Deming, M.D. (GP)
120 Amherst, N.E.
Albuquerque, NM 87106
(505) 266-8876

Dr. Deming walks 35 miles every week.

Robert Larson, D.P.M. (F)
4801 McMahon Boulevard N.W., #260
Albuquerque, NM 87114
(505) 893-2855

Dharma Singh Khalsa, M.D. (PA)
Lovelace Medical Foundation
3939 Rio Grande, N.W. #37
Albuquerque, NM 87107
(505) 262-7197

Dr. Khalsa is an anesthesiologist that specializes in pain management and stress medicine. He walks a fast 10-minute-mile pace for 3 miles, 3 days a week. (S)

W.D. McCarty, M.D. (PS)
610 Graceland Drive, S.E.
Albuquerque, NM 87108
(506) 255-3254

Dr. McCarty is a retired M.D. in obstetrics and gynecology who recently became board certified in addictionology. He does consulting work and prescribes walking to many of his patients. Dr. McCarty walks briskly in rolling terrain 5 to 6 days a week, 4 miles a day.

Carlsbad

Abraham Ellis Goldminz, M.D. (AG)
616 West Pierce Street
Carlsbad, NM 88220
(505) 887-1229

Dr. Goldminz and his wife walk 1½ miles every day. In 1980, he had triple bypass surgery and an artificial valve implanted in his heart. Goldminz was able to withstand the surgery because he had stopped smoking and because of his walking program. (P)

Sante Fe

Joel M. Wilner, D.P.M., (F,S,AG)
665 Harkle Road
Sante Fe, NM 87501
(505) 983-7393

Dr. Wilner prescribes walking to patients of all ages. He has also organized a mall walking program in conjunction with the local hospital for the elderly of Santa Fe. Dr. Wilner walks rugged terrain 3 to 4 days a week, 1 mile a day.

New York

Albany

Jonathan M. Rosen, M.D. (L)
Albany Medical Center
Pulmonary Division A-91
Albany, NY 12208
(518) 445-5196

Dr. Rosen, who specializes in heart disorders, says his heart patients adapt well to walking. He walks 4 to 5 days a week, covering 10 to 15 miles. (P)

Bellerose

Judy Ouziel (W,PE)
Director of Health and Physical
  Education
Cross Island YMCA
238-10 Hillside Avenue
Bellerose, NY 11364
(718) 479-0505

Ms. Ouziel walks 5 days a week, covering 30 miles in 10 hours.

Binghamton

Joseph T. Hogan, D.P.M. (F,O)
41 Oak Street
Binghamton, NY 13905
(607) 723-7454

Dr. Hogan practices podiatric medicine, surgery, and orthopedics. He finds walking to be an excellent form of postoperative rehabilitation and prescribes it to all his postoperative patients. He walks 4 to 5 days week, 3 miles a day.

Bronx

Corby Kessler, M.D. (RM)
Lincoln Medical and Mental Health
  Center
234 East 149th Street
Bronx, NY 10451
(212) 579-5651

Dr. Kessler specializes in physical medicine and rehabilitation and works with the disabled. He feels walking is beneficial exercise for his patients because it promotes increased independence. He walks 4 miles a day, 4 days a week. (P)

Peter Wolstein, D.P.M. (F,S)
1340 Metropolitan Avenue
Bronx, NY 10462
(212) 863-3338

Dr. Wolstein specializes in ambulatory foot surgery and sports medicine. He prescribes walking to his patients recovering from heart bypass surgery. He walks 3 days a week, 9 to 15 miles a week. (P)

Mark Allen Young, M.D. (RM)
2005 Hone Avenue
Bronx, NY 10461-1311
(212) 828-1482

Dr. Young feels walking facilitates mental and cognitive processes and that even leisurely walking can have beneficial effects on preventing osteoporosis. He walks 5 days a week, over a mile a day. (P)

Brooklyn

Mort Malkin, D.D.S. (PM,S)
444 East 19th Street
Brooklyn, NY 11226
(718) 469-6087

Dr. Malkin is a surgical dentist who also teaches aerobic walking for preventive medicine. Author of *Walking, The Pleasure Exercise*, he racewalks a fast 10 minute-mile 3 days a week, 5 miles a day.

Gary Saphire, D.P.M. (F,S)
7516 Bay Parkway
Brooklyn, NY 11214
(718) 236-5253

Dr. Saphire is board certified in foot and ankle surgery. He is an active athlete, walking 6 days a week, 4 to 5 miles a day on backcountry roads. He also enjoys weight training and bicycling.

Roberta Temes, Ph.D. (PS)
262 Coleridge Street
Brooklyn, NY 11235
(718) 646-5537

Dr. Temes is a clinical assistant professor in the Department of Psychiatry at SUNY Health Science Center in Brooklyn. She specializes in psychotherapy and deals with depression as well as using medical hypnosis for weight control and smoking cessation. Dr. Temes's hypnotic suggestions include progressive stages of walking, and her patients find that their urges to eat or smoke tend to disappear after their daily walk.

Clifton Park

Joseph S. Gulyas, D. C. (B)
568 Clifton Park Center Road
Clifton Park, NY 12065
(518) 371-4800

Dr. Gulyas finds walking very useful for his elderly patients, and he also prescribes walking as a rehabiltative treatment for patients in all stages of recovery. Dr. Gulyas walks 3 days a week, 2 miles a day.

Delmar

Mary T. Musso, M.A. (EP,H)
Community Health Plan
250 Delaware Avenue
Delmar, NY 12054
(518) 439-7687

Ms. Musso, director of the cardiac rehabilitation program at the Community Health Plan Center in Delmar, prescribes walking for heart attack patients and bypass patients to help them resume a more normal lifestyle. She bikes and jogs, and she walks 2 miles a day, 2 days a week.

East Hills

Barton Cohen, M.D. (H)
30 Flamingo Road
East Hills, NY 11576
(516) 487-1414

Dr. Cohen, a cardiac specialist, hikes rugged terrain every day, logging 10 miles a week.

Fulton

Marc A. Grosack, D.P.M. (F)
172 South First Street
Fulton, NY 13069
(315) 593-3971
(315) 363-2700

Dr. Grosack specializes in podiatric surgery and sports medicine. He walks 2 days a week for a total of 20 miles.

Hastings-on-Hudson

Howard L. Millman, Ph.D. (PS)
1 Hall Place
Hastings-On-Hudson, NY 10706
(914) 478-5380

Dr. Millman specializes in clinical psychology with an emphasis on drug dependency, depression, anxiety, obesity, and hyperactive children. He has written books on the subject and prescribes walking to help all these conditions. Dr. Millman walks on hills 4 days a week, 2½ miles a day.

Huntington

Roger G. Mazlen, M.D., P.C. (PM)
The Huntington Atrium
775 Park Avenue
Suite 155
Huntington, NY 11743
(516) 424-2050

Dr. Mazlen, who specializes in nutrition and preventive medicine, is a clinical assistant professor of medicine at Mt. Sinai School of Medicine. He walks 4 to 5 days a week, 3 miles a day. (S)

Laurelton

Annie Lee Jones, Ph. D. (AG,PS)
139-20 230 Place
Laurelton, NY 11413
(718) 978-2067

Dr. Jones is a staff clinical psychologist in geriatrics at the Brooklyn Veterans Administration Medical Center in Brooklyn. As a cognitive behavior therapist, she recommends walking to many of her patients. Dr. Jones personally used walking to reduce stress prior to surgery and for rehabilitation after. She walks 7 days a week, 2½ miles a day.

Lewiston

Frank P. Altieri, M.D., P.C. (O,S)
5290 Military Road
Suite 9
Lewiston, NY 14092
(716) 297-1701

Dr. Altieri specializes in orthopedics and sports medicine. He walks 5 days a week, 3 miles a day.

Medford

Richard A. Nebiosini, D.C. (B)
Medford Family Chiropractic
74B Southaven Avenue
Medford, NY 11763
(516) 654-3647

Dr. Nebiosini treats sports injuries, lower back pain, headaches, scoliosis, pinched nerves, and other spinal conditions. He started a Tuesday morning walking club for his patients, and he walks 5 days a week, 3 miles a day.

Mineola

Neal P. Houslanger, D.P.M. (F,S)
220 Mineola Boulevard
Mineola, NY 11501-2540
(516) 746-6464

Dr. Houslanger specializes in foot surgery and sports medicine. He is vice president of the Nassau County Podiatric Medical Association and walks 3 days a week, 4 to 5 miles a day.

Nesconset

Linda Bocchichio-Larese, D.C. (B)
105 Lake Avenue South
Nesconset, NY 11767
(516) 979-9854

Dr. Larese founded the St. James Walking Club, located in St. James, New York, which is now seventy members strong. They meet every day, and Dr. Larese herself walks 7 days a week, 4 to 5 miles a day.

New York

David Balboa, M.S.W., C.S.W. (PS)
Deena Balboa
The Walking Center
140 West 79th Street
New York, NY 10024
(212) 799-4831

Mr. and Mrs. Balboa are codirectors and therapists at The Walking Center, and they also hold a walking club every Saturday in Central Park. David, a sports psychotherapist, and Deena, a lay therapist, diagnose psychological problems and treat them through walking.

Alan M. Farber, D.P.M. (F)
1457 Broadway
New York, NY 10036
(212) 840-1985

Dr. Farber is a doctor of podiatric medicine with interests in ambulatory foot surgery and sports medicine. He is a dedicated walker who paces 4 to 5 miles a day, 7 days a week.

Daniel B. Firshein, D.P.M. (F)
7 Christopher Street
New York, N.Y. 10014

Dr. Firshein specializes in podiatry for all ages. He walks 4 to 5 days a week, a total of 10 miles a week.

Harvey J. Fish, D.C. (B)
222 West 79th Street
New York, NY 10024
(212) 496-0121

Dr. Fish finds that walking helps him both psychologically and physically. He walks 4 to 5 days a week, 4 miles a day.

Susan Fish, M.A. (PT)
30 East 40th Street, Room 403
New York, NY 10016
(212) 686-2826

Ms. Fish holds a master's degree in physical therapy and prescribes walking for osteoarthritis, Achilles tendon tears, hip replacement, and low back pain. She walks 5 days a week, 4 miles a day.

Robert Alan Glick, M.D. (PS)
125 East 84th Street
New York, NY 10028
(212) 472-2223

Dr. Glick had to give up running, so he started walking. He sometimes recommends walking to his patients to alleviate tension. He walks 4 to 5 hours a week, 4 to 5 days. (P)

Herbert H. Greenberg, P.C. (F)
115 West 86th Street
New York, NY 10024
(212) 874-3578

Dr. Greenberg specializes in ambulatory foot surgery. He walks 3 days a week, 3 miles a day.

Joseph E. Kansao, D.C. (B,S)
715 Park Avenue
New York, NY 10021
and
1120 Park Avenue
New York, NY 10128
(212) 988-6240

Dr. Kansao specializes in preventive and rehabilitative sports medicine. He is medical editor of *Running News* and author of a monthly article in *Athletic Magazine*. He walks 6 days a week, 6 miles a day.

Pamela Kovar-Joledano (PT)
515 East 71st Street
S Building, 9th Floor
New York, NY 10021
(212) 606-1128

Ms. Kovar-Joledano treats patients afflicted by musculoskeletal diseases and arthritis. She has been working on her doctorate in health education at Columbia University, where she received a master of arts degree in motor learning. She walks 7½ miles over a 3-day period.

Valerie F. Lanyi, M.D. (AR,RM)
45 East 85th Street
New York, NY 10028
(212) 772-1212

Dr. Lanyi specializes in rehabilitative medicine and is an associate clinical professor at NYU Medical Center. She walks 3 to 4 days a week, 2 miles a day.

Jeffrey Mazlin, M.D. (OB)
1430 2nd Avenue
Suite 101
New York, NY 10021
(212) 517-9048

Dr. Mazlin specializes in obstetrics, gynecology, infertility, and laser surgery. He feels that walking is the best exercise for his pregnant patients and also excellent to induce labor. He walks 6 to 7 days a week, 4 miles a day. (P)

Frances McBrien
Downtown Athletic Club
19 West Street
New York, N.Y. 10004
(212) 425-7000

Ms. McBrien, a fitness instructor, teaches aerobics and aquatics. She walks a half hour every day.

William K. McLaughlin, Ph.D (EP)
The Cardio-Fitness Center
1221 Avenue of the Americas
New York, NY 10020
(212) 840-8240

Dr. McLaughlin works with the Cardio-Fitness Corporation in New York City to create exercise programs primarily for businessmen and women. He walks 6 days per week at a quick 5 to 5½ miles an hour, often on stairs.

Claude H. Miller, M.D. (PS)
7 Park Avenue
New York, NY 10016
(212) 679-7762

Dr. Miller is a psychiatrist who treats substance abuse. He walks 4 miles an hour, 5 days a week. (P)

Ronald E. Ponchak (SM,B)
30 East 60th Street
Suite 1104
New York, NY 10022
(212) 753-5080

Mr. Ponchak is an instructor at the Back Treatment and Learning Center in New York City, where he teaches the causes and prevention of lower back pain as well as body mechanics, resting positions, stress management, and relaxation techniques. He walks 7 miles a week, 4 to 5 days.

James W. Robinson, M.D. (IM)
2186 5th Avenue, #1-D
New York, NY 10037
(212) 283-5150

Dr. Robinson walks 2 to 3 days a week.

Keith W. Sedlacek, M.D., P.C. (PS)
239 East 79th Street
New York, NY 10021
(212) 288-9309

Dr. Sedlacek is a psychiatrist specializing in stress management and biofeedback. He is director of the Stress Regulation Institute, author of the book, *The Sedlacek Technique: Finding the Calm Within You*, and is on the faculty of the Columbia Medical School. He walks 6 days a week, 1 mile a day. (S)

Terry Spilken, D.P.M. (F)
Doctor of Podiatric Medicine
30 East 40th Street, Penthouse
  Southeast
New York, NY 10016
(212) 686-6606

Dr. Spilken specializes in the foot problems of dancers and athletes. He has been the team podiatrist to the New York Islanders hockey team and is now associated with, among other dance companies, the Alvin Ailey American Dance Theater. He walks 20 miles a week.

Ronald Werter, D.P.M. (F,S,O,AG)
160 West End Avenue
New York, NY 10023
(212) 595-1400

Dr. Werter is a doctor of podiatric medicine and is board certified in podiatric orthopedics with a special interest in sports medicine and geriatrics. He walks 4 days a week, 5 miles a day.

Elliot Wineburg, M.D. (PS)
The Associated Biofeedback Medical
  Group
145 West 58th Street, Suite 3F
New York, NY 10019
(212) 582-0720

Dr. Wineburg is a psychiatrist who specializes in stress medicine, biofeedback medicine, and hypnotherapy. He is a dedicated walker, averaging 5 miles daily at a 12-minute-mile pace. (P)

Miriam Yelsky, Ph.D. (PS)
350 West 24th Street
New York, NY 10011
(212) 243-0261

Dr. Yelsky has a Ph.D. in clinical psychology with emphasis on psychoanalysis. In her private practice she works with late adolescents and adults in psychoanalytic psychotherapy, group therapy, marriage and family problems, and therapy for identity problems. She also supervises other psychotherapists. Dr. Yelsky walks 7 miles a week, 1 to 2 miles a day.

Northport

Nadine O'Neill, D.C. (B,S)
691 Fort Salonga Road
Northport, NY 11768
(516) 754-0067

Dr. O'Neill is a chiropractor certified in sports injuries. She has a public service radio program on health and recommends walking to her patients. She racewalks 6 days a week, 4 to 5 miles a day, and she racewalked the New York City Marathon in 1988.

Orangeburg

Neil L. Block, M.D. (GP,PM)
14 Prel Plaza
60 Dutch Hill Road
Orangeburg, NY 10962
(914) 359-3300

Dr. Block is a family physician who specializes in preventive medicine, geriatrics, nutrition, pediatrics, and exercise physiology. He is a fast walker, averaging 6 miles per hour, and includes stair climbing in his program. He walks 3 to 4 days a week, totaling 10 miles. (P)

Port Jefferson

Michael S. Horney, D.C. (B)
656 Main Street
Port Jefferson, NY 11777
(516) 331-1010

Rochester

Carol F. Pizzo, M.S., R.N. (H)
Rochester Cardiopulmonary Group,
 P.C.
Fitness Program
919 Westfall Road
Rochester, N.Y. 14618

Ms. Pizzo, who has a master's degree in pulmonary nursing, walks 15 to 20 miles per week.

Shoreham

Gary P. Milack, D.P.M., F.A.S.P.D.
 (F)
Maple Commons Medical Complex
45 Route 25A
Suite D-1
Shoreham, NY 11786
(516) 744-0022

Dr. Milack writes for numerous podiatric publications. He practices general and surgical podiatry and walks 1 mile, 1 to 2 days a week, on rugged terrain. He likes walking because it can be enjoyed by the whole family.

Smithtown

Herbert I. Silverberg, M.D. (IM)
80 Maple Ave.
Smithtown, NY 11787
(516) 265-0050

Dr. Silverberg walks 4 days a week and uses walking to get his patients into more active exercise regimens.

Staten Island

John R. Addrizzo, M.D. (H)
11 Ralph Place
Staten Island, NY 10314
(718) 981-8880

Dr. Addrizzo has taught at various medical schools and has written many articles on heart disorders and surgery. He likes walking because it is a "low traumatic" cardiovascular workout. Dr. Addrizzo walks 6 days a week covering 24 miles. (S)

Stony Brook

Steven Jonas, M.D. (W)
Department of Community and
 Preventive Medicine
School of Medicine
Health Sciences Center
State University of New York
Stony Brook, NY 11794-8036
(516) 444-2190

Although currently involved full time in academic work, Dr. Jonas also spends considerable time promoting walking to the general public. He is a professor at SUNY Stonybrook and has authored two books on "pacewalking," a highly aerobic form of walking. He pacewalked the 1988 New York City Marathon and walks up to 5 days a week, 5 to 6 miles a day.

Valhalla

Steven Gambert, M.D. (AG,IM)
Professor of Medicine
New York Medical College
Valhalla, NY 10595
(914) 993-4373

Dr. Gambert specializes in geriatrics, internal medicine, and endocrinology and metabolism. He is a professor of medicine at the New York Medical College, director of their Center for Aging, and director of geriatrics at the Westchester Medical Center. A serious walker, he logs 10 miles a day, 4 days a week, at a 10-minute-mile pace.

Warwick

Elmer Platz, P.T. (O,S)
164 Kings Highway
Warwick, NY 10990
(914) 986-6800

Mr. Platz is an orthopedic and sports physical therapist. He walks 7 days a week, 7 to 8 miles a day.

West Rochester

Ronald M. Freeling, D.P.M. (F,S)
2236 Ridge Road
West Rochester, NY 14626
(716) 225-2290

Dr. Freeling is president of the Genesee Valley Sports Medicine Council. He prescribes walking to many of his patients. He plays tennis and walks 3 to 4 days a week, 3 miles a day.

Woodmere

Myron C. Boxer, D.P.M. (F,SM)
2 Woodmere Boulevard
Woodmere, New York 11598
(516) 374-2033

Dr. Boxer believes walking is as effective as jogging as an aerobic exercise without the trauma to joints. He walks 6 miles in 2 hours, 4 days a week, uphill on a treadmill. (P)

Yonkers

Melvyn Grovit, D.P.M., M.S. (F,W)
45 Ludlow Street,
Suite 312
Yonkers, NY 10705
(914) 476-1544

Dr. Grovit is a nutritionist, podiatrist, and diabetes educator who feels walking is most useful in the control of stress, weight management, and general conditioning. He walks 4 miles a day, 2 days a week.

North Carolina

Asheville

Alan S. Baumgarten, M.D., M.P.H.
  (GP)
206 Asheland Avenue
Asheville, NC 28801
(704) 258-8681

Dr. Baumgarten practices family medicine and holds an M.P.H. in nutrition. Dr. Baumgarten recommends walking to all his patients, but biking is his personal favorite form of exercise.

Blowing Rock

David Dauphine, D.C. (B)
P.O. Box 467
Sunset Drive
Blowing Rock, NC 28605
(704) 295-9896

Dr. Dauphine prescribes walking to dyslexic children as part of a rehabilitation program that facilitates neurological development in brain-spinal cord reflexes. He walks 5 days a week, 6 miles a day.

Chapel Hill

Marsha Strahl (PM)
Fitness Coordinator
Holly Hill Hospital
207 Tallyho Trail
Chapel Hill, NC 27514
(919) 942-7375

Ms. Strahl's focus is on preventative medicine. She has given numerous clinics on fitness walking. She walks a solid 5 miles a day, 3 to 4 days a week.

Charlotte

Joseph Estwanik, M.D. (S,O)
1516 Elizabeth Avenue
Charlotte, NC 28204
(704) 334-4663

Walking is Dr. Estwanik's favorite alternative form of aerobic work for those athletic patients with a sports injury that interferes with their primary sport activity.

John C. Simpson, III, Ph.D. (PS)
7621 Little Avenue, Suite 414
Charlotte, NC 28226
(704) 542-1955

Dr. Simpson, a racewalker, walks briskly 5 to 6 miles daily, covering more than 25 miles per week.

Cherokee

Mary Anne Farrell, M.D. (GP,W)
Cherokee Indian Hospital
Cherokee, NC 28719
(704) 497-9163

Dr. Farrell treats a large number of Native Americans with diabetes. Many of her patients have been able to control their disease through proper diet and walking.

She walks 3 to 4 days a week, 2 to 3 miles a day.

Goldsboro

Joyce Wyatt, R.N. (W)
Wayne Memorial Hospital
P.O. Box 8001
Goldsboro, NC 27533
(919) 731-6197

Ms. Wyatt is in charge of employee health at Wayne Memorial Hospital. She prescribes walking for smoking cessation, weight and cholesterol control, and stress management. She controls her own weight through walking and covers 4 miles a day, 3 to 4 days a week. (P)

Raleigh

Douglas I. Hammer, M.D., Dr.P.H.,
   M.P.H. (PM,S,W)
P.O. Box 30786
Raleigh, NC 27622
(919) 847-8821
(919) 781-1371

Dr. Hammer received the M.D. degree from Tufts University Medical School and an the M.P.H. and Dr.P.H in epidemiology degrees from Harvard University School of Public Health. He is medical director at Rex Hospital Wellness Center and practices general preventive and sports medicine. He walks 3 to 5 days a week, 2½ miles a day.

Winston-Salem

Paul Ribisl, Ph.D. (H)
Cardiac Rehabilitation
Box 7628
Winston-Salem, NC 27109-7628
(919) 761-5395

Dr. Ribisl prescribes walking for patients because it is easy to do and tends not to induce back trauma.

Ohio

Cincinnati

G. James Sammarco, M.D.
The Center for Orthopedic Care Inc.
Hospital Medical Building II
2123 Auburn Avenue
Suite 235
Cincinnati, OH 45219
(513) 651-0094

Dr. Sammarco, who specializes in sports medicine and foot and ankle surgery, has organized a group walking program for his patients.

Cleveland

Avrum Froisom, M.D. (B)
26900 Cedar Road
Cleveland, OH 44122
(216) 831-7131

Dr. Froisom is director of orthopedic surgery at the Mt. Sinai Medical Center in Cleveland. An avid jogger for 40 years, he switched to walking because of sore legs. He now walks 6 days a week for a total of 20 miles.

Nancy Ivansen (OC)
University Hospital of Cleveland
Employee Health Services
2074 Abington Road
Cleveland, OH 44106
(216) 844-1601

Ms. Ivansen likes walking because it's a natural activity that's easy on the joints and is good for all ages. She walks 5 hours a week. (P)

Columbus

Dr. Lee D. Pearlman (F)
Dr. Cheryl L. Weiner
Northstone Center
1728 Schrock Road
Columbus, OH 43229
(614) 891-9994

Jessica A. Ross, M.D. (H)
3545 Olentangy River Road
Columbus, OH 43214
(614) 263-5349

Dr. Ross, who specializes in cardiology, believes walking promotes overall health. She bikes 3 to 4 days a week and walks 2 to 3 days a week for 30 minutes each session.

Delaware

Louis C. Huesmann, M.D. (O)
494 West Central Avenue
Delaware, OH 43015
(614) 369-7649

Dr. Huesmann specializes in orthopedic surgery and walks 5 days a week, 3 miles a day.

East Cleveland

George H. Ilodi, D.P.M., Ph.D (F,W)
13944 Euclid Avenue, #104
East Cleveland, OH 44112
(216) 249-9500

Dr. Ilodi practices podiatric medicine and has many diabetic patients to whom he prescribes walking. He walks 3 days a week, 1 to 2 miles a day.

Euclid

Jeffrey D. Lubell, D.P.M. (F)
628 East 222nd Street
Euclid, OH 44123
(216) 731-8052

Dr. Lubell is affiliated with the Ohio College of Podiatric Medicine and Mt. Sinai Medical Center. He walks 2 to 3 days a week, 5 miles a day.

Portsmouth

Jean R. Carlson, R.N., B.S.N.
1248 Kinneys Lane
Portsmouth, OH 45662
(614) 353-2131

Ms. Carlson works in employee health and finds walking immensely helpful as a stress-management tool. She walks over 4 miles an hour, 5 days a week, for a total of 15 miles a week. (P)

Rocky River

Frank M. Strasek, D.P.M. (F,S)
21851 Center Ridge Road
Rocky River, OH 44116
(216) 331-1518

As a sports medicine doctor, Dr. Strasek has treated athletes from American Boxing Federation boxers to runners and walkers. He walks 25 to 30 miles a week, including to and from his office every day, rain or shine.

Shaker Heights

Robert Rosner, M.D. (OP)
3333 Warrensville Center Road
Shaker Heights, Ohio 44122
(216) 991-9044

At 82 years of age, Dr. Rosner is a lifetime walker who believes that walking has been therapeutic for him and has helped him maintain his health. He now walks a half hour almost every day.

South Euclid

Albert F. Paolino, Ph.D. (PS)
Maywood Medical Building
4568 Mayfield Road
South Euclid, OH 44121
(216) 381-0800

Dr. Paolino practices clinical psychology at the St. Vincent Charity Hospital and Health Center, and at the Euclid Meridia Hospital. He prescribes walking to patients, especially depressives, for the chemical changes walking induces, which help them overcome depression. He walks two miles a day, every day. (P)

Worthington

Steven W. Irwin, D.P.M. (F)
37 East Wilson Bridge Road
Worthington, OH 43085
(614) 885-8895

Responsible for making many walking converts, Dr. Irwin has advised many patients with severe running injuries to start a walking program. He himself walks 5 days a week, 10 miles a day.

Carl E. Sharp, D.P.M. (F,S,PD)
37 East Wilson Bridge Road
Worthington, OH 43085
(614) 885-8895

Dr. Sharp practices podiatric medicine with an emphasis on pediatrics, sports medicine, and surgery. He coaches soccer, enjoys bicycling and racketball, and walks 4 days a week, 8 miles a day.

Oklahoma

Oklahoma City

Kathy Brown (PT)
1122 Northeast 13th Street
Oklahoma City, OK 73104
(405) 271-3692

Ms. Brown is a physical therapist at the O'Donoghue Rehabilitation Institute, where she treats children between the ages of 6 to 20, and some adults, often with walking therapy. She walks 9 miles a week, three days a week.

Tulsa

Richard B. Williams, M.D. (RA)
P.O. Box 700863
Tulsa, OK 74170
(918) 493-2642

Dr. Williams is a retired diplomat of the American College of Radiology. He walks five days a week on hilly terrain, 3 to 4 miles a week.

Oregon

Klamath Falls

Steve Bidleman, M.D., P.C. (GP)
2680A Uhrman Road
Klamath Falls, OR 97601
(503) 884-0638

Dr. Bidleman has prescribed walking for many ailments, including depression, diabetes, and obesity, all with positive results. He walks 5 to 7 days a week, covering 15 miles. (P)

Milwaukie

Gerald D. Peterson, D.P.M. (F,S)
Family Foot Health Centers
16239 S.E. McLoughlin Boulevard
Suite 204
Milwaukie, OR 97267
(503) 659-2630

Dr. Peterson prescribes walking as a good cardiovascular and muscle-toning exercise. He walks 4 days a week, 2 to 3 miles a day.

Portland

Joseph A. Cimino, D.C. (B)
3701 S.E. Milwaukie Boulevard
Suite G
Portland, OR 97202
(503) 236-2000

Dr. Cimino walks 6 days a week, 6 miles a day.

John D. Mozena, D.P.M., P.C.
 (F,S,AG)
Town Center Foot Clinic
8305 S.E. Monterey Avenue, #101
Portland, OR 97266
(503) 652-1121

Dr. Mozena practices general podiatry with specialties in sports medicine and geriatrics. He walks 3 miles daily.

Salem

Tomas P. McFie, D.C., Ph.D. (B,W)
5980 Fircrest S.E.
Salem, OR 97306
(503) 581-1801

Dr. McFie specializes in chiropractic medicine with a Ph.D. in nutrition. After suffering spinal and pelvic injuries that prevented him from running or jogging without pain, he now walks 6 days a week, 4 to 7 miles a day in comfort.

Pennsylvania

Allentown

Herbert L. Hyman, M.D. (IM,PM)
401 North 17th Street
Suite 207
Allentown, PA 18104
(215) 434-5300

Dr. Hyman specializes in internal medicine and gastroenterology and stresses preventive medicine with his patients. He trains at a cardiac rehabilitation center three times a week and walks on weekends.

Altoona

Gary A. Raymond, D.P.M.
  (F,S,AG,PD)
719 Logan Boulevard
Altoona, PA 16602
(814) 943-3668

Dr. Raymond specializes in sports medicine, pediatric care, and, geriatric and diabetic care and prescribes walking to many of his patients. He walks 4 to 5 miles every day of the week.

Bala Cynwyd

Gertrude Copperman, M.D. (GP)
Intermediate Level, Suite 51
2 Bala Cynwyd Plaza
Bala Cynwyd, PA 19004
(215) 667-8160

Dr. Copperman walks 25 miles a week, 5 days a week.

Berwick

David R. Campbell, M.D. (S)
1701 Fowler Avenue
Berwick, PA 18603
(717) 759-1228

Dr. Campbell specializes in sports medicine and walks 2 miles a day, 3 days a week.

Broomall

Herbert N. Avart, D.O. (B,RM,AR)
Broomall Rehab Services
Rehab Physicians, Inc.
Suite 10
Delaware County Medical Center
Broomall, PA 19008
(215) 359-1134

Dr. Avart is an osteopathic doctor specializing in outpatient rehabilitation. He is also involved in physical therapy, psychology, and biofeedback technique. He is medical director at Broomal Rehabilitation Services, attending physiatrist at the Drucker Brain Injury Center, and consulting physiatrist at the Philadelphia College of Osteopathic Medicine. He walks 3 days a week, 2 miles a day. (S)

Butler

Leroy M. Potter, D.P.M. (F)
425 North Main Street
Butler, PA 16001
(412) 283-5500

Dr. Potter walks to control his weight and now enjoys the same sense of fitness he had 35 years ago when he was a cross-country runner. He walks on unpaved surfaces for 3 miles every day of the week and uses a treadmill during bad weather.

Charleroi

David E. Brougher, M.D. (OB)
323 McKean Avenue
Charleroi, PA 15022
(412) 489-9521

Dr. Brougher lost 50 pounds by walking and significantly reduced his cholesterol level. He walks 5 to 6 days a week, covering 15 to 18 miles. (P)

Curwensville

Katherine K. Welty, M.D. (GP)
465 State Street
Suite A
Curwensville, PA 16833
(814) 236-1123

Walking to work is included in the 10 to 20 miles Dr. Welty covers every 4 to 7 days. She prescribes walking to reduce cholesterol, hypertension, obesity, depression, stress, and PMS.

Erie

Robert E. Evans, D.O. (B,AR)
1605 West 54th Street
Erie, PA 16509
(814) 866-3063

Dr. Evans has a general practice in osteopathic medicine. He walks 3 to 5 days a week and covers 4 miles a day.

Etters

Todd Pelleschi, D.P.M. (F,S)
564 Old York Road
Etters, PA 17319
(717) 938-5200

Dr. Pelleschi has used walking to improve cardiovascular and lower extremity circulatory efficiency in several of his patients. Biking is his primary exercise, but he also walks 4 days a week, 6 miles a day.

Indiana

Anne Sorrentino Hoover, D.C. (B)
35 North 8th Street
Indiana, PA 15701
(412) 349-7999

Dr. Hoover turned to walking after hurting her knees running. She encourages walking not only for its physical benefits, but also because it's a nice way for families to spend time together. She walks 5 to 6 days a week, 3 to 4 miles a day.

Kingston

George B. Davis, M.D. (H)
Nesbitt Memorial Hospital
562 Wyoming Avenue
Kingston, PA 18704
(717) 288-1411

Dr. Davis, a doctor of cardiology, benefited personally from a walking recovery program after heart bypass surgery. He is now an avid walker who enters two to three walking marathons (26-mile races) a year. He trains 5 days a week, 3 miles a day.

Langhorne

Raymond B. Reinhart, Jr., M.D. (PS)
Saint Mary Medical Building
Langhorne, PA 19047
(215) 757-8558

Dr. Reinhart is a member of the American Board of Psychiatry and Neurology. He is a former jogger who walks 4 miles an hour, 6 days a week. (S)

Malvern

John J. Kraus, M.D. (RM)
Bryn Mawr Rehabilitation Hospital
414 Paoli Pike
Malvern, PA 19355
(215) 251-5690

Dr. Kraus likes walking because it improves cardiovascular endurance, promotes weight loss, and has a low rate of injury. He walks 30 minutes a day, 7 days a week. (S)

Milliersville

Harold L. Godshall, D.C. (AG,GP,PM)
228 Manor Avenue
Milliersville, PA 17551
(717) 872-4636

Dr. Godshall walks 22.5 miles every 3 days. He prescribes walking in conjunction with flexibility exercises. (P)

Philadelphia

Doris G. Bartuska, M.D. (IM)
Professor of Medicine
The Medical College of Pennsylvania
3300 Henry Avenue
Philadelphia, PA 19129
(215) 842-6952

Dr. Bartuska is director of endocrinology and metabolism at the Medical College of Pennsylvania. She walks to work every day, no matter what the weather, and averages 30 miles a week.

Thomas G. Davis, M.D. (H)
1500 Spring Garden Street
Philadelphia, PA 19101
(215) 751-7828

Dr. Smith, an attending physician at the Presbyterian University of Pennsylvania Medical Center, is an executive at SmithKline, a drug company.

Richard H. Kaplan, M.D. (RM)
1015 Chestnut Street
Philadelphia, PA 19107
(215) 923-4001

Dr. Kaplan walks 3 miles a day, 2 days a week. (S)

Howard J. Palamarchuk, D.P.M. (F,S)
Pennsylvania College of Podiatric
  Medicine
Eighth and Race Streets
Philadelphia, PA 19107
(215) 629-0300

Dr. Palamarchuk, director of sports medicine at the Pennsylvania College of Podiatric Medicine, has walked in the Submasters Race Walk Competition since 1987. For exercise he walks, at a 6 mile per hour pace, 20 miles per week.

J. Edward Pickering, M.D. (H)
City Line and Lancaster Drive
316 Lankenau Medical Building
Philadelphia, PA 19151
(215) 642-0100

Dr. Pickering's medical appointments include associate clinical professor of medicine at the Thomas Jefferson University Hospital and Medical School in Philadelphia and the position of associate with the Departments of Internal Medicine and Cardiovascular Disease at the Lankenau Hospital in Philadelphia, where he is a physician. He walks regularly.

Peter C. Toren, M.D. (GP,PM)
5735 Ridge Avenue
Suite 207
Philadelphia, PA 19128
(215) 482-2380

Dr. Toren is a family practitioner and emphasizes preventative medicine. He recommends a walking program to the majority of his patients for a wide variety of medical problems, and he himself walks 4 to 5 miles an hour, varying amounts each week. (P)

Pittsburgh

Diane Dill, M.D. (PM)
619 Mt. Royal Boulevard
Pittsburgh, PA 15223
(412) 487-4422

Dr. Dill, who walks 2 to 4 hours a day, 2 to 3 days a week, considers walking the best form of aerobic exercise with the lowest injury rate. (P)

Westchester

Barry C. Hertz, M.D. (IM,L)
520 Maple Avenue
Suite 3
Westchester, PA 19380
(215) 692-6330

Dr. Hertz is board certified in internal and pulmonary medicine. He walks 7 days a week, 3 miles a day.

York

B. Timothy Harcourt, D.C. (B,PM)
Harcourt Chiropractic Office
1630 West Market Street
York, PA 17404
(717) 843-2542

Dr. Harcourt and his office provide stress-management courses to patients and local businesses, and they recommend walking as a stress reducer. He walks 10 hours and 25 miles a week on rugged terrain. (P)

Rhode Island

Cranston

Deborah J. Rich, M.D. (IM)
88 Massasoit Avenue
Cranston, RI 02905
(401) 941-7834

Dr. Rich is a board-certified internist and enjoys walking in the beautiful countryside of Rhode Island at least three times a week.

Providence

Louis A. Fuchs, M.D. (O)
382 Thayer Street
Providence, RI 02906
(401) 521-2360

Dr. Fuchs started walking to rehabilitate a bad back and has kept at it because walking is a "great emotional outlet." He walks a brisk 4 miles an hour and logs 30 miles a week.

Steven G. McCloy, M.D. (IM)
530 North Main Street
Providence, RI 02904
(401) 331-3000

Dr. McCloy specializes in internal and occupational medicine. He walks 3 to 4 miles a day, 3 days a week.

Stephen J. Richman, M.D. (OP)
444 Angell Street
Providence, RI 02906
(401) 831-3311

Dr. Richman is an ophthalmologist who also treats diabetes. He recommends walking to his diabetic patients because it is a gentle and stress-reducing exercise. He enjoys walking as a "quiet time" or as a time for uninterrupted talks with his wife. He walks 5 days a week, 4 to 5 miles a day. (P)

South Carolina

Greenville

C. David Tollison, Ph.D. (PA)
Pain Therapy Centers
Greenville General Hospital
100 Mallard Street
Greenville, SC 29601
(803) 242-8088

Dr. Tollison is director of Pain Therapy Centers in South and North Carolina, Florida, and Missouri. He walks 8 to 12 miles per week, 4 to 5 days a week.

South Dakota

Rapid City

Suzanne C. Barker, M.S. (H)
Rapid City Regional Hospital
Phase III Cardiac Rehabilitation
2908 5th Street
Rapid City, SD 57701
(605) 399-1211

Suzanne Barker is director of the Phase III Cardiac Rehab Center program, which uses walking as a primary activity for the treatment of heart disease. Ms. Barker walks briskly for 1 hour, 3 days a week.

Steven K. Goff, M.D. (S, RM)
2908 5th Street
Rapid City, SD 57701
(605) 399-1327

Dr. Goff is the Medical Director of the Black Hills Rehabilitation Hospital. Walking is his primary exercise because it can combine low impact activity and aerobic exercises using the major muscle groups, which necessitates complicated motor patterns. He walks 1 to 3 days a week up to 10 miles a day.

Tennessee

Knoxville

Joanne C. Healey, D.V.M. (V)
434 Chicamauga Avenue
Knoxville, TN 37917
(615) 689-7447

Dr. Healey is a doctor of veterinary medicine who finds walking an excellent exercise for both pets and their owners. She walks 3 to 4 days a week, 1 to 2 miles a day. (S)

Memphis

Gary M. Mantell, D.P.M. (F)
376 Perkins Extended
Memphis, TN 38117
(901) 682-4668

Dr. Mantell sees many patients whose problems with diabetes or advanced peripheral vascular disease might have been avoided with proper diet and a regular walking program. He walks 3 days a week, 3 miles a day.

Old Hickory

Donald L. Mynster, D.C., P.C. (B)
4963 Lebanon Road
Old Hickory, TN 37138
(615) 889-0333

Dr. Mynster emphasizes preventive medicine in his chiropractic practice. He walks 5 days a week, 2 miles a day.

Texas

Arlington

Marilee S, Niehoff, Ph.D. (PS)
2416 Heathercrest Drive
Arlington, TX 76018
(817) 467-5496

Dr. Niehoff is a water aerobics instructor. She walks 4 days a week, primarily in water, occasionally on land. (P)

Austin

Jack Wilmore, Ph.D. (EP)
3409 Sanderling Trail
Austin, TX 78746
(512) 471-4405

Dr. Wilmore is an exercise physiologist now based at the University of Texas, Austin, who has in the past been a consultant to every Los Angeles sports team as well as to the California Highway Patrol. He's published many articles on exercise and health and walks, when he doesn't run, 4 to 5 hours at a stretch. (S)

Dallas

Dwight L. Bates, D.P.M. (F)
5510 Abrams Road, Suite 103
Dallas, TX 75214
(214) 369-3969

Dr. Bates walks 2 miles every day of the week.

Steven Blair, P.E.D.
Institute for Aerobics Research
12330 Preston Road
Dallas, TX 75230
(214) 701-8001

Dr. Blair is director of epidemiology at the Institute for Aerobics Research, adjunct professor of epidemiology and biostatistics at the University of South Carolina's School of Public Health, and adjunct professor of epidemiology at the School of Public Health, University of Texas, Houston. He walks 5 miles a week. (S)

Joan Colgin, R.N., C.D.E. (RN,W)
Endocrine Assoc. of Dallas, P.A.
5480 La Sierra Drive
Dallas, TX 75231
(214) 363-5535

Ms. Colgin is a registered nurse who specializes in diabetes, weight loss, and endocrinology. For controlling type II diabetes, she has found walking to be more effective than medication. She walks 3 to 4 days a week, 2 miles a day.

Susan Johnson, Ed.D. (PM)
Institute for Aerobics Research
12330 Preston Road
Dallas, TX 75230
(214) 701-8001

Dr. Johnson is a consultant, coordinator, and instructor of fitness programs nationwide. Among numerous appointments, she is a long-standing clinician/consultant to the President's Council on Physical Fitness and Sports and to the National Fitness Foundation of Orange County, California. Walking, says Dr. Johnson, is the best exercise for the majority of Americans to begin and stick with, because it has the lowest dropout rate of any exercise program. She walks every day.

Norman M. Kaplan, M.D. (H)
5323 Harry Hines Boulevard
Dallas, TX 75335
(214) 684-2103

Dr. Kaplan is professor of internal medicine and heads the Hypertension Division at the University of Texas Southwest Medical Center. He walks 12 hours per week.

George Alfred Monroe, M.D. (PD,GP)
7777 Forest Lane C-525
Dallas, TX 75230
(214) 661-7011

Dr. Monroe walks 6 days a week, totaling close to 30 miles. He says that walking has made his family stronger physically and closer emotionally. He specializes in pediatrics and adolescent medicine and strongly emphasizes walking in any weight-control program for children and adolescents. (P)

Vera R. Stern, D.P.M., M.S. (F,S)
3798 Forest Lane
Suite 10
Dallas, TX 75244
(214) 351-4724

Dr. Stern practices podiatric medicine and surgery and sports medicine. She walks 4 days a week, 2 miles a day.

Ft. Worth

Gerald G. Bronson, D.C., P.C. (B)
Bronson Chiropractic Health Clinic
Bellaire Centre, Suite, 100
5521 Bellaire Drive South
Ft. Worth, TX 76109
(817) 732-4441

Dr. Bronson treats many marathon runners, golfers, and speed walkers. He has walked for the past 21 years and currently follows a walking program using Heavy Hands (hand weights). He walks an average of 30 miles a week.

Houston

Craig S. Heffelman, M.D., P.A. (F,O)
5322 West Bellfort
Suite 118
Houston, TX 77035
(713) 728-0077

Dr. Heffelman recommends walking because it is a safe way to lose weight and because 60 percent of his patients have pain, sprains, aches, and complaints from running. He walks 6 days a week, 2 to 3 miles a day.

Ofelia M. Minor, M.D. (PS)
4114 North Braeswood
Houston, TX 77025
(713) 665-0177

Dr. Minor specializes in psychiatry and walks every day for 30 minutes. She feels that "anybody can do it and enjoy it." (S)

Barry P. Weinstein, D.P.M. (F,S)
6684 Southwest Freeway
Houston, TX 77074
(713) 975-8838

Dr. Weinstein is a podiatrist specializing in sports medicine. He walks 5 days a week, 4 to 6 miles a day.

David S. Wolf, D.P.M. (F)
11515 Chimney Rock Road
Houston, TX 77035
(713) 728-3117

Dr. Wolf feels walking is the best aerobic exercise because it is low-impact. He has racewalked five marathons and walks 5 days a week, 5 to 6 miles a day.

Richardson

Pat Leonard, R.N., F.N.P. (GP)
Student Health Services
University of Texas
P.O. Box 830688
Richardson, TX 75083-0688
(214) 690-2747

Ms. Leonard is a family nurse practitioner and has a master's degree in counseling. She walks 4 days a week during lunch, averaging 4½ miles an hour, for a weekly total of 18 miles. (P)

J.E. Walker, M.D. (PA)
299 West Campbell Road
Richardson, TX 75080
(214) 783-8900

Dr. Walker finds that walking conditions the cardiovascular and musculoskeletal system. He walks 10 miles a week, over a 5-day period.

San Antonio

David N. Toth, M.D., M.P.H. (PM)
203 Baseview Drive
San Antonio, TX 78227-4903
(512) 670-4107

Dr. Toth walks 3 to 4 days a week, 5 miles a day.

Terrell

Robert M. Birenbaum, M.D. (OP)
1024 West Main
Terrell, TX 75160
(214) 887-2020

Dr. Birenbaum specializes in optometry and is a competitive racewalker. He walks a 9-minute-mile for 5 miles, 4 days a week.

Utah

Salt Lake City

M. D. Smithers, D.C. (B)
The Back Clinic
7050 South 2000 East
Salt Lake City, UT 84121
(801) 942-5814

Dr. Smithers has found walking to be one of the best therapies for disk injuries. He walks 5 days a week, 6 miles a day.

Vermont

Burlington

Philip Ades, M.D. (H)
1 South Prospect Street
Burlington, VT 05401
(802) 656-3734

Dr. Ades is an assistant profesor of medicine at the University of Vermont. He prescribes walking to his heart patients.

Virginia

Annandale

Myles J. Schneider, D.P.M. (F,S,PM)
The Podiatry Center
7540 Little River Turnpike
Annandale, VA 22003
(703) 750-1124

Dr. Schneider has authored several books on foot care. He is also involved in sports and preventive medicine. He walks 3 days a week, 5 miles a day.

Culpeper

Robert Rutkowski, M.D. (O,S)
Virginia Orthopaedic Center
663 Sunset Lane
Culpeper, VA 22701
(703) 825-5362

Dr. Rutkowski is chief of staff in orthopedics at Culpeper Memorial Hospital. He walks 7 days a week, 1 mile a day. (S)

Fairfax

Richard Mendelsohn, D.P.M. (F,S)
9918 Main Street
Fairfax, VA 22031
(703) 273-9818

Dr. Mendelsohn in involved in sports medicine and podiatric surgery. He has successfully helped relieve patients of foot pain and excess weight through walking programs. He walks 5 days a week, 6 miles a day.

Manassas

Normood McMahon, D.C. (B,PM)
The Health Development Center
9510 Technology Drive
Manassas, VA 22110
(703) 330-0112

Dr. McMahon is a doctor of chiropractic on the staff of a clinic that offers a team concept in preventive health care. The center provides its own walking trail for patients. Dr. McMahon walks 3 to 4 days a week, 5 miles a day. (P)

Susan J. Shlifer, M.D. (GP)
10633 Crestwood Drive
Manassas, VA 22180
(703) 368-7110

Dr. Shlifer prescribes walking because there is a low risk of injury, no need for special equipment, and it allows people to relax. She walks 10 miles every 4 days. (P)

Richmond

Damien Howell, M.S., P.T. (PT,S,PM)
2nd and East Franklin Street
Richmond, VA 23219
(804) 783-8466

Dr. Howell specializes in physical therapy for sports and preventive medicine. Many of his patients with diabetes, hypertension, and lower back pain benefit tremendously from walking regularly. He walks every day of the week for an hour.

Dr. Marilyn L. Spiro, Ph.D. (PS)
5700 West Grace St., Suite 100
Richmond, VA 23226
(804) 282-6165

Dr. Spiro walks 15 miles a week.

Roanoke

Ms. Alicia Nickens, R.N. (GP)
Gil Memorial Eye, Ear, Nose and
    Throat Hospital, Inc.
P.O. Box 1560
Roanoke, VA 24007
(703) 343-3368

Ms. Nickens specializes in employee health at the hospital and has organized a fun and healthy walking program. She walks a fast 1½ miles, 5 days a week. (P)

Washington

Bellevue

Daniel A. Brzusek, D.O., M.S. (O,RM)
Northwest Rehabilitation Associates Inc.
1515 116th Avenue N.E.
Suite 202
Bellevue, WA 98004-3811
(206) 453-1000

Dr. Brzusek graduated from the Philadelphia College of Osteopathic Medicine and holds a master's degree in rehabilitative medicine. He is also a clinical professor at the University of Washington. Dr. Brzusek walks 2 days a week, 5 miles a day, and does cross training in bicyling, tennis, aerobics, and light weight training.

Bellingham

Clark O. Parrish, M.D. (IM)
2950 Squalicum
Bellingham, WA 98225
(206) 671-7100

Dr. Parrish practices general internal medicine. He walks 3 days a week, 2 miles a day.

Everett

Chris Vance, D.P.M. (F)
1920 North 100th Street, S.E.
Everett, WA 98208-3832
(206) 337-7000

Dr. Vance is an active walker who covers 4 miles a day, 4 days a week. (P)

Puyallup

Leonard S. Allott, M.D. (W)
205 15th Avenue S.W.
Suite D
Puyallup, WA 98371
(206) 848-5559

Dr. Allott is the medical director of a low-calorie diet and exercise program. He walks 1 to 3 days a week, 2 to 3 miles a day. (S)

Renton

John Ball, M.D. (IM)
4509 Talbot Road South
Renton, WA 98055
(206) 235-1950

Dr. Ball is an internist who specializes in endocrinology and metabolism. He walks on hills with Heavy Hands nearly every day of the week.

Seattle

William Phillips, M.D. (GP)
1801 N.W. Market Street
Seattle, WA 98107
(206) 784-7303

Dr. Phillips is board certified in family and preventative medicine and is a clinical associate professor of family medicine at the University of Washington. He walks 3 days a week, about 3 miles a day.

Spokane

Paula A. Lantsburger, M.D. (PT)
Occupational Medical Clinic
West 800 5th Avenue
Spokane, WA 99203
(509) 458-7192

Dr. Lantsburger prescribes walking to patients with back problems. She walks 2 hours a day, 4 to 5 days a week. (P)

Charles R. Wolte, M.D. (PS,PT)
West 800 5th Avenue
Spokane, WA 99210
(509) 458-7192

Dr. Wolte prescribes walking for all back injuries. He walks 7 days a week, covering 15 miles. (S)

Tacoma

Pat Kulpa, M.D. (S,OB)
Feminenergy, P.S., Inc.
1811 South K Street
Tacoma, WA 98405
(206) 572-2212

Dr. Kulpa specializes in sports gynecology and recommends walking to all her patients from adolescent girls to pregnant and postmenopausal women. She enjoys a wide variety of sports, including bicycling, marathon running, racquetball, skiing, hiking, and walking. She walks and hikes on rugged terrain. (S)

Vancouver

John D. Kojis, D.C. (B)
9609 East Mill Plain
Suite B
Vancouver, WA 98664
(206) 254-8866

Dr. Kojis instructs his patients to walk at least 5 minutes after a back adjustment, since walking enhances the effectiveness of the treatment. He also recommends 20 minutes of daily walking. Dr. Kojis walks 5 to 6 days a week with his dog, 3 to 4 miles a day.

Wenatchee

Ben Knecht, M.D. (IM)
P.O. Box 489
Wenatchee, WA 98807-0489
(509) 663-8711

Dr. Knecht prescribes walking to help his patients get over their postoperative "blues." They feel better sooner and have fewer complaints. He walks 3 days a week. (S)

West Virginia

Beckley

Carlos Lucero, M.D. (GP)
403 Carriage Drive
Beckley, WV 25801
(304) 255-7456

Dr. Lucero walks 4 to 6 hours a week and prescribes walking to his patients as a form of weight control.

Morgantown

David J. Withersty, M.D. (PS)
1303 Riddle Avenue
Morgantown, WV 26505
(304) 599-6968

Dr. Withersty practices psychiatry and finds walking to be an excellent method for stress reduction for himself and his patients. (P)

Parkersburg

Daniel P. Pierce, M.S., B.S. (PT,H,S)
19th Street and Murdoch Avenue
Parkersburg, WV 26101
(304) 422-1913

Mr. Pierce holds a bachelor's degree in physical therapy and a master's degree in sports physiology and adult fitness with an emphasis on cardiac rehabilitation. He walks hills 3 to 4 miles a day, 5 days a week, and through walking has lowered his cholesterol.

Vienna

Mary Anne Totten, M.D. (IM)
Primary Health Care, Inc.
23rd Street and Grand Central Ave.
Vienna, WV 26105
(304) 295-3356

Dr. Totten is an internist who specializes in endocrinology and diabetes. She recommends walking to her patients with diabetes to control blood sugar and enjoys walking with her mother on a track 3 days a week.

Wisconsin

Beloit

John D. McCrea, D.P.M. (F)
Associated Foot Clinic S.C.
1517 Huebbe Parkway
Beloit, WI 53511
(608) 362-0758

Dr. McCrea specializes in care and surgery of the foot and ankle. He walks 5 to 6 days a week, 3 miles a day. (S)

Milwaukee

Anna T. Campbell, Ph.D. (PS)
3070 North 77th Street
Milwaukee, WI 53222
(414) 442-7380

Dr. Campbell is an associate clinical professor of psychology at the University of Wisconsin, Madison. She is also in private practice with the Associated Women Psychotherapists, a private practice group formed in 1983. She recommends walking to her patients and walks 15 to 20 miles a week, 4 to 5 days a week.

Jeffrey E. Johnson, M.D. (O)
Department of Orthopedic Surgery
Medical College of Wisconsin
8700 West Wisconsin Avenue
Milwaukee, WI 53226
(414) 257-5433

Dr. Johnson swims and walks 1 to 2 days a week, 2 miles a day.

W. Drew Palin, M.D. (S,W)
3267 South 16th Street
Milwaukee, WI 53215
(414) 383-1700

Dr. Palin specializes in sports medicine and weight control. He is medical director of Competitive Edge Sports Medicine, Take Control, and the Weight Managers Program at Sinai-Samaritan Medical Center, and medical consultant for the Olympic speed skating team.

Saul K. Pollock, M.D. (GP)
700 North Water Street
Milwaukee, WI 53202

Dr. Pollock walks 12 miles a week.

Oshkosh

John F. Aufderheide, M.D. (Radiology)
2616 Fond du Lac Road
Oshkosh, WI 54901
(414) 233-8060

Dr. Aufderheide specializes in radiology. He walks 2 to 7 days a week and averages 5 to 6 miles a day. (P)

Racine

Robert E. Laing, M.D. (O,S)
Racine Medical Clinic
5625 Washington Avenue
Racine, WI 53402
(414) 886-8258

Dr. Laing specializes in orthopedic surgery and sports medicine. For exercise, he uses the Nordic Track and walks 3 days a week, 3 to 4 miles a day.

Sturgeon Bay

Brian E. Palevac
368 Louisiana
Sturgeon Bay, WI 54235
(414) 743-1900

Dr. Palevac walks 5 or more days a week, 2 miles a day.

Wausau

Douglas Olmanson, M.D. (GP)
2727 Plaza Drive
Wausau, WI 54401
(715) 847-3000

Dr. Olmanson finds walking fun, easy, and inexpensive. He walks 10 miles a week.

Canada

Barhead

C.V. Godberson, M.D. (GP)
Barhead Clinic Holdings Ltd.
Box 940
Barhead, Alberta TOG OEO
Canada
(403) 674-2231

Dr. Godberson recommends walking because it is an exercise requiring no costly equipment and is therefore available to everyone. He walks regularly.

Dartmouth

Harold Brogan, D.D.S. (DE)
25 Earnest Avenue
Dartmouth, Nova Scotia B3A 2H6
Canada
(902) 463-0901

A member of the Canadian Volksmarchers Association walking club, one of Canada's largest walking clubs, Dr. Brogan takes a brisk walk everyday.

Edmonton

Art Burgess, Ph.D. (EP)
Room W1-08 Van Vliet Center
University of Alberta
Edmonton, Alberta T6G 2H9
Canada
(403) 492-5607

Dr. Burgess, an avid walker who has lectured in Canada on the subject of fitness walking, is the Director of Fitness and Lifestyle Programs at the University of Alberta. He walks five days a week, covering around 18 miles.

Kingston

Darrel Menard, M.D. (S)
Canadian Forces Base
Kingston, Ontario
(613) 541-5508

Dr. Menard believes in walking because it is the only sport where injury is virtually unheard of. He says men and women are best suited for walking as their exercise choice. He walks 3 days a week, about a mile a day.

Toronto

Dr. Jaan Roos, M.D. (H,L)
Ontario Ministry of Labor Chest Clinic
880 Bay Street, 2nd Floor
Toronto, Ontario M7A 207
Canada
(416) 965-4075

Dr. Roos, a racewalker, is senior medical consultant at the Ontario Ministry of Labor Chest Clinic. He began racewalking in 1981 after a personal injury forced him to give up skiing, and has since become one of Canada's premier racewalkers. Director of the Ontario Racewalker's Club and racewalking instructor at the Toronto Metrocenter YMCA, Dr. Roos walks around 15 hours each week, covering in that time around 100 miles.

Willowdale

Carmel McCartney, R.N. (PM)
50 Hallerown Place
Willowdale, Ontario M2J 1P7
Canada
(416) 499-2009

Ms. McCartney is a certified occupational health nurse who prescribes walking to reduce stress. She walks 1 to 3 miles, 5 to 7 days a week. (P)

International

France

Marc Tourneur, D.C. (B)
44 Rue Labourde
75008 Paris
France
(33)-1-43-87-81-62

Dr. Tourneur, a chiropractor, prescribes walking for patients with back pain because it creates no strain on joints or muscles. He walks 30 kilometers a week.

Japan

Masaru Ikeda, Ph.D. (EP)
National Institute of Fitness and Sports
Kagoshima
Japan
(81)-0994-46-4111

Doctor Ikeda's doctorate is in the field of leisure studies. He walks 18 miles per week, 7 days a week. (S)

Spain

Jose Casas, M.D. (PD)
H. Ruber Internacional
C/ La Maso, 38 Mirasierra
28034 Madrid
Spain

Dr. Casas specializes in pediatrics. He walks 5 to 7 days a week, 5 to 6 miles a day, and enjoys jogging and skiing.

Switzerland

Gmuer Dieter, M.D. (S,O)
Bundesgasse 16
CH-3011 Bern, Switzerland
(41)-031-223666

Dr. Dieter is a general and orthopedic surgeon and belongs to the European and International Association of Knee Surgeons. He walks one day a week for 4 miles.

Walking Health Professional Questionnaire

Please attach resumé or curriculum vitae to the questionnaire.

The following questionnaire is designed to establish a profile of you and your practice as it relates to walking for inclusion in THE WALKING HEALTH PROFESSIONAL to be published by McGraw-Hill Book Company. Please include as much anecdotal information as possible about yourself and the persons to who you recommend walking.

If your primary exercise is not walking, please pass on this questionnaire to an appropriate colleague. If you would like to start a walking program for yourself or your patients, please call and leave your name, organization, address, and telephone. If you are interested in being included in THE DIRECTORY, but would rather be interviewed by phone, please call us at (212) 879-5794 (and send back this form signed).

Name: _____

Office Address: _____

Telephone Number: _____ Fax Number: _____

Age Group of Patients: _____ Your Age: _____

Specialties: (Pediatrics, sports medicine, preventive medicine, etc.) _____

Home Address:*_____ Phone:*_____

Please attach any brochures or printed material describing your practice or programs.

Medical Degrees and Affiliations: _____

_____

PERSONAL WALKING HISTORY

Is it your   Primary _____ Secondary _____ or other exercise? _____

How many miles and hours per week do you walk? _____ How many

days per week? _____

Average speed (mph or minute-miles) _____ Type (fast, weight-loaded, stairs,

rugged terrain) _____

Special exercise training? _____

*Not for publication

Why do you choose walking for yourself and your patients? Tell us a favorite "case history" that shows successful use of prescribing walking.

_____

_____

Would you like to participate in any symposia that relate your health field to walking? Would you like to do local media interviews and/or walking clinics?

_____

Should walkers contact you for: Referral: _____

Treatments: _____

I understand and agree that this information becomes the property of Walking World, to be used at its discretion. I also agree that my name can be used in connection with the publication of this book.

_____   _____
          Signature   Date

Please return this questionnaire to: **Walking World**
P.O. Box K, Gracie Station, New York, NY 10028

Walker's Questionnaire

The following questionnaire is designed to establish a profile of how you and your family and friends have benefited from walking. We are especially interested in using your stories in one of our six books that cover walking and the following topics: arthritis, back and joint problems; heart and pulmonary disease or problems; foot problems; stress reduction and behavior modification; aging; weight control.

Please include stories of how walking has helped you in these areas, and about your walking program. Please pass copies of this questionnaire on to other walkers in your company, walking club, or neighborhood. If you would rather answer these questions by phone, you can contact us at (212) 879-5794.

If you need more room, please attach another sheet.

Name: _____

Address: _____

_____ Phone: _____

Age: ____ Sex: M ____ F ____ Marital status _____ Weight _____ Height _____

Highest level of education completed? _____ Occupation/title _____

Walking club affiliation _____

Please fill in your walking schedule, indicating your reasons for specific time, place, and frequency under the comments section. Please note at what time (or times) you walk in the first column and the number of minutes you walk in the appropriate day of the week column. (For example, if you walk 3 miles in an hour every day you would write: 3 miles, 1 hour in each of the seven columns).

WEEKLY SCHEDULE

Where do you walk? _____ Do you walk in all weather? _____

Time(s) of day	Mon.	Tues.	Wed.	Thurs.	Fri.	Sat.	Sun.
___	___	___	___	___	___	___	___
___	___	___	___	___	___	___	___
___	___	___	___	___	___	___	___
___	___	___	___	___	___	___	___

Comments: _____

How often do you walk each day? _____ Your walking speed (in mph or

minute-miles): _____

Total weekly mileage: _____ How long have you been walking? _____

Age you started? _____Your exercise style? (please check) Fast walking _____

Racewalking _____ Walking in place _____ Weight-loaded: Backpacks

Heavy Hands _____ Ankle weights _____ Climbing: Stairs _____

Hills _____ Nordic track _____

What walking techniques from Gary Yanker's books and tapes do you use (arm pump-

ing, stride stretching, hip swing, heel-toe roll, etc.)? _____

Which techniques have you found most useful, and why? _____

Were there any techniques you found difficult, and why? _____

Have you invented any techniques of your own? _____

Have you participated in walking clinics? _____ If so, who conducted it?

_____

If your company has a walking program, please describe it here: _____

Have you used other walking books or tapes? _____ If so, whose? _____
Do you know any children or teenagers who walk for exercise? If so, please tell us
their walking routine, why they like walking, and how they have benefited from it (if
possible, please give them or their parents a copy of this questionnaire to complete):

_____

_____

Please circle your special medical or health problem or in what situations walking has
helped. For any problems you have encountered, please write the age of onset. To
help us with our genetics chapter, please also tell us if your parents, grandparents,
or siblings have experienced the same problem or disease and, if so, at what age.
Please also note if they died from this disorder and at what age.

Arthritis
Arthritis, back problems, ankle problems, knee problems, hip problems, joint re-

placement, osteroporosis, sports injuries, other: _____

Your age of onset: _____ Relative and age of onset: _____

Heart and Lung Disease

Bypass surgery, hypertension, angina, stroke rehabilitation, asthma, emphysema, other

lung disorders (please specify), varicose veins, high cholesterol, other: _____

Your age of onset: _____ Relative and age of onset: _____
(Note: If you used walking to rehabilitate from a heart attack, bypass surgery, or a stroke, please include your rehabilitation schedule on the back (number of days per week, speed, duration, distance).

Foot Problems

Achille tendons, plantar fascitiis, blisters, calluses, ingrown toenails, bunions, corns,

arch sprain, heel spurs, hammertoes, other: _____

Your age of onset: _____ Relative and age of onset: _____

Emotional, Social Problems

Loss of loved one, divorce, cancer or other major illness (either yourself or loved one), work-related stress, use walking to spend time with spouse, friends, or family, premenstrual syndrome, eating disorder, addiction to cigarettes, alcohol, or drugs, other:

_____

_____

Weight Control

Weight loss, diabetes, body toning, pregnancy, gastrointestinal, other: _____

Your age of onset: _____ Relative and age of onset: _____

Aging

Has walking made you feel younger, increased your energy, made you look younger, other: _____

Miscellaneous Medical Conditions

Enlarged prostate, incontinence, periodontal disease, eyesight problems, hearing loss,

other: _____

Your age of onset: _____ Relative and age of onset: _____

Please provide the name, address, and telephone number of any doctors or health professionals who have prescribed walking to you or worked with you using walking:

_____

_____

_____

Please pick one of more of the situations or problems in which walking has helped you and describe, including your walking program. Use other side of this form or attach additional sheets. Please include before and after statistics (if you know them) for cholesterol count, weight, blood pressure, heart rate, how long it took to see results, etc.

If you use a special walking shoe, what is your favorite brand (or brands) of walking

shoes and why (ample cushioning, good stability, good arch support, etc.)? _____

_____

If you do not, what kind of shoe do you walk in (a sandal, dress shoe, hiking shoe,

casual shoe, or other; please include brand name)? _____

How long has your shoe lasted (number of miles)? _____

What is your least favorite brand of walking shoe and why (falls apart quickly, is too

tight, too hot, etc.)? _____

What improvements do you think are needed in walking shoes? _____

_____

Do you have any special methods of caring for, repairing, or modifying shoes?

_____

*I hereby give permission to Walking World to use my name, likeness, biographical,
and walking information in its publications.*

_____   _____

      Signature   **Date**

Please complete and return to
Walking World
P.O. Box K, Gracie Station
New York, NY 10028

Index

Page numbers in *italics* refer to illustrations. Page numbers followed by t refer to tables.